HEALTH LAW
AND BIOETHICS

ASPEN PUBLISHERS

HEALTH LAW AND BIOETHICS

Cases in Context

Sandra H. Johnson
Professor Emerita of Health Law and Ethics
Saint Louis University School of Law

Joan H. Krause
George Butler Research Professor of Law and
Co-Director, Health Law & Policy Institute
University of Houston Law Center

Richard S. Saver
Associate Professor of Law and
Co-Director, Health Law & Policy Institute
University of Houston Law Center

Robin Fretwell Wilson
Professor of Law and Law Alumni Faculty Fellow
Washington & Lee University School of Law

Wolters Kluwer
Law & Business

AUSTIN   BOSTON   CHICAGO   NEW YORK   THE NETHERLANDS

Aspen Publishers
Attn: Permissions Department
76 Ninth Avenue, 7th Floor
New York, NY 10011-5201

To contact Customer Care, e-mail customer.care@aspenpublishers.com, call 1-800-234-1660, fax 1-800-901-9075, or mail correspondence to:

Aspen Publishers
Attn: Order Department
PO Box 990
Frederick, MD 21705

Printed in the United States of America.

1 2 3 4 5 6 7 8 9 0

ISBN 978-0-7355-7767-1

Library of Congress Cataloging-in-Publication Data

Health law and bioethics : cases in context / Sandra Johnson ... [et al.].
    p. cm.
Includes index.
ISBN 978-0-7355-7767-1
1. Medical laws and legislation — United States — Cases. 2. Medical genetics — Law and legislation — United States — Cases. 3. Bioethics — United States — Cases. I. Johnson, Sandra H.

KF3821.H4344 2009
344.7303'210264 — dc22

                                                                    2008055531

About Wolters Kluwer Law & Business

Wolters Kluwer Law & Business is a leading provider of research information and workflow solutions in key specialty areas. The strengths of the individual brands of Aspen Publishers, CCH, Kluwer Law International and Loislaw are aligned within Wolters Kluwer Law & Business to provide comprehensive, in-depth solutions and expert-authored content for the legal, professional and education markets.

CCH was founded in 1913 and has served more than four generations of business professionals and their clients. The CCH products in the Wolters Kluwer Law & Business group are highly regarded electronic and print resources for legal, securities, antitrust and trade regulation, government contracting, banking, pension, payroll, employment and labor, and healthcare reimbursement and compliance professionals.

Aspen Publishers is a leading information provider for attorneys, business professionals and law students. Written by preeminent authorities, Aspen products offer analytical and practical information in a range of specialty practice areas from securities law and intellectual property to mergers and acquisitions and pension/benefits. Aspen's trusted legal education resources provide professors and students with high-quality, up-to-date and effective resources for successful instruction and study in all areas of the law.

Kluwer Law International supplies the global business community with comprehensive English-language international legal information. Legal practitioners, corporate counsel and business executives around the world rely on the Kluwer Law International journals, loose-leafs, books and electronic products for authoritative information in many areas of international legal practice.

Loislaw is a premier provider of digitized legal content to small law firm practitioners of various specializations. Loislaw provides attorneys with the ability to quickly and efficiently find the necessary legal information they need, when and where they need it, by facilitating access to primary law as well as state-specific law, records, forms and treatises.

Wolters Kluwer Law & Business, a unit of Wolters Kluwer, is headquartered in New York and Riverwoods, Illinois. Wolters Kluwer is a leading multinational publisher and information services company.

To the students, colleagues, patients, and families who taught me so much over the past three decades of health law teaching. — *Sandra H. Johnson*

To Norman Krause, for never doubting that his daughters could be anything they wanted to be; and in loving memory of Barbara Krause, whose spirit lives on in Mikaela. — *Joan H. Krause*

To my parents: Esther Saver, for her wonderful support; and Harry Saver, M.D. (in loving memory), who always appreciated a good health care story and had many to tell. — *Richard S. Saver*

To Mark Ancell, for believing in me and never wavering in his support. — *Robin Fretwell Wilson*

Summary of Contents

Contents

Part II
DEATH AND DYING

Chapter 3
Quinlan and Cruzan
Beyond the Symbols

Part III
REPRODUCTIVE RIGHTS

Chapter 4
Johnson v. Calvert
Technology, Family, and Commerce

Chapter 5
Litowitz v. Litowitz
Feuding over Frozen Embryos and Forecasting the Future of Reproductive Medicine

Part IV
ORGAN TRANSPLANTS, MEDICAL FUTILITY, AND PRESUMED CONSENT

Chapter 6
In re T.A.C.P. and In the Matter of Baby K.
Anencephaly and Slippery Slopes

Chapter 7
Newman v. Sathyavaglswaran
Unbundling Property in the Dead

Part V
PUBLIC HEALTH

Chapter 8
Jacobson v. Massachusetts
The Police Power and Civil Liberties in Tension

Part VI
REGULATORY, ORGANIZATIONAL, AND BUSINESS ISSUES

Chapter 9
United States v. Krizek
Rough Justice Under the Civil False Claims Act

Chapter 10
Utah County v. Intermountain Health Care
Reconsidering the Charitable Status of Nonprofit Hospitals

Preface

To our knowledge, this is the first and only book of its kind in health law and bioethics. In it, leading health law scholars tell the stories behind thirteen landmark cases in the field. Each chapter provides insights and details from the parties, attorneys, and expert witnesses — details that frequently are missing from the public record. We also situate each case in the broader historical, political, and social context in which it unfolded. By placing these cases in context, we not only unpack the background, significance, and impact of each case, but we provide provocative and important new insights into health law and policy more generally.

This book includes renowned, highly influential, widely taught cases that have been drawn from the broad variety of subfields within health law and bioethics. It is divided into eleven chapters covering each of the major areas within the field, including the professional-patient relationship and the quality of care; death and dying; reproductive rights; organ transplants, medical futility, and presumed consent; public health; and regulatory, organizational, and business issues. While we believe that few scholars and teachers would agree on a *single* list of *definitive* cases in health law and bioethics, we have included cases that are widely taught and universally regarded as significant, maximizing the book's overall utility as a teaching tool and resource for research.

We believe the book will stimulate a lively and deeper discussion of the leading cases. For brevity's sake, most casebooks offer only highly edited versions of the cases. Compounding this, appellate opinions typically present a narrow, incomplete set of the "facts," glossing over much of what actually occurred and what the underlying litigation unearthed. These abridged facts represent but a small part of the full human drama and the rich, multi-layered context of each case. By contrast, this book presents more engaging personal narratives and provides essential background information that students can use to form a more nuanced understanding of health law and policy as well as the litigation process. The book is purposefully written in a readable and accessible style, with concise chapters and minimal endnotes.

For law school classes, *Health Law and Bioethics: Cases in Context* can be used to supplement any one of the popular casebooks because it contains many of the cases that appear in these texts. Because the coverage is broad, this book offers considerable flexibility in use, allowing teachers to pick and choose which areas to emphasize. The book's in-depth coverage also makes it well suited to serve as the primary text for law school seminars, courses in legal history, and advanced or specialty courses in health law and bioethics.

In medical schools, schools of public health, graduate health care administration programs, and undergraduate programs in health law, policy, and bioethics, this book can be used as a primary text for courses. It offers a more accessible and intriguing means for exposing non-law students to concepts in health law and bioethics than the traditional law school casebook. The concise, user-friendly format and the presentation of engaging personal narratives make the book well suited for interdisciplinary use. The supporting website for the text (www.aspenlawschool.com/johnsonkrause) includes the original judicial opinions, discussion questions for each chapter, and other materials useful to teacher and student alike.

Behind the stories presented here are interviews with and insights shared by the key figures in the litigation, their families and counsel, and scholars in the field. We are deeply grateful to them for helping us to put flesh on the skeletal record left behind by the courts. Their generosity and willingness to revisit what in many cases were painful times of their lives enriches this book as a teaching and learning opportunity. We are also immensely grateful to Aspen Publishers for believing in this project and to the anonymous reviewers for their candor and constructive suggestions.

Acknowledgments

Our research and publication of this book could not have been accomplished without the much appreciated support of a number of individuals. We want to thank current and former students Jason Alvarado, Susan Briones, Kelly Carroll, Erin Gilmer, Wade Haaland, Joseph Mercer, Michael Myers, Richard Schlauch, Heather Smith, and Michael Smith for their excellent research assistance and helpful comments. University of Houston Law Center reference librarians Peter Egler and Mon Yin Lung displayed expertise and creativity in locating key documents and other sources. April Moreno, Program Director for the University of Houston Health Law & Policy Institute (HLPI), furnished considerable aid in managing the images and many other key materials for the book. HLPI also provided helpful financial support for the research.

HEALTH LAW
AND BIOETHICS

INTRODUCTION

Putting Health Law Cases in Context

A. Health Law's Context

This book's publication occurs as health law enjoys expanded importance, commanding attention and exerting considerable impact on many levels. As a personal matter, virtually all of us will face difficult health care decisions for ourselves and our loved ones. Current legal rules highly influence the process by which such treatment decisions are made and the information disclosed; more fundamentally, the law helps define the nature of the provider-patient relationship. Many of us will face the additional challenge of navigating the Byzantine system that governs payment and access to care, where intricate legal rules figure prominently. At a professional level, issues of health law deeply affect the medical professionals and institutions that provide care, helping to set common standards and practices and also addressing quality problems and unprofessional conduct through liability, regulation, and related means. Health law also affects the businesses that shoulder much of the economic burden associated with making health insurance available to employees and their families. At a societal level, the provision of adequate and affordable health care continues to loom as a major policy and political issue not only in the domestic context, but also internationally. It is no wonder, then, that attention increasingly focuses on the underlying laws and regulations, as well as the broader legal, regulatory, and professional structures and systems, that govern the delivery of health care services.

Yet in many ways health law lacks consistent features and attributes, making it a difficult area in which to conduct research as well to teach. Various legal rules develop seemingly haphazardly or by accident and often change. Issues apparently long settled, such as the whole brain death standard as the legal determination of death, often become contested and unresolved all over again. In short, health law is quite messy. The basic doctrine and rules often appear to be driven more by politics, history, medical culture, institutional and professional power struggles, the emergence of novel technologies, and similar external forces, than internal logic, intellectual refinement, and a commitment to doctrinal consistency. Indeed, the degree of coherence and theoretical unity within the field has been the subject of recurring debate and commentary.[1]

Yet the essence of health law, at its core, concerns how the law accounts for the unique features of medicine and the special relationships that form in medical encounters, especially the interaction of provider and patient.[2] Health law derives its meaning, direction, and content from considering how the healing process occurs and what it means to be ill, including patients' vulnerability and dependency, and by further considering what it means to care for individuals as a health care provider. Thus, conventional legal rules and doctrine, adapted to the medical context, focus on the many special relationships formed in health care between providers, insurers, employers, family members, and many others, with the patient at the center.[3]

Apart from appreciating the field's constant struggle with complexity, change, and imprecision, what is necessary to understanding health law? Most commentators can agree on one core conclusion: *context matters*. As students learning health law soon come to appreciate, the field is more complicated than simply a mix of tort, contract, and other basic legal doctrines applied by chance to the health law setting.[4] Whether to be a successful practitioner in the field, or to explore the theoretical roots of health law, one needs to have a deep understanding of the health care industry and the actual experiences of patients, providers, payers, and other key players. Health law is anything but insular. Context matters, not just a bit, but enormously. This is not to say that the background conditions in which health law operates deterministically define the field; but recognizing and accounting for this context remains indispensable to following the how and the why of health law.

In part, context features so heavily because of health law's close connection to the delivery of health care. Developments that occur within the practice of medicine and the other health professions help determine health law's direction. Consider, for example, the risks and opportunities posed by new medical discoveries, the historically privileged role of medical professionals, the informational problems that exist in evaluating the quality of health care services, the cultivation and powerful influence of medical norms, and the rise of integrated delivery systems and managed health care organizations as viable business structures within the health care market — such diverse phenomena have provided the very basic issues for health law to address. Likewise, the law greatly impacts the experiences of health care providers and patients. But health law is more than just a conduit for reciprocal influence between law and medicine. Health law has historically tried to bridge the gap between law and the health professions, attempting to reconcile differing values, develop further dialogue about critical issues, and improve processes for conflict resolution among patients, health care professionals, payers, and other stakeholders. In performing this connecting function, health law continually looks to, and derives much of its vitality from, the practice of medicine and the other health professions. In short, "[h]ealth law draws its identity as a field from the commitment to work from a deep insight into the [health care] culture and *context* in which the law will operate."[5]

Context matters apart from the close law and medicine connection. Another distinguishing feature of health law is the extent to which many external forces, including political and economic interests, continually become intertwined with and exert pressures on the legal rules and regulatory systems. Health law often implicates not only immediate questions of specific legal duties and ethical obligations within the narrow confines of particular provider-patient relationships, but also much larger societal questions, including the health care system's constant struggle to balance adequately competing considerations of cost, access, and quality. Pertinent examples can be found in nearly all the cases developed in this book, such as when treatment can be withheld and organs harvested from critically ill newborns (discussed in Mary Crossley's chapter, *In re T.A.C.P. and*

In the Matter of Baby K.: Anencephaly and Slippery Slopes), to what obligations health care institutions have to treat under-insured and uninsured patients (discussed in John Colombo's chapter, *Utah County v. Intermountain Health Care: Reconsidering the Charitable Status of Nonprofit Hospitals*). Beyond the immediate parties involved, such cases had important meaning for a much broader and diverse group of stakeholders, including not only health care professionals and their patients, but taxpayers, health care insurers, and businesses. These constituencies, with their distinct agendas, have closely monitored the underlying legal events and have exerted differing degrees of influence on how health law has developed. As Ted Ruger has observed, "[h]ealth law is a legal field shaped dramatically by external dynamics: the surrounding political and economic climate, interest group pressures from various organized actors, and institutional change and interaction among the bodies that apply and shape the law."[6]

Another way in which context matters for health law concerns the social factors and highly personal interests that animate the legal disputes. Many of the issues are related to treatment decisions and the highly individualistic, subjective factors that influence patient decision-making, including the obvious high-stakes questions of life and death, such as deciding when to withhold life-sustaining treatment. How such intimate decisions are made can turn on a party's deeply held personal beliefs, including religious convictions. Moreover, such disputes can often best be understood by looking to the actual relationships formed and the particular family dynamics at play, which can range from supportive to highly charged and volatile (as discussed in Sandra Johnson's chapter, *Quinlan and Cruzan: Beyond the Symbols*).

But as other chapters in this book vividly illustrate, even health law matters seemingly of a less intimate nature, such as compliance with governmental payment rules, can take on a surprising personal dimension. *United States v. Krizek*, one of the leading health care fraud and abuse cases, morphed from a seemingly routine governmental audit into lengthy, expensive, and enormously complicated litigation. To appreciate why the case became so heavily contested and complex, and left the physician-defendant and his family so completely devastated, one must, among other factors, consider the physician's and his wife's personal histories as immigrants who fled a communist regime in Eastern Europe and who remained highly distrustful of governmental authorities (discussed in Thomas Greaney's and Joan Krause's chapter, *United States v. Krizek: Rough Justice Under the Civil False Claims Act*). Such cases reveal how personal struggles, individual pressures, and private grievances figure prominently in the development of substantive health law.

Finally, context matters because of the dynamic quality of health law. The field is in constant motion. Because the health care industry remains highly regulated, a plethora of new laws, administrative rules, professional licensure requirements, and accreditation standards hits the books each year. New advances continually change the very way in which medicine is practiced, forcing reconsideration of existing legal approaches and ethical standards. This elasticity, including a remarkable capacity for reconsideration and reinvention, is what makes health law so bewildering yet also quite exciting to follow. Broader background developments often function as the change agent; this context becomes critical to understanding health law's constant drive and energy.

B. Developing the Context

In light of these considerations, we are very pleased to introduce this book, which centers on the importance of context to understanding health law. The book has related pedagogical and scholarly objectives. First, it is intended to serve as a creative new tool for teaching and learning about health law in a variety of classroom settings. Second, the book makes an important contribution to the academic literature, revisiting some of the most famous cases in the health law field and digging up a fuller contextual record. This reexamination offers fresh insights about each case's background, explores how and why the case developed as it did, considers what happened in the aftermath, and explains why the case achieved such prominence.

Currently, most students of health law approach the subject matter through a highly selective perspective. Most casebooks offer only highly edited versions of the cases. Further, the appellate opinions that appear in many health law casebooks typically present a narrow, incomplete set of the "facts," glossing over much of what actually occurred and what the underlying litigation unearthed. Instead, the opinions often selectively emphasize certain events to better justify the courts' ultimate rulings. Meanwhile, certain key and highly relevant facts may never even make it into the record at all, such as the economic and historical forces at play or the influence of medical norms and interest-group politics. Thus, the "facts of a case" have been selected first by the judges writing the opinions and then by the casebook authors preparing them for the classroom. These abridged facts represent but a small part of the full human drama and rich, multilayered context of each case. Good casebooks of course attempt to provide more than just edited appellate opinions, and good teachers often provide supplemental materials to address some of these matters. But these efforts are necessarily limited.

Teachers can offer only minimal enrichment in this area because, in our view, the scholarly record of the context of many of the leading health law cases has been underdeveloped and the background materials are not available in usable form. A knowledge gap exists in answering many key questions concerning even well-known cases, including: How did the dispute first arise? Why were the parties not able to resolve it outside of the legal system? Why did the parties bring a lawsuit and what did they want to achieve? What happened to the key players after the case resolved? What do they think about the resolution? What other stakeholders entered the dispute and whose interests did they represent? Why has the case achieved such landmark status? Meanwhile, the role of the actual attorneys involved, including the judges as well as the parties' counsel, often remains underdeveloped as well: Why did counsel take on this particular case? What was the litigation strategy at the time? What did they choose to do when the law did not provide a clear answer? How did they view the case's relative merits and decide to argue it? How did they influence the way the case ultimately was resolved, both for their clients and as a matter of precedent? What did the judges think about the arguments, precedent, and how to achieve a just result?

As these questions suggest, there is much to be learned for academic theory, for better ways of teaching, and for engaging in the successful and strategic practice of health law from revisiting famous cases in the field and delving further into their complete context. Accordingly, this book provides a unique treatment of the leading health law cases. To our knowledge, this is the first and only book of its kind in the field. The focus is placed on telling the personal stories behind the disputes, including insights from the parties, attorneys, and expert witnesses. The common endeavor among all the contributing authors is to situate each case in its broader context, including looking at the historical, political, social, and personal factors at play. In doing so, provocative and important new insights are developed, both into these landmark cases and for health law and policy more generally.

Perhaps the biggest challenge that we encountered was selecting the cases. One could debate endlessly which cases should appear on a top-ten or top-twenty list of famous health law cases. We ended up choosing thirteen cases, divided into eleven chapters, with some discussing related cases. It was quite difficult indeed to winnow down our initially longer list. Among the selection criteria, we emphasized first that a case had to appear in several of the leading health law casebooks or in other widely used teaching materials, as we wanted to choose cases that are regularly being taught in the classroom. Second, we selected cases where the background context had not yet been sufficiently developed or where there were novel insights to be gained or new evidence uncovered. Thus, we purposefully avoided cases such as the abortion decision *Roe v. Wade*, where much of the background has already been well covered elsewhere. Third, we tried to pick a broad mix of cases from across the subject matter spectrum within health law.

Conceptually, we ended up dividing health law into the following commonly used categories and included representative cases from each: (i) the professional-patient relationship and the quality of care; (ii) death and dying; (iii) reproductive rights; (iv) organ transplants, medical futility, and presumed consent; (v) public health; and (vi) regulatory, organizational, and business issues. Accordingly, we do not purport to state that the cases included in this book make up the definitive list of leading health law cases; we question whether true consensus could ever be reached on such a list. What we remain confident about, nonetheless, is that this book includes renowned, highly influential, widely taught cases that have been drawn from the broad variety of sub-fields within health law. We believe that this pragmatic approach maximizes the book's accessibility and overall utility.

C. Use of This Book and Supplemental Website

We envision that this book will be used as a secondary text to enrich basic or survey law school courses in health law and bioethics. We also intend this book to be used in non-law school programs covering health law or bioethics on the graduate and undergraduate level.

Outside the law school setting, this book can be used as a primary text for health law and bioethics courses taught in medical schools, schools of public health, graduate health care administration programs, and undergraduate programs related to health law, policy, and bioethics. Compared to a traditional law school casebook, this text offers a more accessible and intriguing means for exposing non-law students to concepts in health law and bioethics. The book's concise, readable, user-friendly format, and its presentation of engaging personal narratives, make it well suited for interdisciplinary use.

We are pleased to provide a supplemental website along with this book: www.aspenlawschool.com/johnsonkrause. The website provides a wealth of additional material for each chapter, including, when available, reproduction of or links to the full written opinions associated with each case, and other interesting primary and background material to help flesh out the full context. Teachers and students will want to consult the website as an ongoing resource for further research and to stimulate additional classroom discussion.

There is one matter of stylistic clarification that we want to mention. This book uses endnotes, not the traditional legal citation method of footnotes, to improve ease of use for all types of readers. We have tried to keep the number of citations to a minimum. The endnotes offer valuable direction to supporting sources and to additional material for readers who wish to pursue further inquiry. Additional textual information appears in some citation notes, as commonly occurs with legal texts. Non-law school readers in particular should be aware of this and, when appropriate, remember to consult the additional textual information in the endnotes.

ENDNOTES

1. *See generally* Symposium, *Rethinking Health Law*, 41 Wake Forest L. Rev. 341 (2006); Theodore W. Ruger, *Health Law's Coherence Anxiety*, 96 Geo. L. J. 625 (2008).

2. *See* Mark A. Hall, *The History and Future of Health Care Law: An Essentialist View*, 41 Wake Forest L. Rev. 347, 362 (2006).

3. *See generally* Mark A. Hall, *Law, Medicine, and Trust*, 55 Stan. L. Rev. 463 (2002); Mark A. Hall, Carl E. Schneider & Lois Shepherd, *Rethinking Health Law*, 41 Wake Forest L. Rev. 341, 342 (2006).

4. *See* Joan H. Krause & Richard S. Saver, *Ethics in the Practice of Health Law*, 32 J.L. Med. & Ethics 766, 767 (2004).

5. Sandra H. Johnson, *Five Easy Pieces: Motifs of Health Law*, 14 Health Matrix 131, 133 (2004) (emphasis added).

6. Ruger, *supra* note 1, at 627–28.

Part I

THE PROFESSIONAL-PATIENT RELATIONSHIP AND THE QUALITY OF CARE

Chapter 1

CANTERBURY
v.
SPENCE

The Inadvertent Landmark Case

ALAN MEISEL*

There is hardly a law student or a medical student who does not encounter, somewhere in the law or medical school curriculum, the subject of informed consent and one of the leading cases on this subject, *Canterbury v. Spence*.[1] Whatever the educational setting, the lesson is the same: medical treatment requires the patient's informed consent. What every student learns, most fundamentally, is that a patient's agreement to be treated by a physician is not legally valid — and hence is a legal wrong for which the physician can be held accountable through the payment of monetary damages — unless the patient's consent is "informed." The ancient duty of obtaining a patient's simple agreement to be treated is still required and the failure to do so is a battery, but the doctrine of informed consent imposes a second mandate. A physician, before obtaining consent, must make adequate disclosure of information about the proposed treatment to the patient — the "informed" part of informed consent.

The *Canterbury* case was hardly the first case to impose this duty. Informed consent was recognized at least 15 years before the *Canterbury* opinion was handed down in 1972, its explicit antecedents in medical practice stretch back at least to the latter part of the nineteenth century,[2] and its legal underpinnings existed in English law so long that "the memory of man runneth not to the

* Alan Meisel is Professor of Law and Dickie, McCamey & Chilcote Professor of Bioethics at the University of Pittsburgh in the Schools of Law and Medicine, where he is the director of the Center for Bioethics and Health Law and the Health Law Certificate Program. His interest in informed consent dates back to the time when he was a law student taking a course from Jay Katz. Professor Meisel relied heavily on information provided by Walter Murphy, Barry Nace, Jack Olender, Irving Schloss, David Schoenbrod, and Thomas Scheuneman in the preparation of this chapter, but without the dedicated assistance of Jerry Canterbury and his sister, Nancy Farahmand, it would not have been possible to have written it, nor would it without the sleuthing skills of Marc Silverman, a reference librarian at the University of Pittsburgh School of Law, who located Jerry Canterbury.

contrary." What *Canterbury* did was to set forth a detailed, elaborate, and thoughtful — though certainly not airtight — discourse on the subject in a form that reads more like a law review article than a judicial opinion. The opinion provides a syllabus of topics that are the mainstay of informed consent: the source of a doctor's duty to provide information to a patient; the standard by which the adequacy of disclosure is to be measured; the requisite causal nexus between inadequate disclosure and the patient's injury; the type of injury that will support recovery; the physician's privilege to withhold information; the role of expert testimony in establishing the inadequacy of disclosure and causation; and the nature of the cause of action for inadequate disclosure, necessary to establish the appropriate statute of limitations and evidentiary rules.

How the *Canterbury* case came to be is a tale of its own. To be certain, no one planned it this way. In fact, one of the prime players — Jerry Canterbury, the injured man at the center of the case — was unaware of its landmark status 35 years after the decision was handed down. Besides Canterbury, the main characters in this tale are his surgeon, Dr. William Spence, and his lawyer, Earl H. Davis; even J. Edgar Hoover has a walk-on part and evidentiary rules.

A. The Plaintiff — Jerry Canterbury

"The record we review tells a depressing tale."[3] And so begins the opinion of the Court of Appeals for the District of Columbia in *Canterbury v. Spence*. The tale of Canterbury may have been depressing, but it was also brief, at least as recounted in the opinion:

> At the time of the events which gave rise to this litigation, appellant [Jerry Canterbury] was nineteen years of age, a clerk-typist employed by the Federal Bureau of Investigation. In December, 1958, he began to experience severe pain between his shoulder blades. He consulted two general practitioners, but the medications they prescribed failed to eliminate the pain. Thereafter, appellant secured an appointment with Dr. Spence, who is a neurosurgeon.
>
> Dr. Spence examined appellant in his office at some length but found nothing amiss. On Dr. Spence's advice appellant was x-rayed, but the films did not identify any abnormality. Dr. Spence then recommended that appellant undergo a myelogram — a procedure in which dye is injected into the spinal column and traced to find evidence of disease or other disorder — at the Washington Hospital Center.
>
> Appellant entered the hospital on February 4, 1959. [Footnote omitted.] The myelogram revealed a "filling defect"[4] in the region of the fourth thoracic vertebra. Since a myelogram often does no more than pinpoint the location of an aberration, surgery may be necessary to discover the cause. Dr. Spence told appellant that he would have to undergo a laminectomy — the excision of the posterior arch of the vertebra — to correct what he suspected was a ruptured disc. . . . [H]is mother was a widow of slender financial means living in Cyclone, West Virginia, . . . [who] could be reached through a neighbor's telephone.[5]

To say that Mrs. Canterbury was a woman of slender financial means was a kind way of saying that the Canterbury family was very poor. Jerry Canterbury was born on March 12, 1939, the third of five children. He grew up in the coalfields of Cyclone, West Virginia, not far from the Kentucky border to the west, and not too far from the interstate heading eastward to Washington, D.C. — where he would catch the Greyhound bus that would take him to the job that eventually would take him to Dr. Spence.

Canterbury was nine when his father died, in what appears to have been a coal mining accident. He and all of his siblings graduated from high school. He followed in the footsteps of his older brothers, Jack and Jim, who left home after graduation to seek their fortune elsewhere because they knew there was none to be found in the coal mines, just a life of danger. Jack joined the Army and Jim the Navy. After high school graduation in June 1957, Canterbury sought a job in a steel mill in Canton, Ohio, near where he had worked summers; failing this, he returned home to Cyclone, where he was attracted to the FBI by a recruitment letter he received in the mail. He believes that the FBI recruited young men and women in rural areas because they were less likely to have criminal backgrounds. He filled out the application, sent it in, "and in no time an agent was knocking on the door."[6]

A photograph of Jerry Canterbury, taken in 1958

Canterbury accepted the FBI's offer, hopped on a bus, and headed for the nation's capital, some 350 miles and untold cultural light years from home. The FBI provided temporary housing for its new out-of-town employees, and Canterbury teamed up with three other new hires and found an apartment in a rooming house on Capitol Hill. He began work in the personnel records department of the FBI on January 6, 1958.[7] By all accounts, he performed his work adequately, made friends on the job, and enjoyed socializing with his roommates and friends.

Just before Christmas of 1958, while walking down a corridor of the FBI building in which he worked, he experienced a sharp pain in his neck.[8] Later that evening, while working the 4 P.M.–12 A.M. shift, "the pain was so aggravating" that he sought and received permission from his supervisor to go home for the evening. At the suggestion of nurses at the FBI dispensary, he contacted the D.C. Medical Society and requested the name of a neurosurgeon; he was given two. The first surgeon was out of town, so he contacted the second, Dr. William T. Spence, and made an appointment for a few weeks later, in late January 1959.[9] Canterbury later testified that Dr. Spence "could not determine the nature of the dull, aggravating pain that I was having,"[10] so he scheduled a myelogram, which required inpatient hospitalization at Washington Hospital Center (WHC). On February 4, 1959, Canterbury was admitted to the hospital and the myelogram was performed.[11] It revealed a "filling defect" in the upper spine.[12] As the Court of Appeals related, Canterbury was told that he needed a laminectomy — the removal of the posterior arch of the vertebra — to treat a suspected ruptured disc.[13]

The laminectomy was performed the following week. The surgery began in the early afternoon and was completed around 6:20 P.M.[14] Dr. Spence found that

Canterbury had "a swollen non-pulsating [spinal] cord and he attempted to relieve the pressure. . . ."[15] Canterbury's next recollection after coming out of anesthesia was in the early hours of the next day, when he was awakened by severe pain in the area of his bladder and needed to urinate.[16] He summoned a nurse, whom he testified:

> took from the night stand beside the bed the urinal. . . . She raised the head of the bed, elevated me, and let down the side rail, handed me the urinal, and walked out of the room. Now, when I woke up prior to summoning the nurse for assistance in the urinal, I was on my right side. Of course, the bed was in full height off of the floor, which I would say would be approximately three and a half feet at least into the air. And lying on my right side I was having a problem putting the urinal in the place to attempt to use it. And the next thing I know I was lying on the floor.[17]

It came out at trial that conflicting orders had been written about how Canterbury was supposed to urinate. Dr. Luessenhop, an associate of Dr. Spence, had written an order that he "may sit up in bed to void."[18] However, Dr. Rubin, a house officer, had written an order stating "Patient to stand at bedside and attempt to void."[19] There is a further conflict as to just what Canterbury did. While he claimed that he tried to urinate lying down in bed and rolled out, the hospital's incident report says that "Mr. Canterbury sat up on side of bed with the intention of being able to void. He slipped off side of bed grabbing onto chair."[20] Curiously, the incident report also says that the bedside rails were up; if that is true, it is unclear how he could have been sitting on the side of the bed. In any event, according to Canterbury:

> as the morning progressed along and shortly before lunch I made mention to my mother in my right leg that I had a stinging numbness sensation, like I had been possibly lying on one side too long. . . . Then later on in the afternoon — this, as I say, started with the right leg, and then it worked its way down into the left leg, and this was mentioned to the nurse on the floor that there was a numbness, tingling sensation, and then approximately in the vicinity of around five p.m., just shortly before dinner was served that evening, I started having chest pain. . . . [P]ossibly ten or fifteen minutes after I ate, I had started getting severe pain in the chest as if I was being bound with a vise or something like someone just cutting off all the oxygen.[21]

Canterbury was taken back to surgery that evening in what must have been thought to have been an emergency. As he had recently eaten a meal, he could not be given general anesthesia and the procedure had to be performed under a local anesthetic.[22] The consultation report after this surgery stated that Canterbury had complete flaccid paralysis of both lower extremities, that "deep and superficial reflexes [were] absent," and that he had no response to a pinprick just above the knee. It further stated that there was no specific therapy to be administered at that time, and that his prognosis was "guarded."[23] Four days later, another consultation report confirmed that "[t]here exist no voluntary movements of lower extremities."[24]

Canterbury's condition did improve somewhat, and he was discharged from WHC, with his legs partially paralyzed,[25] on May 17, 1959, about three and one-half months after he was admitted for a routine operation — one which Dr. Spence had told his mother was no more serious "than any other operation."[26] During his hospitalization, he had physical therapy to teach him how to ambulate and to raise his body using his arms. When he was discharged, he was using two Lofstrand crutches, a type of forearm crutch.[27] FBI employees took him back to West Virginia.[28]

He spent the summer at home in West Virginia, where he did a lot of walking with help from his younger brother and a neighbor boy.[29] He also received a letter from the FBI informing him that he would either need to return to work or resign. The Bureau had advanced him sick leave when he was hospitalized, and that was coming to an end.[30] So in late summer, Canterbury returned to Washington and went directly to the hospital, an arrangement which had been made before he left West Virginia, and spent almost two weeks hospitalized for a cystoscopic study of the urinary problems that were still bedeviling him. When he was discharged, he returned to his prior residence in Washington and began work just after Labor Day, 1959.[31]

His old messenger job was no longer feasible because of the difficulty he had in getting around. Because he had no sensation that he was going to urinate, he had accidents at work and on street cars, which understandably caused him a great deal of embarrassment.[32] A urologist eventually prescribed for him a Cunningham clamp,[33] which put an end to further bladder mishaps, but this did not occur for a few years. In addition to the bladder mishaps, he suffered bladder infections, bowel incontinence, and was subject to falling,[34] either because of leg weakness or problems using the crutches. One of the falls led to phlebitis — inflammation of the veins, which led to swelling in his legs — and another hospitalization.[35] He eventually became reliant on a variety of medications, including Valium, Darvon, and Seconal, resulting in a hospitalization for several weeks in the summer of 1970 to address his drug dependence.[36]

Dr. Spence was concerned about the added difficulties for Canterbury of living in a cold climate and suggested he could more easily get exercise swimming if he were to live in a warm place.[37] Spence told Canterbury that he had some very close friends at the FBI and that he would see about getting him transferred. Canterbury later testified, "[t]hat was the last he told me[,] until right around the latter part of November [when] one of the Special Agents, in charge of the Personnel Department, walked into the Personnel Records Room where I was working and told me that I had been transferred to Miami."[38]

After his initial hospitalization in May 1959, Canterbury moved more than a dozen times — sometimes from one city to another, sometimes within a city — until he eventually settled in Canton, Ohio, at the beginning of 1967. From 1959 to 1962, he worked for the FBI in Washington, Miami, Los Angeles, and Houston. Although at first the FBI exhibited a caring attitude toward Canterbury, over time the agency became less amenable to his transfer requests, which he had made either to be in a warm climate or to be closer to family. Instead of honoring his request to transfer to San Diego from Miami, he was transferred to Los Angeles; instead of being transferred from Los Angeles to Washington, he was transferred to Houston, where he knew no one.[39]

Canterbury resigned from the FBI in June 1962 and returned to Washington, where he took a position as a typist for a few months and then left to work at a better paying job at National Geographic at the behest of a former FBI colleague who was working there.[40] Eventually, he left and returned to West Virginia because of depression. He later recalled that:

during the summer of '64 I was having more problems trying to become adjusted with myself. This had been a great problem since . . . February '59, trying to get adjusted, as to mix and mingle with people, considering my condition, etc. And I became very depressed . . . I did not seek any doctor's advice on this. And I felt that if I could take a leave of absence, which I wanted, approximately a month leave of absence, to try — to go back to my home in West Virginia or to my brother's — I actually wanted to go to my brother's home in Ohio, and be with family, and just relax and see if I could, you know, get myself back together from the depression that I was having, etc. But I was unable to take a leave of absence that long. So, therefore, I resigned because I considered my well-being more important than trying to stay on because I had fallen at the apartment where I lived by myself on two occasions, and at one time severely cut the right hand, had me hospitalized for that.[41]

In the Canton area, he worked on and off for a steel company, for the Ohio state highway patrol, and beginning in January 1967 as a dispatcher at the county sheriff's office, a position he remained in for a bit more than 20 years. Surrounded by family — two of his brothers and their families, his younger brother and sister, and his mother all lived nearby — with a job he found congenial and that provided him with financial security, including health insurance and a pension, Canterbury finally found his niche.[42] He was married in January 1967, but according to the trial transcript the marriage broke up after a few years as a result of some of the after-effects of his accident.[43]

B. The Lawsuit and the Trial

The idea to sue Dr. Spence and WHC crystallized while Canterbury was working for the FBI in Los Angeles in 1962. Canterbury heard about Melvin Belli, then known as the "King of Torts." Belli was at the peak of his career and did not waste much time in brushing him off, but not before giving him the name of another lawyer, whom Canterbury sought out. But his moves to Houston, back home to West Virginia, and then again to D.C. put an end to this arrangement. The Los Angeles lawyer did, however, refer him to Earl Davis, a member of the D.C. bar,[44] with whom he would work for more than a decade through his first trial in 1968, an appeal with the resulting landmark informed consent decision in 1972, and a second trial in 1973 and appeal in 1975.[45]

1. The Attorney

Davis was an old-school trial attorney. He handled mostly personal injury work — he was on retainer to a Washington taxicab company — but also some criminal defense work. Davis was a loner; he never had a partner until the early 1970s, though he shared office space with a variety of other solo trial attorneys. At times those attorneys would work on some of his matters (as some did in helping prepare Canterbury's case for trial) and even try cases together.[46]

By the time he began handling Canterbury's case, Davis was a well-seasoned trial attorney. One of his contemporaries, Jack Olender, claims that "[h]e had more expertise in malpractice than almost any other plaintiff's lawyer. He had a medical library and he used the books. Lawyers constantly called him for advice on cases, including malpractice."[47] Another lawyer, however, observed that Davis had no real expertise in medical malpractice, but neither did many other members of the D.C. plaintiff's bar. At that time, local plaintiffs' attorneys were not eager to take medical malpractice cases because they felt such cases could not be won because they required an expert witness, and doctors would not testify against their peers. To make matters worse, the so-called "locality rule" that applied in medical malpractice law at that time required the expert to be from the same locality as the defendant physician, or at least familiar with the standard of practice there.[48] Davis's inability to obtain a neurosurgeon as an expert witness seemed to make him reluctant to take the case to trial. In a letter to Canterbury, he wrote that "I sincerely hope that this case might be settled, as this jurisdiction is a tough one on medical malpractice cases. . . ."[49]

By contrast, the defense lawyers — including Walter Murphy, who represented Dr. Spence — were part of a "new breed" of lawyers who were increasingly attaining a mastery of medical knowledge, which contributed greatly to the successful defense of their cases. Furthermore, it was difficult at that time to obtain a large damages verdict in D.C. because most accident victims, like most of the residents of the District, had low incomes, which would be reflected in the size of any damages awarded.[50]

Contemporaries recalled that Davis sat behind a desk with mounds of paper on it, yet he knew where every piece was. He wore a green eyeshade and rolled up his sleeves. He worked seven days a week but left his office early on Sundays. Many trial lawyers of that era did a lot of imbibing on the job, but not Davis, who never had a drink during working hours. At night, however, bourbon and steak were his favorites.[51] He loved the law and was married to it, but he was twice married in the conventional sense, too; his first wife died in 1964, and his second wife died just a few years later.[52]

A photograph of attorney Earl Davis, Mrs. Canterbury, and Jerry Canterbury, taken in May 1973. Jerry is supporting himself with a crutch, which is hidden behind his mother.

Although one attorney who knew Davis describes him as "a warm, friendly person loved by his clients and liked and respected by members of the bar," another who worked with Davis described him as a cold person in some respects, saying that he seemed to care more about the law than about the client. However, even this attorney admitted that the *Canterbury* case was different for Davis. After years of working with Canterbury, Davis seems to have developed a genuine fondness for him, which was mutual. Their correspondence is replete with chit-chat interspersed with information about the case: "Am glad to hear that your mother is getting along well after her unfortunate attack of thrombo-phlebitis."[53] However, Davis's sentiment that he "was sorry to hear that you are again a sort of Calamity Joe, what with the happening of that tractor accident, in which you could have been seriously injured were it not for the soft and newly plowed ground acting as a cushion," is immediately followed by "Well, the Record on Appeal (the second go-around) has been finally completed and the case docketed in the U.S. Court of Appeals."[54] And a plea by Davis for some money from Canterbury is immediately followed by news that "[t]he Watergate hearings have had this town in a buzz for the last 13 weeks, and now it look as though Agnew is taking over in the publicity."[55]

Canterbury reciprocated his fondness for Davis in his letters. On February 1, 1975, Davis wrote to Canterbury that he had not been in touch for a while because he had been hospitalized with a heart attack about three weeks earlier. He also reported that the D.C. Circuit had denied his request for oral argument of the second appeal, which could not have been a positive harbinger. In response, Canterbury wrote that "Mother and I are very sadden[ed] to hear of your recent heart attack, but happy to know that you are somewhat better. You are in our thought and prayers always."[56] Beyond these boilerplate thoughts, which anyone responding to such a letter could be expected to include, Canterbury added a heartfelt "You are one heck of a swell man. . . . You know that we have always wanted you, Red and Kitty [Davis's housemates] to come visit us so now that you are on limited duty why don't you just pack up and come to Ohio for at least a few days. I believe the Country air and quietness would be of great benefit to all of you."[57]

Yet Davis was not beyond gossip and *schadenfreude*. After the second trial had been lost, and while preparing for the second appeal, Davis seemed downcast, judging from one of his letters to Canterbury. It is less than a full page, and three of five paragraphs are devoted to the high cost of printing the brief and the appendix and about how he "had to cut down on the Brief, and make it brief" and forgo a reply brief because of the cost. Apart from a closing paragraph sending greetings to Canterbury's mother, the other paragraph reads: "I enclose copy of yesterday's [The Daily Washington] Law Reporter, and if you will look under 'United States Tax Liens', I think you will see a familiar name. He is now apparently in dutch with Uncle Sam," referring to a tax lien against Wm. Thornton Spence for $2,336.58.[58]

Davis frequently referred to the high costs of prosecuting the case and thanked Canterbury enthusiastically when Canterbury sent him a check, although there is no record of his having sent Canterbury a formal bill for expenses. Davis wrote to Canterbury that at the time of the second appeal in 1973, "Things have been pretty tough for me financially since the re-trial of your case, and preparing for the appeal. On the attached list, you will note that I have spent almost $2,000.00 on the re-trial of the case and in preparing for the appeal. Frankly, I do not know where I am going to get the money for the printer, to do the joint appendix and the legal brief. Can you help out on some of this?"[59]

Canterbury kept meticulous records of the money he sent Davis, which was a financial strain for Canterbury. Barry Nace, Davis's associate during the second trial and later his partner, contends that Davis was not in serious financial straits but that he was just tight with money. Davis's attitude toward collecting costs from his clients was that he did not mind if he lost a case, but "I'll be damned if I want to pay for the privilege of doing so."[60]

2. *The Theory of the Case*

Nace began practicing with Davis after the landmark first Court of Appeals decision was handed down in 1972, but before the case was retried in 1973. When he reviewed the file for the second trial, he realized that a medical expert would be important, if not essential, to success. Nace was able to retain the services of Dr. Harold Hirsh to testify on both informed consent and post-op care, and listed him late as a witness. Hirsh was both a lawyer and a physician, renowned in the medico-legal circles of that time, but he was not a neurosurgeon. Nace also realized that this was probably the biggest case of Davis's career, with potentially huge damages given the seriousness and extent of Canterbury's injuries.[61]

However, Canterbury's case was fraught with problems from the outset. The fundamental problem was the issue of what caused Canterbury's paralysis. Was it the very condition for which he sought treatment from Dr. Spence — the pain between his shoulder blades? Was it something that happened during the first surgery, the laminectomy, which was intended to treat this pain? Was it the fall from bed, and if so, was that because the doctors' orders were unclear, inadequate, or conflicting, or because the nurses (who were employees of the hospital, not of the doctors) did not carry them out correctly? Was it instead the second surgery immediately after the fall? Or was it some combination of these?[62]

Closely related to the causation problem was the issue of negligence. Even if the cause of the paralysis was something one of the defendants did, the law said that neither Dr. Spence nor the hospital could be held liable unless what they did was negligent. To establish this, Davis had to show that their conduct failed to meet the standard of care — what a reasonable physician of similar training, education, and experience would have done under the circumstances. To complicate matters even more, in most American jurisdictions at that time (D.C. among them), the locality rule required the plaintiff to establish what a reasonable physician *in that locality* would do, and that required the testimony of an expert witness — another physician from that locality. Unlike today, when it is a relatively simple matter to hire a professional expert witness, in the 1960s and 1970s the "conspiracy of silence"[63] still reigned in many jurisdictions. Getting a doctor to testify against a peer — especially a doctor from the same locality, and perhaps the same hospital staff, same neighborhood, same church, or same country club — was nigh unto impossible.

Because of these difficulties, Davis also advanced legal theories focusing on Canterbury's lack of consent to treatment. One theory was fairly straightforward: Canterbury was, by the law of that time, a minor because he was under the age of 21. Consequently, his consent was not legally valid, and parental consent was necessary. It is clear Dr. Spence did not obtain consent from Canterbury's mother *before* the surgery. But even if legally valid consent to the laminectomy had not been obtained, the one-year statute of limitations on a battery cause of action — the theory that would have had to be pursued for lack of consent — had run by the time the complaint was filed.[64]

However, because the statute of limitations had not yet run on a negligence cause of action, in addition to filing claims for garden variety negligence Davis gambled that he could also bring an action for lack of *informed* consent, couched in the language of negligence — which, while well-accepted today, was somewhat unusual at that time. In a letter to Canterbury, written just after the pre-trial conference for the second trial, Davis told Canterbury that "[s]ince I have been unable to get an expert in neuro-surgery to testify, as a witness for plaintiff, this presents a problem. As I see it, our big point is Dr. Spence's operating without having first secured an 'informed consent', i.e. — fully acquainting you with the risks involved, and then letting you make up your own mind as to surgery."[65]

Prevailing on a negligence-based informed consent claim would be an uphill battle. At the first trial, lack of disclosure had not yet been established as an accepted tort theory in the District of Columbia. Even if it were to be accepted, the claim might still be barred by the statute of limitations if it were treated as sounding in battery rather than negligence. Or the claim might not reach the jury because of a lack of expert testimony. And the garden variety negligence claims were also vulnerable because of the need for expert testimony.

In fact, that is pretty much what happened at the first *Canterbury* trial in March and April 1968, nine years after the accident occurred. Davis "introduced no evidence to show medical and hospital practices, if any, customarily pursued in regard to the critical aspects of the case, and" he had to engage in the risky procedure of calling Dr. Spence as an expert, who testified only on the issue of causation. On this issue, Spence "expressed his opinion that appellant's disabilities stemmed from his pre-operative condition as symptomized by the swollen, non-pulsating spinal cord [which he observed during the laminectomy]. He stated, however, that neither he nor any of the other physicians with whom he consulted was certain as to what that condition was. . . ."[66] Spence did admit "that trauma can be a cause of paralysis," but he qualified this by also testifying "that even without trauma paralysis can be anticipated 'somewhere in the nature of one percent' of the laminectomies performed. . . ."[67]

After Davis finished putting on his case, attorneys for both Dr. Spence and the WHC moved for a directed verdict — that is, they claimed that the plaintiff did not have enough evidence for the jury to find, more probably than not, that either Spence or WHC had been negligent in any way, including by failing to obtain informed consent. The trial court agreed and granted the motion.[68]

3. What Was He Told and When Was He Told It?

Informed consent is a classic "he said, she said" issue. After the fact the patient invariably will say, "the doctor didn't tell me what could go wrong, and if he had, I never would have agreed to that." In contrast, the doctor invariably will say, "I told him that could go wrong, and he said he'd take his chances." As time has gone by and doctors and their lawyers have realized the legal risks of inadequate disclosure, they have devised written forms (the so-called "informed consent forms" widely used today) ostensibly to document that the patient was told exactly what those risks would entail. Some doctors have been surprised to learn that a signed consent form only establishes that the patient signed the form,[69] but not that he really was provided with material information (or that he understood it — which is yet another complexity of the law and practice of informed consent).

The information disclosure made to Jerry Canterbury was meager in the extreme. The Court of Appeals opinion says that Dr. Spence only told Canterbury "that he would have to undergo a laminectomy — the excision of the posterior arch of the vertebra — to correct what he suspected was a ruptured disc."[70] According to testimony in the second trial, Canterbury testified that he asked Dr. Spence about the nature of the proposed surgery, and that Spence "advised me [on the basis of the myelogram] that he had located a filling defect in the area which he had marked on my back, and that I had a possible ruptured disk [sic] and that it would take an operation to correct this."[71] When Davis asked whether the operation he underwent was serious, Canterbury responded:

> I asked him what the nature of the operation was. I am strictly from the country. I had no knowledge of what a disk meant —
> I asked him what a disk consisted of, what the operation consisted of.
> He advised that he would have to go into the area where he had located the trouble to see what the matter was. This was what was explained to me.
> I asked him if this was a serious operation. He said, No more serious than an ordinary, everyday operation.[72]

In other words, there was no evidence that Canterbury was told anything about the surgery or its dangers. Similarly, Spence's exchange with the patient's mother was even more meager:

> Dr. Spence told her that the surgery was occasioned by a suspected ruptured disc. Mrs. Canterbury then asked if the recommended operation was serious and Dr. Spence replied "not anymore than any other operation." . . . The testimony is contradictory as to whether during the course of the conversation Mrs. Canterbury expressed her consent to the operation.[73]

In other words, Canterbury was told very little about the surgery, and his mother was told even less. Even if it wasn't too little, it surely was too late. Consent must be obtained *before* surgery, not after.

C. The Judge

Davis argued the first appeal before the United States Court of Appeals for the District of Columbia on December 18, 1969, before Judges Wright, Leventhal, and Robinson. Ironically, "the problem of informed consent was virtually ignored."[74] The task of writing the opinion was assigned to Judge Robinson. It took two and one-half years for that opinion to see the light of day.

At the time the appeal was heard, the United States Court of Appeals for the District of Columbia was unusual for a federal appeals court in that many of the cases on its docket were the equivalent of "state court" cases — that is, cases arising under local rather than federal law. That was because the federal district court for the District of Columbia heard not only the usual federal matters and diversity cases, but also served as the trial court for all matters arising under District law above a minimum jurisdictional amount. Had it not been for this jurisdictional quirk — one that was abolished while the *Canterbury* case was being litigated[75] — the opinion might have been a far different one, for the case would not have come under the scrutiny of Judge Spottswood W. Robinson III.

Judge Robinson had enjoyed an extremely distinguished legal career. Born in Richmond in 1916, his grandfather had been a slave and though without formal education had achieved considerable success as a businessman. Robinson graduated from Virginia Union University and Howard Law School, where he came under the influence of a group of professors and, after graduation, a group of Howard law graduates who were the leaders of the civil rights movement of that time and the succeeding decades — including Thurgood Marshall and William Hastie, who also went on to become federal judges. Along with the other members of this group, he worked for the NAACP Legal Defense and Education Fund and helped plot the strategy for the U.S. Supreme Court school desegregation cases of the 1950s. Robinson was co-counsel on one of the Brown v. Board of Education companion cases, Bolling v. Sharpe,[76] which originated in the District of Columbia. President Kennedy appointed Robinson to the Civil Rights Commission in 1961, and President Johnson appointed him as a federal trial court judge in D.C. in 1966 and then to the D.C. Court of Appeals.

Judge Robinson, by all accounts, was a scholarly and meticulous judge — "a very academic guy," according to Walter Murphy, Dr. Spence's attorney.[77] In addition to his distinguished career as a legal practitioner, he had been a professor of law and the dean of Howard Law School. His first encounter with serious professional failure was his service as a federal trial judge because he could not do the one thing that trial judges absolutely must do — make decisions expeditiously. It took him 28 days to conclude his first trial, a simple one brought by a passenger against a bus company for an injury to his arm caused by broken glass from the bus window when the bus crashed. Murphy said that "the whole bar was agog over it."[78]

So Judge Robinson, in relatively short order, got kicked upstairs. Appellate courts are far more contemplative places than trial courts, and the Court of Appeals must have been far more congenial to a man of Robinson's scholarly temperament. Speed was less of a virtue on the Court of Appeals, which is fortunate because Robinson still had tremendous difficulty moving the caseload expeditiously.[79] This may have been because, as Walter Murphy observed, "he had to have every citation [in his opinions] God ever created."[80] Irving Schloss, Judge Robinson's clerk who worked on the opinion, added that "Judge Robinson did everything but embroider the opinions."[81] One need look no further to substantiate these observations than the Canterbury opinion, with its 149 footnotes and countless citations in the text.

Schloss further notes that Judge Robinson was also very careful in his personal life. He was one of the first black federal judges in the D.C. Circuit and because of his high profile, did not want to do anything that would bring disrepute on himself or the court. Thus, when he and his wife drove on a trip, they would carefully observe the speed limit and alternate as drivers every two hours so that they would be fresh, able to pay attention, and obey all the rules of the road in order to minimize their chances of being stopped for a traffic violation. "He was careful," Schloss adds, "and meticulous to a fault."[82]

During part of the period between the oral argument and the time the opinion was handed down, there was an "awful bottleneck" in Robinson's chambers because of the Pentagon Papers case.[83] Schloss has a clearer recollection of FBI agents chained to briefcases coming into chambers and sitting there while the judge and clerks looked at the highly classified papers they had brought, and then returning the papers to the chained briefcases before leaving, than he does of the details of the *Canterbury* case. Nonetheless, apart from the Pentagon Papers case, Schloss had a sense at the time that this was an important case, perhaps the most important of the term.[84]

D. The Opinion

Even before Canterbury first met Spence in 1959, and continuing up to May 1972, when the opinion was released, the idea of informed consent was still in its infancy. The phrase *informed consent* was first used by a court in the medical context in 1957,[85] although the idea of informed consent to medical treatment had been gestating for almost 100 years.[86] By 1972, a body of law had begun to grow, but there was still a relatively small number of cases and law review articles on the subject.[87]

There must have been something in the air in 1972, for that was the year that informed consent came into its own — not just in the *Canterbury* decision, but in major opinions from the California[88] and Rhode Island[89] Supreme Courts as well. For whatever reason, Judge Robinson seized on the issue and devoted all but five paragraphs of his 21-page opinion to the discussion of informed consent. In the end, the Court of Appeals recognized a cause of action for inadequate disclosure and held that it sounded in negligence, not battery, and therefore was not barred by the statute of limitations.[90]

Judge Robinson did not have to look far to find a template for a comprehensive approach to informed consent. The source that most influenced the opinion was *Informed Consent to Therapy*, by the late Jon Waltz, a professor at Northwestern University School of Law, and Thomas W. Scheuneman, then a third-year law student at Northwestern working on an independent research project under Waltz's supervision.[91] By the time Canterbury sued Spence — and certainly by the time the appeal was heard — it was just a matter of time as to which case would be the occasion for spinning a full-blown judicial exegesis on the subject. Anyone undertaking a study of informed consent, whether superficial or intensive, is bound to study the *Canterbury* opinion. Even those courts that have rejected one of its core points — the objective standard of care — often recount it in detail. Its thoroughness and tight reasoning alone, however, have not made it the landmark that it is. That is due, in large part, to the elegance of its prose. Judge Robinson's clerk, Irving Schloss, observed that "Judge Robinson had his own style of writing and it was ornate, perhaps one or two generations before our style of writing. His opinion reflects this style and his opinions were always this way."[92]

The core holding of *Canterbury* is that the fiduciary nature of the doctor-patient relationship imposes an affirmative obligation on physicians to disclose information about proposed treatment to patients. The scope of the information that must be disclosed is that which a reasonable person — not the patient in question — would find material to making a decision whether to undergo or forgo the proposed treatment, including information about the risks of treatment, the benefits of treatment, and alternative treatments. The scope of disclosure is most definitely not governed by the professional custom of physicians, for to do so would be completely inconsistent with the ethical underpinnings of informed consent — the patient's right to determine for himself his own medical interests (and, it might be added, because evidence of such a professional custom is completely lacking). The failure to fulfill this obligation constitutes professional negligence and — if it would lead a reasonable person in the patient's situation to undergo treatment and if that treatment causes physical harm to the patient — is the basis for an award of damages to the patient to compensate for his injuries.[93]

In one sense, the *Canterbury* opinion is not original. Many, if not all, of its principal points were previously articulated in other cases or in law review articles. However, it is original in its synthesis of all of these disparate sources into an almost comprehensive essay on informed consent, and it was the first opinion (though hardly the last) to do so. Yet as dramatic as the opinion is, the holding is very narrow. The appeals court merely reversed the defense verdicts and remanded the case to the trial court for a new trial. On the issue of informed consent, the appellate court concluded that:

> the evidence was clearly sufficient to raise an issue as to whether Dr. Spence's obligation to disclose information on risks was reasonably met or was excused by the surrounding circumstances. . . . When, at trial, it developed from Dr. Spence's testimony that paralysis can be expected in one percent of laminectomies, it became the jury's responsibility to decide whether that peril was of sufficient magnitude to bring the disclosure duty into play.[94]

On the issues of whether Dr. Spence negligently performed the laminectomy, the court also concluded that there was evidence from which contrary conclusions could be drawn, and thus it was the jury's province to decide. Similarly, the court found that the case against the hospital — concerning the supervision given to Canterbury when he needed to urinate — also should have gone to the jury.

E. The Retrial and Second Appeal

Given the breadth of the appellate opinion and its partisanship toward the patient's perspective, Canterbury should have been in a far better position on retrial, but it was not to be. He still needed an expert witness for the garden variety negligence claims. Although Davis's new associate, Barry Nace, was able to enlist one, it made no difference — except for the fact that this time the case went to the jury, and the jury found that neither Dr. Spence nor WHC had been negligent.

As to informed consent, the Court of Appeals had held that Canterbury did not even need an expert witness, at least not to establish the standard to be applied in determining what Dr. Spence should have told him about the laminectomy. Nonetheless, at the second trial the testimony of physicians, both for the plaintiff and the defense, was admitted to explain what the custom was in 1959 about disclosing the risks of medical procedures. In the final analysis, however, even that did not matter. What seems to have clinched the case for the defense was that between the end of the first trial and the first appeal, Canterbury underwent another laminectomy in order to relieve new pain that he was experiencing in his back. By this point he was as aware of the risk of a laminectomy as anyone could possibly be because he had experienced it. Nonetheless, he consented to the second laminectomy, which severely undercut the issue of causation at the second trial. Thus, when Canterbury said that he would not have consented to the original laminectomy had Dr. Spence told him of the risk of paralysis, his credibility was impeached by his consent to the second laminectomy — despite the fact that it was far more reasonable for Canterbury to accept the risk of paralysis the second time because he already was partially paralyzed.[95]

The jury returned a verdict for the defendants on the informed consent claim, even though at the second trial Dr. Spence admitted that he did not warn either Canterbury or his mother of the risk of paralysis, but only of "weakness" following the surgery.[96] Again Davis appealed, and this time his and Canterbury's fortunes, intertwined as they always were, bore no fruit whatsoever. Indeed, the appellate court's refusal to let Davis orally argue the case, and its per curiam affirmance — not to mention its observation that Davis's brief was "terse to the point of unintelligibility"[97] — were a setback not only to their fortunes, but probably to Davis's professional pride as well. Davis must have known at that point that after ten years of working with Canterbury, the case was at the end of the line. Nonetheless, in a letter written on February 10, 1975, informing Canterbury of the decision, Davis revealed that he had filed a petition for a hearing en banc, and added that "[w]e will just have to sweat this petition out, and pray that same will be granted. If not, I intend to then file a petition for certiorari to the U.S. Supreme Court. . . ."[98]

F. Conclusion

The case of *Canterbury v. Spence* remains a landmark of informed consent jurisprudence. Today, although only half of American jurisdictions accept its core point that the patient's need for information in order to effectuate self-determination requires a standard of disclosure established by law (i.e., the reasonable patient standard) rather than by professional custom,[99] in almost all other regards the opinion constitutes the bedrock of the law of informed consent.

Why Davis did not petition the U.S. Supreme Court for certiorari is lost to history. He must have realized that this long legal battle was finally over, but couldn't admit it to Canterbury. Canterbury's battle, however, was not over. He continues to this day to battle a variety of medical ailments stemming from his

A more recent photograph of Jerry Canterbury, in his wheelchair

medical mishap, including now being confined to a wheelchair. Though *Canterbury v. Spence* may be a landmark legal case, it is the most Pyhrric of victories for Jerry Canterbury.

ENDNOTES

1. 464 F.2d 772 (D.C. Cir. 1972).
2. *See* State ex rel. Janney v. Housekeeper, 16 A. 382 (Md. 1889). *See also* Pratt v. Davis, 79 N.E. 562 (Ill. 1906); Schloendorff v. Soc'y of N.Y. Hosp., 105 N.E. 92 (N.Y. 1914).
3. *Canterbury*, 464 F.2d at 776.

4. A "filling defect" is the term used to refer to the total or partial obstruction of the flow of dye that has been injected into the spine in a myelogram, "indicat[ing] a herniated disc, blood clot, scar formation, tumor, or vascular malformation." The Spine at Trial: Practical Medicolegal Concepts About the Spine 140 (Jose Kuri & Ed Stapleton eds., 2002).

5. *Canterbury*, 464 F.2d at 776–77.

6. Interview with Jerry Canterbury in New Baltimore, Ohio (Feb. 1, 2008).

7. Joint Appendix at 67, Canterbury, No. 73-1858 (D.C. Cir., Jan. 28, 1975) [hereinafter Joint App.].

8. *Id.* at 67–68. For an extended recounting of the facts by the attorney for Dr. Spence, see Walter J. Murphy, *Canterbury v. Spence — The Case and a Few Comments*, 11 The Forum 716 (1975).

9. Joint App., *supra* note 7, at 69–70.

10. *Id.* at 73.

11. *Canterbury*, 464 F.2d at 776; Joint App., *supra* note 7, at 73–74.

12. *Canterbury*, 464 F.2d at 776; Joint App., *supra* note 7, at 76–77.

13. *Canterbury*, 464 F.2d at 777.

14. Joint App., *supra* note 7, at 79.

15. Murphy, *supra* note 8, at 717.

16. Joint App., *supra* note 7, at 79–80.

17. *Id.* at 80–81. Murphy's account differs. He states that Canterbury successfully used the toilet and the urinal in the morning of the first post-surgical day (February 11) and that the accident occurred in the early morning hours of the second post-surgical day (February 12). Murphy, *supra* note 8, at 717–18.

18. Joint App., *supra* note 7, at 83.

19. *Id.* at 84.

20. *Id.*

21. *Id.* at 85, 87.

22. *Id.* at 89, 100 (for dorsal spinal decompression).

23. *Id.* at 100–01.

24. *Id.* at 110.

25. Murphy, *supra* note 8, at 718.

26. *Canterbury*, 464 F.2d 772, 777 (D.C. Cir. 1972).

27. Joint App., *supra* note 7, at 118. *See also* http://www.walkingequipment.com/lofstrand.htm. This is sometimes referred to as a "Canadian crutch."

28. Joint App., *supra* note 7, at 107.

29. *Id.* at 108.

30. Interview with Jerry Canterbury, *supra* note 6.

31. Joint App., *supra* note 7, at 113.

32. *Id.* at 115.

33. *See* http://www.bardmedical.com/products/loadProduct.aspx?prodID=379.

34. Joint App., *supra* note 7, at 146, 147–51, 158–59.

35. *Id.* at 157–58.

36. *Id.* at 153–54.

37. *Id.* at 115.

38. *Id.* at 116.

39. Interview with Jerry Canterbury, *supra* note 6.

40. *Id.*

41. Joint App., *supra* note 7, at 135–36.

42. Interview with Jerry Canterbury, *supra* note 6.

43. Joint App., *supra* note 7, at 141–43.

44. Interview with Jerry Canterbury, *supra* note 6.

45. *Id.*

46. Telephone Interview with Barry Nace, Esq. (Feb. 12, 2008).

47. Email from Jack H. Olender (Mar. 10, 2008).

48. *See, e.g.*, Brown v. Keaveny, 326 F.2d 660 (D.C. Cir. 1963).

49. Letter from Earl Davis to Jerry Canterbury (Mar. 28, 1967).

50. Telephone Interview with Barry Nace, Esq., *supra* note 46.

51. *Id.*

52. Obituary of Earl Davis, Wash. Post, Sept. 30, 1981, at C8.

53. Letter from Earl Davis to Jerry Canterbury (Aug. 10, 1973).

54. *Id.*

55. *Id.*

56. Letter from Jerry Canterbury to Earl Davis (February 7, 1975).

57. *Id.*

58. Letter from Earl Davis to Jerry Canterbury, *supra* note 53.

59. *Id.*

60. Telephone Interview with Barry Nace, *supra* note 46.

61. *Id.*

62. Dr. Spence's attorney contends that the evidence at the second trial showed that the cause was Canterbury's preexisting condition. *See* Murphy, *supra* note 8, at 721.

63. This term was either invented by or popularized by Melvin Belli. *See* Melvin Belli, *An Ancient Therapy Still Applied — The Silent Medical Treatment*, 1 Vill. L. Rev. 250 (1956).

64. *Canterbury*, 464 F.2d at 793.

65. Letter from Earl Davis to Jerry Canterbury, *supra* note 49.

66. *Canterbury*, 464 F.2d at 778.

67. *Id.*

68. *Id.*

69. *See, e.g.*, Hiddings v. Williams, 578 So. 2d 1192 (La. Ct. App. 1991).

70. *Canterbury*, 464 F.2d at 777.

71. Joint App., *supra* note 7, at 163.

72. *Id.*

73. *Canterbury*, 464 F.2d at 777.

74. Murphy, *supra* note 8, at 720.

75. District of Columbia Court Reform and Criminal Procedure Act of 1970, Public L. No. 91-358, 84 Stat. 473 (1970).

76. 347 U.S. 483 (1954).

77. Telephone Interview with Walter Murphy, Esq. (Feb. 4, 2008).

78. *Id.*

79. Telephone Interview with Professor David Schoenbrod (Jan. 8, 2008). Professor Schoenbrod was one of Judge Robinson's clerks between the time the *Canterbury* case was argued and the time it was decided.

80. Telephone Interview with Walter Murphy, *supra* note 77.

81. Telephone Interview with Irving Schloss, Esq. (Jan. 15, 2008).

82. *Id.*

83. United States v. Washington Post Co., 446 F.2d 1327 (D.C. Cir. 1971), *aff'd sub nom.* New York Times v. United States, 403 U.S. 713 (1971).

84. Telephone Interview with Irving Schloss, Esq., *supra* note 81.

85. Salgo v. Leland Stanford Jr. Univ. Bd. of Trustees, 317 P.2d 170 (Cal. App. 1957).

86. *See* Alan Meisel, *The Expansion of Liability for Medical Accidents: From Negligence to Strict Liability by Way of Informed Consent*, 56 Neb. L. Rev. 51, 77–86 (1977).

87. *See* Jon Waltz & Thomas Scheuneman, *Informed Consent to Therapy*, 64 Nw. U. L. Rev. 628, 628 n.1 (1970) (citing 18 law review articles, notes, and comments published between 1957 and 1968, as well as two treatises).

88. Cobbs v. Grant, 502 P.2d 1 (Cal. 1972).

89. Wilkinson v. Vesey, 295 A.2d 676 (R.I. 1972).

90. *Canterbury*, 464 F.2d 772, 793–94 (D.C. Cir. 1972).

91. Waltz & Scheuneman, *supra* note 87.

92. Telephone Interview with Irving Schloss, Esq., *supra* note 81.

93. *Canterbury*, 464 F.2d at 780 *et seq.*

94. *Id.* at 794.

95. Joint App., *supra* note 7, at 247–48.

96. Brief for Appellant at 7, *Canterbury*, No. 73-1858 (D.C. Cir. 1973).

97. Canterbury v. Spence, No 73-1858 at 2 (Jan. 28, 1975) (per curiam) (unpublished), 509 F.2d 537 (D.C. Cir. 1975) (Table).

98. Letter from Earl Davis to Jerry Canterbury, *supra* note 53.

99. Laurent B. Frantz, Annotation, *Modern Status of Views as to General Measure of Physician's Duty To Inform Patient of Risks of Proposed Treatment*, 88 A.L.R. 3d 1008 (1978).

Chapter 2

DARLING
v.
CHARLESTON COMMUNITY
MEMORIAL HOSPITAL

A Broken Leg and Institutional Liability Unbound

RICHARD S. SAVER*

A. Introduction: Downfall of the High School Quarterback

Pat Darling seems an odd choice to end up as plaintiff in one of the most renowned health care liability cases of all time. He was not the usual patient confronting old age, chronic illness, or severe infirmity. Young, vigorous, and athletic, Darling led an apparently charmed life before the events giving rise to his lawsuit.

Back in the 1950s, Darling enjoyed triumphs in high school that most teenage boys only dream about. He played starting quarterback for the Collinsville High School football team, earned selection for the All-Conference team, and was named the Quarterback of Greater St. Louis. An all-around athlete, Darling lettered in four sports — football, basketball, tennis, and

A high school portrait of Pat Darling

* Associate Professor & Co-Director, Health Law and Policy Institute, University of Houston Law Center. I thank Heather Smith for helping me dig up much of the background and for her dedicated work as research assistant. Reference librarians Peter Egler and Mon Yin Lung provided much appreciated aid in locating key documents and materials. Joan Krause, as usual, offered invaluable support and excellent advice in so many ways. Finally, I am grateful to John P. Ewart and, especially, Pat Darling for agreeing to be interviewed and sharing their perspectives on the case.

Pat Darling in his basketball uniform, playing for the Collinsville High School Kahoks

track — the first Collinsville High School student to do so in over 30 years.[1] Meanwhile, handsome looks and an engaging manner complimented his athletic talents. The female editors of his high school yearbook nearly gushed in writing his photo caption: "a real sportsman . . . nice-looking . . . in fact, he pretty well lives up to his last name."[2] Indeed, Darling's success extended to the romantic front. He steadily dated Carol Ackermann, a popular student in the Honor Society, during his junior and senior school years.

Appropriate to his All-American boy-next-door persona, Darling grew up in a small Midwest town. Collinsville, Illinois, only ten miles from St. Louis, had once been an industrial and mining area. But by the time Darling attended high school in the 1950s, most of these businesses had closed and the town had transformed itself into the bedroom community that it remains today, featuring rolling hills, large homes, and shaded streets. Collinsville also enjoys a unique agricultural distinction. Called "the horseradish capital of the world," the town and surrounding areas produce much of the world's horseradish supply.[3]

In Collinsville, the Darling name was and remains well known; Pat's father, Dorrence Kenneth Darling, became Superintendent for the local school system in 1944 and enjoyed a distinguished career.[4] This meant the son could not glide by on just athletic talent; he had to treat his academic work seriously too. Following his father's example, Darling intended to work as a teacher and coach.

When Darling arrived as a freshman at Eastern Illinois University (EIU) in the fall semester of 1960, he seemingly had everything going for him. But his good fortune changed horribly on Saturday, November 5. On that day, the EIU Panthers played a home football game against Central Michigan University (CMU) at Lincoln Field. Darling played defensive left halfback. A CMU player, trying to block, came in from the right side. Darling later testified that the CMU player "threw the block low; my cleats were in the ground and I couldn't push him off."[5] Darling was hit hard and fast. He realized almost immediately that his leg had broken: "I heard the bone snap . . . and the leg — it just wouldn't work."[6] Making a bad day even worse, Darling's team ended up losing the game by a wide margin, 35-12.[7]

Darling was taken by ambulance to the emergency room of nearby Charleston Community Memorial Hospital. Dr. John Alexander, the medical staff physician on emergency call, came to the hospital and attended to Darling on an inpatient basis over the next two weeks. Complications arose in treating the injury, eventually resulting in Darling having to undergo a leg amputation eight inches below the knee. The Darling family filed a lawsuit against Dr. Alexander and the hospital, which led to the landmark court ruling.

B. The Familiar Holding of the Case

Darling v. Charleston Community Memorial Hospital[8] has been called a "watershed"[9] event in health law, "the symbol of a major change in the relation of physicians and hospitals,"[10] and even the equivalent of the "Big Bang" because it "gave rise to a new and still expanding universe"[11] of liability for health care institutions. First, *Darling* is most recognized for its ruling on direct liability (sometimes referred to as "corporate" liability). The Illinois Supreme Court held that hospitals are not empty shells and actually do treat patients and have duties to them directly regarding the quality of medical services. In the pre-*Darling* era, hospitals enjoyed limited exposure to liability for the actions of medical staff physicians. Among other reasons, the common law "corporate practice of medicine" doctrine prohibited laypersons and business entities from engaging in or exercising control over the practice of medicine. Courts therefore tended to view the licensed professional — the physician — as the necessary (and ultimately responsible) party directing the course of medical care. Also, many medical staffs operated as semi-autonomous entities, distinct from their affiliated hospitals, subject to their own bylaws and often performing functions beyond the reach and control of the hospital's board of directors. More generally, hospitals were seen as secondary players, furnishing equipment and space in which physicians practiced independently, rather than complex institutional health care providers in their own right that directed or influenced medical care. Thus, before *Darling*, case law recognized only very limited direct duties by hospitals to patients, such as accountability for custodial/administrative functions involving the physical structure and equipment. But *Darling* clearly announced for the first time that a hospital can incur direct liability to patients in a much broader sense for the overall quality of care rendered within the institution and that hospitals have some responsibility to ensure that independent contractor physicians on the medical staff are selected and reviewed with care.[12]

Second, *Darling* also arguably expanded hospitals' liability via non-direct channels. Even before *Darling*, hospitals had been found vicariously liable for the acts of medical staff in certain cases under application of the respondeat superior doctrine (holding employers vicariously liable for certain acts of employees), such as where employed physicians acted as agents for the hospital. *Darling* stated that patients reasonably expect that hospitals act, along with the physician staff, to cure them. Later courts relied upon this patient expectation view to find hospitals vicariously liable for acts of independent contractor staff physicians, even when actual agency did not exist. Doctrines such as apparent agency and agency by estoppel, generally invoked by courts when patients might reasonably assume that the hospital controls the staff physician or where the hospital has given such an impression, were applied to expand vicarious liability for health care institutions in these instances. Such cases follow *Darling*'s general logic by looking to what the patient reasonably expects when receiving institutional-based care.[13]

C. The Events at Charleston Community Memorial Hospital

How did what appear to be an unremarkable, garden-variety football injury — a broken leg — lead to such unexpected, drastic results? *Darling*'s

case was not "a train wreck" from the start, as some malpractice incidents tend to be. The ambiguous record suggests that Darling received customary care, indeed even excellent care, along with possibly very poor care. But as each complication arose, the situation worsened in escalating fashion, with no change in course until too late.

When Dr. Alexander arrived at the hospital, he took x-rays and diagnosed a comminuted, or spiral, fracture of the right tibia and fibula. Working with a surgical scrub nurse and other hospital employees, he applied traction and counter-traction by pulling the leg towards the body while pulling the foot away from the body. After starting to apply the cast material, he took further x-rays to make sure of good alignment. The cast ended up covering the leg from a few inches below Darling's groin down to his toes, but it left the toes exposed.[14]

Although questions were later raised during the litigation about whether Dr. Alexander should have used padding or cleansed the leg more thoroughly before applying the cast, there were no criticisms about his actual diagnosis or suggestions that he manipulated the bones improperly. Indeed, the orthopedic surgeon who later testified for Darling, Dr. Fred C. Reynolds, stated in deposition that "as to the reduction [of the fracture] . . . the position was excellent."[15] Instead, the central issues turned out to be possible early misapplication of the unpadded cast, before swelling had subsided, and leaving it on too long.

The first evening at the hospital, Darling developed intense pain. Despite receiving repeated prescriptions of Demerol for pain relief, and occasional prescriptions of Carbital as a sedative and tranquilizer, his agitation and distress increased. Rather meticulous nursing notes documented an ominous cycle over the next few days. Darling continued to complain of pain. His toes became swollen and discolored, and the foot eventually became cold to the touch. Dr. Alexander did visit with him and partially cut the cast on at least two different occasions. Yet the pain, swelling, and discoloration continued. Around midnight of the second evening at the hospital, Darling was "irrational" with pain according to the nursing notes. Dr. Alexander partially cut the cast again the next day. Yet his third evening in the hospital, nurses observed Darling "moaning" and "unable to settle down."[16]

On the third day at the hospital, Dr. Alexander decided to partially split the cast on the sides and retape the leg. While doing so, he accidentally cut Darling's leg with a Stryker saw. Darling recalls, "I grabbed his hand and said 'you're cutting me.'" Dr. Alexander allegedly replied that was impossible. As Darling protested, one of the nurses gave him a "hypo" to calm him down. On the next morning, blood was discovered under the pillow. After the cutting incident, Darling began to lose faith in Dr. Alexander. Darling had worn casts before, for a separated knee and a broken arm, but had never experienced these difficulties or this type of pain.[17]

Apart from the pain, swelling, discoloration, and lack of sensation in the toes, a foul odor emanated from the injured leg, a likely sign of infection. Darling's visitors described it with great consistency. His cousin, Rex Darling, Jr., testified that by Wednesday there was a "rather putrid stench" in the room. His father said that by the second weekend there was a 'terrifically foul stench" in the room. Family friend Joy Schelling observed that the room smelled like "burnt flesh." His uncle, Rex Darling, testified that he smelled an odor like decaying flesh.[18]

Darling recalls few other details about his hospital stay as he generally felt "out of it" and completely "worn down." He does remember, however, that his cousin went looking, without success, for a nurse to give him more pain medication. Although confined to bed, Darling proved resourceful. He let out a piercingly loud whistle to attract attention, and a nurse came quickly to the room. "The poor, very elderly man in the bed next to me said, 'please don't do that again!'"[19] Darling recalls.

It is certainly not the case that Dr. Alexander was inattentive to Darling. The physician regularly visited with Darling, sometimes several times a day. Dr. Alexander prescribed medicines for the pain and swelling and also prescribed antibiotics to control infections. He testified that he thought that circulation was satisfactory, as discoloration and pain were normal complications following a fracture.[20] Yet Dr. Alexander, a general internist, did not at any point seek a consultation from the two orthopedic surgeons who served as consulting members of the hospital's medical staff. Nor is it the case that the nurses ignored Darling. The nursing notes indicated a pattern of regular observation and attempts to comfort Darling in dealing with the pain.[21] Nurse Anna Meyers testified that she talked with Dr. Alexander about the odor and other observations regarding Darling's pain and the discoloration of the foot.[22]

Nonetheless, as the days marched on, the Darling family became increasingly concerned, and Darling's mother, Marjorie, in particular, grew agitated. According to Darling, when the occasion called for it, his mother could prove quite assertive. Despite being surrounded by athletic men, she was the "true quarterback" in the family. By the second weekend, Marjorie Darling had enough. He recalls that his mother declared, "This is it. You're out of here, whether we have to put you in a car and drive you ourselves."[23]

Soon thereafter, Darling's tumultuous stay at the hospital came to an end. His parents arranged for his transfer to Barnes Hospital in St. Louis on November 19, nearly two weeks after his admission to Charleston Community Memorial.

D. Follow-Up at Barnes Hospital and the Partial Amputation

At Barnes, Dr. Fred C. Reynolds, the same orthopedic surgeon who later testified for Darling, took over the case. The contrasts could not have been more great: Charleston Community Memorial, a small, semi-rural, community hospital, could hardly compare to Barnes, a large, urban academic medical center affiliated with Washington University Medical School. Dr. Alexander was a general internist; Dr. Reynolds, meanwhile, chaired the Orthopedic Surgery Section at Washington University, served as President of the American Board of Orthopedic Surgeons, and, around the time of Darling's case, the St. Louis Cardinals football team appointed him as its head orthopedic surgeon.[24]

As Dr. Reynolds later testified, Darling's problems all likely arose due to interference with circulation under the cast. He said that a point of no return usually occurs about six to twenty-four hours after circulation is impaired, when the muscles cannot survive even if circulation is restored. According to this view, Darling had already crossed the point of no return well before he got to Barnes. The earlier accidental cutting of Darling's leg with the saw likely exacerbated the problems. Dr. Reynolds explained "that tipped the scale and tied our hands" because there was dead tissue complicated by infection in the cuts.[25]

Dr. Reynolds tried to prepare the family for what might follow from a case of severe gangrene. Darling recalls Dr. Reynolds saying, "I don't know if we can save the leg. My problem right now is to save the life."[26]

Over the next several weeks, Dr. Reynolds tried successive stripping away of dead tissue, insertion of a metal screw and wire sutures, and other unsuccessful attempts to save some usefulness of the leg. Eventually, he concluded that preventing the spread of deadly infection required more drastic action. On January 23, he amputated Darling's leg about eight inches below the knee.

While obviously distressed about the amputation, Darling and his family believed that an even worse fate had been avoided. As Darling views it, "Another week in Charleston and the gangrene would have got me."[27]

E. Bringing in the Big Legal Guns and Filing the Lawsuit

Although the dispute appeared to be an undistinguished malpractice case originating in the "backwaters" of downstate Illinois, it attracted big gun legal talent from the start. This may partially explain why it gained momentum, as the adept counsel for each side creatively litigated the dispute. Darling's father contacted Stanford Meyer, a well-regarded local area attorney in Belleville, to take on the case. Meyer, in turn, suggested bringing in John Alan Appleman of Urbana as co-counsel. Appleman, a former Dean of the International Academy of Trial Lawyers, had litigated many cases and was also a prolific legal writer, authoring the noteworthy treatise *Appleman on Insurance* (subsequent editions still in print) among other books, as well as numerous articles in publications such as *Tort and Medical Yearbook*.[28]

On the defense side, the hospital retained Jack E. Horsley and John P. Ewart of the Craig & Craig law firm in Mattoon. Horsley, a Fellow of the American College of Trial Lawyers, also had an active trial practice and handled many medical malpractice defense cases, both within Illinois and nationally.[29] He was as prolific a legal writer as Appleman, authoring many medical-legal columns for the journal *Medical Economics*.[30] Appleman and Horsley were used to facing off against each other; they had tried many cases as opposing counsel but remained personal friends.[31]

The litigation started with a big offensive push. On June 14, 1961, Appleman and Meyer filed a Complaint seeking $207,430 in damages, the largest single person injury claim ever initiated in Coles County. The lawsuit named Dr. Alexander and the hospital as defendants.[32] Also, and very significant to the eventual outcome of the case, Darling's attorneys pressed a theory of hospital negligence and direct liability to the patient right from the start. Count 1 of the initial Complaint alleged that the hospital breached a duty owed directly to Darling and catalogued more than 10 specific breaches by the institution, including acting negligently in permitting Dr. Alexander to perform orthopedic surgery when he lacked the necessary skills and qualifications and employing inexperienced nurses who did not properly recognize and report the significant symptoms of infection in Darling's leg.[33]

As Darling's attorneys are now deceased, one can only speculate regarding their strategy at the time. Undoubtedly, they wanted the hospital in the case because the institution had deeper pockets. The attorneys no doubt were concerned about Dr. Alexander's ability to cover any judgment. Such concern would prove appropriate. Dr. Alexander had malpractice insurance coverage for only up to $25,000. He eventually agreed to settle the case for $40,000 before trial, a small portion of the overall damages sought. It is unclear whether the physician paid for the rest of the settlement out of his own personal funds or if the insurer agreed to pay above the policy limits.[34] Given Dr. Alexander's limited resources, all roads led back to the hospital as a matter of litigation strategy.

What is less clear is why Darling's attorneys pushed aggressively for a theory of direct liability? The facts seemingly supported making the hospital vicariously liable for any negligent acts of the nurse-employees and for the conduct of Dr. Alexander, although not a hospital employee, if the attorneys could successfully argue the physician nonetheless acted as an actual agent of the institution. Quite likely, Darling's attorneys thought it prudent to leave no liability angle against the hospital unturned.

Moreover, Appleman probably viewed the case, which featured a quite sympathetic plaintiff, as a strategic opportunity to push for a change in the law. This appears to be an instance where a creative, energetic attorney lay primed and ready to pursue a larger agenda along with winning the client's claim. Appleman had decades earlier authored an article in the American Bar Association Journal, *The Tort Liability of Charitable Institutions,* which severely questioned continued application of the charitable immunity doctrine (holding charitable institutions such as nonprofit hospitals not liable in tort). In the same article, he showed similar skepticism for the inflexibility of the respondeat superior doctrine and expressed concern about patient injuries that might go uncompensated. Appleman clearly preferred a broad public policy rationale for imposing institutional liability rather than having liability turn on technical legal distinctions in each situation[35] — as might occur with vicarious liability claims that could succeed or fail based on a staff physician's status as an agent of the hospital. With the *Darling* litigation, Appleman was finally matched to a case with a favorable enough set of facts. The *Darling* dispute, which featured a quite sympathetic plaintiff, likely seemed a very good vehicle to test Appleman's views that the common law should adapt to changing times, including the need for courts to recognize that, unlike in decades past, modern hospitals increasingly operated as complex health care entities and did far more than simply furnish facilities for independent physicians to practice in. More generally, the lawsuit offered a further opportunity to argue that greater deterrence and accountability pressures imposed on health care institutions could improve the quality of care and address undercompensation problems.

F. The Trial

The trial began on October 30, 1962 and lasted about two weeks. Because Dr. Alexander settled before trial, the hospital's conduct became the principal area of focus. Darling's attorneys scored a key tactical advantage by convincing the trial judge to admit into evidence the hospital's bylaws, the Joint Commission on Accreditation's (Joint Commission) accreditation standards for hospitals, and the Illinois Hospital Licensing Act's rules and regulations. This procedural development had significant impact on the substantive merits of the case; it enabled the jury to look to these provisions, and not just what similar hospitals did, as evidence of the standard of care expected from hospitals.[36] In this respect, Darling's attorneys were somewhat lucky in the choice of trial judge assigned to the case. Judge Robert F. Cotton proved quite receptive to allowing extensive use of such evidence. Before this case, custom for health care institutions was typically determined by referencing only the standards of comparable institutions in the community — the so-called "locality" rule. Judge Cotton thought it was no longer sufficient to evaluate hospitals' action in this manner. In later reflections about the case, he observed that Illinois had a largely unregulated hospital system through the early 1950s, at which point the legislature enacted detailed hospital licensing laws. He regarded this change as significant, providing firm support for moving beyond the locality rule and subjecting hospitals to other external standards.[37] Had the locality rule been applied, the outcome may have been quite different. Defense counsel John Ewart recalls that "we were confident that the hospital followed the customary standard for hospitals in like areas."[38]

In another interesting strategic aspect to the case, the trial almost did not come to pass. Judge Cotton called a conference in chambers before the selection of the jury to explore whether the dispute could be resolved. Darling's attorneys, having already settled with Dr. Alexander for $40,000, and notwithstanding their hopes to argue for an expansion of the law, said they would dismiss the suit if the hospital agreed to pay another $25,000. According to Judge Cotton, the hospital "firmly rejected" the $25,000 offer.[39]

Using the logic of hindsight, this was a costly tactical decision as the jury ended up finding the hospital liable for six times that amount.[40] But at the time, both sides likely questioned the strength of the claims against the hospital given Dr. Alexander's more apparent culpable role. Also, the limited precedent finding institutional liability for the actions of staff physicians likely affected the hospital's willingness to settle.[41] In the end, the case's landmark holding might very well have been avoided altogether if the parties had pursued different negotiation tactics to settle what each side must have perceived as, at best, uncertain claims. This illustrates the many intrinsic vagaries of civil litigation and the odd twists and turns often taken along the road in the making of legendary case law.

The trial featured numerous witnesses. Much of the relevant testimony is discussed in the lengthy opinion of the lower appellate court and will not be repeated here. The witnesses generally painted a consistent portrait of Darling in constant pain, the foul odor, the discoloration, coldness, and insensitivity to touch of the leg and toes, and related complications. Plaintiff's counsel also tried to portray Dr. Alexander as an elderly general internist who lacked experience with complicated bone breaks. From 1957, when the hospital had opened, to 1960, when Darling was hospitalized, Dr. Alexander had worked on only two fracture cases. Both were ankle injuries and one resulted in a nonunion. Dr. Alexander could not recall the names of any books he had looked at in the last ten years to update his orthopedic skills.[42] Among other trouble spots, Dr. Alexander gave less than convincing testimony in claiming Darling's pain was not alarming because pain was an expected complication and "his mother says he is an awful baby and can't stand pain." Dr. Alexander also said he did not notice the foul odor because "[t]here was another patient in the room. You know odors, it's hard to distinguish between odors."[43]

The hospital's general trial strategy was to avoid linkage with Dr. Alexander. As hospital counsel John P. Ewart recalls, "if we got into bed with Dr. Alexander, we could have trouble." He says that the aim was "to educate and convince the jury that Dr. Alexander's conduct and duties were different from the hospital's conduct and duties." Also, the hospital tried to emphasize that it would have been improper, and against custom, for the institution to interfere with the clinical judgment of a physician. "Our position was that the hospital could not intrude on treatment decisions of licensed physicians like Dr. Alexander,"[44] says Ewart.

Along these lines, the defense witnesses included Anthony J. Perry, administrator for Decatur-Macon County Hospital, a comparable health care institution. Perry was called to speak to the custom for hospitals, and, in accord with the defense's theory of the case, he testified that hospital officials do not practice medicine and do not interfere with the clinical judgment of staff physicians. Appleman pressed Perry on this point forcefully during a blistering cross-examination, one of the notable highlights of the trial:

> MR. APPLEMAN: Do we understand from you that it is commonplace in hospitals, where broken legs are placed in casts, to have blood in the cast, blood on the pillows, a foul odor in the room, the foot to be dark, toes to be tight and insensitive to touch, and continuing complaints of pain? Is that commonplace in your opinion?
>
> MR. PERRY: I would not say commonplace. However, I am not qualified to judge the course of events.
>
> ———————————
>
> MR. APPLEMAN: And, if you found out from your examination that the doctor was seeing the patient regularly and the condition kept getting worse, wouldn't you, as hospital administrator, begin to wonder what kind of a doctor —
>
> MR. HORSLEY (defense counsel): We object, Your Honor.
>
> THE COURT: Yes, sustained. That word "wonder."
>
> MR. APPLEMAN: Would you do anything about it?
>
> MR. PERRY: I said what I would do about it. I would check.
>
> MR. APPLEMAN: Just check with the doctor and that's all?
>
> MR. PERRY: I would check with my personnel, the nursing personnel, to see if the physician was seeing the patient regularly as required by the medical staff and the hospital.
>
> MR. APPLEMAN: But, if he was seeing the patient regularly and the complaints kept getting worse, you, as hospital administrator, would do nothing about it?
>
> MR. PERRY: If I was convinced that the attending physician was a qualified man who had been practicing successfully in the community for a number of years, I would probably not do anything about it.
>
> MR. APPLEMAN: Assume that the odors kept getting worse, the complaints of pain kept getting worse; you would not go beyond talking to that man, the attending physician?
>
> MR. PERRY: Probably not.
>
> MR. APPLEMAN: Do you still have the Code of Ethics hanging on your wall?
>
> MR. HORSLEY (defense counsel): Objection.
>
> THE COURT: Sustained.
>
> MR. APPLEMAN: You feel you are bound by that, don't you, sir?
>
> MR. HORSLEY (defense counsel): We object. Argumentative and repetitious.

THE COURT: He may answer. Objection overruled.

MR. PERRY: They are a guide.

MR. APPLEMAN. That's all.[45]

The "Code of Ethics" referred to sarcastically in the exchange was the American Hospital Association's Code of Ethics, which, among other provisions, stated that "no members of the medical staff or other practitioner shall be permitted to undertake any procedure for which he is not fully competent. . . . For the protection of the patient in all serious or doubtful cases, there should be adequate consultation."[46]

Similarly, Wayne Annis, the Administrator of Charleston Community Memorial, gave troubling testimony suggesting the hospital's apparent disregard and unconcern as to whether Dr. Alexander had the requisite skills to handle Darling's care. Annis stated that he had little involvement in decisions about the medical staff:

> I did nothing to see that Dr. Alexander reviewed his operating techniques for the handling of broken bones. So far as I know, Dr. Alexander may not have reviewed his operating techniques since he was first licensed to practice in 1928. . . . The governing board, neither through me nor through any other designated administrative representative, ever checked up on Dr. Alexander as compared by medical text books.[47]

Although somewhat tangential to the central issue of the hospital's duties, the testimony of Darling and his mother likely helped earn a great deal of general sympathy from the jury. Darling described how, well after the amputation, he continued to have phantom pains and his leg stump was still tender and formed blisters. He also talked about how he had to give up athletics.[48] Meanwhile, Marjorie Darling explained, in brief but emotionally powerful testimony as only a mother could, how Pat had difficult personal adjustments after the amputation. He sometimes had to leave off his artificial leg because of soreness. He also had a disturbing change in mood: "He was [before] a very considerate boy and tried to help me in every way. Now he is sharp tempered and, of course, he can't help with a number of things. . . ." She also described how she had to regularly wash blood off Pat's stump socks, which resulted from the breaking of blisters.[49]

Apart from their words, Darling and his mother provided powerful images for the jury. When Darling took the witness stand, his counsel had him remove the artificial leg, to show the full extent of his injury and how the prosthesis had to be awkwardly strapped on. Darling recalls feeling self-conscious at the time, aware all the jurors were looking at his leg stump.[50] Meanwhile, Marjorie Darling sat "openly weeping" while she faced the jury during the closing arguments.[51]

The trial also had its share of litigation tactics and theatrical presentation. Both plaintiff and defense counsel made dramatic, and potentially improper, closing arguments. For example, Horsley, arguing for the hospital, tried to play to the jurors' local pride, emphasizing that the plaintiff and his counsel were from outside Coles County whereas the jurors, the hospital, and hospital's counsel were part of the local community: "I think our doctors in Coles County are as competent as those any place else to reduce a broken leg and put a cast on it. . . . Ladies and Gentlemen, when it's all over — when the Darling family has gone back to Collinsville, Mr. Appleman to Urbana, Mr. Meyer to Belleville, I to Mattoon, you to your respective homes. . . ."[52]

Similarly, Appleman, arguing for the plaintiff, crossed the line in injecting his personal opinion. He told the jury that, as he saw it, this was the worst record of any hospital in the entire State of Illinois. He scoffed at the testimony of Wayne Annis, the hospital administrator: "What he [Annis] is saying to you, in effect [is] We [The hospital] owe no obligation to anybody except to take their money. Otherwise, we owe them nothing." Appleman also presented Darling as a young man full of promise that had tragically come undone: "And then this thing happens to him. And here he is today. I have never felt so sorry for anybody in my life."[53] Meanwhile Appleman's co-counsel, Meyer, made highly emotional remarks during his rebuttal argument. Meyer detailed for the jury the terrible lifestyle changes Darling would experience because of the amputation and even questioned whether Darling would ever be able to find a girlfriend and eventual wife.[54] The Illinois Supreme Court ultimately concluded that both sides engaged in improper argument, but it could not say that one side's improprieties out-weighed the other so as to become prejudicial error.

In instructing the jury, the trial judge was ambiguous on the critical issue of law: what were a hospital's direct duties, if any? Among the many instructions given, Instruction 12a referred to the duty of a hospital to use reasonable care to see that only persons duly qualified to perform orthopedic surgery were retained upon the medical staff for performing such surgery. However, the trial judge also gave an instruction which advised the jury to weigh the accreditation and licen-sure provisions "along with all other evidence in the case in determining whether there was a duty upon the [hospital] to make a decision in the field of the practice of medicine."[55] This could have allowed the jury to find that the hospital, a lay entity, could not legally practice medicine and therefore should not override a staff physician's medical judgment.

The jurors were undoubtedly sympathetic to Darling. The hospital's counsel recalls that several jurors cried during the plaintiff's final argument.[56] Deliber-ating for only three hours (after a two week trial), the jury returned a verdict in favor of Darling for $150,000 (worth approximately $1,035,546 in 2007 dollars).[57] After the verdict was read, several jurors came up to Darling, shook his hand, and told him, "We're sorry that this happened."[58] For Coles County, known as a somewhat conservative jurisdiction for jury verdicts, this was indeed a very big win. The $150,000 verdict was a record in the county.[59] Upon defendant's motion, the judgment against the hospital was reduced by the $40,000 that Dr. Alexander had earlier agreed to pay in his settlement.

G. Reconsidering the Facts and the Jury's Verdict

As the *Darling* case has been summarized and rehashed by later courts and academic commentators, a typical story arc emerges of a young man entering the hospital with an ordinary broken leg but receiving obviously poor care. Yet, upon closer examination, some of the points were likely a much closer call. First, Darling's bone break was not simple. A comminuted, spiral fracture, which involves multiple shattered fragments, with the bone twisted around, can be difficult to treat. Dr. Malachi Topping, an orthopedist, testified for the defense that certain fractures can directly lead to spasm and pressure in the blood ves-sels, shutting off blood to the extremity. He said that this condition, known as "Volkmann's ischemic contracture," occurred more often with comminuted fractures and that the condition can arise from the fracture itself, not the cast being too tight. If this occurred with Darling, it was possible that nothing done by Dr. Alexander or the hospital in setting the cast contributed to the ultimate complications.[60] Even current medical opinion recognizes that Volkmann's ischemic contracture can arise for many reasons independent of cast constriction, including any process that leads to increased compartmental pressure.[61] At the end of the day, the jury simply found plaintiff's arguments concerning constriction from the cast more persuasive than the hospital expert's possible alternative explanation of causation.

Second, even if plaintiff's version of the law was correct — that institutions do have a direct *duty* to patients regarding the overall quality of medical care — the defense nonetheless had a reasonable argument that the hospital did not actually *breach* the duty because it still conformed to the standard of care. What should have been the standard of care applicable to Charleston Community Memorial Hospital? Assume that the accreditation, licensure, and bylaw provisions admitted into evidence made clear that an institution had some responsibility for evaluating the quality of care rendered by nominally independent contractor physicians on the medical staff. Surely the effort required to reasonably discharge this duty, even if defined by such external standards and not custom alone, would still vary for each institution depending on the actual circumstances.

Charleston Community Memorial Hospital was a small, semi-rural institution. It had only a 46-bed capacity, an average census of about 35 patients, and a limited supply of physicians in the area. It could not reasonably be expected to undertake and bear the same monitoring obligations for medical staff that a large, tertiary care institution like Barnes Hospital could, nor could it, at the end of the day, reasonably be expected to provide the same level of expert orthopedic care. As commentators noted at the time, *Darling* seemed particularly harsh to small institutions. Large hospitals had medical directors, full-time clinical department chiefs, and sometimes directly employed physicians on staff. At these institutions, monitoring and evaluation of a medical staff member's privileges was "usually a day-to-day occurrence."[62] For a small institution such as Charleston Community Memorial, staff physicians often practiced as multiple, disconnected solo practitioners rather than departmental colleagues; in such a setting, oversight became, as a practical matter, much more difficult to perform. Moreover, expecting that a hospital more readily restrict staff privileges glosses over the fact that in some small hospital communities there simply were not many physicians to begin with; in order to remain open, these institutions often had few alternatives but to work with the local physicians.

So perhaps the hospital had a legitimate point in arguing that the effort it exerted in evaluating its medical staff was reasonable in light of its overall size and resources. From the available record, it is not entirely clear to what extent Dr. Alexander's previous patient care experiences should have been cause for alarm at the time. In any event because the medical staff was so small, the hospital had *no* regular orthopedics department and only a few community orthopedists served as "consulting" members of the medical staff. Thus, it was not so unusual to expect that a regular internist on the medical staff, handling emergency on-call duty, would undertake a broken bone case.

This may be an instance where bad facts were used to make good law. In other words, the general precedent established by *Darling* may make more sense than the actual result in the case. While the opinion's reasons for imposing broader direct duties on health care institutions as a general matter may have been sound and forward-looking, and while public policy considerations may likewise support this change in the law, the *Darling* litigation was an odd vehicle to bring about this transformation. Accounting for the hospital's size and geographic location, its limited resources, and the few expert orthopedists available to serve on the medical staff, the justification for finding the hospital liable on the actual facts was arguably far less clear.

H. What Really Was the Holding?

The Fourth District Appellate Court opinion, affirming the result below and totaling 77 pages, was one of the longest court decisions in Illinois history.[63] The eventual Illinois Supreme Court opinion was much shorter. The contrasting brevity, although welcome, also contributed to later confusion. The Illinois Supreme Court's somewhat choppy, abbreviated opinion actually had several key parts. First, it clarified that charitable immunity no longer applied to hospitals. Second, in doing so, it rejected the long-standing view that hospitals have only limited duties to patients regarding chiefly administrative and custodial functions. Quoting from the earlier New York case of *Bing v. Thunig*, which had also rejected charitable immunity and applied respondeat superior to find a hospital potentially liable for the actions of hospital-employed nurses, the Illinois Supreme Court adopted the view that hospitals do much more than furnish facilities to independent medical staff:

> The conception that the hospital does not undertake to treat the patient, does not undertake to act through its doctors and nurses, but undertakes instead simply to procure them to act upon their own responsibility, no longer reflects the fact. Present-day hospitals, as their manner of operation plainly demonstrates, do far more than furnish facilities for treatment. . . . Certainly, the person who avails himself of 'hospital facilities' expects that the hospital will attempt to cure him, not that its nurses or other employees will act on their own responsibility.[64]

Although the opinion suffers somewhat from being opaque and cryptic, the *Darling* ruling actually went even farther than the New York *Bing* case by suggesting that a hospital has a *direct* duty to patients that extends to ensuring the overall quality of care rendered within the institution. The Illinois Supreme Court reasoned that such a duty could be found because "[t[he Standards for Accreditation, the state licensing regulations and the [hospital's] bylaws demonstrate that the medical profession and other responsible authorities regard it as both desirable and feasible that a hospital assume certain responsibilities for the care of the patient."[65]

Third, the Illinois Supreme Court approved of the use of accreditation standards, licensing provisions, and the hospital's own bylaws as further guidance, in addition to custom, for helping the jury determine what the standard of care should be regarding dealings with the medical staff. Finally, the Illinois Supreme Court found that the jury verdict ultimately could have been justified on either of two grounds: (a) if the hospital had employed a sufficient number of trained nurses, they would have recognized the progressive gangrenous condition of

Darling's leg and brought their concerns to the attention of the medical staff and hospital administration; or (b) the hospital did not require Dr. Alexander to consult with surgical specialists and failed to review and properly address the treatment Darling actually received.

It is curious why the Illinois Supreme Court chose to emphasize the first ground, relating to the nurses' actions, to partially uphold the jury verdict. If the nurses had acted negligently, the hospital's liability could have resulted simply from vicarious liability under respondeat superior doctrine because the nurses were hospital employees. But if this was so, arguably the Illinois Supreme Court did not need to reach at all the more controversial points of law concerning direct liability by the hospital for physician oversight.

Moreover, as a matter of the facts, was it even clear that the nurses acted negligently regarding insufficient observation or reporting? The nurses did keep regular observation notes that detailed Darling's worsening condition and occasionally updated Dr. Alexander by phone. In some cases, the front-line nurses reported their concerns not to Dr. Alexander directly but up through the chain of command to their nursing supervisors. Yet at least one nursing supervisor, Doris Potts, did discuss Darling's condition with Dr. Alexander, although possibly not reporting all the symptoms such as the foul odor. Also, Nurse Anna Meyers testified that she talked with Dr. Alexander about the odor, Darling's pain, and the discoloration of the foot.[66]

Was it unreasonable not to report everything about the patient's condition to the hospital administrator, Wayne Annis, when the nurses had revealed enough for him to know that the patient was in distress and when the nurses knew that the treating physician was more fully informed? The opinion seems to find it unreasonable that the nurses did not "speak up" enough, in effect bypassing Dr. Alexander and going directly to hospital administration or other physicians on staff with their concerns. This might have been a preferable course of action, but it also may be somewhat unrealistic, given traditional professional roles and power hierarchies, to expect that the nurses would challenge the treating physician to this degree.[67]

Identifying perhaps a stronger claim of negligence, Darling's counsel also argued that the nurses should have watched the toes constantly for color, temperature, and movement, including pinching the toes every ten to twenty minutes for blanching and return of blood. Yet such tests were never done.[68] Still, the nurses evidently told Dr. Alexander enough about the leg's condition to already raise serious clinical concerns about possible infection. All together, it seems that any deficiencies in reporting and observation arguably represented only incremental, marginal variances from ordinary nursing practice. It seems reasonably debatable whether this actually breached the nursing standard of care.

In any event, the Illinois Supreme Court's second ground for upholding the jury verdict — the hospital's failure to require a consultation and failure to review Dr. Alexander's care — proved far more novel and controversial. The court essentially ruled that a hospital had direct duties to the patient in a much broader sense than previously understood. The hospital's direct duties reached beyond upkeep of the facilities and equipment, and general oversight of nurse-employees, to the overall quality of care rendered within the medical center, including some institutional responsibility to ensure that independent contractor physicians on the medical staff were selected and reviewed with care. Given that the courts at the time firmly embraced the corporate practice of medicine doctrine, the legal rule which restricted lay persons and business entities from exercising control over the practice of medicine, and the courts more generally viewed medicine as a learned profession that should enjoy considerable clinical autonomy, placing such responsibility on lay hospital administrators was "indeed surprising."[69]

I. Reaction at the Time and Ongoing Impact of the Case

The full revolutionary impact of the *Darling* decision took some time to set in. Interestingly, there was at first some confusion among commentators and other courts about the potential breadth of the holding. Some initially misunderstood the facts and assumed that Dr. Alexander had been employed by the hospital, viewing the result in the case as merely an additional occasion of imposing vicarious liability on an institution for the acts of an employee.[70] Only with time, and reexamination through later cases, did *Darling*'s groundbreaking implications for institutional responsibility become more widely appreciated and the case more frequently cited.

In any event, it was perhaps somewhat naïve for the Illinois Supreme Court to state that ". . . the medical profession . . . regard[s] it as both desirable and feasible that a hospital assume certain responsibilities for the care of the patient."[71] A logical concern among many staff physicians was whether lay hospital administrators, in light of the decision, would seek to influence or direct clinical decisions. For example, the American Medical Association (AMA) warned that "[t]he effect of this decision is unfortunate since it appears to place a hospital in a position where it must exercise control over the practice of medicine by physicians on its attending staff in order to avoid liability. This is apt to encourage control of the practice of medicine by persons who are not licensed physicians."[72] The hospital industry did not react any more favorably. At the time, the decision's suggestion of continually expanding institutional liability certainly caused much worry and concern in many hospital boardrooms.[73] Just how far institutional responsibility extends for the actions of nominally independent medical staff was not clearly answered by *Darling*. The opinion seemingly opened the door to at least two different prongs of direct duties for hospitals: (1) to select, credential, and retain physicians on the medical staff with reasonable care; but also (2) to reasonably supervise the ongoing care of the physicians already on staff (as opposed to retroactive review of staff physicians' care that occurs with renewal of credentials).

Despite this interpretation, later courts have not as forcefully embraced the suggested second prong as part of the *Darling* legacy. Many jurisdictions today recognize that hospitals have a duty to reasonably select, credential, and retain members of the medical staff. Yet far fewer courts have ruled that a hospital had a duty to supervise and intervene in the ongoing care provided by an independent contractor physician.

As for its overall impact, *Darling* has proven quite influential. As of 2007, it has been cited in at least 344 cases and 350 journal articles.[74] Many jurisdictions today recognize some form of action against hospitals for negligent credentialing and many jurisdictions recognize more general forms of direct liability for health care institutions. By creating more fertile opportunities for plaintiffs to bring malpractice cases against deeper-pocketed institutions, *Darling* helped usher in an era of increased liability generally for health care providers — perhaps a mixed blessing for health policy as this increased institutional interest in quality improvement while also escalating costs. The malpractice insurance availability crisis in the 1970s, one of the first of periodic episodes of instability in the malpractice system,[75] can be partly traced back to the forces unleashed by *Darling*. Moreover, *Darling*'s impact has not been limited to hospitals. Its ruling logically applies to many health care institutions with medical staffs, such as nursing homes and ambulatory surgical centers. More recently, courts have relied on *Darling* to extend direct institutional liability to health maintenance organizations.[76]

Another clear consequence of the liability pressures introduced by *Darling* can be found in the more complex process of medical staff credentialing that occurs today. Most hospitals now have administrative departments that engage in regular reviews and delineate privileges in detail for new and current staff physicians. At many institutions, hospital administration delegates much of this activity, while retaining some authority, directly to the medical staff itself. A considerable body of case law and statutory law has developed to address the credentialing function in some detail. Also, the opinion's reliance on the Joint Commission accreditation standards clearly raised the prominence of the accreditation provisions; these standards have now become central to understanding how hospitals conduct medical staff reviews and establish clinical privileges.

As for the case's impact on hospital-physician relations more generally, the AMA's initial worries about *Darling* — that lay hospital administrators would exert control over staff physicians — foreshadowed power struggles still at play today. The bizarre system of governance at most modern hospitals, with separate and sometimes conflicting lines of authority for the board of directors, hospital executives, and the quasi-independent medical staff, makes for an overall inefficient structure that has been called a "three-legged monster without a head."[77] *Darling* held out promise of unifying the three-legged system by recognizing that institutional responsibility for business matters (typically a board of directors concern) could not be neatly divorced from quality of care issues (traditionally within the purview of the medical staff).[78] But complete centralization of authority within the hospital board has not completely come to pass. Instead, hospital administration and staff physicians have continued to struggle over traditionally contested areas such as the type, cost, and quality of services rendered.

More recently, the hospital-physician battles have spilled over to newer arenas. Hospitals now view certain medical staff members as potential economic competitors, threatening to take profitable lines of service outside the institution to other care settings, such as physician-owned specialty hospitals and ambulatory surgery centers. In today's market, many hospitals require staff physicians to undergo not only *Darling*-type quality credentialing, but also "economic credentialing" — where a hospital considers factors related to the efficient operation of the institution, not quality factors, to determine a physician's staff membership and privileges, including the physician's utilization costs, payor mix, impact on hospital reimbursement, and whether the physician competes with the hospital in certain service lines.[79] More generally, institutional quality improvement encounters serious obstacles as hospitals and physicians all too often work in an environment featuring misaligned incentives, fragmentation, and detachment.[80]

J. Other Observations About the Case

1. Medical Error as Systems Problem?

Increasingly, the phenomenon of medical error is understood to occur for reasons other than merely the conduct of "bad apple," substandard practitioners. Instead, analysts describe larger "systems" problems as the root cause for many medical errors, which often involving multiple parties and implicate numerous institutional policies. Such systems problem–driven errors can occur, for example, when pertinent clinical information about patients is not communicated between providers taking over different shifts of a case or when medication is dispensed in dosage amounts that vary from what the physician actually ordered due to complicated procedures for translating and applying the order in the clinical setting. The Institute of Medicine's influential *To Err Is Human* report concluded that 44,000 to 98,000 deaths occur in hospitals each year due to medical errors, many of which result from such systems problems.[81]

These new perspectives on medical error underscore why it is far too simplistic to view what happened to Darling as simply the result of Dr. Alexander delivering botched care. Indeed, *Darling* seems a perfect example of many systems problems at work. First, the case demonstrates miscommunication and lack of coordination among the entire health care team. There was an apparent incomplete flow of information from the nurses. No clear procedures existed for the nurses to bypass Dr. Alexander with any concerns, or for their reports to be regularly reviewed and double-checked by anyone other than the attending physician. Meanwhile, no clear procedures were in place for when to contact the consulting orthopedists and when, at a minimum, to involve the chief of the medical staff. Also, suitable policies apparently did not exist for indicating the standard observational tests that the nurses should run on Darling's leg. More generally, hospital administration and Dr. Alexander seemed to be operating in completely different spheres, rather than responding to aligned incentives for ensuring quality of care.

2. Reflecting the New Realities of Medical Care Delivery

Darling certainly broke new ground to the extent that it expanded the scope of health care institutions' duties and, therefore, potential liabilities. However, a ruling like *Darling* was perhaps inevitable. The 1965 opinion merely reflected the very changed environment for delivering health care. By the late 1950s, the proportion of physicians in private practice had declined over previous decades. More physicians practiced at least part of the time in institutional settings such as hospitals, including as direct employees, notwithstanding any corporate practice of medicine prohibitions. Also, small community hospitals, such as Charleston Community Memorial, would eventually become almost obsolete as forces at work in the 1960s market later led to the consolidation of hospitals, formation of larger health systems, and the overall growth of "corporate" style medicine.[82]

Thus, *Darling* may have simply confirmed in law what was already occurring in practice: more complex medical care delivery; the blending of business issues with clinical issues; and increasing provision of care in larger institutional settings, requiring health care entities to engage in skillful coordination, oversight, and management of diverse personnel and resources. Accordingly, hospitals evolved from being mere "workshop[s]" where individual physicians practiced their craft to complex, technological systems with their "own goals, character, and momentum."[83] In such an environment, it seemed natural that some type of direct liability should attach because "[i]nstitutionalization of medicine results in institutionalization of responsibility for the patient's welfare."[84]

3. *Part of the General "Tort Revolution"*

Darling not only reflected changes in medical care delivery. It also resonated with larger, revolutionary changes in legal doctrine then occurring outside the narrow confines of medical malpractice law. It is significant that the Illinois Supreme Court rendered the *Darling* opinion in September 1965; a mere four months earlier it applied the concept of strict liability to product defect cases in *Suvada v. White Motor Corp.*[85] Also in 1965, the Illinois Restatement (Second) of Torts clarified that a contractor could be held liable under certain circumstances for the actions of independent contractors under his control. Each of these developments made it easier for plaintiffs to reach deeper-pocket defendants and obtain more comprehensive relief. Seen in its proper context, *Darling* was but a small part of the larger "tort revolution" of the mid-1960s. The right political climate, social consensus, a savvy plaintiffs' personal injury bar, and receptiveness of the judiciary combined in sync to create doctrinal changes that increased access to the courts, expanded concepts of liability, and provided fuller compensation to injured parities.[86]

4. *Limits to Institutional Liability?*

Following *Darling*, institutional liability has not become completely unbound as courts have arguably not gone as far as even the case logically suggests. First, as previously noted, many courts find hospitals directly liable with regard to negligent selection and retention decisions involving the medical staff, but far fewer courts recognize negligent supervision claims.

Second, if there is a deterrence and patient welfare rationale for imposing direct liability on a hospital for the overall quality of care rendered within the institution, why stop at direct liability? Arguably, the current system of mixed vicarious and direct liability, the legacy of *Darling*, should be replaced by a rule of "enterprise liability" for hospitals. Under this approach, hospitals would exclusively bear liability for all malpractice claims brought by hospitalized patients, regardless whether the treating physician was an independent contractor, employee, or had some sort of ostensible or apparent agency authority, and regardless of whether the hospital itself had directly been negligent. Leading enterprise liability proponents such as professors Kenneth Abraham and Paul Weiler argue that this approach would be cleaner and cheaper, ensure a more sensible system for compensation, provide greater transparency, and more strongly encourage institutions — often in the better position to engage in refined monitoring and coordination of care — to improve quality.[87] Nonetheless, the liability expansion initiated by *Darling* has not yet reached to enterprise liability.

Third, another doctrinal step yet not taken, but certainly suggested by *Darling*, is the imposition of informed consent obligations directly on hospitals. Most courts today still follow the traditional common law rule that hospitals do not have the responsibility to obtain the informed consent of patients before treatment, viewing it as a duty solely of the treating physician. But *Darling*'s reasons for recognizing hospitals as health care providers in their own right, with direct duties to patients for the overall quality of care, would seemingly also justify recognizing hospitals as having informational duties to patients independent of what the treating physician may do. Yet, institutional informed consent claims rarely succeed under common law.[88] In some respects, the pre-*Darling* view of hospitals as more custodial and administrative in nature than directly responsible for the provision and process of care still persists.

5. The Imprecise Nature of Awarding Damages

The medical malpractice system continues to struggle in finding an optimal approach to awarding damages, including recent experimentation with damage caps, especially for non-economic damages. There likely will never be firm consensus on the best approach as so much of the damages question inevitably depends on a large degree of quite imprecise speculation.

Indeed, the *Darling* verdict illustrates this problem. The jurors awarded Darling $150,000 (later reduced by the $40,000 from Dr. Alexander's settlement), a record amount for conservative Coles County. Most of the award seems to have been for "hard," "tangible" damages, such as Darling's medical expenses and lost income, and not for the often more controversial "soft," "intangible," non-economic, pain and suffering component that has been the subject of much current malpractice reform. Yet, Darling's total damage award seems, in retrospect, not well matched to the nature of the injuries.

On the one hand, the overall award did not likely account for the true non-economic pain and suffering caused by Darling's inability to continue with competitive athletics. When the context of his family background is considered, this loss must have been simply devastating. Athletics was the Darling family tradition. His father had been a coach and manual arts instructor in the Collinsville school system before becoming Superintendent of Schools and, earlier, had been a star college athlete. A captain of Illinois State's conference championship basketball team in 1931, Darling's father earned selection to the Illinois State Redbirds' Hall of Fame.[89] Meanwhile his uncle, Rex Darling, also a member of the Illinois State Redbirds' Hall of Fame, was a distinguished basketball and tennis coach at Eastern Illinois University (EIU). Indeed, EIU would eventually name its tennis courts after Rex Darling.[90] Pat Darling had gone to EIU in large part because his uncle coached there. After the injury occurred, Darling withdrew from EIU; he simply did not want to be at the university when pursuing the athletic programs that had meant so much to him would no longer be possible.

On the other hand, the jury award may have overestimated the injury's impact in terms of lost income. Much of the information on damages presented to the jury assumed Darling, if not injured, would have earned the lion share of his income from a teacher's salary and earned some additional money as a coach.[91] Yet today Darling himself acknowledges that, even if not injured, he likely would not have pursed teaching over the long haul. He found that he had little patience for maintaining discipline with the sometimes rebellious, unruly students. He says that he may have continued to work as an athletic coach in some form, but not as a teacher.[92]

K. Epilogue

Following the decision, Dr. Alexander continued to practice in the Charleston, Illinois community without further serious incident. There are no other major cases or reported settlements involving his medical care. It is not known if and to what extent Charleston Community Memorial Hospital restricted his privileges. In 1967, he died of a heart attack at the age of 65.[93]

The liability ruling likely caused the hospital to change its credentialing practice, but it clearly still had a resource problem in attracting a full range of qualified medical staff, and was often in precarious circumstances. In 1968, for example, it had only seven physicians on the active medical staff and had a net loss of approximately $72,000.[94] In 1976, the hospital merged with nearby Mattoon Memorial Hospital, and the two institutions formed the Sara Bush Lincoln Health Center. Ironically, Sarah Bush Lincoln Health Center would itself become famous in the annals of health law as a party to a noteworthy case, *Berlin v. Sarah Bush Lincoln Health Center*,[95] in which the Illinois Supreme Court questioned the continued viability of the corporate practice of medicine doctrine as applied to hospitals. The building that was the old Charleston Community Memorial Hospital is now used as administrative headquarters for the Coles County Public Health Department.[96]

After the accident, Darling transferred to another college and studied speech education and psychology. After deciding teaching was not for him, he transitioned altogether and, at the suggestion of a family friend, went into the insurance business. He eventually set up his own business, "Your Insurance," an agency dealing with commercial and property liability insurance.

Happily (and despite plaintiff's counsel's arguments to the jury about how the injury would ruin his romantic prospects), Darling also ended up marrying Carol Ackermann, his high school sweetheart. They eventually returned to Collinsville where Pat ran his insurance agency and Carol worked as a nurse in the school system. Married over 44 years, they have a son, Scott, and two granddaughters.

A common criticism of the malpractice system is that it does not offer aggrieved parties a sense of closure. Along these lines, Darling says that he never received any apology from Dr. Alexander or from hospital officials; moreover, he never heard from them again after the trial. Darling admits that he did have feelings of unresolved anger and frustration, consistent with his mother's testimony about his change in personality. He recalls a difficult episode at home shortly after the amputation. He went to answer the phone while not wearing his artificial limb and fell on the floor. "That really aggravated me to no end. It took me a long time to get over that," he says.

He also recalls being despondent when in Barnes Hospital, thinking: "Ok. You're gonna lose a leg — the world's gonna come to an end."[97] But he eventually adjusted through a combination of perseverance and stoicism. He worked hard at his physical rehabilitation; his athletic ability and strength likely helped a great deal. Shortly after being fitted with the artificial limb, he learned to walk without a cane and has never needed one. His mood improved once he gained more mobility and resumed school: "Well, as I progressed the world was not coming to an end and things like that you work through and go about your business."[98]

Indeed, his physical recovery has been quite strong. Now many years after the accident, he has occasional sores and blisters around the leg stump and still experiences phantom pains. But overall, Darling remains remarkably active and athletic for his age, let alone his disability. He enjoys the outdoors, including regular camping and fishing trips. He also hunts waterfowl and makes periodic expeditions to Canada for wild geese hunting accompanied by his trusted black Labrador retriever. Over the years, he also has enjoyed occasional coaching for Little League baseball and elementary school basketball.

Given the horrible medical complications that he endured, Darling remains remarkably equanimous and good-natured about his fate. He is proud of his family and the life that he ended up making for himself, despite the unexpected change in paths. He says he has no feelings of ill will toward Dr. Alexander or the hospital: "We're all

Pat Darling — the sporting outdoorsman

human. When you walk on water, then you shouldn't make mistakes. But most of us can't do that."[99]

Darling has been somewhat aware of the case's great renown. He first began to appreciate its impact when one of Carol's colleagues, a hospital employed nurse, mentioned that the case had been discussed at a training session with the nursing staff. As he works in the insurance field, Darling also has dealt with many attorneys over the years; occasionally a lawyer would recognize his name and ask about the case. But Darling is a private person and prefers to keep a low profile; until now, he has declined to comment publicly about the litigation in any detail.

Indeed, Darling remains a rather reluctant agent for change. He seemingly abhors the idea of serving as a figurehead symbol of the broadening of

Pat Darling and his wife, Carol Darling

institutional liability, and he demonstrates ambivalence about the case's impact. He believes that medical institutions should have direct responsibly for the patient's overall care. At the same time, he has some sympathy for health care providers from the experiences of his wife, who also worked as a hospital nurse before becoming a school system nurse. Darling recognizes that medical errors can occur even with diligent health care providers. Also, as an insurance man, he appreciates the connection between litigation exposure and higher insurance expenses and wonders how this impacts access to and cost of health care.[100]

Accordingly, Darling worries to some degree about his case's ultimate legacy. He does not want the malpractice system to "go overboard" where hospitals incur liability for understandable mistakes. He ultimately remains optimistic, however, about the new environment his case helped create. He doubts a medical misadventure like he experienced would occur in a hospital today. Darling hopes that his case has something to do with that: "I don't think what happened to me would likely happen to another patient now. I think there's probably many checks and balances which go through . . . [hospital] system[s] now, and, if my experience led to some of this, I guess that's a very good thing for all."[101]

ENDNOTES

1. *See* Collinsville High School Yearbook (1960); Abstract of Record at 111, Darling v. Charleston Cmty. Mem'l Hosp., 211 N.E.2d 253 (Ill. 1965) (No. 38790). Darling was born on St. Patrick's Day. Relatives therefore called him "Pat," a nickname that stuck. Named after his father, his actual birth name is Dorrence Kenneth Darling II.

2. Collinsville High School Yearbook (1960).

3. *See* Collinsville Historical Museum, Collinsville in Vintage Postcards 7–8, 78 (Neal Strebel ed., 2005).

4. *See* Abstract of Record, *supra* note 1, at 113.

5. *Id.* at 219.

6. Interview with Pat Darling in Collinsville, Ill. (Oct. 22, 2007).

7. *See Suit Against Hospital Starts*, The Charleston-Courier News, Oct. 30, 1962; *Central Michigan Routs Eastern, 35–12*, Eastern State News (Charleston, Ill.), Nov. 9, 1960, at 6.

8. 211 N.E.2d 253 (Ill. 1965).

9. Clark C. Havighurst, *American Health Care and the Law*, in The Privatization of Health Care Reform 9 (M. Gregg Bloche ed., 2003).

10. James E. Ludlam, *The Impact of the Darling Decision upon the Practice of Medicine and Hospitals*, 11 The Forum 756 (1976).

11. Mitchell J. Wiet, *Darling v. Charleston Community Memorial Hospital and Its Legacy*, 14 Annals Health L. 399 (2005).

12. *See* John D. Blum, *Feng Shui and the Restructuring of the Hospital Corporation: A Call For Change in the Face of the Medical Error Epidemic*, 14 Health Matrix 5, 8–9 (2004).

13. *See* Wiet, *supra* note 11, at 404–05.

14. *See* Defendant's Brief at 20–21, Darling v. Charleston Cmty. Mem'l Hosp., 211 N.E.2d 253 (Ill. 1965) (No. 38790).

15. Abstract of Record, *supra* note 1, at 184–85.

16. 200 N.E. 2d 149 at 158–63 (Ill. App. Ct. 1964); 211 N.E.2d 253 at 255, 258 (Ill. 1965).

17. Interview with Pat Darling, *supra* note 6. *See also* Brief of Appellee at 37, Darling v. Charleston Cmty. Mem'l Hosp., 211 N.E.2d 253 (Ill. 1965) (No. 38790).

18. *See* 200 N.E. 2d at 167–68 (Ill. App. Ct. 1964).

19. Interview with Pat Darling, *supra* note 6.

20. *See* Abstract of Record, *supra* note 1, at 284, 287–29, 303–05.

21. *See* Defendant's Brief, *supra* note 14, at 60; 200 N.E. 2d at 159–61 (Ill. App. Ct. 1964).

22. *See* 200 N.E. 2d at 166–68 (Ill. App. Ct. 1964).

23. Interview with Pat Darling, *supra* note 6.

24. *See* Seyed Behrooz Mostofi, Who's Who in Orthopedics 286–87 (2005).

25. 200 N.E. 2d at 169 (Ill. App. Ct. 1964).

26. Interview with Pat Darling, *supra* note 6.

27. *Id.*

28. *See* Biography- John Alan Appleman, Contemporary Authors: A Bibliographical Guide to Current Writers 21, *available at* www.galegroup.com/pdf/facts/ca.pdf; Appleman on Insurance 2d (2007).

29. *See* Jack E. Horsley, One Lawyer's Fifty Eight Years as an Attorney 133–35 (2d ed. 1997); *Remembrances: An Autobiography*, The Charleston-Courier News, Dec. 31, 1998; *Names in the News*, The Charleston-Courier News, Aug. 15, 2001.

30. He would go on to write numerous books, including Jack Horsley & John Carlova, Testifying in Court: A Guide for Physicians (Medical Economics Company, 2d ed. 1983).

31. *See* Horsley, *supra* note 29, at 156.

32. *See Charleston Hospital, Doctor Defendants in $207,430 Circuit Court Damage Suit*, The Charleston-Courier News, June 14, 1961.

33. *See* Complaint at Count 1, Darling v. Charleston Cmty. Mem'l Hosp., No. 61-L-108 (Coles County Cir. Court, Ill. June 14, 1961).

34. Telephone Interview with John P. Ewart, Counsel, Craig & Craig, in Mattoon, Ill. (July 30, 2008).

35. *See* John A. Appleman, *The Tort Liability of Charitable Institutions*, 22 A.B.A. J. 48, 52–55 (1936).

36. *See* Robert Charles Clark, *Does the Nonprofit Form Fit the Hospital Industry?*, 93 Harv. L. Rev. 1417, 1489 & n.177 (1980).

37. *See* Robert F. Cotton, *The Anatomy of Darling v. Charleston Community Hospital*, 11 The Forum 727, 727–28 (1976).

38. Telephone Interview with John P. Ewart, *supra* note 34.

39. *See* Cotton, *supra* note 37, at 727.

40. The trial court ended up reducing the jury's $150,000 verdict against the Hospital to $110,000, to offset the $40,000 that Darling settled with Dr. Alexander.

41. Telephone Interview with John P. Ewart, *supra* note 34.

42. *See* 200 N.E.2d at 168–70 (Ill. App. Ct. 1964).

43. Abstract of Record, *supra* note 1, at 303, 305.

44. Telephone Interview with John P. Ewart, *supra* note 34.

45. John Alan Appleman, *Cross-Examination Relative to Hospital Duties*, Personal Injury Annual, 212, 242–43 (1963) (reproducing trial transcript of the cross-examination).

46. *Id.*, at 212, 222.

47. Abstract of Record, *supra* note 1, at 72–73.

48. *See* Plaintiff's Brief at 37, Darling v. Charleston Cmty. Mem'l Hosp., 211 N.E.2d 253 (Ill. 1965) (No. 38790); Interview with Pat Darling, *supra* note 6.

49. Abstract of Record, *supra* note 1, at 217–18.

50. Interview with Pat Darling, *supra* note 6.

51. *See* Defendant's Brief, *supra* note 14, at 92.

52. *See* Plaintiff's Brief, *supra* note 48, at 126.

53. *See* Defendant's Brief, *supra* note 14, at 92–93.

54. Telephone Interview with John P. Ewart, *supra* note 34.

55. *See* 200 N.E.2d at 189–90 (Ill. App. Ct. 1964).

56. Telephone Interview with John P. Ewert, of Counsel, Craig & Craig, in Mattoon, Ill. (July 23, 2008).

57. *See* BLS inflation calculator, which uses the Consumer Price Index, *available at* http://www.bls.gov/cpi/.

58. Interview with Pat Darling, *supra* note 6.

59. *See $150,000 Verdict Returned by Jury*, The Charleston-Courier News, Nov. 12, 1962.

60. *See* 200 N.E.2d at 175 (Ill. App. Ct. 1964).

61. *See* John A. Kare, *Volkmann Contracture* (2004), *available at* http://www.emedicine.com/orthoped/topic578.htm; C.E.A. Holden, *The Pathology and Prevention of Volkmann's Ischaemic Contracture*, 61 J. Bone & Joint Surgery 296 (1979) (noting that during the 1960s, the time of the Darling case, there was some support for the view that the condition was due solely to arterial injury with reflex spasm of the collateral vessels and that tight splintage was merely contributory).

62. Kenneth B. Babcock, *Darling Case Raises Issue of Staff Privileges*, 107 Modern Hosp. 138 (1966).

63. *See* Darling v. Charleston Cmty. Mem'l Hosp., 200 N.E.2d 149 (Ill. App. Ct. 1964); *Court Upholds $150,000 Award to Ex-EIU Athlete*, The Charleston-Courier News, June 30, 1964.

64. 211 N.E.2d at 257 (Ill. 1965) (quoting Bing v. Thunig, 143 N.E.2d 3,8 (N.Y. 1957)).

65. 211 N.E. 2d. at 257 (Ill. 1965).

66. *See* 200 N.E. 2d at 166–68, 176 (Ill. App. Ct. 1964); Defendant's Brief, *supra* note 14, at 60; Defendant's Petition for Rehearing at 4, Darling v. Charleston Cmty. Mem'l Hosp., 211 N.E.2d 253 (Ill. 1965) (No. 38790).

67. *See* Trotter Hardy Jr., *When Doctrines Collide: Corporate Negligence and Respondeat Superior When Hospital Employees Fail to Speak Up*, 61 Tul. L. Rev. 85, 94 (1986).

68. *See* Plaintiff's Brief, *supra* note 48, at 85.

69. Havighurst, *supra* note 9, at 9.

70. *See* Arthur F. Southwick, *The Hospital as an Institution — Expanding Responsibilities Change Its Relationship With the Staff Physician*, 9 Cal. W. L. Rev. 429, 446–47 (1973); James E. Ludlam, *The Impact of the Darling Decision Upon the Practice of Medicine and Hospitals*, 11 The Forum 756 (1976).

71. 211 N.E.2d. at 257 (Ill. 1965).

72. Mark A. Hall et al., Health Care Law & Ethics 463 (7th ed. 2007) (quoting AMA 12 Citation 82 (1965)).

73. *See* Joel Edelman, *How To Adapt to The Charleston Decision*, 107 Modern Hosp. 137 (1966).

74. Westlaw search of multiple databases (last visited Dec. 31, 2007).

75. *See* William M. Sage, *The Forgotten Third: Liability Insurance and the Medical Malpractice Crisis*, 23 Health Affairs 10, 12 (2004).

76. *See* Jones v. Chicago HMO Ltd. of Illinois, 730 N.E.2d 1119 (Ill. 2000).

77. Mark A. Hall, *Institutional Control of Physician Behavior: Legal Barriers to Health Care Cost Containment*, 137 U. Pa. L. Rev. 431, 505–06 (1988) (quoting Smith, *Two Lines of Authority Are One Too Many*, Modern Hosp., March 1955, at 59, 60).

78. *See* Thomas L. Greaney, *New Governance Norms and Quality of Care in Nonprofit Hospitals*, 14 Annals Health L. 421, 431–33 (2005).

79. *See* Elizabeth A. Weeks, *The New Economic Credentialing: Protecting Hospitals from Competition by Medical Staff Members*, 36 J. Health L. 247 (2003).

80. *See* Greaney, *supra* note 78, at 431–32.

81. *See generally* Committee on Quality of Health Care in America, Institute of Medicine, To Err is Human: Building a Safer Health System (Linda Krohn et al. eds., 1999).

82. *See* Paul Starr, The Social Transformation of American Medicine 355, 362–63, 429 (1982).

83. Rosemary Stevens, In Sickness and in Wealth: American Hospitals in the Twentieth Century 241 (rev. ed. 1999).

84. Arthur Southwick, *The Hospital's New Responsibility*, 17 Clev.-Marshall L. Rev. 146, 161 (1968).

85. 210 N.E.2d 182 (Ill. 1965).

86. *See* Sara Parikh & Bryant Garth, *Philip Corboy and the Construction of the Plaintiffs' Personal Injury Bar*, 30 Law & Soc. Inquiry 269, 282–84 & n.16 (2005).

87. *See* Kenneth S. Abraham & Paul C. Weiler, *Enterprise Medical Liability and the Evolution of the American Health Care System*, 108 Harv. L. Rev. 381, 393–94, 399–415 (1994).

88. *See generally* Robert Gatter, *The Mysterious Survival of the Policy Against Informed Consent Liability for Hospitals*, 81 Notre Dame L. Rev. 1203 (2006).

89. *See* Player Biography: Dorrence Darling, *available at* http://goredbirds.cstv.com/genrel/darling_dorrencered00.html.

90. *See Area Deaths*, The Journal Gazette Times-Courier (Charleston, Ill.), Oct. 16, 1996.

91. *See* 200 N.E.2d at 176 (Ill. App. Ct. 1964).

92. Interview with Pat Darling, *supra* note 6.

93. *See Dr. John Alexander Dies Monday Night*, The Charleston-Courier News, Oct. 31, 1967.

94. *See A Dream Realized: Sarah Bush Lincoln Health Center Serves the Entire Area with Modern Medical Facility*, The Journal Gazette Times-Courier (Charleston, Ill.), Sept. 28, 2005.

95. 688 N.E.2d 106 (Ill. 1997).

96. *See* Bonnie Clark, *This Won't Hurt a Bit: Health Department Nurse to Give Retirement a Shot*, The Journal Gazette Times-Courier (Charleston, Ill.), Nov. 11, 2004, at C1.

97. Interview with Pat Darling, *supra* note 6.

98. *Id.*

99. *Id.*

100. *Id.*

101. *Id.*

Part II

DEATH AND DYING

Chapter 3

QUINLAN

and

CRUZAN

Beyond the Symbols

Sandra H. Johnson*

Karen Ann Quinlan, Nancy Beth Cruzan, and Terri Marie Schiavo are iconic figures. Remarkably similar in appearance, familiar photographs show all three — young, white, twenty-something, pretty, dark-haired women — prior to the medical catastrophes that eventually claimed their lives. Each of these three women — and their families and caregivers — existed for a time within a vortex of public conflict, media attention, and legal battles over unavoidable decisions about the course of their medical treatment.

In many respects, Ms. Quinlan, Ms. Cruzan, and Ms. Schiavo present identical cases. All three shared the same diagnosis and prognosis — the persistent vegetative state (PVS), the paradigmatic mental condition through which advocates, courts, and legislatures developed and challenged fundamental ethical, social, and legal principles. For all three, decisions concerning life-sustaining treatment would be made by family members without the benefit of specific advance directives.

These three cases, however, are not entirely the same. The Quinlan family was the prototype for the idealized surrogate decisionmaker that forms the foundation for our current framework for end-of-life decisionmaking. For Terri Schiavo, in contrast, the painful and destructive split among her family members — a scenario that perhaps was narrowly avoided in Nancy Cruzan's case through divorce — challenged idealized notions of family that had been

* Professor Emerita of Law and Health Care Ethics, Center for Health Law Studies, Saint Louis University School of Law. Professor Johnson signed an amicus brief filed with the United States Supreme Court in support of the Cruzan family. Brief of Missouri Hospitals, Hospital Ethics Committees, Medical Schools, Hospital Chaplains, Hospice Organizations and Law Professors, Cruzan v. Director, Missouri Dept. of Health, 497 U.S 261 (1990) (No. 88-1503), 1989 WL 1115257. I gratefully acknowledge the research assistance of Kelly Carroll, M.A., J.D./Ph.D. candidate, Saint Louis University.

Karen Ann Quinlan. With permission of Mrs. Julia Quinlan.

so conveniently and intuitively accepted. An unrelenting and startling legal battle in the courts and in the state and federal legislatures marked Terri Schiavo's case. Missouri trial and appellate courts, in contrast, uniformly closed the door on challenges filed by strangers to the Cruzans, spared the difficulty of dealing with litigation by family members against one another. Finally, for Karen Quinlan, the medical intervention targeted for withdrawal was the ventilator. The dispute did not include nutrition and hydration, which the family continued in some form for nearly ten years after withdrawing the ventilator. For Nancy Cruzan and Terri Schiavo, however, nutrition and hydration was the only form of life support at issue, an intervention that itself was and remains loaded with emotional, political, and religious significance.

Some of these differences reveal the fragility of the legal framework for end-of-life decisionmaking, a framework that relies on a theory of highly individualized inquiry. In this framework, each case requires an inquiry into the individual

Nancy Beth Cruzan. With permission of William Colby on behalf of the Cruzan family.

patient's precise medical condition and her known or inferred desires — as those wishes are communicated by appointed or default surrogates. In each case, these surrogates are themselves subject to examination and challenge as to whether they are acting in good faith on the patient's behalf. These stories, however, are not entirely about legal standards:

> Though the stories played out in the court system, they are really about how decisions are made in a democratic society on our hardest questions. . . . And the

heart of the . . . story is about what happens to human beings who are caught in the middle of that decision making process.[1]

While Terri Schiavo's tale is well known and well documented, memories of Karen Quinlan and Nancy Cruzan have dimmed with the passage of time. It is

in their narratives rather than in their iconography, however, that the notion that Terri Schiavo's case defied the consensus developed by *In the Matter of Karen Quinlan*[2] and *Cruzan v. Director, Missouri Department of Health*[3] can be tested with a deeper understanding.

This chapter begins by telling the stories of Karen Quinlan and Nancy Cruzan and their families as their journey led them into the public arena. It begins with their youthful experiences and walks through the catastrophic events and early treatment decisions, their medical diagnoses and prognoses, how the parents reached the decision to withdraw life-sustaining treatment, and the events that then triggered litigation. As happened for the Quinlan and Cruzan families, the focus of

Terri Marie Schiavo. Used with permission of Getty Images/Getty Images News.

the chapter then widens to bring in the media forces and protests, the court decisions, and the role played in each case by thought leaders in the Catholic Church and medicine. Finally, the story centers again on the two families and the withdrawal of life-sustaining treatment, the deaths of their daughters, and the aftermath for the Quinlans and the Cruzans.

A. Youth and Family

Julia Quinlan, Karen's mother, suffered three miscarriages and a stillborn child during the first years of her marriage to Joseph Quinlan, the childhood sweetheart she married after World War II. Told by doctors that it would be impossible for Julia to bear a live child, Julia and Joe adopted their infant daughter in 1954 and named her Karen Ann.[4] Shortly after bringing her home, the Quinlans rushed their new baby to the hospital, suffering from dysentery. After three days, the doctor told them: "I can't give you any hope. I'm afraid the illness has gone too far." Julia prayed for her child "harder than she had for anything else in her life." When they returned to the hospital after a church service, the same doctor told them, "I don't understand it, but Karen has passed the crisis."[5]

The Quinlans' image of their daughter Karen was fixed by this memorable incident; her family knew her ever after as a survivor and a fighter — their own little "miracle." Karen confirmed that image when she "walked away without a scratch" from an accident in 1974 in which her little VW bug flew off the edge of the road into a ravine, totaling the car that Karen later rebuilt and put back into service.[6] Like many patients in judicial cases concerning the discontinuation of life-sustaining treatment, Karen was described as vivacious and sociable, with a special enthusiasm for climbing, running, sports of all kinds, and her friends. According to Julia, Karen "was so full of life" and had a laugh that "was just contagious."[7] Karen's resistance to her parents' desire that she attend college after high school and her interest in working as a car mechanic marked her as a determined young woman.[8]

Joe and Julia Quinlan were devoutly Catholic, and their three children were raised in the Catholic faith.[9] Joe, who worked in the accounting department at Warner Lambert, was known as "a quiet man, gentle, carefully controlled; the kind of man people lean on."[10] Joe Quinlan took the public lead for his family in what was to come, just as Joe Cruzan would a decade later.

Nancy Cruzan's family was a "salt of the earth, God-fearing, blue-collar, southern Missouri family."[11] Nancy Cruzan, like Karen Quinlan, was known by her family and friends as a vibrant and determined character. Her nieces described Aunt Nancy as "the greatest aunt anybody could ever have in the whole world" and as "ornery" and "funny."[12] Her father remembered that when he watched her perform as co-captain of the twirlers for the high school marching band, his "eyes would fill up" and he "couldn't hardly see through the camera."[13] Nancy was the firstborn and the "free spirit" of the three Cruzan girls. She "loved speed," whether riding with her father on his motorcycle or driving her car on the two-lane country roads around the Cruzan home in little Carterville, Missouri, population 2000.

Nancy, like Karen, did not always follow the path her parents would have chosen for her. She married Danny Hayes while a senior in high school, mistakenly believing that she was pregnant, and later moved with him to Florida while he served in the Navy. Her first marriage ended in divorce three years later, and she moved back to her parents' home — a twenty-year-old who loved to party. Nancy met Paul Davis in 1980, and they married in 1982 and moved to a small home on Krummel Nursery Road.[14]

Joe Cruzan did not approve of his daughter's new husband. Like Joe Quinlan, Joe Cruzan, a construction worker, was the man everyone relied on. His younger brother called him "The Wagonmaster" because of his role in planning and executing the Cruzans' extended-family outings. Although Joe Cruzan spoke in measured tones, he was opinionated and engaged in active correspondence with politicians and newspapers concerning behavior he thought was wrongheaded.[15] According to daughter Christy, her father was a fixer and could fix anything.[16] Joe Cruzan could not repair the devastation that befell his own daughter, however, and neither could Julia and Joe Quinlan.

B. The Catastrophic Events and the Early Decisions

Karen Ann Quinlan had just turned 21 and was living with friends in April, 1975, when her parents received the phone call that all parents of young adults dread — their daughter was in the emergency room of a local hospital in dire condition. According to her friends, Karen had had no more than three gin and tonics at their party when she "passed out" and they put her to bed.[17] They knew that she had been on a "crash diet" to fit into a bikini and hadn't eaten all day. When her friends checked on her later, though, she had stopped breathing for who knows how long.

Karen was first admitted to Newton Memorial Hospital emergency room. A few days later she was transferred to St. Clare's Hospital, which had more sophisticated facilities and which the Quinlans loved because it was in that New Jersey hospital that their daughter had survived dysentery as an infant.[18] For weeks, the Quinlans maintained hope of their daughter's recovery, even as her body "folded itself into a tight little fetal figure" and her weight dropped from 120 pounds, to 90 pounds, and then to 70 pounds. By late June, Karen was immobile except for her head and her aimlessly darting eyes.[19] Despite her condition, Joe Quinlan expected her to pull through as she had before: "I knew Karen — she's such a determined, strong girl. If anyone could pull out of this, it's Karen."[20]

Nancy Cruzan's family also received a call in the middle of the night that would "change their lives forever."[21] On January 11, 1983, Nancy Davis, *nee* Cruzan, was a 25-year-old newlywed, married nearly one year, when her husband received the call that his wife was being taken to Freeman Hospital with head injuries after a car accident. Nancy's car had run off the road at a curve on Krummel Nursery Road. A neighbor heard a crash around 12:30 A.M. and discovered the car resting on its roof, with no sign of a driver inside. He later found Nancy lying "facedown and motionless on the hard ground" where she had been thrown from the car.[22] Some time later, police arrived on the scene; concluding that Nancy was dead, as she had no pulse and was not breathing, the officers made no effort to resuscitate her.[23] Instead, police and neighbors continued to look for other passengers who might also have been thrown from the car, until the ambulance arrived and paramedics began efforts to resuscitate Nancy.[24]

Paul Davis called Nancy's sister, Christy, at 2:25 A.M. to tell her the news, and Christy called her parents. They all rushed to Freeman Hospital to await Nancy's arrival; however, the Cruzans didn't recognize Nancy as she was carried through the emergency room but for her socks — special socks that Joyce had given each of her daughters for Christmas.[25] Joe remembered that "when the nurse came out and said that she was going to be all right, I turned . . . to Joyce and I said 'I feel like I can breathe again.'"[26] Unfortunately, it turned out that "all right" wasn't exactly accurate.

Nancy's husband Paul, and Joe and Joyce Cruzan when Paul wasn't available, consented to all interventions recommended by the doctors. These included a gastrostomy, a surgical procedure to insert a tube into Nancy's stomach to deliver nutrition. Joyce later recalled that they signed anything that the hospital asked them to, often without reading the document: "When it's just been three or four weeks after the accident, you think . . . that there's a good chance she's going to get better."[27] Joe said, "I had no idea I was signing away anybody's rights [when he permitted the gastrostomy]. I would have signed anything. We were just waiting for Nancy to wake up."[28] Christy recalls that the gastrostomy was to be "a bridge to allow Nan to recover. We had great hopes that she would be able to recover and return to consciousness."[29]

In February 1983, Brady Rehabilitation Center agreed to admit Nancy for intensive interventions, including attempts at spoon feeding, to try to stimulate her to consciousness. After four weeks with no change, the Center discharged her. Paul didn't want his wife to be in a nursing home, or apparently at the Cruzans' home, and instead arranged to have her stay with his grandmother in Oronogo, Missouri. Paul's family cared for Nancy there, in a tiny home without air conditioning throughout an intensely hot Missouri summer. After a brief hospitalization, Nancy was admitted to the Missouri Rehabilitation Center (MRC), a state facility in Mount Vernon, Missouri.[30]

C. Medical Diagnosis and Prognosis: PVS and "Sleeping Beauty"

Both Karen Quinlan and Nancy Cruzan, like Terri Schiavo after them, were eventually diagnosed as being in a persistent vegetative state. At the time of Karen's diagnosis in 1975, recognition of the syndrome was quite new. PVS had been described first by Jennett and Plum in the Lancet just three years earlier[31] in an attempt to find a less offensive term for patients who were sometimes crassly called "locks" or "goons" in the medical slang of the time.[32] At the time of his testimony in the *Quinlan* case, Plum testified that he had personally examined no more than 25-30 persons in PVS and had complete records on only 40-50 more around the world.[33]

In a prominent article published just a few years before the Lancet article on PVS, a Harvard committee had coined the term "irreversible coma" to describe the irreversible cessation of all brain activity, including activity in the brain stem. The Harvard committee proposed to bring irreversible coma within the definition of death.[34] Naturally, some confusion arose over whether Karen Quinlan was dead or alive because her coma was also described as "irreversible." These new brain death standards had not been accepted in law by many states, including New Jersey, so their legal status was ambiguous.[35] In a significant but now unappreciated aspect of their decision, the *Quinlan* court accepted the new brain death standards and declared that, under those standards, Karen was alive as her brain stem continued to function. The recognition of PVS by the New Jersey Supreme Court in *Quinlan* also catapulted this new category of unconsciousness into the public — as well as the legislative and judicial — arena and gave it significance beyond medical circles. As courts developed the law on a case-by-case basis after *Quinlan*, and as legislatures responded tentatively at first with advance directive statutes, PVS became a legally significant category, distinct from other non-terminal conditions such as advanced dementia or minimal consciousness, in analyzing withdrawal of life-sustaining treatment.

Although the sleep-wake cycles, the contractures of the limbs, the aimless eyes, and in Karen's case bedsores "so deep that the hipbone could be seen beneath,"[36] had all been described in court opinions and news articles, Karen Quinlan remained a "sleeping beauty" in the public imagination. This was exactly the image of their beloved daughter that the Quinlans wanted to convey: "Although we knew that . . . Karen's condition was nothing like the glorified image of a 'sleeping beauty' — we nevertheless wanted her to be remembered as such. No one needed to see what Karen really looked like."[37]

In part because of the Quinlans' decision to keep Karen's physical condition private, film of Nancy Cruzan, broadcast on the evening news, was the first encounter with a PVS patient for most of the general public. Bill Colby, the Cruzans' attorney, recalls that his first visit to Nancy was "among the most unsettling and disquieting experiences of my life." He says: "I think maybe I expected to see Sleeping Beauty: eyes closed, skin white, serenity embodied. If the cases about other families I'd read in the law books had told me what to expect, somehow I missed it."[38]

Perhaps the most startling characteristic revealed to the public in these broadcasts was that Nancy's eyes were open. Unconscious, but with her eyes "open in the promise of speech,"[39] breathing on her own, grimacing, and startling at loud noises — the dissonance between the appearance and the diagnosis is dramatic. Similarly, Julia Quinlan recalls one evening with her daughter years after the withdrawal of the ventilator: "As I kissed her good night, . . . I told her I loved her and wondered if she heard me, maybe just this once. I knew the answer, but sometimes your heart, not your intellect, rules you." More disturbing was the grimacing and thrashing and the response to pinches and cold water; Julia Quinlan says that she "sat by Karen's bedside day and night and watched her grimace as though she was in pain. The doctor assured me she was not. But I was not convinced."[40]

Controversy over Karen's situation included conflict over whether she truly was in a persistent vegetative state and whether her condition was irreversible. Critics charged that Karen would recover consciousness. As it would be many years later for Terri Schiavo, newspapers covering Karen's case constantly reported stories of individuals who had come out of comas. One such individual, in fact, came to New Jersey and held a press conference reporting how his coma of one-month's duration had been "like Utopia," and how he, and likewise Karen, had to be forced to return.[41]

It was no different for Nancy Cruzan. One doctor called to testify by the state had said in an earlier deposition that Nancy was in a chronic vegetative state and had only a "minuscule probability of ever having any cognitive function." Nonetheless, at trial the doctor testified that while examining Nancy once again just before his testimony, she had fixated on his face, responded to sound, had a pain response higher than mere reflex, and was not in PVS.[42] In contrast, Dr. Ronald Cranford, the expert witness for the Cruzans on the issue of PVS generally and Nancy's diagnosis in particular, testified that there was "no hope of recovery" in her case. On cross-examination, however, the state's attorney probed a notorious situation in which a patient that Cranford had diagnosed as being in PVS had later recovered some cognitive function.[43] The debate spread outside the courtroom: in the popular media, Pat Robertson reported on his *700 Club* television show that Nancy Cruzan could cry and could smile as she felt pain and joy.[44]

As their daughter's future became clearer to the family, however, the Cruzans began to consider some difficult decisions, as had the Quinlans before them.

D. Coming to a Decision

By May 1975, approximately a month after Karen's collapse, Julia Quinlan had concluded that "there was no medical help for Karen . . . [and] the time that the respirator could help her had passed." Still, Julia felt she could not share this view with her family, as "they were not prepared to listen to any hints that [Karen] might not recover." Karen's sister Mary Ellen told Julia much later that she "didn't really understand at first why we were going to turn off the machine. It was kind of a shock. . . ." But Mary Ellen "gradually recognized the futility of the machines," and Karen's brother John "accepted the fact that she was not going to make it."[45]

Joe Quinlan was "the last holdout."[46] He was hostile to any suggestion that Karen might not recover, and had responded to a gentle suggestion by Julia of the futility of additional care in a "low, taut tone she'd never before heard: 'I don't ever want to hear that.' "[47] When a nurse and close friend of the Quinlans tried to talk to Joe and explain that this wasn't an "ordinary coma," that "the thinking part of her brain is dead," and that what they observed were only "primitive reflexes," Joe was absolutely furious. Finally, in mid-June, Karen's neurologist at St. Clare's, Dr. Robert Morse, responded to another of Joe's reports that Karen was getting better. Dr. Morse told Joe: "What am I going to say to you, Joe? . . . Even if God did perform a miracle so that Karen would live, her damage is so extensive that she would spend the rest of her life in an institution!" Only then did Joe Quinlan begin to accept that Karen would not recover, and he wept in his car as he drove home, carefully wiping his eyes before he went inside.[48]

Joe and Julia Quinlan sought counsel from Father Thomas Trapasso, the pastor of the Catholic parish where Julia worked as the priests' secretary. Father Tom assured the Quinlans that "God has made the decision that she's going to die. You're just agreeing with God's decision, that's all."[49] Father Tom's advice was confirmed by Father Paschal "Pat" Caccavale, St. Clare's chaplain.[50]

On July 31, three-and-a-half months after his daughter's collapse, Joe Quinlan gave Dr. Morse permission to remove the respirator. According to Joe, Dr. Morse said, "I think you have come to the right decision."[51] Joe signed the documents provided by the hospital authorizing them to discontinue "all extraordinary measures, including the use of a respirator" and releasing the hospital from liability.[52]

The Cruzan family made a similarly reluctant journey. It was when Joe and Joyce Cruzan brought Nancy home from MRC for Christmas in 1984, in the hope that the return home for the holidays would trigger some response from her, that Christy lost all hope for her sister's recovery.[53] Nancy's father also began his own investigation into brain injuries and comas at this time, reading everything he could find. When Joe Cruzan came across an article on PVS, he told Joyce that the description fit perfectly,[54] a diagnosis later confirmed by MRC's medical director. Armed with a name for her condition, Joe began calling people all around the country to learn as much as he could. He spoke at length with doctors, medical ethicists, priests, preachers, lawyers, and family members of PVS patients, like Patricia Brophy[55] and the parents of Nancy Jobes,[56] whom he had read about in a newspaper column.

Joe's investigation and consultations over the next two years led to a conclusion that he and Joyce kept to themselves for a time. In October 1986, however, when Sue Rowell, a nurse at MRC, related her experience with the health crises of her own son, the Cruzans shared with her that they had decided to stop the feeding tube, nearly four years after it had been inserted.[57] Word about the Cruzans' decision spread quickly through MRC, and the ripples of conflict that would become a torrent appeared almost immediately. Both the Quinlans and the Cruzans ultimately would turn to the courts for resolution.

E. Trigger for Litigation

July 31, 1975, when Joe Quinlan gave permission for withdrawal of the ventilator from his daughter, might have been the end of the story for the Quinlans had Dr. Morse and the family been of the same mind about finding some way to accomplish what they wanted — as other families and doctors had done with this new respirator technology.[58] Instead, after consulting with his former teacher, Dr. Morris Bender, chief of neurosurgery at Mt. Sinai Hospital in New York, Dr. Morse decided that he would not terminate ventilator support after all because he was convinced that no established medical custom or standard supported that action.[59]

At this point, the decision over Karen's future left the intimacy of the bedside. The Quinlans met with administrators and legal counsel for St. Clare's to pursue their decision. The hospital's attorney noted that Joe Quinlan was not his adult daughter's legal guardian. The attorney informed Joe that he would have to go to court to be formally appointed, even though the hospital had accepted Joe's consent on his daughter's behalf for all of her prior medical treatment. Moreover, the hospital's attorney didn't know whether the hospital would comply with the family's request to withdraw the ventilator even if Joe were appointed guardian. This was the first time that St. Clare's had dealt with such a situation, and it was moving cautiously.[60]

The Quinlans found an attorney, Notre Dame alumnus Paul Armstrong — a Legal Aid lawyer who decided to take the case on his own time without pay, but ended up devoting his full time to the cause.[61] Armstrong offered the Quinlans an option that might have avoided the public spotlight and the landmark case that followed. Paul suggested to Joe Quinlan that he could petition to be his daughter's guardian but not ask specifically for authority to discontinue the ventilator, as St. Clare's stated objection so far was only that he lacked legal authority for the decision. Joe Quinlan rejected this approach, saying: "I don't think that would be honest, and I don't think it would do much good. What I'd like is for everything to be open and aboveboard. . . . I think that would help the doctors, too. They wouldn't have to worry or to feel guilty. . . ."[62] And so it was that the Quinlans' time in the courts began.

Joe and Joyce Cruzan had been appointed formally as co-guardians for their daughter Nancy in January 1984, more than two years before they made their decision concerning life-sustaining treatment. Nancy's husband Paul did not attend the guardianship hearing in 1984, but didn't oppose the appointment. Six months later, Joe and Joyce petitioned the court for a divorce on behalf of their daughter. Tension between Joe and Paul had been building throughout Nancy's hospitalization: "Joe was at the hospital all of the time, day and night; Paul visited and left."[63] Nancy's father thought her husband should be just as attentive. Once Nancy was transferred to MRC, about 45 miles from Carterville, Paul's visits waned, and he did not oppose the divorce. Nancy's sister Christy believed that Paul probably realized that his life with Nancy was gone forever, whether or not they divorced.[64]

Joe Cruzan had developed a cordial relationship with Judge Charles Teel, the probate judge who had jurisdiction over Nancy's guardianship. In September 1986, when Joe and Joyce Cruzan first decided that they wanted to stop the nutrition and hydration, Joe told Judge Teel that he had heard that some families had taken patients like Nancy home to die. Judge Teel advised against it, saying, according to Joe's notes of the conversation: "Every rinky-dink politician is out to make a name for himself," and the prosecutor would surely act if it became known. The judge added that he would have to intervene himself because removing the tube would be "murder."[65] Thus, the option of simply taking Nancy home, which some suggested should have been done, was out of the question.

Transferring Nancy to a private facility that would support the family's decision was still a possibility, one that the MRC staff had been trying to persuade the Cruzans to do for some time.[66] In 1984, when Don Lamkins became the administrator of what was then known as the Missouri State Chest Hospital (MSCH), caring for persons with chronic respiratory illnesses, he confronted a failing enterprise. Lamkins refocused MSCH's efforts on the care of an emerging class of brain-damaged patients who had been saved by the greater capacities of the emergency room, the intensive care unit, and outside-of-hospital CPR,[67] dealing with what one nurse called "the aftereffects of what heroics are done on the roadside."[68] MSCH had a notably high success rate in weaning respirator-dependent patients, and changed its name to the Missouri Rehabilitation Center in 1985 to reflect its new purpose.[69] After the Cruzans' conversation with Nurse Rowell concerning their decision to stop delivery of nutrition and hydration became known, Lamkins intensified efforts to transfer Nancy out of this state-owned facility.[70]

Joe and Joyce Cruzan resisted all efforts to transfer their daughter, fearing that the quality of care for Nancy would decline and perhaps viewing the state hospital where she had lived and they had visited for so long as her home. At one point, they went to Judge Teel for help. The Republican judge called his powerful friend, Missouri Senator Dick Webster, who with one call to the Department of Health assured that the talk of transferring Nancy would stop.[71] Ironically, the Senator's son, Bill Webster, would later lead the case for the state against the Cruzans as Missouri's Attorney General.

On May 28, 1987, the Cruzans met with administrators from MRC, and Joe delivered a letter he had written himself detailing their request for withdrawal of the feeding tube. Don Lamkins, a "devout member of the conservative Church of Christ," disagreed with the Cruzans' decision, viewing it as a violation of the Commandment that "thou shalt not kill," but believed that "it was their decision to make."[72] He wondered, though, why the Cruzans would resist a transfer for fear of their daughter developing bedsores, when on the other hand they wanted to remove the feeding tube and let her "starve to death."[73] Lamkins informed the Cruzans at that meeting that he sympathized with them, but would have to take the decision to his superiors at the Department of Health. Robert Northcutt, general counsel for the Department, responded in a memo to Lamkins' request for guidance, saying that the Department would not proceed without a specific court order but that he doubted that "a Missouri Court, while it may be willing to remove life-support systems, w[ould] be willing to authorize the deliberate dehydration and starvation of a comatose or coma patient."[74]

Joe and Joyce Cruzan searched for an attorney to represent them and were referred to Shook, Hardy & Bacon, a large Kansas City law firm willing to do pro bono work. Young Bill Colby, a fifth-year associate, took the case with the support of his firm. As was the experience of the Quinlans' attorney Paul Armstrong, this case would consume Bill Colby for many years.[75] As Armstrong did for the Quinlans, Bill offered the Cruzans one last option to avoid litigation: they could move their daughter out of Missouri to another state where withdrawing nutrition and hydration would not be an issue. Joe would not hear of it, arguing that "If we're doing what is right, why do we need to move her somewhere? . . . We're Missourians. Why should we have to move her out of Missouri?"[76] With Joe's mind made up, Bill Colby turned to preparing for trial.

The Cruzan litigation began, prior to filing any petition, with Judge Teel and Bill Colby having lunch at a local restaurant near the courthouse. There, the Judge reported that he had already talked "on another matter" with Attorney General Bill Webster, whom the Judge had known as a child and still called "Billy." The Judge told Colby that he didn't expect a problem from the Attorney General, although he advised Colby to include the State and the hospital as defendants in his petition. Colby then met with Robert Northcutt and recalls that Northcutt said: "We want this to be a friendly suit. We need clarification as much as you do on what the law is. We'll oppose you at trial, and if you win, we'll appeal, but we don't want it to be adversarial. . . . We just need to know what the rules are."[77] Northcutt said he didn't want the process to be hard on the family; but it could not have been otherwise, and the friendly suit did not stay that way for long.

F. Media Force and Protests

For years, the Quinlans and Cruzans spent every moment with television cameras and reporters camped out at their homes, at the institutions where their daughters lived, and surrounding them whenever they moved from one place to another. The day after Joe Quinlan filed the petition for guardianship, the newspaper delivered to his front door had a banner headline: "Father Asks the Court to Allow Him to Kill His Daughter."[78] Although Paul Armstrong had made a plea for privacy for the family, they watched their "front lawn . . . crush under an army of reporters and photographers, TV cameras and sound equipment. . . ."[79] Julia recalls that the family was "inundated" by the press, with one reporter tapping on her car window to offer her $100,000 or more for a current photo of Karen. Karen's graduation picture was "as recognizable in Japan, Mexico, England, and most European countries as it is in this country,"[80] and the Quinlans' story was covered each day on the evening news. When the New Jersey Supreme Court's decision was announced, 100 reporters attended a press conference at Our Lady of the Lake Elementary School, which was carried live on all three television networks, and the New York Times published the full text of the court's opinion.[81] Karen's ultimate transfer from St. Clare's to the Morris View Nursing Home was a secret, strictly orchestrated affair, complete with a decoy ambulance and other efforts to assure that the press, and protesters, would not threaten or harm Karen.[82] For nearly ten years, the press kept what Julia Quinlan calls a "death watch" outside the nursing home where Karen lived out her life.[83]

Similarly, film of the Cruzans captures crowds of reporters surrounding Joe, Joyce, Christy, and Nancy's young nieces as they walked together to court. At one point, Joe is heard warning the reporters in a low growl: "If you get into my granddaughter here, there is gonna be a problem."[84] Otherwise, though, he felt helpless, complaining that "[T]here's not a damn thing I can do about it. Except just watch." He longed for the day when he would be able to go home and "watch the evening news without seeing 'Cruzan' splashed all over it."[85]

Yet both the Quinlans and the Cruzans also used the media to tell their stories in the way they wanted. The Quinlans wrote a book and were advisors for a television movie dramatizing their experience. The Cruzans told their story on the PBS series, *Frontline*. Elizabeth Arledge, a *Frontline* producer who was about the same age as Nancy, had contacted the Society for the Right to Die — one of the organizations that Joe Cruzan had consulted — for suggestions of families who would be facing controversial end-of-life decisions.[86] The Cruzans allowed *Frontline* to film their experiences, including their visits with Nancy, interviews with the staff of MRC, and the events surrounding Nancy's last days.

Both Karen Quinlan and Nancy Cruzan became the objects of public protests and attempted interventions, just as Terri Schiavo would become years later. The Morris County Sheriff responsible for security at the courthouse during the Quinlan guardianship proceeding reported that, "Everybody was getting letters, sometimes packages. . . . The people who wrote seemed to take two basic views. One was 'Don't let Karen die, or we'll kill you.' The other was 'Let her die, or we'll kill *her*.'"[87] Wells Fargo guards kept at bay the "hundreds of faith healers who came to the hospital pleading to see and cure Karen."[88]

Protesters also set up camp at MRC during the course of the Cruzan litigation, and several were able to enter the facility before security was increased. One man walked through the halls carrying a cup and saying "I have a friend upstairs and I was trying to give her a cup of water. . . . [T]here are policemen up there and they won't let me give her a cup of water." The police removed protesters occupying the stairs leading to Nancy's floor, and Joyce Cruzan described how "a number of times Joe leaned against the door [of Nancy's room] and held it shut. . . . [Y]ou could hear that there was stuff going on out there." Don Lamkins commented that the MRC staff, too, were "feeling like we're being attacked by all these people coming in and that means that we band together a little closer and try to take care of each other."[89]

G. The Courts Decide

In November 1975, Judge Robert Muir denied Joe Quinlan's petition for appointment as the guardian of his daughter with authority to remove her from the ventilator.[90] Joe Quinlan was "enormously sad" after that decision and began to visit his daughter three to four times a day. In fact, Dr. Morse asked him to reduce his visits because it made the nurses "so deeply sad" for him, a suggestion that outraged the Quinlans.[91] They continued the visits, but had no contact thereafter with the doctor. The Quinlans appealed Judge Muir's decision to the New Jersey Supreme Court. That court, in a unanimous decision, authorized Joseph Quinlan to decide on behalf of his daughter that the ventilator should be discontinued.[92] After a close examination of his character, the court decided that Joe Quinlan was a worthy decisionmaker for his daughter. The court also decided, however, that Karen's reported conversations concerning her desires, which were and remain typical for a young person, were too remote and nonspecific to be relevant and that a specially constituted hospital committee had to review her prognosis before withdrawal of the ventilator.

The Cruzans had a longer legal road to travel than did the Quinlans. Judge Teel issued his order on July 27, 1988. I was teaching a class for state court judges about legal issues in life-sustaining treatment that day, with the man who would be writing the law for our state sitting as a student in our classroom. At the beginning of a break, he announced, "Ma'am, I have my decision in the Cruzan case here if you would like to look at it."

Judge Teel, who first believed that removing nutrition and hydration would be murder, had written an opinion ordering MRC to comply with the Cruzans' decision. In discussion in our class, it was clear that he had focused his efforts primarily on establishing the right to withdraw nutrition and hydration. The Judge relied on a liberty interest — "as in give me liberty or give me death," the Judge said in class discussion that day. He had rejected the right to privacy because, he said, Cruzan's case "had nothing to do with abortion."

Thad McCanse, who had acted as Nancy's guardian ad litem and who had filed a report with Judge Teel supporting the Cruzans' decision, filed an immediate appeal of the decision that had followed his recommendation, possibly at the request of Judge Teel.[93] The Missouri Supreme Court wanted to hear the *Cruzan* case, and initially scheduled argument for the same day that the court expected to hear arguments in an appeal of a trial court decision that a hospital had the right to stop ventilator support for a brain-dead patient over the objections of the family. As it turned out, that patient's heart stopped and he was not able to be resuscitated. That case was removed from the docket, and the court considered the *Cruzan* case standing alone.[94]

The Missouri Supreme Court, in a 4-3 decision written by Chief Judge "Chip" Robertson, reversed Judge Teel's order. The court held that state law required life-sustaining treatment be continued unless Nancy's desires regarding treatment were proven by clear and convincing evidence, which was lacking in the record.[95] Robertson later called *Cruzan* an "excruciating case for everybody involved," a case that has "haunted" him since. Indeed, Robertson later said he did not pay much attention to the *Schiavo* case "because it brings up too many difficult memories for me." As he explained, "I may well have reached under those circumstances the same decision that [the Cruzans] had reached, but I had to make sure that the fact that I would have reached that would not have deprived Nancy Cruzan of what her wishes would have been."[96]

The Cruzans appealed to the U.S. Supreme Court, which in a plurality opinion upheld Missouri's evidentiary requirement against constitutional challenge.[97] Perhaps because he had to write a decision for a fractured court, or perhaps because a claim to a constitutional right to physician-assisted suicide was on the horizon, Justice Rehnquist's opinion was quite tentative on the issue of the content of a constitutional right to make decisions regarding life-sustaining treatment and whether nutrition and hydration could be treated differently from other medical treatments. The Supreme Court held that the Missouri requirement of clear and convincing evidence was constitutional. While the scope of the constitutional rights involved was ambiguous, for the Cruzans the decision was clear enough — they had lost.

Yet the Cruzan's lawyer, Bill Colby, regrouped from defeat and focused on eight words in the Court's plurality opinion in which Justice Rehnquist justified the high standard of proof of intent. The high standard, according to the opinion would protect against erroneous termination of treatment while preserving the possibility of subsequent medical developments or the "*discovery of new evidence regarding the patient's intent.*"[98] The case was placed before Judge Teel once again to test only whether there was clear and convincing evidence that Nancy would want the feeding tube removed. Two new witnesses had come forward to report on relevant conversations they had had with a co-worker they had known only as "Nancy Davis," and not as "Nancy Cruzan," when they worked with very seriously impaired children.[99] There has always been some speculation that there really was no new evidence; Colby describes one reporter telling him that the new evidence seemed incredible and that others felt the same.[100] Judge Teel himself, at a conference at Saint Louis University Law School, said that he resented the implication that he would assist in manufacturing evidence.

Attorney General Webster decided that the state would not participate in the one-day trial. According to Colby, Don Lamkins objected to Webster's decision, saying "[W]hen this went back to court, *nobody* represented us."[101] Finding clear and convincing evidence of Nancy's choice, Judge Teel ordered MRC to carry out the Cruzans' decision.

H. Intellectual Leadership

Protesters weren't the only ones with strong opinions about the ethics and morality of the issues that the courts were considering. Both cases were also significantly influenced by thought leaders in the Catholic Church and in medicine.

1. Catholic Views

The Catholic perspective had a direct influence on the result of the Quinlan litigation, through the counsel of a parish priest for the family, the support of the local bishop, and a then-twenty-year-old papal statement. Parish priest Tom Trapasso counseled Joe and Julia Quinlan that they were not required to continue ventilator support when there was no hope of recovery, and the hospital's chaplain agreed.[102] Bishop Lawrence Casey, head of the Paterson diocese in which the Quinlans resided, supported them publicly and consistently throughout the process, and the New Jersey Catholic Conference (the organization of the bishops of the state) filed an amicus brief to support the Quinlans' claim on moral grounds.[103] The *Quinlan* opinion describes the Catholic position at length, ostensibly solely to evaluate Joe Quinlan's character as guardian of his daughter.[104] Yet the court's extensive exposition, with direct quotation of nearly all of the New Jersey bishops' statement on the case, belied the denial of greater significance and provided a powerful showcase for the Catholic perspective.

In supporting the Quinlans, the New Jersey bishops relied upon a 1957 address by Pope Pius XII describing the new capacity for resuscitation and mechanical respirator support in terms very much like the Quinlan situation itself. The statement observed that when a doctor resuscitates a patient, "the family usually considers this improvement an astonishing result and is grateful to the doctor." Over time, however, the doctor may find that "the family considers that the efforts he has taken are improper and opposes them . . . when the patient's condition, after a slight improvement at first, remains stationary and it becomes clear that only automatic, artificial respiration is keeping him alive."[105] The papal statement relied on a distinction between ordinary and extraordinary means, with extraordinary means being those that impose a "grave burden for oneself or another," to conclude that there is no obligation to continue the use of the ventilator in this circumstance. The 1957 papal statement, however, did not address the issue of nutrition and hydration, and the application of the ordinary-extraordinary distinction to that treatment, though anticipated by some,[106] was not clear at the time the New Jersey bishops filed their brief.

By the late 1980s, *Cruzan* revealed significant disagreement within Catholic circles regarding the termination of nutrition and hydration for PVS patients. A number of Catholic health care organizations, led by SSM Health Care System in St. Louis, submitted an "important" amicus brief to the Missouri Supreme Court supporting the Cruzans.[107] This group, together with health care systems representing more than 100 Catholic hospitals, later submitted a second amicus brief to the U.S. Supreme Court, but this time formally in support of neither party.[108] At the same time, however, the U.S. Catholic Conference (USCC), the organization of all bishops in the United States, also filed an amicus brief with the U.S. Supreme Court, but in support of the state of Missouri.[109] A comparison of these briefs shows significant disagreement within the Catholic Church on whether withdrawal of such treatment is morally permissible.

The SSM brief noted that the amici did not represent "the official teaching authority" of the Church; indeed there had been no "authoritative statement" by the Catholic Church on the issue of the withdrawal of nutrition and hydration. This brief argued that "the dignity and sanctity of life" did not require the "assertion of an absolute value in the maintenance of biological life regardless of other human values"; that "both under-treatment, especially of the disabled or unprotected, and overtreatment of the dying" are to be avoided; and that persons in PVS are distinguishable from those who are merely impaired.[110]

In contrast, the USCC brief argued that "food and water are necessities of life" and that "negative judgments about the 'quality of life' of unconscious or otherwise disabled patients have led some in our society to propose withholding nourishment precisely in order to end these patients' lives."[111] Notably, at the same time the USCC filed its brief, a guide published by the Catholic Health Association for priests and nuns executing durable powers of attorney for themselves included a form that provided for the withdrawal of nutrition and hydration when the intervention would "only prolong my inevitable death or irreversible coma."[112]

The conflict within these "Catholic" briefs was also being played out in revisions to the bishops' Ethical and Religious Directives for Catholic Health Care Services (ERDs), undertaken during the course of the *Cruzan* litigation, beginning in 1987. The first draft of revisions to the ERDs' section on "Issues in Caring for the Dying Patient," produced in May 1991, included no explicit reference to nutrition and hydration, implying that it should be evaluated on the same terms as any other life-sustaining intervention. This draft addressed PVS specifically, however, by calling it "partial brain death" and recognizing that the condition was relevant in determining proper treatment. A later draft in February 1992 referred to persons in PVS as "dying patients" rather than as partially brain dead, and described "life-sustaining technology" as including "respirators, antibiotics, artificial feeding and hydration." This 1992 draft, according to one commentator, did not require that nutrition and hydration be provided "simply because it kept the person alive."[113]

While the revision process was underway, bishops in various dioceses in the U.S. were taking conflicting public positions on the permissibility of removing nutrition and hydration from PVS patients. This conflict among the bishops loomed over the ERD revision process. Rather than choose one position definitively over the other, as the USCC brief had done two years earlier, the ERDs instead directed that physicians and patients were to be guided by instructions from the local bishop.[114] Throughout 1993 and 1994, different committees within the bishops' national organization responsible for the ERDs continued to battle over the permissibility of withdrawing nutrition and hydration from PVS patients. In the end, however, this process did not resolve the question, and it remained open in the ERDs.[115]

In 2004, however, Pope John Paul II delivered a public address intended to support Terri Schiavo's Catholic parents in opposing discontinuation of nutrition and hydration for their daughter.[116] In 2007, the U.S. Conference of Catholic Bishops, the successor to the USCC, asked the Vatican's Congregation for the Doctrine of the Faith (CDF) to answer more formally questions concerning provision of nutrition and hydration to persons in the vegetative state. The 2007 CDF response repeated the message of the 2004 papal address that persons in PVS must receive "ordinary and proportionate care which includes, in principle, the administration of water and food even by artificial means."[117] Significant disagreement still persists on this point among Catholic theologians and ethicists, with some arguing that the 2004 and 2007 Vatican statements regarding nutrition and hydration, which by their own terms apply only to PVS patients, are to be construed quite narrowly and allow for a range of decisions even in such cases.[118]

2. Medicine

The Quinlan controversy occurred at a time of significant change in medical standards and practices regarding new resuscitative capacities and the use of ventilators. Karen Quinlan's neurologist had refused to remove the ventilator because he could not "break medical tradition."[119] Another physician-witness testified, "No physician . . . will ever interrupt a device which is performing a lifesaving measure. . . ."[120] The Quinlan court, however, recognized manifestations of change — the evidence of hidden practices; questionable line-drawing; conflict among thoughtful physicians as to the demands of medical ethics; a growing professional debate; and fears that legal standards would not reflect emerging medical practice, putting individual doctors at risk for criminal prosecution.[121]

The Quinlan opinion elicited strong negative reactions from some members of the medical community, especially as to the involvement of the courts in such cases.[122] Although some argue that Quinlan reaffirmed physician power,[123] it is just as likely to have accelerated change and determined the course of that change by legitimizing one perspective (i.e., that withdrawal of life-sustaining treatment is morally sound) and by its claim that such decisions are subject to the "common moral judgment of the community" rather than to medicine alone.[124] Yet by the time of Cruzan, the leadership in medicine had embraced the position adopted in Quinlan as to the permissibility of withdrawing life-sustaining treatment. Although some pockets of dissent persisted among physicians on the issue of nutrition and hydration for PVS patients, major medical organizations presented a united and vocal force in Cruzan — a voice that some believe was too restrained in Schiavo.[125]

I. Withdrawing Treatment

The courts had made their decisions in *Quinlan* and *Cruzan*, and their orders were clear. Yet the withdrawal of treatment in each case still met with resistance and conflict.

The struggle between the Quinlan family on the one side and Dr. Morse and St. Clare's Hospital on the other continued for a full six weeks after the state supreme court's decision. Even after attorney Paul Armstrong intervened, St. Clare's would not cooperate with the court's order as the facility disagreed with the bishop's statement concerning the morality of the decision.[126] Shortly thereafter, however, the doctors took the Quinlans aside and told them that they would begin the process of weaning Karen off the respirator, assuring the parents that it would be a "slow, but safe process."[127] As a result of this weaning process, Karen began to breathe entirely on her own on May 22, 1976.

Karen was transferred to the Morris View Nursing Home, the only one of the 22 facilities contacted by the Quinlans that would accept their daughter. Joe and Julia continued to visit each day. Julia has said that even then her husband "was not ready to face the reality of Karen's ordeal. [H]e still thought that God would perform a miracle and bring his daughter back."[128] More than nine years after being weaned off the ventilator, and more than two years after Nancy Cruzan went into PVS, Karen Quinlan died of pneumonia on June 11, 1985. Her mother said goodbye: "When I kissed my daughter for the last time, I thanked God for blessing me with this beautiful child and for the twenty-one happy years we shared, as well as the ten painful ones."[129] Although it has been reported that Karen had continued to be treated with antibiotics and "feeding,"[130] her mother writes that Karen received no antibiotics, at least for this final episode of pneumonia.[131] In an interview some time after Karen's death, Julia also reported that the family had never permitted "tube feeding" for Karen.[132]

The Cruzans did not experience the delay that the Quinlans had between the court's order permitting withdrawal of treatment and compliance with that order, although some at MRC had tried to persuade the Cruzans to wait several days until after Christmas. Within two hours of Judge Teel's final opinion in the case, however, Dr. James Davis simply went to Nancy's room himself and removed the tube from her stomach, placing a bandage over the wound.[133] Nancy was moved to the hospice section of MRC. The next day, Don Lamkins informed Dr. Davis that Governor John Ashcroft had called and asked to have the tube reinserted so that the Governor's office could have some time to consider alternatives. Soft-spoken Dr. Davis replied that "there was no medical reason" to reinsert the tube; he had a court order authorizing its removal; and he would not reinsert it.[134] Dr. Davis had testified in the first hearing before Judge Teel that he was not certain that it was appropriate to remove the feeding tube.[135] But "through a lot of reading, introspection and meditating, whatever you want to call it," Dr. Davis had come to the conclusion that sometimes "you cannot relieve suffering while you are prolonging life," and that the two goals of medicine are not "mutually compatible" in this type of case.[136]

The action left the MRC staff in turmoil. A head nurse told reporters that "we don't want her blood on our hands"; another said that she felt as if she had "been beaten with a club";[137] and some argued that it would be more humane to allow Nancy to die quickly by using a lethal medication.[138] Don Lamkins suffered a crisis of conscience:

> The hardest part has been deciding how much blame I have, how much moral responsibility I have for being in charge of the whole thing. What part am I playing in her death? Am I causing it? Should I have stopped it? . . . I could have gotten myself out, but somebody else would have come in and done it. [H]ow far should I have gone?[139]

Colby observed, however, that Lamkins remained polite, proper, and professional throughout the ordeal, although "the strain showed on his face."[140]

Protests intensified outside MRC with many different groups participating, including Operation Rescue. In addition, several individuals and groups filed petitions for emergency writs with state and federal courts. The courts dismissed each of these petitions, with one judge issuing a ruling stating that further filings would be considered an abuse of process.[141]

Nancy died on the day after Christmas in 1990. Nancy's dying process was no different than the family had expected from talking with other families who had experienced similar situations. Patricia Brophy had described how her husband had passed away peacefully, with no sign of suffering whatsoever.[142] And so it was with Nancy.[143] Her father Joe wrote his goodbye while his daughter was dying. It said in part, "Though brilliant, her life was terribly short lived, but she has left a flaming trail, a legacy . . . and I'm damned proud of her. . . . Now we walk with her to the door of death so that she may at last pass through and be free. So fly away, little sister, and have fun."[144]

J. The Aftermath

Their lives were never the same. The Quinlans and the Cruzans could not return to life as they had known it before the battles over their daughters' lives.

Julia Quinlan feared for the survival of her marriage and the health of her other children, Mary Ellen and John, after the litigation was over.[145] Eventually, she was able to find a greater peace. She and Joe used the proceeds from their book to establish the Karen Ann Quinlan Hospice, which opened in 1980, at a time when the hospice movement was just beginning to develop in the United States. Joe Quinlan died of cancer in 1996, at home and with the care and support of the hospice that bears his daughter's name. Julia is proud of what her family accomplished and of what she views as Karen's legacy. She says that she has no regrets: "We would do the same thing all over again. . . . I thank God that we were able to make the decision as a family and still be a close loving family after it all."[146] The Karen Ann Quinlan Hospice celebrated its Silver Anniversary in 2005, serving 700–800 patients each year.[147]

For Joe Cruzan, however, life became unbearable, and he committed suicide on August 17, 1996. Joe left a note, saying that he loved his wife, daughters, and granddaughters and that "I love Nancy and am sorry about what happened." What did he mean — that it took so long and cost his family so much to do what they believed was right for their daughter? Or that they had done the wrong thing?[148] Joe Cruzan's frustration and pain during the years of litigation were palpable. Photographs before the fight show a man with a broad smile and twinkling eyes. That man had disappeared, a fact documented by later photos showing him as drawn and taut. He had said:

> It's made a very pessimistic, angry person out of me. . . . I feel like I'm in a sack and I want to get out of it, but I don't know where to hit. . . . I don't know what to do. . . . I've wondered, is my obsession for me now, that I'm not going to take no for an answer, or is it for Nancy? And in reality, I know that it's not for Nancy. It's for everyone that's in this condition. And to have the state come in and say "No you can't do this."[149]

In the year after Nancy's death, Joe worked tirelessly with a number of groups, including state bar associations, medical associations, and the lobbying arm of the Catholic dioceses of Missouri to persuade the Missouri legislature to enact legislation to recognize a durable power of attorney for health care, including instructions concerning the withdrawal of nutrition and hydration.[150] Late the night before the vote, however, Joe called me and said, "I just don't think this is enough." He wanted to go to Jefferson City in the morning and tell them not to enact the legislation, convinced that no one would sign these documents and that the legislature would lose interest thereafter. He was passionate and didn't want to settle for less than what was necessary. He finally acquiesced to arguments that the legislation's statement concerning nutrition and hydration offset the more restrictive language of the state's earlier living will statute, on which the Missouri Supreme Court had relied in finding a public policy against withdrawal in his own daughter's case. The Missouri legislature passed the legislation, but it has yet to return to the matter to adopt a broader family consent statute, as many other states have done.

Joyce Cruzan died of cancer two years after Joe's death, having refused chemotherapy or other aggressive treatment and dying at home with the support of hospice. Before she died, she said that she had lived "an ordinary life" and that her family was actually unremarkable.[151]

K. Conclusion

Quinlan, Cruzan, and their progeny established a highly individualized inquiry for end-of-life decisionmaking — what would this particular person (rather than the ordinary, typical, or "reasonable" person) want; what is her medical condition, and does it fit the categories that have been identified in the state's statutes or cases or in her advance directive; is her family acting in good faith; and do all family members tell the same story of what she would want? That approach opens the door to honest, loving disagreements and, of course, to rancorous disputes, which fortunately are uncommon. Unlike Terri Schiavo's circumstances, most families and physicians come to some agreement about the course of life-sustaining treatment.

Claims of public consensus on the issue of the withdrawal of nutrition and hydration from someone in PVS prior to the Schiavo controversy are overstated. The stories of Karen Quinlan and Nancy Cruzan illustrate the persistent presence of sharp dissent, from different quarters at different times, but there nonetheless. They also illustrate that public strategies meant to challenge the patient's diagnosis and prognosis, the patient's own desires, and the character of family members did not arise for the first time in the Schiavo conflict.

Principles aside, however, the Quinlan and Cruzan stories teach us most poignantly about the awesome suffering of families caught in legal conflict over these most painful of decisions. The stories confirm the intimacy of such decisions as well as the burdens these families bear — burdens that have their own moral significance. They reaffirm the intuition that families should decide such matters, just as much as Terri Schiavo's story reminds us that this will not always be possible.

ENDNOTES

1. William H. Colby, *From Quinlan to Cruzan to Schiavo: What Have We Learned?*, 37 Loy. U. Chi. L.J. 279, 287 (2006) (referring specifically to the Cruzan family).

2. 355 A.2d 647 (N.J. 1976).

3. 497 U.S. 261 (1990).

4. Joseph & Julia Quinlan, Karen Ann — the Quinlans Tell Their Story 36–38 (1977).

5. Julia Duane Quinlan, My Joy, My Sorrow — Karen Ann's Mother Remembers 23–24 (2005).

6. Joseph & Julia Quinlan, *supra* note 4, at 11.

7. Karen Ann Quinlan Memorial Foundation, History, www.karenannquinlanhospice.org/History.htm [hereinafter History] (quoting Julia Quinlan) (last visited Mar. 7, 2008).

8. Julia Quinlan, *supra* note 5, at 29.

9. Julia gave birth to a daughter (Mary Ellen) and a son (John) after adopting Karen. *Id.* at 27–28. As the couple explained, "There is one thing that I am absolutely sure of — you cannot force religion on your children . . . But we did expect each of the youngsters to be thoughtful, humane human beings, and they are. Karen was the most religious of the three." Joseph & Julia Quinlan, *supra* note 4, at 54.

10. History, *supra* note 7; Phyllis Battelle, *"Let Me Sleep" The Story of Karen Ann Quinlan*, Ladies Home J., Sept. 1976, at 69.

11. Colby, *supra* note 1, at 285.

12. *Frontline, The Death of Nancy Cruzan* (PBS television broadcast Mar. 24, 1992) (transcript available at http://www.pbs.org/wgbh/pages/frontline/programs/transcripts/1014.html).

13. *Id.*

14. William H. Colby, The Long Goodbye: The Deaths of Nancy Cruzan 3–6, 79 (2002).

15. *Id.* at 7, 11, 264–67.

16. *Frontline, supra* note 12, at 10.

17. Joseph & Julia Quinlan, *supra* note 4, at 12–13. One individual who had been with Karen that night reported that she had used drugs, a report that Dr. Robert Morse, Karen's neurologist, completely discounted. *Id.* at 14, 77, 169. Other news reports based on interviews with friends describe Karen as having experimented with marijuana and "uppers" and "downers." *A Life in the Balance*, Time Mag., Nov. 3, 1975, *available at* http://www.time.com/printout/0,8816,913631,00.html. Morse testified in court that laboratory tests showed only aspirin, very small and "normal therapeutic" amounts of barbiturate, and "traces" of Valium but no "hard drugs." In the Matter of Karen Ann Quinlan: The Complete Briefs, Oral Arguments, and Opinion in the New Jersey Supreme Court, vol. I, at 236 (1975) [hereinafter Complete Vol. I] (testimony of Dr. Robert Morse).

18. Joseph & Julia Quinlan, *supra* note 4, at 79.

19. Battelle, *supra* note 10 at 70–71.

20. *Id.; see also* Complete Vol. I, *supra* note 17, at 239 (testimony of Dr. Robert Morse).

21. *The Other Side of "Persistent Vegetative State"* (NPR radio broadcast Oct. 24, 2003) (interview with Christy Cruzan White), *available at* http://www.npr.org/templates/story/story.php?storyId=1477805.

22. Her 1963 Rambler, a gift from her father who thought it was safer than the van she had been driving, did not have seat belts. Karen J. Donnelly, Cruzan v. Missouri: The Right to Die 8 (2003).

23. *Id.* at 9.

24. Colby, *supra* note 14, at 8–9. Estimates on the time until resuscitation range from 14 to 22 minutes. Donnelly, *supra* note 22, at 9.

25. Colby, *supra* note 14, at 12.

26. *Frontline, supra* note 12, at 2.

27. Colby, *supra* note 14, at 22.

28. *Id.*

29. *The Other Side of "Persistent Vegetative State", supra* note 21.

30. Colby, *supra* note 14, at 24, 27, 28.

31. Brian Jennett & Fred Plum, *Persistent Vegetative State After Brain Damage. A Syndrome in Search of a Name*, 1 Lancet 734 (1972).

32. Complete Vol. I, *supra* note 17, at 486 (testimony of Dr. Fred Plum); Classics in the Courtroom: Cruzan v. Director Missouri Department of Health 112 (1992) [hereinafter Classics] (testimony of Dr. James Dexter).

33. Complete Vol. I, *supra* note 17, at 486 (testimony of Dr. Fred Plum).

34. *Report of the Ad Hoc Committee of the Harvard Medical School to Examine the Definition of Brain Death, A Definition of Irreversible Coma*, 205 JAMA 337 (1968); Robert J. Joynt, *A New Look at Death*, 252 JAMA 680, 682 (1984) (noting that the use of the term "irreversible coma" for brain death was "unfortunate").

35. The pretrial order in *Quinlan* specified that one of the questions to be addressed was "what is or should be the legal definition of death" and "assuming the proof shows Karen Quinlan is legally dead, is the only relief cessation of the extraordinary devices." Complete Vol. I, *supra* note 17, at 28–29 (pretrial order).

36. Battelle, *supra* note 10, at 71.

37. Julia Quinlan, *supra* note 5, at 46–47.

38. Colby, *supra* note 14, at 85.

39. Dr. Plum in his testimony refers to his colleague's use of this phrase to account for the fact that the "emotional impact of someone in a vegetative state opening the eyes is so overwhelmingly strong." Complete Vol. I, *supra* note 17, at 488 (testimony of Dr. Fred Plum).

40. Julia Quinlan, *supra* note 5, at 66, 40.

41. Joseph & Julia Quinlan, *supra* note 4, at 251.

42. Classics, *supra* note 32, at 120, 102, 104, 108 (testimony of Dr. James Dexter).

43. *Id.* at 56, 87–90 (testimony of Dr. Ronald Cranford).

44. Colby, *supra* note 14, at 281–82.

45. Julia Quinlan, *supra* note 5, at 41–43.

46. *Id.* at 43.

47. Battelle, *supra* note 10, at 70.

48. Joseph & Julia Quinlan, *supra* note 4, at 100–103.

49. Battelle, *supra* note 10, at 71.

50. Complete Vol. I, *supra* note 17, at 413 (testimony of Fr. Pascal Caccavale).

51. Joseph & Julia Quinlan, *supra* note 4, at 72.

52. In the Matter of Karen Quinlan: The Complete Briefs, Oral Arguments, and Opinion in the New Jersey Supreme Court, vol. II, at 40 (1976) [hereinafter Complete Vol. II] (plaintiffs' exhibit P-6).

53. Colby, *supra* note 14, at 40.

54. *Id.* at 41.

55. Brophy v. New Eng. Sinai Hosp., 497 N.E.2d 626 (Mass. 1986).

56. In the Matter of Jobes, 529 A.2d 434 (N.J. 1987).

57. Colby, *supra* note 14, at 46.

58. Melvin D. Levin, *Disconnection: A Clinician's View*, 6 Hastings Center Rep. 11 (1976); Matt Clark, *A Right to Die?*, Newsweek, Nov. 3, 1975, at 58; Battelle, *supra* note 10, at 72; M.L. Tina Stevens, *The Quinlan Case Revisited: A History of the Cultural Politics of Medicine and the Law*, 21 J. Health Pol. Pol'y & L. 347 (1996).

59. Battelle, *supra* note 10, at 72; Joseph & Julia Quinlan, *supra* note 4, at 118–19.

60. Stevens, *supra* note 58, at 358; Battelle, *supra* note 10, at 72, 76.

61. Battelle, *supra* note 10, at 76.

62. Joseph & Julia Quinlan, *supra* note 4, at 126.

63. Colby, *supra* note 14, at 21.

64. *Id.* at 29.

65. *Id.* at 61.

66. *Id.* at 40.

67. Missouri Rehabilitation Center, A Century of Progress, Phase II, *available at* http://www.muhealth.org/MOrehab/history2.shtml (last visited April 6, 2008).

68. Frontline, *supra* note 12, at 4.

69. University of Missouri, Missouri Rehabilitation Center, http://www.muhealth.org/MOrehab; Missouri Rehabilitation Center, A Century of Progress, Phase III, *available at* http//www.muhealth.org/MOrehab/history3.shtml (last visited Mar. 9, 2008).

70. Colby, *supra* note 14, at 46.

71. *Id.* at 48.

72. *Id.* at 49.

73. *Frontline, supra* note 12, at 6.

74. Colby, *supra* note 14, at 48.

75. Bill Colby is now Senior Fellow — Law and Patients' Rights at the Center for Practical Bioethics in Kansas City. Paul Armstrong litigated several subsequent end-of-life cases and became a trial judge in New Jersey.

76. Colby, *supra* note 14, at 67.

77. *Id.* at 64, 68–69.

78. Julia Quinlan, *supra* note 5, at 45–46. Others report that the headline said "Father Seeks the Legal Right to Let His Gravely Ill Daughter Die." *See, e.g.,* Battelle, *supra* note 10, at 76.

79. Joseph & Julia Quinlan, *supra* note 4, at 146.

80. Julia Quinlan, *supra* note 5, at 75, 90–91, xv.

81. Joseph & Julia Quinlan, *supra* note 4, at 277.

82. *Id.* at 317–26.

83. Julia Quinlan, *supra* note 5, at 88.

84. *Frontline, supra* note 12. This comment can be heard on the film itself, but is not included in the written transcript.

85. *Id.* at 10, 14.

86. Colby, *supra* note 14, at 75–76.

87. Joseph & Julia Quinlan, *supra* note 5, at 172.

88. Battelle, *supra* note 10, at 174.

89. *Frontline, supra* note 12, at 12–13.

90. 348 A.2d 801 (N.J. Ch. Ct. 1975).

91. Julia Quinlan, *supra* note 5, at 63–64.

92. *Quinlan,* 355 A.2d 647 (N.J. 1976).

93. Colby, *supra* note 14, at 236.

94. *Id.* at 236–42.

95. Cruzan v. Harmon, 760 S.W.2d 408, 426 (Mo. 1988).

96. *Echoes of Earlier Right to Die Battle in Schiavo Case* (NPR radio broadcast Mar. 28, 2005) (interview with Chip Robertson), *available at* http://www.npr.org/templates/story/story.php?storyId=4563884. Robertson left the bench in 1998 to return to law practice.

97. *Cruzan,* 497 U.S. 261 (1990).

98. Colby, *supra* note 14, at 322; *Cruzan,* 497 U.S. at 283 (emphasis added).

99. Colby, *supra* note 14 at 334–36.

100. *Id.* at 333.

101. *Id.* at 341.

102. *See* discussion *supra* notes 49 and 50.

103. Rev. Fr. Frank J. Rodimer, Bishop Emeritus of Paterson, *Foreword* to Julia Quinlan, My Joy, My Sorrow — Karen Ann's Mother Remembers, at xi (2005); Complete Vol. II, *supra* note 52, at 197 (Brief for the New Jersey Catholic Conference).

104. 355 A.2d 647, 657 (N.J. 1976).

105. Pope Pius XII, Address to an International Congress of Anesthesiologists (Nov. 24, 1957). *See also* Complete Vol. I, *supra* note 17, at 263 (testimony of Dr. Robert Morse, commenting on the Quinlans' change in position).

106. *See, e.g.,* Gerald Kelly, S.J., *The Duty to Protect Life,* Theological Studies, Jan. 1950, at 218 (asserting the permissibility of withdrawal).

107. Colby, *supra* note 14, at 240; Cruzan v. Harmon, 760 S.W.2d 408 (Mo. 1988) (listing amicus briefs).

108. Brief for SSM Health Care System et al. as Amici Curiae, Cruzan v. Dir., Missouri Dep't of Health, 497 U.S. 261 (1990) (No. 88-1503), 1989 WL 1115245. Many other religious organizations filed briefs in *Cruzan.* For example, Agudath Israel and Christian Advocates Serving Evangelism filed briefs supporting the State of Missouri, and the General Board of Church and Society of the United Methodist Church and the Lutheran Church in America filed briefs supporting the Cruzans.

109. Brief of the United States Catholic Conference as Amicus Curiae in Support of Respondents, *Cruzan,* 497 U.S. 261 (No. 88-1503), 1989 WL 1128124.

110. Brief for SSM Health Care System et al. as Amici Curiae, *supra* note 108, at 6, 8.

111. Brief of the United States Catholic Conference as Amicus Curiae, *supra* note 109, at 2.

112. Bro. Peter Campbell, CFX, Choices for the Journey 30 (1989).

113. Rev. Thomas R. Kopfensteiner, *Developing Directive 58,* 81 Health Progress 3 (May-June 2000), *available at* http://www.chausa.org/Pub/MainNav/HP/Archive/2000/05MayJun/Articles/Features.

114. *Id.*

115. Ethical and Religious Directives for Catholic Health Care, USCCB, 2001, *available at* http://www.usccb.org/bishops/directives.shtml#partfive (noting that the question requires "further reflection"). The ERDs also note that there should be a presumption in favor of the provision of nutrition and hydration as long as there is sufficient benefit to outweigh burdens to the patient.

116. Pope John Paul II, Address to the Participants in the International Congress on "Life-Sustaining Treatments and Vegetative State: Scientific Advances and Ethical Dilemmas" (Mar. 20, 2004).

117. Congregation for the Doctrine of the Faith, Responses to Certain Questions of the United States Conference of Catholic Bishops Concerning Artificial Nutrition and Hydration (Sept. 14, 2007).

118. *See, e.g.,* Daniel P. Sulmasy, *Preserving Life? The Vatican and PVS,* 134 Commonweal, Dec. 7, 2007, *available at* http://www.commonwealmagazine.org/article.php3?id_article=2083; *see also* Ellen Horan, *Vatican Affirms Care Requirements for Patients in Persistent Vegetative States,* Catholic Health World, Oct. 1, 2007 (describing reactions of Catholic health care leadership), *available at* http://www.chausa.org/Pub/MainNav/News/CHW/Archive/2007/1001/Articles/w071001c.htm.

119. Complete Vol. I, *supra* note 17, at 245, 264 (testimony of Dr. Robert Morse).

120. *Id.* at 495 (testimony of Dr. Sidney Diamond, referenced in *Quinlan,* 355 A.2d 647, 657 (N.J. 1976)).

121. *Quinlan,* 355 A.2d at 657 (referring to "unwritten and unspoken standard of medical practice") and (describing "judicious neglect"), 666–68 (describing the literature).

122. Joseph & Julia Quinlan, *supra* note 4, at 280 (noting negative responses from the American Medical Association (AMA)).

123. *See generally* Stevens, *supra* note 58.

124. *Quinlan,* 355 A.2d at 665.

125. Arthur Caplan, *What Can We Learn from the Schiavo Case?,* Mar. 31, 2005, *available at* http://www.msnbc.msn.com/id/7289351/ (accusing organized medicine of "inexcusable silence") (last visited April 6, 2008).

126. Joseph & Julia Quinlan, *supra* note 4, at 291.

127. *Id.*

128. Julia Quinlan, *supra* note 5, at 61.

129. *Id.* at 106.

130. *See, e.g.,* Battelle, *supra* note 10, at 180.

131. Julia Quinlan, *supra* note 5, at 104.

132. "[Y]ou also don't want to continue with aggressive care — the feeding tube and so on. We refused to have a feeding tube in Karen. But she still lived for 10 years. . . ." End-of-Life Decisions, *available at* http://fathom.lib.uchicago.edu/2/10701024/ (comments by Julia Quinlan) (last visited Mar. 9, 2008).

133. *Anger in Hospital at a Death Order,* N.Y. Times, Dec. 16, 1990.

134. Colby, *supra* note 14, at 364.

135. *Id.* at 350–51.

136. *Frontline, supra* note 12, at 14.

137. Colby, *supra* note 14, at 362–63.

138. *Frontline, supra* note 12, at 16.

139. *Id.* at 16.

140. Colby, *supra* note 14, at 361.

141. Colby, *supra* note 1, at 286 n.22; Colby, *supra* note 14, at 380.

142. Paul W. Armstrong & B.D. Cohen, *From Quinlan to Jobes: The Courts and the PVS Patient,* 18 Hastings Center Rep. 37, 37 (1988) (describing Patricia Brophy's experience).

143. *Frontline, supra* note 12, at 12, 16–17.

144. *Id.*

145. Julia Quinlan, *supra* note 5, at 60.

146. History, *supra* note 7.

147. Elizabeth Hendler, *Julia Quinlan Says Growth of Hospice "Beyond my Vision,"* Daily Record, Mar. 24, 2005.

148. Colby, *supra* note 14, at 393–94.

149. Frontline, *supra* note 12, at 10.

150. Mo. Rev. Stat. §404.800 (2007).

151. Colby, *supra* note 14, at 394.

Part III

REPRODUCTIVE RIGHTS

Chapter 4

JOHNSON
v.
CALVERT

Technology, Family, and Commerce

LISA C. IKEMOTO*

A. Introduction

The dispute between Anna Johnson and Mark and Crispina Calvert presented the first opportunity for a court to determine the parental rights of parties to a gestational surrogacy agreement. Previous surrogacy disputes had arisen from traditional surrogacy agreements, in which the woman who carries the pregnancy also provides the eggs. She is, therefore, the only woman who has a biological relationship with the child born of the agreement. In traditional surrogacy cases, the issue of whether or not the contract is enforceable determines maternity. If the contract is not enforceable, as the New Jersey Supreme Court decided in *Baby M.*,[1] the woman who gave birth to the child is the legal mother. If the contract is enforceable, the intended mother, who has no biological relationship with the child, is the legal mother.

The Calverts had agreed to pay Anna Johnson $10,000 for undergoing an embryo transfer with embryos created by in vitro fertilization (IVF) with Crispina Calvert's eggs and Mark Calvert's sperm. Seven months into the resulting pregnancy, tensions among the parties led both sides to file claims for parental rights. Over a three-year period, the consolidated case wound its way up to the California Supreme Court.[2] The Court had to decide who was the legal mother, given that both women had a biological relationship with the child. Paternity was undisputed and, in fact, never discussed. In 1993, the Court issued an opinion that first applied the Uniform Parentage Act (UPA) — a piece of model legislation designed to resolve questions of parentage over which states had sometimes

* Professor of Law, UC Davis School of Law. I greatly appreciate the skilled and thoughtful research assistance provided by Karen Lai and Derek Sinclair, both of King Hall Class of 2008, and Asha Jennings, Class of 2009.

Anna Johnson. Photograph taken by Ken Hiveley. Copyright, 1990, Los Angeles Times. Reprinted with permission.

taken conflicting approaches, to determine that both Crispina Calvert and Anna Johnson were natural mothers under the law. The Court's discussion began with an account of the purpose of the UPA — to eliminate the distinction between legitimate and illegitimate children by setting out the bases for establishing parentage, especially paternity, regardless of marriage.[3] This led to the Court's acknowledgment that the UPA was not intended to address parentage determinations arising from surrogacy agreements. Despite that, the Court asserted, the UPA was the appropriate starting point for determining maternity,[4] but added the caveat, "[y]et for any child California law recognizes only one natural mother, despite advances in reproductive technology rendering a different outcome biologically possible."[5] The Court then used the parties' initial intent to raise the child as the tiebreaker. Under that rule the tie went to Crispina, who intended to parent the child. Thus, Anna Johnson was found to have no legal relationship with the child to whom she had given birth.

The use of assisted reproductive technologies (ARTs) permits the slicing and dicing of family relationships in ways that challenge longstanding norms. The results are often unsettling. In *Johnson v. Calvert*, differences in racial identity among the parties highlighted the unsettling aspects of bifurcating biological parenthood. While the Court's opinion scrupulously avoided mentioning race, the media regularly noted that Anna Johnson was African American, Crispina Calvert was Filipina, and Mark Calvert was white.

In terms of social implications, *Johnson* presented the Court with the question of whether it would decide the legal issue in a way that reinforced longstanding norms, or whether it would upend them. To some, the Court's decision accomplished the former: it protected the marital family, and it forestalled the disturbing possibility that a white child could have a black mother. On the other hand, the use of initial intent, a rule derived from intellectual property law, seemed to reintroduce an old, rejected concept — that children are property. In addition, the determination that Anna Johnson was not the child's mother seemed inconsistent with the common law rule that deems the birth mother

Mark and Crispina Calvert. Photograph taken by Jose Barrera. Copyright, 1990, Los Angeles Times. Reprinted with permission.

the child's legal mother. To some, the determination devalued the experience of pregnancy and childbirth, particularly that of black women, and treated the woman who bore the child as a mere vessel to be used by others.

Surrogacy arrangements are made within a larger context — they are a product of the fertility industry. The fertility industry provides a combination of access to ARTs, biological resources, legal services, and the possibility of family formation. Explanatory narratives accompanying ART use have shaped how we understand and feel about ARTs. In addition, the medical practices of ART use have become intertwined with commercial practices. Thus, the medical facts, explanatory narratives, and commercial practices are interwoven into the personal aspects of *Johnson* in a way that may have shaped the role of law in this case.

B. The Setting

When the Calverts met Anna Johnson, they were unable to have children on their own. At that time, the medical profession defined "infertility" as failure to conceive after one year of unprotected intercourse. Because Crispina Calvert had undergone a hysterectomy, she was unable to carry a pregnancy. The Calverts were, therefore, "infertile." While infertility was understood to be a medical condition, the use of ART as treatment formed the basis of a highly profitable industry.

1. The Fertility Industry

There is no chicken or egg question in the fertility industry: sperm came first. That is, the sale of sperm for assisted insemination was the first sector of the fertility industry to form. The first for-profit sperm bank opened in 1970.[6] In 1973, the National Conference of Commissioners on Uniform State Laws promulgated the UPA, which included a rule that acknowledged and enabled the use of assisted insemination by sperm obtained from a third party.[7] The rule had two important effects. First, it declared that a third party who provided sperm was not the legal father. This protected men who sold sperm to commercial banks, and thus facilitated the commercial trade in sperm. Second, the rule stated, "[i]f, under the supervision of a licensed physician and with the consent of her husband, a wife is inseminated artificially with semen donated by a man not her husband, the husband is treated in law as if he were the natural father of a child thereby conceived."[8] Conferring legal status on the husband also enhanced the marketability of assisted insemination services.

In the next step of the fertility industry's formation, the market for fertility drugs expanded.[9] Fertility drugs are taken by women. In fact, most of the ARTs are administered to women, even when low sperm count or other male factors are the most probable reason for failure to conceive. The most well-known fertility drugs are follicle stimulating hormones, which prompt the woman's ovaries to produce ova, usually two or more per cycle. By doing so, the drugs increase the chance that the woman who takes them will become pregnant. For the pharmaceutical companies that sell them, fertility drugs have become a substantial product line.

In 1978, two English fertility specialists announced the birth of Louise Brown, the first child conceived through IVF. The medical aspects of the typical IVF process start when a woman takes a series of three hormones, usually by injection, over a period of about two weeks. The drugs, respectively, shut down the woman's ovaries; stimulate the development of several ovarian follicles and, therefore, of several ova; and trigger maturation and release of the ova. At that point, a doctor retrieves the ova from the woman's fallopian tubes, typically by inserting a glass syringe through her cervix to reach the fallopian tubes. Obviously, the procedure is invasive. In the meantime, the intended father or a third party has provided sperm. Ova and sperm, also called gametes, are mixed together in a laboratory. If all goes well, one or more fertilized eggs result. The first stages of meiosis, or cell division, take place in the lab. Then two to three days after the eggs are retrieved, pre-embryos are transferred to a woman's uterus. The woman becomes pregnant if one or more of the pre-embryos implants in her uterus and cell division continues.[10]

While neither the commercialization of sperm nor the stepped-up marketing of fertility drugs prompted much public attention, the birth of Louise Brown provoked great controversy.[11] International headlines reflected the public's mixed reactions, which ranged from the belief that science had produced a miracle to the fear that science had gone too far and that IVF might cause harm to the child. The media dubbed Louise Brown the first "test-tube baby," a phrase that persisted for years. Despite the persistence of the phrase, the medical profession's characterization of the technology as "infertility treatment" quickly became the dominant narrative. Thus, IVF use came to be understood as medically and socially necessary for infertile couples.[12]

This narrative had two consequences. First, the needs of infertile couples made concerns about IVF use seem less important. As a result, little effort was made to track the medical risks of IVF to women and children.[13] Second, IVF became a big part of the fertility business, even though it initially offered low odds of success. By the early 1990s, when Mark and Crispina Calvert were looking for a surrogate, the fertility business was full-fledged and booming.

2. Surrogacy

Commercial surrogacy followed closely on the heels of commercial sperm banks. Enterprising individuals set themselves up as surrogacy brokers, starting in the mid-1970s.[14] Initially, the market was aimed at infertile married couples. Surrogacy brokers arranged contracts between the couple who wanted a child and a woman who would bear a child for them. During the first few years, surrogacy contracts provided for impregnation by assisted insemination. As a result, the woman who carried the pregnancy and gave birth to the child provided the egg. Sperm was obtained from the male party to the contract or purchased from a third-party donor through a commercial sperm bank. These arrangements are now called "traditional surrogacy."

In a "traditional surrogacy" contract, the surrogate promised to relinquish her parental rights after the child's birth, and the other woman who was party to the contract agreed to adopt the child. These two promises were legally suspect. Every state has an adoption law, and while the specifics of the law vary from state to state, every state prohibits "baby selling,"[15] or paying parents to relinquish their parental rights. Yet in commercial surrogacy arrangements, the parties who contract to become parents to the child pay fees to both the broker and the surrogate. Paying the surrogate raises the issue of whether these arrangements violate the ban on baby selling. Some state legislatures have addressed this issue by banning surrogacy contracts, by banning commercial surrogacy contracts, by declaring surrogacy contracts to be void and unenforceable, or by expressly allowing and regulating surrogacy.[16]

Paternity is more easily established for the male party, especially if he provides the sperm for insemination. Every state has adopted the UPA, which states that paternity may be established by blood tests showing a genetic relationship between man and child.[17] Therefore, if the male party to the contract provided the sperm for assisted insemination, he would be deemed the legal father. Adoption is unnecessary for the man in those circumstances.

Like the birth of Louise Brown, commercial surrogacy provoked controversy from the start. That controversy rose to the level of national debate in the *Baby M.* case.[18] The case arose from a traditional surrogacy arrangement made by Richard and Elizabeth Stern, the couple seeking a child, and Mary Beth Whitehead, the surrogate mother. The contract was executed by Richard Stern, Mary Beth Whitehead, and her husband, Richard Whitehead. Elizabeth Stern was not party to the contract, presumably so that the arrangement would avoid the baby selling prohibition. By its terms, Richard Stern agreed to pay Mary Beth Whitehead $10,000 and she agreed to undergo insemination with his sperm, carry the pregnancy, and give birth to the child. She also promised to give up her parental rights so that Elizabeth Stern could adopt the child. Richard Whitehead agreed to do whatever was necessary to rebut the presumption of paternity.

Mary Beth Whitehead changed her mind about relinquishing her parental rights, and Richard Stern sued to enforce the contract and for custody. The case worked its way up the New Jersey court system. In 1988, the New Jersey Supreme Court held that the contract was void as a matter of public policy because it violated the state ban on baby selling. The Court accepted that Richard Stern was the legal father by virtue of his genetic relationship with the child. It recognized maternity in Mary Beth Whitehead because under traditional family law, a woman who gives birth to a child is the child's legal mother. The Court granted custody to Richard Stern and remanded the case for determination of visitation rights. On remand, the lower court granted visitation rights to Mary Beth Whitehead.

The case received national media attention. The public debate over the case did not address the particular technology — assisted insemination — but focused on the commercial aspects, including the use of contract and the offer of money. Ultimately, however, the parentage issues drew the most attention. To a large extent, the media coverage blamed Mary Beth Whitehead for her change of heart. She was castigated for reneging on the contract, the commercial aspect of the arrangement. At the same time, the Sterns were portrayed in sympathetic terms as the infertile couple who desperately wanted a child of their own. Their yearning for a child, not Mary Beth Whitehead's decision to keep her child, was characterized in private, non-commercial terms. Much of the media coverage expressed class bias. The Sterns were married professionals; Mary Beth Whitehead was working class. She was portrayed as crass and grasping, and the Sterns as caught in a nightmare that she had created. As a result, when the New Jersey Supreme Court found that the contract was void, it contradicted the public's judgment; the outcome of the custody and visitation decisions, however, seemed ultimately to vindicate the public's judgment.[19]

The combination of IVF and surrogacy contracts yielded a new type of arrangement called gestational surrogacy. When IVF is used, the egg can be supplied by the woman who contracts to raise the child or by a third-party donor. The surrogate undergoes IVF, and if a pregnancy results, carries the pregnancy and gives birth to the child. The surrogate has a biological relationship formed by pregnancy and birth, but the child does not share her genes. Instead, the ova come from the intended mother or a third party. Gestational surrogacy seems to allocate more control to the intended parents, who can choose both sperm and ova. In addition, the elimination of a genetic tie between the birth mother and child arguably lowers the risk of a *Baby M.* scenario. A woman who gave birth to a child with whom she had no genetic relationship would be less likely to claim the child as her own, or so the argument goes. Gestational surrogacy, then, enhanced the appeal of surrogacy and expanded the market for IVF.

3. ART Use and the Law

ART use is subject to surprisingly little legal regulation. State laws typically require some testing of sperm for transmissible diseases. A few Food and Drug Administration regulations address laboratory practices and handling of embryos.[20] As mentioned, every state has adopted some version of the UPA that can be used to establish paternity by presumption or genetic testing. Generally, however, the statutes and cases that do exist are scattered across the states and vary in approach. For example, in the wake of the *Baby M.* case, many legislatures considered bills to regulate surrogacy, but surprisingly few enacted them.

In California, several bills had been proposed and ultimately defeated in the years preceding the *Johnson* case. For example, in 1982, Assembly member Mike Roos proposed one of the nation's first surrogacy bills. The "Surrogate Parenting Act" would have made surrogacy contracts legal and enforceable.[21] The bill never made it out of committee in either the assembly or senate. In 1985, the state assembly approved a bill that would have legalized commercial surrogacy,[22] but the state senate defeated the bill. Shortly after the New Jersey Supreme Court decided *Baby M.*, the California legislature created a Joint Legislative Committee on Surrogate Parenting. The Committee set up an advisory panel to review legal, ethical, social, and practical issues that arise from commercial and noncommercial surrogacy. In July 1990, the Advisory Panel issued a majority and a minority report. The majority report recommended prohibiting commercial surrogacy and allowing non-commercial surrogacy to proceed without making the contracts enforceable. The minority report stated that "legislation relating to surrogate parenting would be useful as a matter of public policy."[23] The minority report also recommended legislation that declared surrogate parenting agreements void and supported using the "best interests" standard to determine parentage.[24] The Joint Legislative Committee did not adopt either report. In August 1992, the California legislature did pass Senate Bill 937, which would have established the Alternative Reproduction Act. That Act would have authorized and

regulated commercial surrogacy. However, Governor Wilson vetoed the legislation. In his accompanying public statement, Governor Wilson said, "No state
has adopted regulations on this matter. Comprehensive regulation of this difficult
moral issue is premature in California as well."[25]

The lack of regulation means that courts often must decide disputes arising
from ART use by adapting existing law — law not originally crafted with this
scenario in mind. The most provocative cases still arise from parentage disputes.
Consider, for example, the various problems that have arisen because of gamete
and embryo mix-ups. These are the cases in which the wrong eggs were mixed
with the wrong sperm, or the cases in which the wrong embryos were implanted
in a woman undergoing IVF. Perhaps the most controversial cases of all are those
in which racial difference is at stake: the woman who gave birth to twins, one
white and one black, because of an embryo mix-up; or the black woman who gave
birth to a white child after choosing gametes from white donors.[26] The last scenario created more outrage than a story that broke at nearly the same time — a
story about a 59-year-old woman who gave birth to twins as the result of ART
use.[27] In the public debate, racial difference seemed to trump the relationship
formed by pregnancy, birth, and desire to have a child.

C. *Johnson v. Calvert*: The Third-Party Actors

1. *The Arrangers*

> On January 15, 1990, Mark, Crispina, and Anna signed a contract providing
> that an embryo created by the sperm of Mark and the egg of Crispina would be
> implanted in Anna and the child born would be taken into Mark and Crispina's
> home "as their child."[28]

The judicial opinions and the media coverage of *Johnson* focused on the roles
of Mark Calvert, Crispina Calvert, and Anna Johnson. There were, however,
third-party actors who made this sentence in the California Supreme Court's
opinion possible. In fact, the line-up of third-party actors reads like a *Who's
Who* of the West Coast fertility industry. A close look at the third parties provides context for understanding the facts of the case.

Bill Handel drafted the contract that Mark, Crispina, and Anna signed on
January 15, 1990. Handel was one of the early entrepreneurs of surrogacy, having been the founding director of the Center for Surrogate Parenting, Inc. (CSP),
an agency that facilitates surrogacy. CSP's website states that Handel, a lawyer,
started his surrogacy practice in 1980. CSP itself was incorporated in 1986. Its
website also states that, "[i]n 1992, CSP and the California Bar Association co-
sponsored Senate Bill 937" [29] — the surrogacy bill that would have authorized
commercial surrogacy but for the governor's veto. Handel has had national
influence through two mediums. As of 2008, he continues as Director of CSP,
which now provides services in California and Maryland. In addition, he hosts a
nationally syndicated radio show, "Handel on the Law," on which he offers advice
and ridicule on a wide range of legal issues, including family law. If Mark and
Crispina Calvert's willingness to undertake the risks of surrogacy and IVF typify
the consumer-patient side of the industry, then in many ways, Handel and CSP
typify the commercial-medical side. CSP provides services on the cutting edge of

medicine and commerce. It describes itself as a leader in best practices by offering psychological and medical screening of surrogates and by recommending independent counsel.[30] The business operates knowingly and openly in the gray area of the law.

The Calverts did not arrange the surrogacy through CSP. According to media accounts, they were "[u]nable to afford the $40,000 minimum fee charged by a surrogate agency," and so conducted their own search for a surrogate.[31] Crispina Calvert and Anna Johnson both worked as nurses at the same hospital. Anna Johnson had said that she had been accepted as a surrogate at CSP. Coworkers who knew of Crispina's search for a surrogate introduced the two. While Bill Handel wrote the contract for the Calvert-Johnson arrangement, he later stated that CSP had no record of Anna Johnson.[32] The contract provided that the Calverts would pay $10,000 to Anna Johnson in installments, by trimester. The Calverts obtained the money for this fee, plus the $10,000 fee for the IVF, by taking out a $20,000 second mortgage on their home.

Dr. Ricardo Asch performed the IVF procedure, using the gametes of Mark and Crispina to create three embryos that were transferred to Anna Johnson on January 19, 1990. In 1984, Asch and Jose Balmaceda had achieved international fame in the world of fertility medicine when they published an article describing a new procedure. The procedure, called Gamete Intrafallopian Transfer or GIFT, produced higher success rates than standard IVF. As a result, Asch and Balmaceda were in great demand. In 1986, the University of California, Irvine (UC Irvine) recruited Asch to a faculty position in the Department of Obstetrics and Gynecology. In 1990, Asch was appointed Director of the UC Irvine Center for Reproductive Health. He worked there with Balmaceda and another doctor, Sergio Stone. Like many university medical centers, UC Irvine affiliated with or established fertility clinics, in part because fertility clinics are profit centers for universities. UC Irvine and the Calverts sought out Asch for the same reason — his reputation for fertility success. In this case, Asch lived up to his reputation: Anna Johnson became pregnant on the first try.

When IVF is used in the context of gestational surrogacy, both women must take hormones to coordinate their cycles. Crispina Calvert would have received the regimen of drugs described above. Dr. Asch would have started her on daily Lupron injections to shut down her ovaries. A little over a week later, he would have added a daily injection of follicle stimulating hormone to cause multiple follicles to develop. After perhaps nine or ten days, he would have given her one shot of a drug that causes the eggs to mature and release. The egg retrieval is typically performed two days later. IVF with Mark Calvert's sperm would have been performed in the laboratory. In the meantime, Anna Johnson would have been taking hormones to prepare her body to receive an embryo two or three days after egg retrieval. The actual length of this process varies, but it usually takes at least three weeks from the first Lupron injection to embryo transfer. One newspaper account referred to "two months of daily hormone shots."[33] The Calverts and Johnson signed the agreement only four days before Dr. Asch performed the embryo transfer. Whether or not the process took two months, it is noteworthy that the parties signed the informed consent forms and started the medical procedure long before they executed the legal contract.

In 1995, Asch became famous for another reason. He and Balmaceda were forced to resign from UC Irvine after allegations and an internal investigation revealed irregularities in their practice. The two most troubling allegations were that Asch had used an imported non-FDA-approved drug in lieu of Lupron and that he had transferred eggs and embryos from patients who had not consented to their use by others. According to the allegations, most of the transfers were made to other fertility patients, some of whom became pregnant as a result. Some also learned, as a result of the investigations, that Asch sent some embryos to researchers for experimental purposes.

Asch, Balmaceda, and their colleague Stone, were indicted. Asch departed to Mexico before he could be prosecuted. However, the fallout from the UC Irvine fertility center scandal, as it is now known, has lasted for years. At least 139 patients filed lawsuits against UC Irvine. There were also custody suits and whistleblower claims. As of 2007, UC Irvine had paid a total of $23.2 million to fertility clinic patients whose eggs or embryos were transferred to others or were never found.[34]

In the same year, Gerald Schatten, a well-established researcher in reproductive medicine and cloning who received eggs from Asch in the 1990s, made international headlines. When the UC Irvine fertility center scandal broke, Schatten was investigated and cleared of any wrongdoing. In 2005, he was listed as co-author with cloning expert Hwang Woo-Suk of a scientific article that falsely reported success in cloning human embryonic stem cells. Because he had not directly participated in the research, Schatten was cleared of scientific fraud, although he was rebuked for agreeing to co-author an article he did not produce.[35]

In addition to Schatten, what links the two stories are eggs: the scientists who actually conducted the fraudulently reported research also used unethical practices to obtain eggs from women. It would be unfair to say that Asch's unauthorized use of eggs and embryos is typical of fertility practice. Some have argued that overregulation of ART use to prevent one bad actor would hamper good medicine. Others, however, have argued that the breach was inevitable, given the unregulated setting in which ARTs are used.[36] In the wake of the UC Irvine fertility center scandal, the California legislature enacted one statute, which criminalizes the use or implantation of human gametes or embryos without the written consent of those who provide the gametes.[37]

2. The Lawyers

Unfortunately, relations deteriorated between the two sides. . . . Mark and Crispina responded with a lawsuit, seeking a declaration they were the legal parents of the unborn child. Anna filed her own action to be declared the mother of the child, and the two cases were eventually consolidated.[38]

The Calverts were represented by Christian Van Deusen and Robert Walmsley. The Calverts contacted them on Friday, August 10, 1990, immediately after Anna Johnson stated her intention to sue for custody. Van Deusen and Walmsley are family law practitioners. As of 2008, they practice as Van Deusen, Youmans & Walmsley in "adoption, surrogacy, and related litigation." The law firm website lists *Johnson* as one of the firm's principal cases.[39] When the Calverts first contacted him, Van Deusen was representing another California couple in a traditional surrogacy case that first went to court in 1987, when the surrogate petitioned to withdraw her consent to adoption eight months after she signed it. In 1991, the Court of Appeals decided that case in favor of the intended parents.[40] Robert Walmsley also represented Luanne Buzzanca in a surrogacy dispute that arose in 1995. In that case, the decision of the intermediate appeals court used *Johnson* as precedent. The Calverts' lawyers, in other words, have established a niche practice in family law issues arising from ART use.

Anna Johnson was represented by Richard Gilbert and Diane Marlowe. Gilbert and Marlowe have a practice that is broader in focus than Van Deusen and Walmsley's, but still largely concentrated in family law. Gilbert and Marlowe also represented Elvira Jordan, the surrogate in *Marriage of Moschetta*, another post-*Johnson* surrogacy case.[41] It is probably more titillating than relevant to note that Gilbert and Marlowe contended in the *Moschetta* oral argument that "this court should ignore *Johnson*, which counsel compared to *Dred Scott v. Sanford*."[42] The *Moschetta* court, in a footnote, declined "counsel's invitation to stage an insurrection against the rule of stare decisis"[43] — that is, the notion that precedents that are squarely on point should be followed. The court then carefully reviewed the majority's opinion in *Johnson*, and relied on the majority's analysis of the UPA. It recognized Elvira Jordan, the surrogate in a traditional surrogacy arrangement, as the natural and legal mother.

On behalf of Anna Johnson, Gilbert and Marlowe appealed to the California Supreme Court from a decision issued by Judge David Sills, who was presiding judge of the 4th District, Division 3, of the California Court of Appeals. Judge Sills has decided more surrogacy cases than any other California judge. In addition to *Johnson*, Judge Sills also decided *Moschetta* and *Jaycee B. v. Superior Court*, two post-*Johnson* cases.[44]

3. The Media

OC Couple Battle Surrogate Mother for Custody of Fetus/ Lawsuit Likely Breaks New Ground on Issues of Legal and Biological Parentage[45]

The media coverage of the dispute between the Calverts and Johnson began before either party filed a complaint. On Friday, August 10, 1990, the media got wind of Anna Johnson's intent to file a claim for custody. She was seven months into her pregnancy at the time. When television crews started showing up at Bill Handel's office, he called the Calverts to warn them. They called attorney Christian Van Deusen to make an appointment for Saturday. Shortly after that meeting, they gave their first media interview, to the *Orange County Register*. The headline quoted above appeared on the first page of the *Register*'s Sunday morning edition. On Monday, August 13, Anna Johnson filed her complaint.

The opening sentence of the August 12 story pinpoints the source of the legal dispute and its newsworthiness: "An Orange County couple whose embryo was implanted in a surrogate mother are battling the woman for custody of the unborn child, the first dispute involving a surrogate mother who has no genetic tie to the child she is carrying."[46] Neither *Baby M.*, nor the two surrogacy decisions in California's lower courts prior to that date, had arisen from a gestational surrogacy arrangement. While the legal issue was novel, the *Register*'s opening line shows that ART use, and IVF in particular, had already produced common understandings of the interests the parties had at stake. The sentence begins by characterizing the embryo as belonging to the Calverts. It ends by emphasizing the absence of a "genetic tie" between the surrogate and the "unborn child." The fact that Anna Johnson was pregnant with the "unborn child" at the time seems irrelevant, or at least invisible.

Both print and television news media covered the story intensely from August 10, 1990, to October 4, 1993, when the U.S. Supreme Court denied Anna Johnson's writ of certiorari.[47] The story attracted national attention. But two local newspapers shaped public opinion in California. The *Orange County Register* published the greatest number of stories during this period. But the *Los Angeles Times*, with its wider circulation, arguably had greater influence.

Coverage by both newspapers reflected deeply embedded assumptions about race, gender, and class. There were parallels between media portrayals of the Sterns and Mary Beth Whitehead in the coverage of *Baby M.* and the newspapers' portrayals of the Calverts and Anna Johnson. The portrayals seemed to be based on archetypes. The Calverts, like the Sterns, were depicted as "The Infertile Couple" — married, middle class, desperately yearning for a child of their own. The depictions of Whitehead and Johnson, in contrast, focused on the acts and words that made them seem selfish, grasping, and manipulative. For example, the *Register* published a story on August 23, 1990 — the thirteenth day of media coverage — about the intensity of the media coverage. The story stated the Calverts' position that "their baby was being held hostage by a publicity-hungry woman," and then focused on the Calverts. It described them as "intensely private" and, without irony, recounted the number of interviews they had given since August 10, 1990. The list included the *Orange County Register*, "five TV networks, a morning TV show, two radio call-in shows, TV's 'Inside Edition.'"[48] The story also mentioned a four-hour interview with *People Magazine* that included a nine-hour photo shoot. It was apparent from the quotes of Mark Calvert that the story itself was based on an interview.

Race played a different role in media coverage of the two cases. Richard Stern, Elizabeth Stern, and Mary Beth Whitehead were white. There was mention of Richard Stern's desire to have a biologically related child because he had lost family in the Holocaust. And so he was identified as Jewish. Beyond that, the identity differences used to contrast the Sterns and Whitehead tapped into assumptions about class. In covering *Johnson*, the media made much of the parties' racial identities. Mark Calvert was white; Crispina Calvert was Filipina; Anna Johnson was African American. The newspaper stories often overlooked that Crispina Calvert was non-white. It was as if she was nominally white by virtue of her marriage to a white man. The *Los Angeles Times* coverage, in particular, seemed to highlight racial differences, perhaps to emphasize the notion of genetic parentage, or perhaps to sell newspapers. The *Los Angeles Times* photos that accompanied the print stories often featured Mark Calvert and Anna Johnson, or just Anna Johnson. As a result, the racial difference was framed as black versus white.

The newspaper depictions of Anna Johnson included coverage of welfare fraud charges brought against her. From August 15, both the *Orange County Register* and the *Los Angeles Times* ran a series of stories about the charges. The stories explain the relevance of the charges to the parentage issue from the Calverts' point of view. "Lawyers for Mark and Crispina Calvert, the couple whose baby Johnson is due to deliver in October, said the revelations about her alleged conduct show that Johnson cannot be trusted when she claims that the couple mistreated her."[49] The stories provided space for emphasizing certain facts: Anna Johnson was a single mother; she was on welfare; she committed fraud by continuing to accept benefits after she returned to work. The stories do not explicitly state her race, but they were accompanied by photos of Johnson. Taken together, the photos and facts position Johnson as an archetypal "welfare mother." Yet other facts countered the stereotype: Johnson had educated herself and become a licensed vocational nurse; she had returned to work after her daughter's birth, thus obviating her need for government assistance; as a nurse, she earned only $400 a week. Within the stories, however, these were background facts used to explain the fraud charges.[50]

D. After *Johnson v. Calvert*

1. *The UPA*

The National Conference of Commissioners on Uniform State Laws has revised the UPA since its 1973 debut. The most recent version, the Uniform Parentage Act of 2002 (UPA of 2002), adds two sections that expressly address parentage issues arising from ART use. Article 7 addresses children of assisted conception and Article 8 addresses parentage under gestational agreements. In addition, the revised Article 2 states that the legal mother is the woman who gave birth to the child, with three exceptions: a woman who is adjudicated as the legal mother, adopts the child, or is the legal mother under a gestational agreement, where enforceable.[51] As of 2008, only a small handful of states have adopted the revised UPA. In most states, then, the parentage issues arising from gestational surrogacy agreements remain unaddressed. California has not adopted the UPA of 2002, and so *Johnson* remains prevailing law.

2. *Parentage Disputes Arising from ART Use*

For over a decade now, the courts have been wrestling with the legal and social significance of *Johnson*. The decision left many legal questions unanswered, such as whether and when surrogacy contracts could be enforced and whether genetics, intent, or birth would be determinative in other situations. The decision also triggered concerns about the social implications of the court's analysis. Unlike the California Supreme Court's decision, the California Court of Appeals had used genetics as the tiebreaker,[52] and did so in a way that diminished the significance of pregnancy and birth, as well as bonds formed through adoption and childrearing: "[T]he whole process of human development is set in motion by genes. There is not a single organic system of the human body not influenced by an individual's underlying genetic makeup."[53] In using intent as a tiebreaker, the California Supreme Court's majority moved away from the notion of genetic determinism. Yet, as Justice Kennard's dissent points out, the result — recognizing Crispina Calvert as the legal mother — still suggested the devaluation of childbearing and childbearers.[54]

The legal questions left by *Johnson* have not been fully resolved. Indeed, because ART use and family formations continue to evolve, there will always be new questions. However, the California courts have followed the logic of *Johnson* to some interesting ends. In general, the courts have more often distinguished *Johnson* than followed it. Yet, in most (but not all) of those cases, the courts have also adhered to its analytical approach. That is, in most cases, the courts have used the UPA despite the fact that it was written without ART use in mind. In addition, the courts have applied the UPA's paternity provisions on a gender-neutral basis.

a. Traditional Surrogacy

Judge Sills may have given *Johnson* its strictest and its loosest reading in the two cases mentioned above: *Moschetta* and *Jaycee B.* In *Moschetta*, the court addressed the "who is the mother" question in a traditional surrogacy situation. The intended parents argued that *Johnson* was directly applicable. Judge Sills, however, rejected the argument that the intended mother and the surrogate were equally mothers under the UPA, and that intent broke the tie in the intended mother's favor. Instead, the court determined that under the UPA, the intended mother, Cynthia Moschetta, was not the child's legal mother at all.[55] The judge also provided a careful reading of *Johnson* and concluded that the Supreme Court had not said that surrogacy contracts were enforceable.[56] Judge Sills then determined that traditional surrogacy contracts are not enforceable, and therefore the surrogate, or birth mother, was the child's legal mother.[57]

b. Gestational Surrogacy with Third-Party Gametes

In *Jaycee B.*, Judge Sills took the rule of intent to its extreme. The arrangement itself took gestational surrogacy a step beyond the one at issue in *Johnson*. In *Jaycee B.*, the intended parents and the surrogate agreed to a gestational surrogacy arrangement, but third-party egg and sperm donors provided the gametes used to create the embryos.[58] During the surrogate's pregnancy, the intended parents split up. The intended father, John Buzzanca, denied paternity. The case arose as a child support claim filed against him after the child, Jaycee, was born. The issue before the court was its authority to issue a *pendente lite* child support order before John Buzzanca's parentage was determined. The intended mother, Luanne Buzzanca, wanted the child. The surrogate did not. The trial court decided that Jaycee had no parents and refused to issue the support order. The trial court's holding outraged the public and the appellate court. The California Court of Appeals reversed the lower court's decision. In addition, Senator Diane Watson proposed a new version of the Alternative Reproduction Act, but the bill never made it out of committee.[59]

In his opinion, Judge Sills did not make ultimate determinations of parentage, but assessed the probable outcome on the parentage determinations in order to establish the court's authority to issue the support order. He applied to both gamete donors the UPA rule that cuts off paternity for a man who provides sperm for use by a woman other than his wife. Without ruling that the contract was enforceable, Judge Sills then used the rule of intent, together with the surrogate's expectations and the "but for" logic of *Johnson,* to conclude that the surrogate should also not be deemed the legal mother, despite the fact that she was the birth mother. Judge Sills also determined that, based on the parties' originally expressed intent, John Buzzanca probably would be deemed the legal father, despite the absence of a biological relationship between him and Jaycee.

c. Two Mothers

More recently, the California Supreme Court decided a trio of cases in which the parentage disputes arose not from surrogacy contracts, but from parenting arrangements formed by lesbian women in committed relationships. In each case, the Court determined that a child can have two mothers. It reached that conclusion, in part, by distinguishing that part of *Johnson* in which the Court refused to recognize both Anna Johnson and Crispina Calvert as the child's legal mothers. In *Elisa B. v. Superior Court,*[60] *K.M. v. E.G.,*[61] and *Kristine H v. Lisa R.,*[62] there were two potential parents. Therefore, the refusal to recognize both women as mothers would have resulted in a one-parent family. In these cases, the Court limited the use of intent as a tiebreaker to the situation where there are three potential parents. The Court pointed to the public policy of providing children with two parents, where possible.

In each of the cases, the Court adhered to its gender-neutral use of the UPA to determine that both women were parents. In *K.M.*, for example, K.M. had provided the eggs that enabled her former partner to have children through IVF. There were, therefore, two biological mothers. In *Elisa B.*, Elisa and Emily decided to have children together.[63] By agreement, they chose a sperm donor and each underwent insemination. Elisa gave birth to Chance. A few months later, Emily gave birth to twins, Ry and Kaia. They raised the children together, but shortly after they separated, Elisa refused to continue providing support for the twins. This case, therefore, arose as a claim for support. The Court determined that both women were legal mothers of the twins under the UPA — Emily by virtue of having given birth to them, and Elisa because she held the children out as her own. The latter conclusion was reached by applying a paternity establishment provision in a gender-neutral way. As in *K.M.*, because the UPA cut off paternity of the sperm donor, there were only two possible parents, and therefore no need to use a tiebreaker.

3. The Fertility Industry

As recently stated by our Supreme Court in a case involving a surrogacy contract: It is not the role of the judiciary to inhibit the use of reproductive technology when the Legislature has not seen fit to do so; any such effort would raise serious questions in light of the fundamental nature of the rights of procreation and privacy.[64]

Less than a month after *Johnson*, the California Court of Appeals cited the opinion for the proposition that it is not for the courts to restrict ART use. In the later case, the court considered the fascinating question of whether it could enforce a testamentary transfer of the decedent's cryogenically stored sperm to his surviving girlfriend, for her use in assisted insemination. (The court said yes).[65] But the statement quoted above indicated the implications of *Johnson* for the fertility industry.

Had the Supreme Court recognized Anna Johnson, or both Anna Johnson and Crispina Calvert as the legal mother(s), the legislature might have felt compelled to respond with legislation. Indeed, Senator Diane Watson did propose a new version of the Alternative Reproduction Act, but the bill did not go forward. Public opinion ran with the Calverts, in large part because of the media portrayals of the parties. If the Calverts had lost, the public may have supported another attempt to pass an Alternative Reproduction Act. Industry may also have supported legislation if CSP's earlier support for the 1991 version of the Act was indicative. But the outcomes in *Johnson* and *Jaycee B.*, in granting custody to the intended parents, accorded with public judgment of the cases. As a result, the courts seemed to reach the correct outcomes in absence of legislation.

As a result of *Johnson* and the accompanying lack of legislation, the fertility industry continues to flourish in California and elsewhere. To a large extent, the industry operates in the gray area of the law. The issue of whether or when a surrogacy contract would be enforced has not yet been determined. But in a gestational surrogacy like that in *Johnson*, the outcome is predictable. The rule of intent carries out the most important provision of the contract. *Jaycee B.*, as a Court of Appeals decision, is not binding. The outcome nevertheless reassures those considering gestational surrogacy.

The recent two-mother cases illustrate at least two points. First, they illustrate the potential that ART use has for challenging the dominance of the heterosexual, marriage-based model of family. Second, they show that the fertility industry has expanded. In addition to technological innovations, the fertility industry has expanded its market in at least two directions: niche markets, such as services for gay and lesbian families and single-parent families, and the global market. The media has coined the term "fertility tourism" to describe the phenomenon of intended parents who travel to other countries to obtain access to ART services. Due in large part to the absence of substantial restrictions in California and the near-certainty that the UPA and *Johnson* provide, as well as cultural and political factors, California has become a destination spot for those living in the United States and abroad who seek fertility services.

E. Epilogue

In 1990, Crispina Calvert, Mark Calvert, and Anna Johnson entered an agreement that was both intimate and entrepreneurial in nature. The California Supreme Court's opinion provides a glimpse of how the surrogacy agreement broke down: "Unfortunately, relations deteriorated between the two sides. Mark learned that Anna had not disclosed she had suffered several stillbirths and miscarriages. Anna felt that Mark and Crispina did not do enough to obtain the required insurance policy. She also felt abandoned during the onset of premature labor in June."[66] Within weeks, the parties moved their conflict into the public arenas of the courts and the media. Over the next three years and ten months, the Calverts and Johnson pursued the parental rights claim and various civil lawsuits through both venues.

All parties experienced hardship during this period. Anna Johnson's repeated requests for visitation time with the baby were denied. She married in 1991, but divorced two years later.[67] By 1991, the Calverts had incurred more than $60,000 in medical and legal fees. In order to manage that debt, they sold their home in Tustin and their Mercedes Benz, and acquired less expensive substitutes.[68] Yet, both sides persisted. Both the Calverts and Johnson sued several parties who participated in arranging the surrogacy, including each other, on grounds other than parental rights. Johnson sued the Calverts,[69] Bill Handel, and Asch.[70] The Calverts sued Johnson, Handel, and CSP.[71]

In July 1993, Anna Johnson appealed the California Supreme Court decision to the United States Supreme Court. Three months later, the Court denied her writ.[72] In June 1994, the *Orange County Register* reported that the Calverts and Johnson had agreed to drop their civil suits against each other.[73] At the time, Christopher Michael Johnson was 3 years and 9 months old. Today, he is a teenager.

ENDNOTES

1. In the Matter of Baby M., 537 A.2d 1227 (N.J. 1988).
2. Johnson v. Calvert, 851 P.2d 776 (Cal. 1993).
3. *Id.* at 778–79.
4. *Id.*
5. *Id.* at 781.
6. Debra Spar, The Baby Business: How Money, Science, and Politics Drive the Commerce of Conception 35 (2006).
7. National Conference of Commissioners on Uniform State Laws, Uniform Parentage Act (UPA), §5(a) (1973).
8. *Id.* §5(a).
9. Spar, *supra* note 6, at 39–40.
10. Michelle Meadows, *Facing Infertility*, FDA Consumer Mag. (Nov.-Dec. 2004).
11. Jose Van Dyck, Manufacturing Consent: Debating the New Reproductive Technologies 62–65 (1995).
12. *Id.* at 69–77.
13. One Australian study found that infants conceived with ART are more likely to be born by Caesarian section, born before term than naturally-conceived infants, and have low birth weight. Michèle Hansen et al., *The Risk of Major Birth Defects After Intracytoplasmic Sperm Injection and In Vitro Fertilization*, 346 New Eng. J. Med. 725, 726–27 (2002). Infants conceived via IVF also have a higher prevalence of major birth defects than naturally conceived infants and ART infants also have a higher incidence of musculoskeletal and chromosomal defects. *Id.* at 727–29. *See also* Robin Fretwell Wilson, *Uncovering the Rationale for Requiring Infertility in Surrogacy Arrangements*, 29 Am. J.L. & Med. 337 (2003) (summarizing empirical literature about risks of birth defects following ART).
14. Spar, *supra* note 6, at 75–78.
15. *See* Lynn D. Wardle & Laurence C. Nolan, Fundamental Principles of Family Law 310 (2d ed. 2006).
16. For a complete list of state statutes addressing surrogacy, see Jessica Arons, Center for American Progress, Future Choices: Assisted Reproductive Technologies and the Law, Appendix: Surrogacy Laws (2007).
17. UPA, *supra* note 7, §12.
18. In the Matter of Baby M., 537 A.2d 1227 (N.J. 1988).
19. In the Matter of Baby M., 542 A.2d 52 (N.J. Super. Ch. 1988).
20. *See, e.g.*, 21 C.F.R. §884.6160 (classifying labware used in IVF as requiring "special controls").
21. *See* Susan Markens, Surrogate Motherhood and the Politics of Reproduction 31–34 (2007).
22. Assemb. Bill No. 1701 (1985-1986 Reg. Sess.).
23. Sen. Bill No. 1160 (1993-1994 Reg. Sess.).
24. *Id.*
25. *Id.*
26. Van Dyck, *supra* note 11, at 184.
27. *Id.*
28. Johnson v. Calvert, 851 P.2d 776, 778 (Cal. 1993).
29. http://www.creatingfamilies.com/IP/IP_Info.aspx?Type=5 (last visited Aug. 7, 2008).
30. http://www.creatingfamilies.com/IP/IP_Info.aspx?Type=9 (last visited Aug. 7, 2008).

31. Susan Peterson & Susan Kelleher, *OC Couple Battle Surrogate Mother for Custody of the Fetus*, Orange County Reg., Aug. 12, 1990, at A1.

32. Susan Peterson, *Surrogate Sues for Child Custody in Case That Could Set Precedent*, Orange County Reg., Aug. 14, 1990, at A1.

33. Peterson & Kelleher, *supra* note 31.

34. For a general overview of the UC Irvine Fertility Scandal and its aftermath, see Kimi Yoshino, *UC Irvine Fertility Scandal Isn't Over*, L.A. Times, Jan. 20, 2006, at A-1, *available at* http://articles.latimes.com/2006/jan/20/local/me-uci20 (last visited Aug. 8, 2008).

35. *See Panel Finds That Dr. Schatten Committed No Scientific Misconduct, available at* http://www.upmc.com/Communications/MediaRelations/NewsReleaseArchives/By+Subject/S/Stem+Cell+Research/SchattenPanelRelease.htm (last visited August 8, 2008).

36. George J. Annas, *Crazy Making: Embryos and Gestational Mothers*, 21 Hastings Center Rep. 35 (Jan.-Feb. 1991).

37. Cal. Penal Code §367g (1996).

38. Johnson v. Calvert, 851 P.2d 776, 778 (Cal. 1993).

39. http://www.familybuilding.com/profile.php (last visited Aug. 8, 2008).

40. Adoption of Matthew B., 232 Cal. App. 3d 1239 (1st Dist., Div. 3 1991).

41. 25 Cal. App. 4th 1218 (4th Dist., Div. 3 1994).

42. *Id.* at n.14.

43. *Id.*

44. *Id.*; 42 Cal. App. 4th 718 (4th Dist., Div. 3 1996).

45. Peterson & Kelleher, *supra* note 31.

46. *Id.*

47. Johnson v. Calvert, 510 U.S. 874 (1993).

48. Susan Peterson, *Surrogate-Case Pair Bears Up Under Media Frenzy*, Orange County Reg., Aug. 23, 1990, at A1.

49. Catherine Gewertz, *Surrogate Mother in Custody Fight Accused of Welfare Fraud*, L.A. Times, Aug. 16, 1990, at A3.

50. Susan Peterson, *Surrogate Mom Charged with Welfare Fraud*, Orange County Reg., Aug. 15, 1990, at B1; Gewertz, *supra* note 49.

51. National Conference of Commissions on Uniform State Laws. Uniform Parentage Act, Article 2 (2002) (2002 UPA).

52. Anna J. v. Mark C., 12 Cal. App. 4th 977 (4th Dist., Div. 3 1991).

53. *Id.* at 996.

54. Johnson v. Calvert, 851 P.2d 776, 797–98 (Cal. 1993).

55. 25 Cal. App. 4th 1218, 1231 (4th Dist., Div. 3 1994).

56. *Id.* at 1230.

57. *Id.* at 1231.

58. 42 Cal. App. 4th 718, 720 (4th Dist., Div. 3 1996).

59. Alternative Reproduction Act of 1996, Cal. S.B. 2024 (introduced by Watson), 1995-1996 Reg. Sess.

60. 117 P.3d 660 (Cal. 2005).

61. 117 P.3d 673 (Cal. 2005).

62. 117 P.3d 690 (Cal. 2005).

63. 117 P.3d at 663.

64. Hecht v. Superior Court, 16 Cal. App. 4th 836, 860 (2d Dist., Div. 7 1993).

65. *Id.*

66. 851 P.2d 776, 778 (Cal. 1993).

67. Susan Peterson, *What Makes a Mother?*, Orange County Reg., Feb. 1, 1993, at B1.

68. Susan Peterson & Susan Kelleher, *The Legal Limelight Returns for Surrogate-Case Figures*, Orange County Reg., Aug. 28, 1991, at A1.

69. Jonathan Volzke, *Calverts, Johnson End Bitter Lawsuits*, Orange County Reg., June 21, 1994, at B1.

70. Pat Brennan, *Surrogate Mother Sues for $5 Million for Emotional Pain*, Orange County Reg., Dec. 8, 1990, at B1.

71. *Surrogate Mother Sued for Breach of Contract*, S.F. Chron., Sept. 17, 1992, at A24.

72. Baby Boy J. v. Johnson, 510 U.S. 938 (1993).

73. Volzke, *supra* note 69.

Chapter 5

LITOWITZ
v.
LITOWITZ

Feuding over Frozen Embryos and Forecasting the Future of Reproductive Medicine

JUDITH DAAR*

Any marriage that ends with the husband asking a court to consider evidence that his wife paid a third party to have him killed was probably not a happy one. Strangely and sadly, this murder-for-hire allegation is not what made the divorce proceedings of Washington residents David and Becky Litowitz the subject of extensive newspaper and television coverage. Instead, the feuding couple was foisted into the public eye because of the high-tech nature of their marital assets. Only months before the pair separated, they had contracted with two Southern California women to serve as an egg donor and a gestational carrier to enable the Litowitzes to have a child. A baby girl was born of this arrangement, but tempers flared over the disposition of the two embryos that remained in frozen storage, with Becky and David adopting irreconcilable positions on the fate of their would-be offspring.

By the time the Litowitz dissolution reached the Supreme Court of Washington in June 2002,[1] the subject of frozen embryo disposition was well known in the world of assisted reproductive technologies (ART),[2] having been the subject of several state court decisions.[3] Likewise, the notion of creating embryos using in vitro fertilization (IVF)[4] and then freezing them for later use was hardly novel, coming more than two decades after the birth of the world's first so-called "test tube" baby[5] and in a year in which nearly 46,000 children were conceived using IVF in the United States.[6]

---

* Judith Daar is the Associate Dean for Academic Affairs and Professor of Law at Whittier Law School, where she was named the Harry S. Zekian Scholar in 2008.

97

What is unique about the Litowitz case is not so much its jurisprudence on embryo disposition at divorce, but rather its potential applicability to two behemoths in the world of reproductive technologies — third-party reproduction and embryonic stem cell research. Though generally discussed and regulated as distinct practices, procreation with the aid of third-party gamete (sperm and egg) donors and scientific research using nascent human embryos are currently struggling with the same dilemma because of their shared reliance on donated gametes. Participants in both the reproductive and research realms are being called upon to determine the scope and extent of dispositional authority that gamete donors retain over their excised tissue. Allocating enduring control over gametes and the product of those gametes to those who contribute the raw ingredients could significantly impact the future of reproductive and regenerative medicine. Delving into the mostly ordinary, albeit occasionally explosive, divorce saga of David and Becky Litowitz provides a glimpse of possible judicial reactions to future schemes allocating control over the products of reproduction.

A. The Marriage, The Divorce, The Lingering Dispute

Theirs is a common story.[7] Boy meets girl, girl has boy's baby, baby makes five counting girl's two children from a prior relationship, boy and girl marry. Nearly two decades pass, and boy and girl decide to have another baby using an egg donor and gestational carrier, boy and girl's marriage crumbles as new baby is about to arrive, boy accuses girl of illicit drug use and plotting his murder, and finally boy and girl divorce but continue their bitter battle over two embryos frozen in Southern California. Though one could tweak these highlights into a plot line ripe for the silver screen, taken individually each event is a rather humdrum occurrence (except maybe for the drugs and murder) in an era of frequent divorce,[8] frequent infertility,[9] and frequent use of assisted reproductive technologies.[10]

In the 1970s, David Litowitz, the son of a real estate developer who followed in his father's career footsteps,[11] met Becky Baily, the mother of two children (Ann Marie, born in 1976, and Lucas, born in 1978).[12] A son, Jacob, was born to the couple on July 15, 1980. Some twenty months later David and Becky married, tying the knot on February 27, 1982. The months between Jacob's birth and the couple's wedding were probably difficult, as Becky underwent a hysterectomy during that time that left her unable to produce eggs or to give birth naturally to another child. After their nuptials, for fourteen years the Litowitz family enjoyed life in the Pacific Northwest.

As Jacob approached his teenage years, the couple began to feel a strain in their marriage; though no cause and effect is suggested, most couples with adolescent children can empathize with the rearing challenges this developmental period poses. Perhaps as a way to divert the strain, or as a potential salve to smooth over the marital fissures, in or around 1995 Becky and David agreed to have another child.[13] While the production of a marriage-saving baby is as old as the institution of marriage itself, for the Litowitzes such a notion was far easier to conceive in their minds than in their bodies. With Becky unable to contribute to the genetic or gestational development of another child, her only option was to recruit other women to supply the necessary ingredients to create and gestate the next Litowitz offspring.

1. The Surrogacy Process

As if tensions on the home front and the lack of ovaries, eggs, and a uterus weren't enough of a disincentive to proceed with their procreative plans, the Litowitzes faced another barrier that was clearly designed to prevent just the type of arrangement the couple ultimately forged: Washington law outlawed payment to gestational carriers and voided any contract that called for compensation in exchange for gestational services. In 1989, Washington became one of the first states to address via legislation the then-novel practice of surrogate parenting, in which a woman is inseminated with the sperm of an intended father whose wife is infertile or serves as a gestational carrier of an embryo formed with the wife's or a donor's egg. The relevant statute provides:

> No person, organization, or agency shall enter into, induce, arrange, procure, or otherwise assist in the formation of a surrogate parentage contract, written or unwritten, for compensation.[14]

The Litowitzes initially sought treatment at the University of Washington, but upon learning of the state's legal barrier to commercial surrogacy, the couple had to reconsider their options. Since the likelihood of encountering a volunteer gestational carrier was remote, the couple became fertility tourists, traveling to what many in the ART world refer to as "Surrogacy Central," the great State of California. The Golden State earned this reputation partly by enterprise and partly by law. Of the over 400 ART clinics in the U.S., about fifteen percent are located in California, and virtually all offer gestational surrogacy services.[15] In addition, California law is friendly to commercial surrogacy, both because it has no prohibitory legislation and because the state supreme court declared in *Johnson v. Calvert* in 1993 that surrogacy contracts are not "inconsistent with public policy."[16] Buoyed by the welcoming, laissez-faire ART practices to the south, the Litowitzes contacted the Center for Surrogate Parenting in Beverly Hills.[17]

Typically, when an individual or couple contacts an egg donation or surrogacy agency, the intended parents are shown profiles of prospective donors and surrogates, with basic information such as age, height, weight, eye color, education, ethnicity, religion, and pregnancy or prior donative experience. A current photo and a baby photo are also part of the profile packet. In March 1996, the Litowitzes selected Jennifer Yocom, a twenty-something married woman, as their egg donor. Becky, David, Jennifer, and her husband Eric signed what was then a standard egg donor contract, in which the donor and her spouse waived any parental rights to a child born of the donation. In exchange, the intended parents agreed to pay the donor for her "pain and suffering," in this case valued at $2,500.[18] Jennifer is described by Colleen Grady, the attorney for Becky Litowitz, as good-hearted and earthy, a woman who both "did it for the money" and also out of a sense of wanting to help the couple have a child. These dual mercenary and altruistic motivations are common among third-party gamete donors.[19]

Whatever her motivation, Jennifer went on to produce a sufficient number of eggs to yield five embryos for the Litowitzes. Three of the embryos were transferred into the uterus of a gestational carrier named Tammy McColley, and two were frozen for potential later use. These two frozen embryos later spawned the Litowitz litigation, but they proved to be controversial from the start. The embryos were produced in the ART clinic at the Loma Linda Center for Fertility and In Vitro Fertilization (Loma Linda Center), where the Litowitzes went with their entourage for treatment. When Jennifer's eggs and David's sperm melded into five healthy embryos, doctors urged that all five be transferred to the carrier's uterus to maximize the chance for pregnancy. This advice was rejected because, according to Becky Litowitz's brief to the Court of Appeals, all of "the mothers: biological, surrogate and, intended parent, Ms. Litowitz chose to limit the implantation to three pre-embryos to avoid the possibility that multiple conception would place the participants involved in the untenable position of selective reduction which was abhorrent to Ms. Litowitz."[20]

The women's approach proved successful when Tammy became pregnant with only one of the embryos. Tammy gave birth to an infant girl, Micah Litowitz, on January 25, 1997. By the time Micah was born, the couple had physically separated, with Ms. Grady remarking that Becky was "served with divorce papers as she was about to board the plane" to witness her daughter's birth.[21]

2. The Egg Donor Arrangement

Before turning to the ensuing divorce proceedings and dispute over the frozen embryos, it is worth pausing to highlight two noteworthy aspects of the egg donor arrangement between the Litowitzes and Mrs. Yocom. One pertains to the egg donor contract and the other to the parties' relationship. As to the contract, the parties negotiated the dispositional authority over the eggs by agreeing:

> All eggs produced by the Egg Donor pursuant to this Agreement shall be deemed the property of the Intended Parents and as such, the Intended Parents shall have the sole right to determine the disposition of said egg(s). In no event may the Intended Parents allow any other party to use said eggs without express *written* permission of the Egg Donor.[22]

Anecdotal evidence suggests the last sentence in the excerpted paragraph is a highly debated provision in egg donor contracts. According to Steve Masler, CEO of The Donor Source, an Orange County agency specializing in egg donor and surrogacy services, the vast majority of egg donor contracts provide that the intended parents retain total control over any donated eggs. The egg donor surrenders the right to control the fate of her eggs once they leave her body, such that a provision requiring the written consent of a donor to any use the intended parents wish to make of the eggs would be unusual.[23]

In contrast, several attorneys working in the ART field report an increasing desire on the part of their egg donor clients to control both the primary and secondary dispositions of their eggs and resulting embryos. For example, some women do not want their genetic material re-donated to couples who are unmarried, or of the same sex, or for use in medical research. If this request for control is made, the intended parents have the opportunity either to accept these terms or to begin searching for another donor. For the most part, intended parents tend to accept these terms or ask the donor to reconsider in the hopes of reaching a compromise, in order to preserve the donor choice they struggled to make.[24]

Assuming an agreement is reached whereby the donor relinquishes all rights to control the disposition of her eggs and any resulting embryos, are the intended parents free to re-donate the eggs to another couple? The act of distributing a donor's eggs to more than one set of intended parents is known as "egg sharing," a practice that has garnered its share of bad publicity. In 2002, an egg donor from Houston sued two couples who used her eggs to form embryos. One couple, the Does, entered into a contract with the donor, but the second couple, the Rhodes-McBrides of Texas, obtained the donor's eggs from their doctor, who "assured Ms. Rhodes-McBride that it was legal and that physicians are actually encouraged to promote egg sharing among patients."[25] The attorney for the ART physician, also named in the suit, reasoned "[o]nce you donate those eggs, you have no rights to those eggs or to the child of those eggs."[26] The donor disagreed, arguing that her agreement with the Does was exclusive and she had never, and would never, give consent for any couple other than the Does to use her eggs. While the donor eventually settled her lawsuit against the ART physician, the case continues to raise concerns about the unspoken practice of egg sharing.

In the summer of 2007, a follow-up newspaper article on the Texas lawsuit began, "More than 100 fertility doctors in dozens of states may have brokered unauthorized transfers of human eggs, according to the bankruptcy court filing of a local company and its former records supervisor."[27] The article detailed the saga of the Southern California egg donor agency that brokered the agreement between the Houston donor and the Does, ultimately filing for bankruptcy in 2003 after being named in the donor's lawsuit. Over the next several years, the agency's medical records supervisor combed through the records of known egg donations, seeing if the disposition of donor eggs matched with the number of eggs retrieved. In nearly 100 cases the numbers did not add up, showing discrepancies in the number of eggs retrieved, fertilized, transferred, frozen, or disposed of. As of this writing, investigations are underway to determine if unauthorized egg sharing did occur and whether children were born of these arrangements.

The Texas legal battle highlights the gender differences in third-party reproduction. Under current practices, egg and sperm donations differ significantly. When a man donates his sperm to a commercial sperm bank, he relinquishes all rights to control his sperm from the moment it is handed over to the technician. Sperm sharing is common, meaning that banks routinely sell one man's sperm to many recipients. Distributions over a period of time, at least several years, are possible because sperm can be frozen for long periods.[28] While there are no laws that govern the number of recipients or children that can attach to one donor's sperm, each program does have its own set of criteria for determining when a particular man's sperm should be "retired." Newly developed websites allow children conceived with donor sperm to search for half-siblings, and some report finding at least a dozen such kin.[29]

Egg donation does not operate under this model of total donor relinquishment, partly because eggs are used fresh, as soon as they are retrieved. Typically, a couple or individual will select the donor from a profile booklet, and the donor will be consulted as to her willingness to donate to a particular recipient.[30] The donor may receive some demographic information about the recipient, such as marital status, number of existing children, religion, or ethnicity. She can consent or decline the match, and as noted in the Litowitz agreement, reserve the right to direct her eggs exclusively to the selected recipient. Thus, unlike male donors, female donors have some sense about the recipients of their eggs, though they may not know the outcome of their donation. If embryos are left over from the fresh IVF cycle they belong to the intended parents, and the donor — absent a contractual agreement, as in *Litowitz* — has no control over the disposition of these frozen embryos.

Recent technological advances could work to equalize the treatment of male and female gamete donors, placing women in the same position as men. Improving outcomes for egg freezing, previously an elusive science, may allow commercial egg banks to operate in the same fashion as sperm banks, attracting donors and preserving their gametes for years in the future. A milestone in egg freezing was achieved in 2007, when an Orange County, California hospital announced the birth of the world's first child conceived using frozen eggs and frozen sperm.[31] While the child was born to a mother using her own frozen eggs, certainly the possibility for storing and selling donor eggs to multiple recipients, as occurs with the sperm model, is approaching.

Clearly, the *Litowitz* case did not involve egg sharing, as all of Mrs. Yocom's eggs were used by Becky and David. But it is important to realize that the egg donor contract did anticipate, and reject, the possibility of egg sharing, requiring the donor's written permission if her eggs were to be used by any other party. This directed donation from Mrs. Yocom to the Litowitzes suggests a certain personal relationship between the parties, in addition to a legal relationship based in contract. This personal relationship is the second noteworthy aspect of the egg donor arrangement between the Litowitzes and Mrs. Yocom.

Again, looking to standard practices, typically egg donors and intended parents do not meet, do not exchange contact information, and do not communicate in any way before or after the egg retrieval and embryo transfer.[32] In this sense, egg donation more resembles sperm donation as to the anonymity of the parties to one another. True, donors and recipients do learn basic information about each other, but the process is set up to preserve as much privacy for the parties as possible. Thus, the *Litowitz* case appears as an aberration.

Court records and newspaper accounts paint a picture of Becky, Jennifer the egg donor, and Tammy the gestational carrier as having a close relationship. In May 2000, Becky appeared on national television, telling Diane Sawyer on *Good Morning America*, "we're all three very close. Micah's middle name [Amber] is named after all three of us women, it's a mix of our names."[33] When the *Litowitz* case reached the Washington Court of Appeals, both Jennifer and Tammy flew to Tacoma to attend the oral arguments on May 4, 2000, as a show of their support for Becky. "The three women have become fast friends and staunch supporters of Becky's desire to gain control over the embryos," one local reporter noted.[34] After the arguments, Jennifer appeared with Becky on a National Public Radio program, expressing her frustration that the Washington appeals court did not permit her to speak during the session. She voiced her position to reporter Tom Banse, explaining, "I do want Becky to have these children, as they were intended to. They were adopted to Becky. Maybe the contract says 'Becky and David,' but, obviously, David doesn't need any eggs and Becky does."[35]

Jennifer's post-retrieval relationship with Becky hints at another dimension of third-party reproduction — the role of gamete donors and surrogates in the lives of the offspring they help to produce. The records do not reveal whether Jennifer was close to Micah, though Colleen Grady reported that Jennifer and Becky "had a falling out" at some point after the litigation ended and no longer speak. Even if the social relationship did not last, Jennifer's genetic relationship to the family is forever sealed in Micah's genome. As Table 5.1 illustrates (see page 113), *Litowitz* was the first, and remains the only, case to test not just the relationship between donor and recipient, but also to examine the intended parents' relationship to their offspring-in-waiting when only one of them is genetically related to the embryos. This fact was given different weight by each of the three courts to consider the Litowitz divorce case, to which we now turn.

B. The Trial

When solo practitioner Colleen Grady took her seat at counsel's table for the first day of the Litowitz divorce trial on October 21, 1998, Pierce County Superior Court Judge Waldo Stone commended her for taking on the matter, opining that she was "swimming upstream" against her opposing counsel. As a seasoned, but solo, family law attorney, she had agreed to represent Becky in the divorce the prior year, when the matter of the frozen embryos was not in dispute. Her opposing counsel was Bart L. Adams of Adams & Adams, a Tacoma attorney who, according to Ms. Grady, had taken over the case when his father became ill. Also appearing for David was Kathryn J. Nelson, an attorney with Eisenhower & Carlson, a firm with offices in Seattle and Tacoma that traces its roots to President Dwight Eisenhower's older brother Edgar, who founded the firm in 1914. Ms. Nelson later became a judge on that same court, the Pierce County Superior Court.

The trial and its aftermath reflect a common human attribute that is not uncommon in lengthy marital dissolution proceedings — a change of heart or position. The record reflects that while Becky consistently maintained her desire to gestate the remaining embryos in a surrogate,[36] David's position on the embryos' fate changed at various times throughout the proceedings. Before the trial, David was amenable to Becky taking control of the frozen embryos. This is evidenced by a report submitted to the trial court by Steve Downing, appointed to serve as a guardian ad litem for the two embryos on January 9, 1998.[37] In his Report of the Parenting Investigator, Downing said of the spouses' dispositional wishes, "Becky Litowitz would like to be awarded the embryos for their potential future use. David Litowitz did not dispute during my discussions with him regarding the embryos, the award to Becky."[38]

At some point in the ensuing months, David had his first change of heart about the embryos, evidenced by his attorney's opening statement asking the court to "award custody of the frozen preembryos to Petitioner, David Litowitz, who is strongly opposed to bringing those to life."[39] Later in the trial, David's position morphed again as he took the stand for direct examination. When asked what his wishes were, he testified, "Well, at this time I would put them up for adoption. They have a bank there [referring to the frozen storage facility at the Loma Linda Center where the embryos were housed]."[40] According to Ms. Grady, this new position came as a surprise to everyone in the courtroom, including David's own attorney.[41] Still later, David's position changed again, reverting back to his request that the embryos be destroyed.[42]

David Litowitz's hopscotching across the options for embryo disposition is emblematic of the struggle divorcing couples endure when their would-be offspring rest somewhere between conception and implantation. Freezing embryos in liquid nitrogen halts the reproductive process, giving prospective parents a technical time-out to reconsider their procreative goals. The literal freezing of the pregnancy process offers spouses both choices and ethical dilemmas they simply would not face if traditional methods of procreation were employed. If the wife in a soon-to-be divorced couple were pregnant, she alone could decide whether to continue or terminate the pregnancy. Her husband would have no say in the matter, from a procreative rights perspective.[43] But embryos that have yet to reach the dark recesses of the uterus are in a legal limbo, where both spouses seem to have equal say over continuing or suspending the procreative process.

The adage "timing is everything" certainly is apt in the context of frozen embryo disputes. A couple's shared hope and optimism when they agree to freeze surplus embryos can become bitterness and derision over their fused gametes when discord replaces marital bliss. The time between harmony and disharmony need not be long, as a recent case demonstrates. In *Roman v. Roman*, a Texas couple began IVF in March 2002, following five years of a childless marriage.[44] On the day of the egg retrieval, doctors were able to extract thirteen eggs from Mrs. Roman, of which six were fertilized with Mr. Roman's sperm. As is routine, a fresh embryo transfer was scheduled three days later, but the night before the implantation Mr. Roman told his wife he had concerns about the marriage. The next day, Mr. Roman withdrew his consent for the IVF treatment, agreeing only to freeze the three embryos that had developed to the eight-celled stage. Predictably, the *Roman* divorce action focused on the fate of the frozen embryos. The Texas Court of Appeals ordered the embryos destroyed, based on a provision in the Romans' embryo cryopreservation contract providing for discard in the event of divorce.

While the decision in *Roman* will eventually take its place in the line of frozen embryo cases, all of which favor the party wishing to avoid procreation, it is noteworthy as the only case in which the spouse's change of heart came *before* the embryos were frozen. In all of the other cases, including *Litowitz*, the couples went through IVF with fresh embryos, presumably hoping for the best. In the main, embryo disputes come long after the woman has undergone surgical retrieval of eggs, the stage marking the beginning of an assisted reproductive process. But Mrs. Roman's procreative process was cut short while the embryos were continuing to develop in the laboratory. If the Romans were fertile and had intercourse three days before their break-up, any resulting embryo would be within Mrs. Roman's womb and under her exclusive control. But the fortuity of technology relocated the Romans' embryos and repositioned their respective procreative rights. Query whether a woman's inability to conceive within her body should also deprive her of a right enjoyed by her fertile counterparts — the right to control the fate of early embryos destined for her uterus?

In *Litowitz*, it seems that the trial judge, Judge Stone, may have sympathized with the notion that an embryo frozen in time should be given the opportunity to continue along its developmental path. His order, awarding the two embryos to Mr. Litowitz, invoked a legal standard normally reserved for custody disputes involving existing children, the "best interest of the child." In ruling from the bench, Judge Stone told the courtroom that his "decision on the preembryos has very little to do with property, very little to do with constitutional rights, everything to do with the benefit of the child."[45] He ruled as follows:

> This court makes the following decision awarding the preembryos to father in the best interest of the child. If this child is brought into the world here in

Tacoma or Federal Way, Washington the alternatives are not in the child's best interest. In the first alternative the child would be a child of a single parent. That is not in the best interest of a child that could have an opportunity to be brought up by two parents. In the second alternative, the child may have a life of turmoil as the child of divorced parents. Also, both parties here are old enough to be the grandparents of any child, and that is not an ideal circumstance. The court awards the preembryos to Father with orders to use his best efforts for adoption to a two-parent, husband and wife, family outside the State of Washington, considering the egg donor in that, as Father is required.[46]

Judge Stone's views of marriage and parenthood can be gently described as "traditional." In an amicus brief filed with the Supreme Court of Washington, the Northwest Women's Law Center (NWLC) took exception to Judge Stone's characterization of the embryos and the parties. First, the NWLC argued that embryos were not children, despite Judge Stone's repeated references to "the child."[47] Then, the amicus chided the judge for preferring a hypothetical married couple of David's choice to "a single, middle-aged mother raising a child without a father."[48] Judge Stone did little to redeem himself in the matter of nonmarital children. In speaking about the prejudice that children of single women encounter, he opined, "I recognize the stigma isn't the same as it was years ago and we don't refer to them as bastards or anything of that sort, but still, there's a stigma to a child without a father."[49]

On December 11, 1998, Judge Stone issued an order staying the embryo award pending all appeals in the matter. After the trial court handed down its decision, Becky moved for reconsideration, incorporating a written declaration from the egg donor, Jennifer Yocom. Though Mrs. Yocom did not testify at the trial, she did agree to show her support for Becky's position after the fact, submitting an affidavit requesting "[i]n the event that the court fails to award the [preembryos] to [Becky], I insist that the court award the [preembryos] to me or return the eggs to me in accordance with the contract."[50] The trial court denied the motion for reconsideration, but insertion of the egg donor's request for return of the embryos help set the stage for the Court of Appeals decision. As noted earlier, for the first time, a state appellate court was asked to decide the fate of frozen embryos that bore a genetic relation to only one of the intended parents.

C. The Court of Appeals Decision

Nearly two years passed between the day Judge Stone stayed his order awarding the embryos to David and October 17, 2000, when the Court of Appeals of Washington handed down its decision in the case. Both parties used the time to formulate their contrasting legal arguments, but they were united on one point: the appellate court should reject Judge Stone's "best interest of the child" standard for resolving the dispute. Instead, they urged the court to rule on the basis of the legal documents signed in connection with their ART plan. However, each spouse emphasized different documents.

In the main, David Litowitz urged the court to uphold the terms of the IVF contract, signed by the parties on March 25, 1996.[51] By any measure, the contract is not a model of comprehensive drafting because it fails to address the most common condition under which embryo disputes arise: divorce of the intended parents. Instead, the contract contains a general directive to resolve disputes in "a Court of competent jurisdiction."[52] Then, the contract lists four possible "events or dates" that could require advance direction from the parties: death, withdrawal from the program, shuttering of the IVF clinic, and the passage of five years. No mention is made of divorce.

Only one additional provision seems relevant to the parties' circumstances, and it is the one most cited by David. In language giving consent to the program to freeze sperm for purposes of the IVF, David (along with Becky as a signator) agreed: "I agree that the [sperm] specimen can only be used by me for the purpose of artificial insemination, *in vitro* fertilization or assisted reproductive technique involving my lawful spouse."[53] David truly sought to parse the words of the contract, advising the court that since Becky Litowitz was no longer his "lawful spouse" he had effectively withdrawn his consent to proceed with the IVF, and thus he alone was entitled to control the remaining product of his specimen.[54]

Becky parsed the words of a different document: the agreement signed by the couple and the egg donor. Becky argued that the case should be decided strictly according to the terms of the egg donor contract, which disallowed transfer of the donor's eggs to anyone other than the Litowitzes without the consent of the donor. Once Jennifer Yocom provided a post-trial declaration that she favored an award to Becky and opposed adoption out to third parties, the egg donor contract was moved front and center. In a bold move, Colleen Grady argued that the court should rely strictly on the egg donor contract and "should not consider the IVF contract. It is not an agreement which includes all of the necessary parties."[55] In the end, this argument not only failed, it was met with outright hostility by the Court of Appeals.

In briefly addressing Becky's argument that the egg donor retains the right to control the frozen embryos, the court knocked down the claim with two jabs. First, the court observed that the eggs no longer existed, having developed into embryos post-fertilization. Any control the egg donor had over her own gametic material was lost when their genetic identity as single-celled eggs morphed into multi-celled embryos. The donor's attempt to trace the raw ingredient to the higher order product was outside the scope of the court's contemplation. Second, the court scoffed that the donor "is not a party to the Litowitz dissolution" and therefore had no standing to voice her position in the matter.[56]

The appellate court ruled unanimously in David's favor, awarding him the embryos to do with what he wished. While the three-judge panel upheld the core of the trial court's ruling, it abandoned Judge Stone's order that David "use his best efforts for adoption to a two-parent, husband and wife," and rejected his reasoning that such an award was in the best interest of the child. Instead, the appellate court focused on the parties' constitutional rights surrounding procreation, rights which it determined arose only in the context of genetic reproduction. Since Becky did not contribute any gametes to the embryos, the court deemed that "she does not have a constitutional right to procreate."[57] David, as the sperm provider, was "a progenitor and, therefore, he has a constitutional right not to procreate."[58] With this holding, the Washington appellate court reinforced the prevailing common law in the U.S., which uniformly favored procreation avoidance in embryo disputes, as Table 5.1 illustrates.[59]

Colleen Grady described the Court of Appeals decision as "very disappointing," adding that "once someone donates sperm, he should not be able to change his position."[60] In petitioning for review by the state's highest court, Ms. Grady hoped to persuade the justices to give greater weight to the woman's role in this high-tech case of arrested reproduction. In a sense, she asked the court to treat the egg donor and the intended mother as a single entity, represented by Becky Litowitz, whose procreational autonomy rivaled that of the genetic/intended father. When the high court granted review, the female voice was in fact amplified, but the sound it made came as a surprising one and a disappointment to the appellant.

D. The Supreme Court of Washington Decision

The case was argued on the fateful day of September 11, 2001, and the decision was handed down on June 13, 2002. In a ruling that granted neither party's requested disposition, the court took a lead from a different constituency, the NWLC. As amicus curiae, NWLC urged the court to decide the case strictly on the basis of contract law, arguing "no constitutional rights are implicated in this case."[61] The main, and ultimately winning, argument set forth by amicus was that the IVF contract contained an enforceable advance directive from the parties. Though failing to mention the contingency of divorce, the IVF contract did solicit the parties' mutual direction regarding disposition of the embryos "upon the occurrence of any one of the following four (4) events or dates:"

A. The death of the surviving spouse or in the event of our simultaneous death.
B. In the event we mutually withdraw our consent for participation in the cryopreservation program.
C. Our pre-embryos have been maintained in cryopreservation for five (5) years after the initial date of cryopreservation unless the Center agrees, at our request, to extend our participation for an additional period of time.
D. The Center ceases it's [sic] *in vitro* fertilization and cryopreservation program.[62]

The couple indicated that under any of the forgoing, their embryos were to be thawed. In its brief filed August 20, 2001, NWLC argued that the five-year time limit for cryopreservation set forth in subsection C had expired, given that the contract was signed on March 25, 1996. Thus, it urged the court to hold the couple to their signed expression of intent and allow the embryos to be thawed. In an 8-1 decision, the court upheld the NWLC's position, reversing the decision of the Court of Appeals and upholding the terms of the IVF contract limiting the parties' procreative opportunity to five years.[63] Though the court did not specifically order the Loma Linda Center to thaw the embryos, it sanctioned such a result if the embryos still existed, reasoning that the parties themselves had long ago agreed on this eventuality. "Under the five-year termination provision of the cryopreservation contract, the Center is directed by the Litowitzes to thaw the preembryos and not allow them to develop any further."[64]

The court's opinion drew praise from Lisa Stone, executive director of the NWLC. The amicus' emphasis on contract law was also a way of diverting attention from the preeminence of biology in reproductive rights. Ms. Stone told reporters that NWLC "worried that the court would focus on David Litowitz' biological link to the embryos."[65] With contract elevated over genetics, individuals in nontraditional relationships can be more secure in their rights to procreate through assisted conception. "We are delighted because [the court's opinion] does not have a negative impact on infertile people and lesbian and gay couples," Stone said.[66]

Colleen Grady was not expecting the contract-oriented result, and in fact did not even brief the issue of the five-year term because she concluded that filing a lawsuit over the future of the embryos would toll the contractual time period.[67] She expressed her dismay over the court's narrow approach, charging, "[t]hey don't give the citizens of this state any help at all. They sidestepped and avoided the issue. We look to these nine supreme scholars to give us direction, and they dropped the ball."[68] The sole dissenting opinion, authored by Justice Sanders, likewise lamented the court's unwillingness to tackle the merits of the parties' procreative claims. As to the majority's holding, he seethed, "nor has either party even argued for that unimagined result."[69]

Becky Litowitz was mortified by the result and immediately began to consider her legal options. Colleen Grady initially told reporters that her client was considering seeking reconsideration by the Washington court, but no formal motion was ever filed.[70] Instead, Mrs. Litowitz appealed to the U.S. Supreme Court, but certiorari was denied in 2003.[71] About a year after the end of the litigation, Becky explained why she pursued the case to the highest court in the land: "I did it because of my core belief that life begins at conception."[72]

David Litowitz was pleased with the outcome, even though the court reversed the Court of Appeals' order awarding him control over the embryos. Bart Adams, counsel for Mr. Litowitz, called the decision "as good as a victory." He explained, "[t]he primary issue is that he did not want to have more children with Becky Litowitz."[73] By this time, David Litowitz had gained custody of his daughter Micah, with Becky having visitation rights following a modification of the couple's original child custody agreement at the time of the dissolution.[74] A 2007 conversation with Colleen Grady revealed that both David and Becky Litowitz have remarried, but neither had additional children with their new spouses.

As for the disputed embryos, by all accounts they remain in frozen storage in Loma Linda, California. After failing to get relief in the Washington courts, Becky Litowitz turned to a foundation in California that offered to assist in her quest to protect the embryos from destruction. Under a legal settlement, the parties agreed that the embryos could be offered to another patient, whose identity would not be divulged. This result, according to Roland Bainer, attorney for the Loma Linda University Gynecology and Obstetrics Medical Group, "works for all sides. . . . Becky . . . gets the satisfaction of knowing that the embryos have a chance to become human life" and "David Litowitz has that satisfaction, as well as the knowledge he won't be made a parent against his will."[75]

While neither party got the result each originally sought — parenthood for Becky and the right to adopt out for David — neither realized their worst fears. Becky declared that had the embryos been destroyed, she "would have been devastated."[76] David's dogged efforts to keep the frozen material out of Becky's reach is testament to his bottom-line goal to avoid establishing further ties with his ex-wife. Today, according to Ms. Grady, with both Becky and David remarried, they have managed to work out an amicable custody arrangement over their daughter Micah, who is described as a terrific girl.

E. Lessons for Third-Party Reproduction

The travails of David and Becky Litowitz yield at least three important lessons for those brave enough to venture into the world of reproductive technologies. First, beware of unintended consequences when signing IVF contracts. Second, be mindful of the relative weight accorded genetics and intent in assigning procreational rights. Third, understand the distinction between the raw ingredients and the downstream product in assisted conception.

1. Unintended Consequences

The unintended consequences of *Litowitz* are best described by dissenting Justice Sanders, who referred to the high court's decision to enforce an obscure five-year thaw provision in the IVF contract as "that unimagined result."[77] In retrospect, the Washington high court was not the first court, nor will it likely be the last, to interpret the words of an IVF agreement outside the scope of the parties' intentions and expectations.

In Massachusetts, the state high court disregarded seven jointly signed IVF consent forms providing that any disputed embryos be "returned to the wife for implant."[78] Elevating public policy that disfavors forced procreation over contract interpretation, the court addressed the mores of the Commonwealth rather than the expressed intent of the litigating parties. In New York, the Court of Appeals waded through a complex set of consent forms, fixating on a provision that called for donation of disputed embryos to research. Though the wife urged consideration of other equally prominent provisions, the court declared its favored term an unequivocal manifestation of the parties' intent. To this day, the wife begs to differ.[79]

The case law urges ART participants to thoughtfully contemplate their dispositional choices, taking care to select consistent outcomes across a range of possible unforeseen events. Of course, even with an airtight document that truly reflects a meeting of the minds, a court could decide to disregard the IVF agreement for reasons beyond the contemplation of the parties. Placing one's prospective children in frozen—and legal—limbo continues to carry risk all around. While that risk can be reduced, the possibility of unintended consequences remains so long as there are parties to dispute agreements and courts to interpret them.

2. Genetics vs. Intent in ART

The *Litowitz* court treated Becky as a second-class procreator, saying she was "not a progenitor" and therefore any rights she had to the embryos "must be based solely upon contract."[80] Becky's ability to assert procreational rights seemingly was lost when her ovaries and uterus were removed during a long-ago hysterectomy. Her efforts to create the embryos, her intent to parent, and her role in rearing the earlier product of those embryos were disregarded by an assignment of rights based solely on genetics. With her lack of the necessary reproductive parts, Becky joined other women whose recruitment of egg donors and gestational carriers have diminished their procreational autonomy when measured against genetic contributors.

In a California case of switched embryos, a married couple sought parental rights to a baby boy who was the whole blood genetic sibling to their daughter, but born to a different mother. The couple hired an egg donor whose gametes were mixed with the husband's sperm to create a batch of embryos. On the day of transfer to the wife's uterus, three of the couple's embryos were mistakenly transferred to a single woman who was scheduled to receive unrelated donor embryos at the same time. Once the child was born to the single woman and the mishap revealed, the couple declared their mutual paternity, based on their intent to parent any children born of their embryos. While the court acknowledged the husband's paternity arising from his genetic tie to the child, it dismissed any parental claim on the part of the wife. Though the wife intended to parent any children born of the embryos, her lack of a genetic tie translated into a lack of standing to assert parental rights.[81] Like Becky Litowitz, the wife's role in orchestrating the birth of the child was ignored.

The case law and statutory authority governing assignment of parental rights in ART is a jumble of presumptions favoring genetics, gestation, intent, and rearing, depending upon the situation at hand. One lesson from *Litowitz* is that genetics can trump intent in the exercise of ART procreational rights. The Washington court viewed Becky as devoid of procreational rights because she was not a progenitor — a source of gametic material. Imagine the outcome if the Litowitz embryos were created with Becky's eggs and donor sperm. If David objected to Becky's use of the embryos, he should not prevail under a rubric that accords rights strictly on the basis of a genetic tie. Since David would not be considered a progenitor, he would have no procreational rights at stake. Neither his right to engage in procreation, nor his right to avoid it, should be at issue.

Despite the attraction of a bright-line rule that accords procreational rights along genetic lines, we simply do not know how a frozen embryo dispute pitting a procreation-seeking, egg-supplying wife against a procreation-avoiding, non-sperm-supplying husband would be resolved. Would a court favor procreation avoidance as preemptive in all circumstances? To date, every U.S. court to decide a frozen embryo dispute has landed squarely in the procreation avoidance camp.[82] Why is this? Is the desire to avoid creating or expanding families amid marital strife so strong that the law should wedge itself into the technological gap that ART creates between conception and gestation? If Becky were pregnant at the time of dissolution, even with the aid of donor eggs, no judge would order her to abort the coming child. But her lack of a physical and genetic relationship to the embryos made Becky's nonparental status an easy call for all three Washington courts, though each had a different rationale for its ultimate disposition.

Litowitz does not so much resolve the genetics-versus-intent debate as it highlights a pitfall of third-party reproduction. When donor gametes are used, the rights of both the donor and the intended parents get swallowed up in the confusion over the relative weight of each party's contribution. From the perspective of biological development, the parties' rights are fixed and certain at some points, yet vague and undefined at others. For example, once ova are surgically retrieved from an egg donor and mixed with sperm to form embryos, the donor generally loses all dispositional authority over those genetically related embryos. Once pregnancy occurs, the intended mother (or the gestational carrier) is imbued with all the procreational autonomy accorded women who conceive naturally — until fetal viability the pregnant woman alone has the right to decide whether to continue or terminate the pregnancy.[83] At the end of the pregnancy when the child is born, the rights of the egg donor generally are subrogated to the rights of the intended mother in determining parental rights. But in the interim, when embryos remain unimplanted, a rights vacuum appears that has yet to be filled by comprehensive law or policy. *Litowitz* suggests that in the case of frozen embryo disputes, genetics trump intent, perhaps because DNA creates a more tangible, easily measured relationship between progenitor and prospective child. Query, though, whether a single case isn't far too thin a reed on which to rest the myriad ART scenarios that are yet to be undertaken?

3. Raw Ingredients and the Downstream Product

The egg donor in *Litowitz* tried mightily to trace her dispositional rights to the resulting embryos, to no avail. Using a classic property construct, the Washington Supreme Court held that the egg donor had no rights in the embryos because the character of the property was different from that of the eggs. The eggs "were later fertilized by the Respondent's sperm and their character was then changed to preembryos."[84] Any dispositional rights the egg donor had disappeared as her eggs transformed into early embryos.

The court's decision to recognize the embryos as newly created property, without regard for the provenance of the raw materials, is consistent with other cases in which providers of human tissue are denied property rights in any resulting products. The famous case of John Moore, whose surgically excised spleen and other bodily tissues were converted by medical researchers into a potentially lucrative cell line, exemplifies judicial reluctance to trace raw materials beyond their original form. In *Moore v. Regents of the University of California*, the California Supreme Court dismissed Mr. Moore's claims for conversion which, if proven, could have entitled him to share in any profits generated by the new product.[85] Because he "did not expect to retain possession of his cells following their removal" and because "the patented cell line [was] both factually and legally distinct from the cells taken from Moore's body," the court refused to extend any ownership to the source patient.[86]

While the decision in *Moore* may best be understood as a mechanism to preserve and incentivize medical research, its message about the transformation of legal rights through biologic change is clear. When a gamete donor surrenders eggs or sperm with the intent to relinquish parental rights over any resulting children, such relinquishment will likewise apply to any rights over the resulting embryos. Like Mr. Moore, gamete donors do not expect to retain control of their excised gametes, and once fertilized the gametes are "factually and legally distinct" from the source cells. But query whether a nascent human being should be equated with a pharmaceutical or other biotech product?

The downstream product made from somatic cells and tissues will bear little or no resemblance to the raw ingredients used in its development, and its users will have no need to trace the origin of its building blocks. A person, on the other hand, may find many reasons to trace the origin of the sex cells that contributed to his or her genome — hereditary diseases, genetic predispositions to illness, or just plain curiosity, to name a precious few. Dismissing the dispositional authority of a gamete donor in a frozen embryo dispute may prove inconsistent with later rulings that allow the children of third-party ART to seek out their genetic roots. Viewing *Litowitz* not just as an embryo dispute, but as an opportunity to anticipate and begin to address future dilemmas over privacy and genetics, helps highlight the case's import in the burgeoning field of reproductive medicine.

F. Lessons for Stem Cell Research

At first blush, *Litowitz* would appear to have nothing to do with stem cell research. Neither party called for the embryos to be donated to research, as has been requested in prior cases,[87] nor did any of the Washington courts even mention the possibility of such disposition. But the rejection of the egg donor's right to control the secondary disposition of embryos formed with her gametes is highly relevant to the current debate over embryos donated for stem cell research.

Today, a growing handful of states have established institutes for the study of embryonic stem cells, thought to hold promise for the treatment of numerous deadly and disabling diseases.[88] In a nutshell, embryonic stem cells (ESC) are the 30 or so cells that make up the inner cell mass of a five-day old human embryo, known as a blastocyst. The unique aspect of ESC is that they are pluripotent, meaning they have ability to create all of the tissues that make up the human body.[89] In recent years, scientists have discovered ways to extract ESC from the blastocyst and have begun experimenting with ways to prompt these cells to differentiate into various tissues, with the goal of creating transplantable tissues or other therapeutics for use in treating human ailments. Embryos, as the source for ESC, can either be created in the lab specifically for research, or they can be donated by ART patients who have spare embryos resulting from their fertility treatments.

In the states where ESC research is ongoing, lawmakers have begun to grapple with the legal rights of patients who donate their embryos or gametes for research. In California, for example, the California Institute for Regenerative Medicine, the entity which oversees the state's voter-approved ESC initiative, requires that research embryos formed using donor eggs be accompanied by the express consent of the egg donor.[90] This means that couples undergoing ART using donor eggs must procure the donor's written consent for a secondary donation to research at the time of donation, or face the task of tracing the egg donor long after their typically brief and generally anonymous encounter in order to secure her permission to donate spare embryos to research.

ART practitioners and their legal counsel are only now beginning to add language to egg donor contracts which give express permission to donate unused embryos to research. For the roughly half million embryos that are currently in frozen storage in the U.S.,[91] presumably at least some of those were formed using donor eggs. Moreover, a number of these embryos were formed prior to the development of ESC research as a viable destination for spare embryos. The likelihood that intended parents had the foresight to anticipate the possibility of donating their embryos for stem cell research, and obtaining the egg donor's consent for such secondary donation, is quite low. Witness the Litowitz egg donor contract executed in 1996: while the agreement does allocate the authority to dispose of the eggs, at no point does it mention the secondary disposition of any resulting embryos, to research or otherwise.

The Washington ruling that the egg donor has no right to control the secondary disposition of embryos formed for reproductive purposes runs counter to current guidelines on secondary donation to research. For reproductive purposes, egg donors are dismissed from the equation once embryos are formed.

TABLE 5.1. A Catalog of Frozen Embryo Disputes

CASE NAME AND CITATION	FACTS	DISPOSITION
Davis v. Davis, 842 S.W.2d 588 (Tenn. 1992)	No IVF contract in place. W sought donation to a childless couple. H wanted embryos destroyed.	Award to H, based on three-part test. Favor, in order: 1) preferences of progenitors, 2) prior agreements, 3) procreation avoidance.
Nachmani v. Nachmani, CA 2401/95 Nachmani v. Nachmani [1996] IsrSC 50(4) 661	W sought control of embryos to implant in gestational surrogate. H objected to W's proposed use, asked clinic to retain embryos.	Award to W, reasoning once IVF is begun it can only be stopped with consent of both parties. Israeli court found "no value . . . in the absence of parenthood."
Kass v. Kass, 696 N.E.2d 174 (N.Y. 1998)	Complex four-part IVF contract. W sought embryos for implantation. H argued for donation to IVF clinic for research.	Award to research, based on court's interpretation of the contract. "Agreement between progenitors . . . should generally be presumed valid and binding."
A.Z. v. B.Z., 725 N.E.2d 1051 (Mass. 2000)	Seven signed IVF contracts stated that upon separation, embryos would be awarded to wife for implantation. H sought injunction to prevent W from accessing embryos.	Award to H. Public policy disfavors enforcement of agreements that force parenthood on gamete donor.
J.B. v. M.B., 783 A.2d 707 (N.J. 2001)	H sought embryos "to be implanted or donated to another infertile couple" based on religious beliefs. W sought to discard.	For W; ordered embryos destroyed. Court upholds procreation avoidance for W. Since H can father additional children, "party choosing not to become biological parent will prevail."
In re Marriage of Witten, 672 N.W.2d 768 (Iowa 2003)	W sought custody of embryos at divorce trial, agreeing to have H's parental rights to any child terminated. H sought injunction to prevent W's access to embryos.	For H, enjoining use of embryos without joint consent of parties. Court adopts "contemporaneous mutual consent model."

CASE NAME AND CITATION	FACTS	DISPOSITION
Roman v. Roman, 193 S.W. 3d 40 (Tex. App. 2006), *rev. denied* (Tex. Aug. 24, 2007), *cert. denied*, 128 S. Ct. 1662, *reh'g denied*, 128 S. Ct. 2469 (2008)	H withdrew consent for IVF night before scheduled fresh transfer; embryos frozen. Upon divorce, W sought control of embryos for implant, H favored discarding.	For H, allowing discard. Court upholds cryopreservation agreement authorizing discard in event of divorce, as "mutual intention of the parties."

Yet for research purposes, egg donors retain dispositional control over embryos long into the future. If reproductive-minded egg donors understand that they retain no control over any resulting embryos, is it a good idea for dispositional rights to materialize when intended parents have a change of heart about their reproductive needs and decide to donate embryos to research? The answer is no.

Two rationales support a no-tracing policy. First, upon donation, an egg donor's expectation is that she will not be contacted by the parents or by any resulting child. Her services are finite and explicitly exclude future obligations. If properly counseled, egg donors know that intended parents may fulfill their family needs with less than all of the embryos created and may discard spare embryos in the future. The fact that these embryos may meet their demise in a research lab versus an ART lab is not significant enough to justify contacting a long-ago egg donor for consent. Second, the intended parents' expectation with egg donation is that they will be accorded full dispositional authority over the resulting embryos. For gamete donation to work for family formation, intended parents must feel secure that once embryos are formed, they step into the shoes of any genetic contributors for purposes of parenting the resulting embryos. To feel secure in their parental rights, at some point in the procreative process ART participants must receive equal treatment to fertile parents whose reproductive rights are firmly established.

G. Conclusion

The *Litowitz* case offers lessons to contemporary ART participants that may help prevent similar disputes in the future. Comprehensive contract drafting, coupled with an appreciation for the preemption of genetics over intent when couples engage in third-party reproduction, can shape more realistic expectations on the part of prospective parents. In the end, neither Becky nor David obtained their desired results, which leads one to wonder whether the four-year court battle was worth the financial and emotional toll it wreaked on both parties. In her most recent statement to the press, Becky revealed that she spent $1 million on the fight.[92] Just knowing that the embryos were not destroyed may have made it the best seven figures she ever spent.

ENDNOTES

1. Litowitz v. Litowitz, 48 P.3d 261 (Wash. 2002).

2. The term ART refers to the medical techniques used to achieve pregnancy other than through sexual intercourse. This definition of ART is broader than that adopted by prominent authorities such as the Centers for Disease Control and Prevention (CDC), which produces an annual report on the use and success of certain reproductive technologies. The CDC report defines ART as "all fertility treatments in which both egg and sperm are handled. In general ART procedures involve surgically removing eggs from a woman's ovaries, combining them with sperm in the laboratory, and returning them to the woman's body or donating them to another woman. They do NOT include treatments in which only the sperm are handled (i.e., intrauterine — artificial — insemination) or procedures in which a woman takes drugs only to stimulate egg production without the intention of having eggs retrieved." CDC, U.S. Dep't of Health and Human Services, 2005 Assisted Reprod. Tech. Success Rates: Nat'l Summary and Fertility Clinic Reports, 3 (Oct. 2007). The CDC's definition of ART, derived from the 1992 Fertility Clinic Success Rate and Certification Act, 42 U.S.C. 263a-1 (mandating that fertility clinics report pregnancy data to the CDC), is more narrow than the one adopted herein. The broader definition includes techniques such as artificial insemination and intrauterine insemination, which do not involve the mixing of both male and female gametes. While the federal and CDC definitions of ART have been adopted for purposes of mandatory clinic reporting, the broader definition enjoys support among law and policymakers. See, e.g., Assisted Reprod. Tech.: Analysis and Recommendations for Public Policy, The New York State Task Force on Life and the Law 1 (1998).

3. Four cases had been decided by state high courts, Davis v. Davis, 842 S.W.2d 588 (Tenn. 1992); Kass v. Kass, 696 N.E.2d 174 (N.Y. 1998); A.Z. v. B.Z., 725 N.E.2d 1051 (Mass. 2000); and J.B. v. M.B., 783 A.2d 707 (N.J. 2001). A fifth case was heard at the trial court level in April 2002, according to the later appellate decision in In re Marriage of Witten, 672 N.W.2d 768 (Iowa 2003). For a description of every reported frozen embryo case through 2007, see Table 5.1.

4. In vitro fertilization (IVF) is a medical technique in which embryos are created outside the body by placing the female's egg and the male's sperm in a laboratory Petri dish. The goal of IVF is to treat infertility by assisting fertilization of the egg in the laboratory. Once the sperm fertilizes the egg, the resulting embryo is nurtured in the lab for several days and then transferred into a woman's uterus where it will, hopefully, implant and develop until birth. See generally Peter R. Brinsden, A Textbook of In Vitro Fertilization and Assisted Reproduction (1999).

5. The world's first "test tube" baby, Louise Brown, was born outside London on July 25, 1978. See Peter Gwynne, All About That Baby, Newsweek, Aug. 7, 1978, at 66.

6. According to the CDC, which tracks and reports on the use of IVF and other reproductive technologies in which egg and sperm are mixed in the laboratory (collectively referred to as ART), in 2002 there were 45,751 babies born in the U.S. as a result of ART, comprising approximately 1% of the total U.S. birthrate. See CDC, U.S. Dep't of Health and Human Services, 2002 Assisted Reprod. Tech. Success Rates: Nat'l Summary and Fertility Clinic Reports 11 (Dec. 2004).

7. Some of the details described herein were obtained via telephone interviews with two of the attorneys who worked on the case: Colleen Grady, attorney for Becky Litowitz, and Patricia Novotny, attorney for the Northwest Women's Law Center as Amicus Curiae. Telephone Interview with Colleen Grady, Law Offices of Colleen Allen Grady (Aug. 14, 2007); Telephone Interview with Patricia Novotny, Adjunct Professor, University of Washington School of Law (Sept. 21, 2007).

8. The 2002 Census Bureau fixes the U.S. divorce rate at 50%. See Divorce Reform Page, Divorce Rates, available at http://www.divorcereform.org/rates.html (last visited Feb. 20, 2008).

9. The American Society for Reproductive Medicine (ASRM) indicates that infertility affects about ten percent of the reproductive-age population in the United States (about 6.1 million people). See ASRM Frequently Asked Questions About Infertility, available at http://www.asrm.org/Patients/faqs.html (last visited Feb. 20, 2008).

10. According to the CDC, the use of ART has seen a steady increase. The number of IVF cycles nearly doubled during the period between 1996 and 2004, jumping from 65,000 in 1996 to 128,000 in 2004, while live births also increased from 21,000 in 1996 to nearly 50,000 in 2004. See CDC, 2004 Assisted Reprod. Tech. Success Rates: Nat'l Summary and Fertility Clinic Reports 57 (Dec. 2006).

11. David is described as a "wealthy Federal Way property developer." See Court Orders Embryos in Dispute Be Destroyed, Seattle Post-Intelligencer, June 14, 2002, at B8. In her brief to the Court of Appeals, Becky Litowitz averred that her ex-husband had an annual income in excess of $600,000. Reply Brief of Appellant at 21, Litowitz v. Litowitz, 48 P.3d 261 (Wash. 2002) (No. 70413-9), 1999 WL 33955016.

12. David adopted Becky's children after the couple married. According to Colleen Grady, as of August 2007, Lucas was a member of the U.S. Armed Services, deployed to Iraq.

13. Mr. Litowitz's brief describes the decision to have a fourth child as a way "to bring their marriage closer together." Brief of Respondent at 8, *Litowitz*, 48 P.3d 261 (No. 70413-9), 1999 WL 33955015.

14. Wash. Rev. Code §26.26.230 (West 2007). The law further declared that any "surrogate parenting contract entered into for compensation, whether executed in the state of Washington or in another jurisdiction, shall be void and unenforceable in the state of Washington as contrary to public policy. *Id.* §26.26.240.

15. According to the CDC, as of 2004 California housed 54 of the nation's 411 ART clinics. *See* CDC, 2004 Assisted Reprod. Tech. (ART) Reports: Fertility Clinic Rep. by State: State Clinic Lists, *available at* http://apps.nccd.cdc.gov/ART2004/clinlist04.asp?State=CA (last visited Feb. 20, 2008).

16. 851 P.2d 776, 783 (Cal. 1993).

17. Now known as the Center for Surrogate Parenting & Egg Donation, the agency advertises that as of April 1996, the time the Litowitz egg donation contract was signed, the Center had "celebrated 456 births with the help of a surrogate mother." *See* Featured Surrogacy Resource: The Center for Surrogate Parenting and Egg Donation, Inc., *available at* http://www.surrogacy.com/agencies/csp/(last visited Feb. 21, 2008).

18. Much ado is paid in the popular press to the amount of money paid to egg donors, typically women in their twenties, whose need for cash is reported to exceed their exercise of judgment when signing on the dotted line. Stories of $50,000, even $100,000 eggs have been reported, though none of those reports have ever been verified. Proven donors, those whose past donations have resulted in the birth of a healthy child, do earn a premium and can garner around $15,000, but the average amount paid to an egg donor hovers around $5,000. *See* Sharon N. Covington & William Gibbons, *What Is Happening to the Price of Eggs?*, 87 Fertility & Sterility 1001 (2007) (reporting the national average for donor compensation in 2006 was $4,217).

19. *See* Judith Daar, Reproductive Technologies and the Law 201-205 (2006) (reprinting sperm donors' answers to questions about their motivations for donating, ranging from "I want to help others" to "I am donating to make money").

20. Reply Brief of Appellant, *supra* note 11, at 4. Selective reduction, or multifetal pregnancy reduction, refers to a medical procedure used to reduce twin, triplet or higher order multiple pregnancies with the purpose of improving the outcome for the remaining fetuses. The procedure is generally performed between the 9th and 12th weeks of gestation and commonly involves the insertion of a needle guided by ultrasound through the abdominal wall, followed by the injection of potassium chloride into the thorax of a fetus to stop its heart. *See* Nanette Elster, *Less is More: The Risks of Multiple Births*, 74 Fertility & Sterility 617 (2000).

21. David Litowitz filed for divorce on January 16, 1997. Alex Fryer, *Which Comes First: Family or the Eggs?*, Seattle Times, May 5, 2000, at B1.

22. Answer to Brief of Northwest Women's Law Center as *Amicus Curiae* app. at 5, *Litowitz*, 48 P.3d 261 (No. 70413-9), 2001 WL 34801593 (emphasis in original).

23. Telephone Interview with Steve Masler, CEO of The Donor Source (Aug. 16, 2007).

24. Telephone Interview with Steven Lazarus, a Los Angeles area attorney specializing in ART and adoption law (Aug. 16, 2007). Mr. Lazarus explains, "when the intended parents have an objection to the requested encumbrance, they usually do not need to choose another donor; rather the donor often reconsiders the demand or a compromise is reached."

25. *See* Jo Ann Zuniga, *Fertile Grounds for Disputes*, Hous. Chron., June 1, 2002, at A33. According to the suit, the reason the ART physician suggested the McBrides use the donor's eggs was because the Does didn't have the money to complete the transaction. If the couples split the cost of the donor cycle and then divided up the eggs, both couple's interests would be met. Of course, the egg donor knew nothing of this arrangement at the time, according to her complaint. *See* Teri Sforza, *Bankrupt Egg-Donor Registry Says Fertility Doctors May Have Transferred Eggs Without Permission*, Orange County Register, July 22, 2007.

26. Zuniga, *supra* note 25.

27. Sforza, *supra* note 25.

28. The current known record for conception and birth using frozen sperm is 21 years, reported in 2004. *See* Jenny Hope, *21 Today: Baby's Amazing Journey From Father's Sperm In the 1970s*, Daily Telegraph, May 26, 2004, at 11.

29. *See* Amy Harmon, *Sperm Donor Father Ends His Anonymity*, N.Y. Times, Feb. 14, 2007, at A15 (describing how "one of the sperm bank's most requested donors," six feet tall and blue-eyed, has located at least seven offspring so far).

30. Egg donors are typically recruited in one of two ways — by egg donor agencies such as the Center for Surrogate Parenting in *Litowitz*, or by ART Clinics (physician practices specializing in reproductive medicine) who recruit women to supply eggs to infertile patients. According to Steve Masler, CEO of The Donor Source, around 75% of all ART practices have their own egg donor

recruitment program, but an almost equal percentage will look to outside agencies for donors. These figures are explained by the fact that donor agencies generally have much larger pools of available donors. An ART practice may not be able to provide a patient with her preferred donor from its own database, and thus will have to turn to an agency for additional donor options.

31. *See Orange County Woman Makes History by Giving Birth to the Nation's First Frozen Egg/Frozen Sperm Baby*, Biotech Week, April 25, 2007.

32. According to the CEO of a Southern California egg donor agency, "The Donor Source has NO matches wherein the Donor and the [intended parents (IP)] exchange contact information. There are a few selected cases where an in person meeting of the IP and donor is arranged, but without exchange of contact information. This may be the case for say 5% or less of our matches (we do about 250 matches per year)." E-mail from Steve Masler, CEO of The Donor Source (Aug. 16, 2007) (on file with author).

33. The name, Amber, is taken from T<u>am</u>my, <u>Be</u>cky, and Jennif<u>er</u>. *Becky Litowitz and Lori Andrews Discuss Legal Battle Over Frozen Embryo*, Good Morning America (ABC television broadcast May 10, 2000) (transcript on file with author).

34. Fryer, *supra* note 21.

35. *Legal Battle Between a Divorced Couple to Gain Custody of Two Frozen Embryos* (National Public Radio, May 13, 2000) (on file with author).

36. Colleen Grady attributes Becky's position on the fate of the embryos partly to her religious beliefs. Ms. Grady describes Becky as "a very religious person" who would not have signed a contract authorizing the embryos to be destroyed under any circumstances.

37. Litowitz v. Litowitz, 48 P.3d 261, 265 (Wash. 2002).

38. Reply Brief of Appellant, *supra* note 11, at 1.

39. *Id.*

40. Corrected Opening Brief of Appellant at 2, *Litowitz*, 48 P.3d 261 (No. 70413-9), 1999 WL 33955014.

41. Reply Brief of Appellant, *supra* note 11, at 2.

42. Answer to Brief of Northwest Women's Law Center as *Amicus Curiae*, *supra* note 22, at 11-12 (arguing that contract law, public policy and constitutional principles call for "the preembryos to be thawed and not allowed to develop").

43. *See* Planned Parenthood of Central Missouri v. Danforth, 428 U.S. 52 (1976) (striking down a spousal consent provision in a state abortion law, giving the woman sole authority to decide the fate of her pregnancy); *accord* Planned Parenthood v. Casey, 505 U.S. 833 (1992) (striking down a spousal notification provision in a state abortion law).

44. Roman v. Roman, 193 S.W. 3d 40 (Tex. App. 2006), *rev. denied* (Tex., Aug. 24, 2007), *cert. denied*, 128 S. Ct. 1662, *reh'g denied*, 128 S. Ct. 2469 (2008).

45. Litowitz v. Litowitz, 10 P.3d 1086, 1089 (Wash. Ct. App. 2000) (quoting trial court opinion).

46. 48 P.3d 261, 264 (Wash. 2002) (quoting trial court opinion).

47. Brief of Northwest Women's Law Center as *Amicus Curiae* at 2, *Litowitz*, 48 P.3d 261 (No. 70413-9), 2001 WL 34801593. The Supreme Court of Washington agreed with this critique, noting that Judge Stone's "characterization of frozen embryos as children is of dubious legal or scientific correctness." 48 P.3d at 264.

48. Brief of Northwest Women's Law Center as *Amicus Curiae*, *supra* note 47, at 2.

49. *Id.* In her brief to the Court of Appeals, Becky Litowitz also remarks on Judge Stone's commentary about the modern family, charging his "decision was based on an outdated value system including age, gender and single parent biases." Reply Brief of Appellant, *supra* note 11, at 18. Interestingly, and perhaps ironically, it may be that Mrs. Litowitz had her own outdated value system. In Judge Stone's original ruling from the bench, he awarded the embryos to Mr. Litowitz "to use his absolute best effort for adoption to a two-person family outside of the state of Washington." In her written objections to the wording of the judge's order, Mrs. Litowitz revealed her concern that "adoption to a two-person family" left open the possibility of adoption by persons in same sex relationships, not married heterosexual couples." Brief of Respondent, *supra* note 13, at 7. Apparently Judge Stone shared this concern, as his modified order referred to adoption by a husband and wife.

50. 10 P.3d at 1090.

51. "The IVF contract" actually refers to two separate documents, "Consent and Authorization for Pre-embryo Cryopreservation (Freezing) Following *In Vitro* Fertilization" and "Agreement and Consent for Cryogenic Preservation (Short Term)." *See* Answer to Brief of Northwest Women's Law Center as *Amicus Curiae*, *supra* note 22, app. at 1, 12, 17.

52. *Id.*

53. *Id.* at 17.

54. Mrs. Litowitz labels this argument "misleading" because "it was always the intent of the Litowitz's that a surrogate be used to create children and at no time in the process was the availability of Mr. Litowitz's 'lawful wife' as the recipient of his sperm contemplated by the parties." Reply Brief of Appellant, *supra* note 11, at 9.

55. *Id.* at 7.

56. Litowitz v. Litowitz, 10 P.3d 1086, 1093 (Wash. Ct. App. 2000).

57. *Id.* at 1092.

58. *Id.* In a concurring opinion, Justice Bridgewater emphasized that the decision should be based on the right to procreate, and not the right to parent. "I would decide this case based solely on the genetic connection to the husband and his fundamental right to reproductive autonomy." *Id.* at 1094.

59. The Washington appellate court relied on four prior cases in reaching its decision, all of which awarded frozen embryos to the spouse wishing to avoid procreation. Though the reasoning in each case varied, the results were the same. See Table 5.1 for a description of the case law.

60. Telephone Interview with Colleen Grady, *supra* note 7.

61. Brief of Northwest Women's Law Center as *Amicus Curiae*, *supra* note 47, at 10.

62. Answer to Brief of Northwest Women's Law Center as *Amicus Curiae*, *supra* note 22, app. at 14.

63. "We base our decision in this case solely upon the contractual rights of the parties under the preembryo cryopreservation contract with the Loma Linda Center for Fertility and In Vitro Fertilization dated March 25, 1996." 48 P.3d at 271.

64. *Id.* at 269.

65. *See* Paul Queary, *Court Decides Frozen Embryos Should Be Destroyed*, Columbian (Vancouver, WA), June 14, 2002, at 2.

66. *Id.*

67. In the sole dissenting opinion, Justice Sanders agreed with this view: "That by today more than five years has passed since the cryopreservation commenced is irrelevant because the judicial action which provided for the disposition of the preembryos was commenced well within the five-year window thereby tolling the contracted period of limitations." 48 P.3d at 273.

68. *See* Carol M. Ostrom, *Court: Destroy Frozen Embryos; State's Justices Base Ruling on Contract*, Seattle Times, June 14, 2002, at A1.

69. 48 P.3d at 274.

70. *See* Ostrom, *supra* note 68.

71. Litowitz v. Litowitz, 537 U.S. 1191 (2003).

72. *See* Cathy Kightlinger, *Couples Fight Over Custody of Embryos*, Indianapolis Star, July 11, 2004, at 1A.

73. *See* Queary, *supra* note 65.

74. *See* Reply Memorandum in Support of Motion to Allow Additional Evidence on Review at 3, *Litowitz*, 48 P.3d 261 (No. 70413-9).

75. Kightlinger, *supra* note 72.

76. *Id.*

77. Litowitz v. Litowitz, 48 P.3d 261, 274 (Wash. 2002).

78. A.Z. v. B.Z., 725 N.E.2d 1051 (Mass. 2000).

79. Kass v. Kass, 696 N.E.2d 174 (N.Y. 1998).

80. 48 P.3d at 267.

81. Robert B. v. Susan B., 109 Cal. App. 4th 1109 (2003).

82. *See* Daar, *supra* note 19, at 599-666 (reprinting and discussing reported frozen embryo cases).

83. *See* Planned Parenthood v. Casey, 505 U.S. 833 (1992).

84. 48 P.3d at 269.

85. 793 P.2d 479 (Cal. 1990).

86. *Id.* at 489, 492.

87. *See, e.g.,* Kass v. Kass, 696 N.E.2d 174 (N.Y. 1998) (husband argued for embryos to be donated to research).

88. California became the first state to enact, through popular initiative, a statewide institute for regenerative medicine. Proposition 71, passed by voters in November 2004, provides for $3 billion in general issue bonds over ten years to fund stem cell research. Other states with state-sponsored stem cell programs include Connecticut, Illinois, Massachusetts, Maryland, and New Jersey. See Russell Korobkin, Stem Cell Century 54-55 (2007).

89. *Id.* at 8.

90. The California Institute for Regenerative Medicine's Medical and Ethical Standards Regulations provide that when embryos are donated for research, "If the procurement of oocytes involves

a donor providing oocytes for another woman's reproductive use, then the donation to research must be expressly permitted by the original donor." Cal. Code Regs. tit. 17, §100095(b)(4) (2007).

91. It is estimated that 400,000 embryos are currently housed in sub-zero facilities in the United States alone. *See* Rick Weiss, *400,000 Human Embryos Frozen in U.S.: Number at Fertility Clinics Is Far Greater Than Previous Estimates, Survey Finds*, Wash. Post, May 8, 2003, at A10.

92. Kightlinger, *supra* note 72.

Part IV

ORGAN TRANSPLANTS, MEDICAL FUTILITY, AND PRESUMED CONSENT

Chapter 6

IN RE T.A.C.P.

and

IN THE MATTER OF BABY K.

Anencephaly and Slippery Slopes

MARY CROSSLEY*

A. Introduction

Unlike most of the other chapters in this volume, this chapter tells the story of two cases. These two cases share neither a single legal issue or doctrine, nor a particular individual. Instead, the common element in the cases is a medical condition. Because of this medical condition, the individual by whose name each of these cases is known expressed no opinion about the litigation she was involved in. Indeed, in each case, the litigation revolved around the legal status and protections accorded to a baby girl who never experienced any consciousness.

The medical condition that makes *In re T.A.C.P.* and *In the matter of Baby K.* a natural pairing is anencephaly. This condition is defined as "a congenital absence of a major portion of the brain, skull, and scalp" that begins developing during the first month of pregnancy.[1] Infants born with anencephaly have a brain stem, but no functioning cerebral cortex. As a result, although their brain stems regulate some neurological functions such as breathing and feeding, anencephalic infants are permanently unconscious and are unable to see, hear, or experience their environments in any way. The appearance of an infant with anencephaly is striking because large portions of its skull and scalp are absent, leaving exposed a mass of nerve tissue.** Prenatal screening, including non-invasive procedures such as ultrasounds, can detect anencephaly. Detection is most often followed by termination of the pregnancy, although the parents in both of these cases elected not to terminate. Anencephaly is relatively rare, with a recent estimate indicating that only 3 of every 10,000 births involve an infant

* Mary Crossley is Dean and Professor of Law at the University of Pittsburgh School of Law.
** For a photograph of an anencephalilc infant, see the supplemental website accompanying this book, available at www.aspenlawschool.com/johnsonkrause.

with anencephaly. Most infants born with anencephaly survive no more than several days.

It is perhaps the very extreme nature of anencephaly that caused these two cases — which presented different legal issues — to capture the public's attention during a two-year period of time in the early 1990s. In each case, the commonplace occurrence of a pregnancy filled with hope and expectation turned into a remarkable public drama revolving around the responses of the parents, doctors, and the law to the birth of a hopelessly incomplete infant. Parents in the two cases responded to their private tragedies by seeking medical interventions that pushed the proverbial envelope in two very different directions. While the parents in *In re T.A.C.P.* sought a judicial declaration that their baby was dead, notwithstanding her breathing, beating heart, and functioning brain stem, the mother in *Baby K.* sought aggressive medical intervention to prolong her daughter's life. Despite this obvious difference, these cases share the capacity to illustrate vividly how the medical profession, the legal system, and the public mind have struggled to define the limits of parents' medical decisionmaking and of appropriate medical treatment.

B. "Little Angel": Teresa Ann Campo Pearson

When Laura Campo and Justin Pearson learned in 1991 that Laura was pregnant, nothing suggested that the birth of their child would rivet the public's attention.[2] Laura had been a waitress for a number of years at The Feed Bag restaurant in Coral Springs, Florida, and Justin was an asphalt worker. They already had two healthy preschoolers, and Laura also had a thirteen-year-old son from a previous marriage. But in the eighth month of pregnancy, an ultrasound revealed that the fetus Laura was carrying had anencephaly.

Although they were counseled about the condition's incompatibility with life and the advisability of terminating the pregnancy, Justin and Laura decided to carry the pregnancy to term so that after the doomed infant was delivered, its organs could be removed and donated to other children or infants awaiting life-saving organ transplants. Their hope was to make something life-affirming flow from their sorrow. At one point after their infant was born, Laura stated, "There was no possible chance for my baby at all, but there were other babies out there who could have lived from her organs. It seems senseless to have five babies die when four could live."[3] Motivated by this desire, Laura even chose to deliver the baby by Caesarean section so that its organs would be less likely to be damaged during birth.

And so, on Saturday, March 21, 1992, four-pound Teresa Ann Campo Pearson was born at Broward General Medical Center near Fort Lauderdale. Her physical presentation confirmed the prenatal diagnosis of anencephaly, but by the day after her birth she was breathing without medical support. Laura and Justin quickly learned of a major roadblock in their quest to have Teresa Ann's healthy organs transplanted to needy recipients. As long as the infant was breathing and had a heartbeat, doctors feared that the removal of organs would be the legal cause of her death and thus would be considered murder. Laura and Justin responded by going to court and requesting a ruling that their infant, because of her anencephaly, was already legally dead. So began an intensely emotional and widely followed legal odyssey that continued past their daughter's short life.

Their legal advocate in seeking this ruling was perhaps an unlikely candidate for the job. Walter G. "Skip" Campbell was an attorney who had attended Catholic seminary for a number of years before going to college and later law school at the University of Florida. Advocating for a position that would be attacked vigorously by pro-life groups, Campbell's decision to take the case on a pro bono basis was strongly influenced by the infant's physical appearance, which convinced him that the parents were doing the right thing. In an interview conducted during the litigation, Campbell explained, "I know, you look at the pictures and see a child. But there is no skull. Remove the gauze cap, and you look right into the brain stem. The child feels nothing, and we want the court to recognize that."[4]

An anencephalic infant

The parents sought a judicial ruling that their daughter was legally dead, filing a petition with the Circuit Court of Broward County, but Judge Estella Moriarty rejected their request on Thursday — just five days after their daughter's birth. Although the judge identified a Florida statute relating to the determination of death for persons on life support as the basis for her order, her ruling from the bench at the end of a "tearful hearing with the parents" captured the judge's fundamental unease with the prospect of defining away the legal protection of Teresa Ann's life for the benefit of others: "I can't authorize someone to take your baby's life, however short, however unsatisfactory, to save another child."[5]

With this ruling, the media began to cover the story of Campo and Pearson's efforts to secure legal authority for the removal of their daughter's organs for transplantation before it was too late for those organs to benefit potential recipients. While local papers covered the story, so too did national outlets like the *New York Times, USA Today,* and the *Los Angeles Times.* The media reports included interviews with medical experts and medical ethicists not only on the immediate legal issue in the case — whether the baby could be declared legally dead for purposes of organ retrieval while her heart and lungs were still working — but also on the nature of anencephaly and the broader implications of the case's outcome. As the story attracted national and international attention, strangers started leaving donations at The Feed Bag to support the parents' efforts. Laura and Justin received supportive cards and letters from as far away as Italy.

But while the parents were being encouraged by strangers who sympathized with their efforts to produce something good from their daughter's terrible condition, the courts continued to rebuff their efforts to obtain legal sanction for their plan. Immediately after Judge Moriarty's ruling, Laura and Justin requested an emergency order from the Fourth Circuit Court of Appeal in West Palm Beach to overturn the ruling. A three-judge panel of that court denied the parents' request without comment on Friday, and later that day Campbell filed an appeal with the Florida Supreme Court. At that point, the baby was still breathing independently, which according to Campbell the parents interpreted as a sign that God wanted the infant to last until her organs could be used. In language that betrays the irony of describing the baby's struggle to stay alive long enough to be declared legally dead, Campbell told one reporter on Friday, "Physicians this morning said for some reason this baby, this body is just fighting.

The parents think it's a sign from God that this baby is going to be around until this thing is decided ultimately."[6] Over the weekend, though, the infant's condition deteriorated, and by Sunday she was on a ventilator in critical condition. On Monday morning, the Florida Supreme Court rejected an appeal for an emergency hearing, and at 3:45 that afternoon nine-day-old Teresa Ann Campo Pearson died after her lungs failed. At that point, doctors believed that her organs had deteriorated to the point that they could no longer be transplanted. She was buried under a headstone that read "Little Angel."

With Teresa Ann's death, Justin and Laura failed in their quest to have her short existence provide a lifeline to other gravely ill children. Despite that failure, they continued the legal effort to obtain a judicial declaration that because of her anencephaly their daughter should have been considered legally dead. They pursued their appeal to the Florida Supreme Court, but in an opinion issued by the Court on November 12, 1992,[7] their arguments met with no greater success than in the lower courts.

After reviewing medical descriptions of anencephaly and noting that the Court was addressing a question of first impression regarding the legal status of anencephalic infants, the Court examined Florida law regarding the definition of death. Although the Court found no authority showing that Florida courts previously had adopted as a matter of common law the traditional cardiopulmonary definition of death (which defines death as occurring when all circulatory or respiratory function ceases irreversibly), the Court accepted that definition as part of the state's common law. That traditional definition was supplemented by a Florida statute allowing, in cases when a patient's breathing or circulation is artificially supported, a determination of death when the entire brain has irreversibly ceased functioning.[8] Consequently, the Court found that Florida law effectively mirrored the approach embodied in the Uniform Definition of Death Act (UDDA), a model staute issued by the Conference of Commissioners on Uniform State Laws, a law reform body that provide states with model legislation to clarify important areas of the law. The UDDA provides that an individual is dead if he has sustained either "irreversible cessation of circulatory and respiratory functions, or . . . irreversible cessation of all functions of the entire brain, including the brain stem."[9] Thus, under existing Florida law, because Teresa Ann's brain stem functioned, she was not legally dead until her breathing and heartbeat ceased irreversibly on March 30.

The real question advanced by Campo and Pearson, though, was whether the law *should* include an additional approach to defining death, one unique to anencephalic infants. To address that question, the Court considered whether some public necessity or fundamental right would be served by recognition of a common law standard defining anencephalic infants as dead. While commending the parents for their altruism, the Court characterized the questions regarding anencephalic infants' legal status and their use as sources of transplantable organs as generating controversy rather than consensus. The Court found the medical community divided on both the utility and the ethics of retrieving organs from anencephalic infants and pointed to legal and constitutional concerns regarding the proposed practice. Given the "utter lack of consensus" on the question, the Court declined to create a new common law definition of death for infants with anencephaly.[10] The Court thus found that as long as Teresa Ann was breathing and her heart was beating, she was not dead under Florida law and the retrieval of her organs would not have been legal.

C. The Background for an "Utter Lack of Consensus"

As told so far, the story of Laura Campo and Justin Pearson's mission to have their daughter's organs retrieved for transplantation may appear to be nothing more than the story of two people seeking to draw meaning from a senseless loss. Taken in context, though, their story represents a chapter in an ongoing debate about which humans are morally entitled to the protections that flow from personhood. Questions about the medical, ethical, and legal suitability of anencephalic infants as sources of organs arose more than two decades before Teresa Ann's birth and erupted into a national controversy in the late 1980s.[11]

The broader backdrop to that controversy was provided by advances in medicine during the 1980s that made organ transplantation an increasingly viable response to organ failure in both adults and children. But as transplantation became a more successful therapy, demand outstripped the available supply of transplantable organs. Indeed, the development of the UDDA in the early 1980s, cited by the Florida Supreme Court in *In re T.A.C.P.*, sought in part to clarify the point at which organs legally could be retrieved from individuals whose respiratory and circulatory functions were being artificially maintained following a devastating injury. The "whole brain death" approach embodied in the UDDA permitted the retrieval of organs from someone whose brain had ceased to function, without requiring that the person's respiration and circulation cease. Harvesting organs while respiration and circulation continue means that the organs do not deteriorate, which lessens the chances of a successful transplant.

Because children engage less frequently in the types of activities that produce traumatic injuries resulting in brain death, the shortage of pediatric organs became particularly acute. Many children died each year while waiting for an organ. In that situation, transplant specialists considered using organs from anencephalic infants for transplantation into infants and children. The stumbling block, of course, was the question of how soon after the delivery of an anencephalic infant could surgeons, legally and ethically, retrieve the organs. As a pair of reporters described the scenario when *In re T.A.C.P.* was in the news, "Because anencephalic babies have perfect organs and are on the brink of death, doctors have been tempted to have rules bent so the organs can be retrieved while healthy."[12]

Experiments using organs from anencephalic infants began as early as 1963. In 1967, the first unsuccessful attempt at human heart transplantation in the U.S. used a heart from an anencephalic infant.[13] Then in 1987 a successful heart transplant generated widespread media coverage and sparked a public debate on the topic. Surgeons at Loma Linda University Medical Center removed the heart from a Canadian baby, "Baby Gabrielle," and transplanted it into "Baby Paul," a newborn with hypoplastic left heart syndrome.[14] The surgeons maximized the chances of a successful transplant by placing Baby Gabrielle on a respirator shortly after birth until her brain stem ceased functioning a few days later, at which point she was legally dead and her heart could be removed for transplantation.

It was not only the success of this transplantation, but also the protocols subsequently adopted at Loma Linda that generated attention and concern. These protocols involved placing anencephalic infants on respiratory support either at birth or once they developed respiratory difficulty and maintaining the support for some limited period of time until brain death occurred, allowing for organ retrieval. Ultimately these protocols produced no additional successful transplantations and were suspended less than a year later. Furthermore, the protocols raised concerns in the medical community and public about the morality of artificially sustaining anencephalic infants to keep their organs healthy and of blurring the boundary between life and death to increase the number of transplantable organs. Coinciding with an early attempt at fetal tissue transplants in Mexico, the Loma Linda protocols prompted *Time* magazine to ask, "Should laws defining death be rewritten to allow the 'harvesting' of anencephalic donors? Should their existence be prolonged solely to enable doctors to take their organs?"[15]

By 1990, Dr. Robert Truog, a leading medical ethicist and pediatric anesthesiologist, characterized "[t]he use of anencephalic newborns as sources of transplantable organs" as "one of the most debated issues in contemporary medical ethics . . . attract[ing] a wide audience and appear[ing] prominently in newspapers as well as in medical and ethical journals." Proponents focused on anencephalic infants' absolute lack of cognitive ability and short life span as distinguishing them from other potential sources of organs. Such characteristics justified a frankly instrumentalist approach to advancing the welfare of patients needing transplants. These proponents advocated several different approaches to surmounting the legal obstacles to retrieving organs, ranging from proposals to:

  - redefine "death" to include anencephalic infants (the approach pursued by the parents in *In re T.A.C.P.*);
  - recognize "brain absence" as an alternative to "brain death" that would carry the same medical and legal implications; and
  - create an exception to the "dead donor rule" (which states that organs can be retrieved only once a donor is legally dead) solely for anencephalic infants so that organs could be retrieved from living infants.[16]

Indeed, the year before the Loma Linda transplant, a law was proposed in California that would have amended the state's definition of death to provide that an individual born with anencephaly is legally dead.[17]

Other voices argued against any change in the law or medical protocols to accommodate a desire to increase the transplantable organs available from anencephalic infants.[18] Critics tended to emphasize the Kantian ethical principle that an individual should never be treated simply as a means to another's ends. They asserted that making an exception to this rule for anencephalic infants might make it seem acceptable to use persons with other conditions impairing their cognitive abilities and shortening their life spans to lesser degrees in similar ways. Thus, groups concerned with the rights of persons with disabilities objected to any move that would erase legal protections based on the extreme disability of anencephaly. These groups pointed to reports that physicians from around the country had contacted Loma Linda seeking to enroll newborns with less severe cognitive disabilities in the organ-preservation protocol. Opponents also noted that any benefit from such a morally perilous change would be insignificant, given the small number of infants born each year with anencephaly and the lack of consistent success in transplanting their organs.

Against this background, the unfolding of the personal and legal drama involving Teresa Ann appears not simply as a personal tragedy that inexplicably turned into a court case, but as a logical — if emotionally laden — next step in testing the permeability of the "dead donor rule." Any woman who learns in the eighth month of a pregnancy that the baby she is carrying will either be stillborn or die shortly after birth inevitably asks "Why?" Laura Campo and Justin Pearson found some answer to that question in the hope that other children could live longer, fuller lives as a consequence of their baby's terrible malformation. And if it took going to court to produce that meaning, they felt compelled to do so.

The expert reactions in the media to the parents' decision to push for a judicial determination that their daughter was dead simply rehashed points made the decade before. The medical ethicists and advocates quoted in the major media outlets covering the story had ample practice addressing this issue. As a result, the public heard well-rehearsed refrains. These ranged from those distancing anencephalic infants from the rest of humanity (noting that because of the similarity between human brain stems and fish brain stems, Teresa Ann "has more in common with a fish than a person"[19]), to those warning of a slippery slope ("Are we going to use some people, because they have severe disabilities, as a means to save lives that we think are worth saving?"[20]). The focus of this story, though, was the grief-stricken but determined parents pushing ahead to benefit other people's children. Who could help but admire their fortitude in seeking some kind of silver lining to the situation? And what kind of law would stymie such good intentions? As described below, notwithstanding the parents' failure to persuade the Florida courts, *In re T.A.C.P.* provided significant momentum for one final push towards the acceptance of retrieving organs from anencephalic infants. But before that push occurred, the public would hear the story of another baby born with anencephaly who became the center of a legal battle.

D. Futility Emerges

At the same time that the public was hearing about the moral and legal issues associated with retrieving organs from anencephalic infants, another debate was brewing less publicly within the medical community — a debate that would be thrust into the public forum by the case of another infant with anencephaly. This debate was over the meaning and implications of medical futility — that is, care that provides no benefit to the patient. In brief, articles in the medical literature in the late 1980s began questioning whether physicians had an ethical or legal obligation to provide treatment requested by a patient or a patient's family if the physician believed that care to be futile.[21] In the preceding decades, patient autonomy eclipsed physician beneficence and paternalism as the predominant ethical principle in medicine. As a result, questions increasingly arose over whether doctors were obligated simply to do the bidding of empowered, autonomous patients, or whether some principle acted as a check on patient autonomy, permitting physicians to refuse to provide care they believed to be medically inappropriate because it conferred no benefit on the patient.

The debate in the medical and bioethical literature concerned both the definition of futile care (i.e., on what basis might a particular treatment legitimately be deemed futile) and the extent to which futility served to excuse physicians from complying with a patient's request for the treatment. Concerns of varying types found their way into the debate. Some physicians objected to having to provide care they deemed futile, viewing the obligation as an intrusion on their professional autonomy or an inappropriate and potentially even harmful use of their expertise. Other proponents of recognizing futility highlighted the sense-lessness of diverting expensive medical resources to pointless ends, while those more deontologically inclined pointed out that the futile application of medical technology could rob a patient of the dignity of a natural death. Underlying the futility debate was a more fundamental question about the goals of medicine, and whether physicians were rightfully the sole arbiters of those goals or whether patients might demand treatment to advance goals that might be non-medical in nature. Family, for example, might demand life support in order to extend a terminally ill patient's life briefly to permit her to witness an important family event. Another concern was the potential that allowing refusals to treat on futility grounds would effectively permit rationing of care based on physicians' subjective valuations of patients' quality of life.

E. Every Breath You Take: Stephanie Keene

Almost exactly a month before the Florida Supreme Court issued its opinion in *In re T.A.C.P.*, another baby was born with anencephaly, this time at Fairfax Hospital in Falls Church, Virginia.[22] In some ways this infant's story was similar to that of Teresa Ann Campo Pearson. The infant's mother, Contrenia Harrell, received a diagnosis of anencephaly during her pregnancy and, as a result, was counseled regarding the advisability of terminating the pregnancy. She rejected this counsel, though, and decided to continue the pregnancy. At this point, the stories diverge and the differences seem to overwhelm the common thread of anencephaly binding the two stories together.

When the diagnosis of anencephaly disrupted her pregnancy, Contrenia Harrell, a cafeteria worker, had already recently faced emotional and spiritual challenges. She was pregnant without being married, and her relationship with the father, Stephen Keene, was not strong. Indeed, it would not survive the story that unfolded. A year earlier her nine-year-old child had died at Fairfax Hospital following a car accident, and she still grieved that loss deeply. After she lost one child, it is perhaps not surprising that she wanted to play no role in losing a second. Instead, she relied on her religious faith and looked to God for a possible miracle. She refused to terminate her pregnancy and instead sought aggressive treatment for her infant.

When the baby girl was born on October 13, 1992, she experienced diffi-culty breathing. In accordance with their discussions with Contrenia prior to the delivery, doctors at Fairfax Hospital intubated the newborn, whom Contrenia named Stephanie, and placed her on a mechanical ventilator. This type of life support was typically not provided to anencephalic newborns, for whom the medical standard of care was to provide only comfort care. Still, the doctors took the step both to confirm the diagnosis of anencephaly and in hopes that the visual impact of the anencephaly would lead the mother to reconsider her insistence on aggressive treatment.

Those hopes were not realized. Despite physicians' attempts at persuasion, Contrenia continued her efforts to extend her child's life. Physicians recom-mended that a "do not resuscitate" order be entered for Stephanie so that the next time she had trouble breathing, she would be allowed simply to die. They explained that infants with anencephaly inevitably die soon after birth and that providing further aggressive forms of life support would serve no purpose in helping the infant's condition. Contrenia disagreed. The hospital explored the possibility of transferring the baby to another hospital nearby, but could not find one providing pediatric intensive care that was willing to accept the transfer.

Unable to penetrate Contrenia's determination to provide her daughter with maximal care, physicians requested a consultation with the hospital's ethics committee, which consults with and advises health care providers, patients, and their families when they face an ethical dilemma. When Stephanie was ten days old, her mother met with a subcommittee made up of a family practitioner, a psychiatrist, and a minister. Apparently, this meeting did nothing to resolve the impasse. Committee members attempted to persuade Contrenia that her daughter's hopeless condition could not be improved through aggressive life support, yet apparently failed to give serious consideration to her viewpoint and how it might be accommodated in a way acceptable to the physicians. As a result the mother's resolve remained unbending, and the ethics committee recommended that the hospital pursue legal action to resolve the impasse between mother and doctors regarding the infant's care.

In the meantime, Stephanie's condition stabilized, and she regained — for a time — the ability to breathe without assistance. Her vital physical functions controlled by her brain stem — heart rate, blood pressure, liver function, digestion, and kidney and bladder functions — were all normal. When she was a month old, doctors at the hospital inserted a gastrostomy tube through which she received nutrition and hydration. Although doctors argued that they should not be required to provide aggressive resuscitation, the Child Abuse Amendments of 1984, a federal law passed to protect disabled infants, required the provision of nutrition and hydration.[23]

At this point, in contrast to the media coverage of Teresa Ann Campo Pearson's brief life, the conflict between Contrenia and Fairfax Hospital remained largely private; but Birthright, an organization protecting disabled infants, somehow heard about it and reached out to Contrenia. The group put her in touch with the state's Department for Rights of Virginians with Disabilities (DRVD), which sent lawyers to warn the hospital about potential violations of antidiscrimination and child neglect laws if it refused to provide the treatment sought. Hoping to avoid negative legal consequences, the hospital transferred Stephanie to a nearby nursing home at the end of November, a transfer her mother agreed to only on the condition that the hospital would readmit Stephanie if she developed breathing problems again.

Those problems developed again in January. By this time, Stephanie — at three months old — was one of the longest surviving infants with anencephaly in medical history. Her readmission to Fairfax Hospital set in motion the legal action styled *In the matter of Baby K.* Seeking to avoid the repetition of a cycle of readmissions for mechanical breathing support, the hospital filed suit in federal district court in Alexandria, Virginia, seeking a declaratory judgment reflecting the court's determination that its refusal to readmit Stephanie despite her mother's request would not violate five specific federal and state laws discussed below. The hospital named Stephanie and her parents as defendants.

Initially, DRVD represented both Contrenia and her daughter in responding to the lawsuit, but then the hospital successfully petitioned to have the state's attorneys disqualified on conflict of interest grounds, since Contrenia's interests and those of her daughter might diverge in the matter. As a result, attorneys from the firm of Covington & Burling stepped in to represent Contrenia, and the court appointed a guardian ad litem to represent Stephanie. Stephen Keene, who supported the hospital's position that the baby should not receive further aggressive interventions, had his own lawyer. The court also entered a protective order maintaining the privacy of the parties' identities and the medical information at issue, thereby permitting the case to continue under the radar of public attention until the district court released its opinion.

In its lawsuit, the hospital sought to cover all of its legal bases. It requested the court to rule that its refusal to grant Contrenia's demand for future readmissions and mechanical ventilation would not violate the Emergency Medical Treatment and Active Labor Act (EMTALA), the Rehabilitation Act of 1973 (Rehabilitation Act), the Americans with Disabilities Act (ADA), the Child Abuse Amendments of 1984, or the Virginia Medical Malpractice Act.[24] Although the case proceeded on an expedited basis, it moved at nothing like the pace at which *In re T.A.C.P.* had moved to trial the previous year. The parties prepared their cases and engaged expert witnesses prior to the two-day trial before the federal district court judge, Claude Hilton.

At the trial, both of Stephanie's parents and her treating physicians testified. In addition, the guardian ad litem testified that he agreed with the physicians' position to deny further treatment on ethical grounds. Each side also presented an expert witness on the medical ethics issues in the case, hoping that an understanding of the ethical complexity of the dispute between Contrenia and the hospital would inform the judge's interpretation of the statutes at issue. Dr. John C. Fletcher, a professor of biomedical ethics at the University of Virginia's medical school, testified for the hospital. He explained his opinion that requiring the hospital to provide treatment that its treating professionals believed was futile and medically and ethically inappropriate would violate the doctors' and nurses' professional integrity, which entailed a right to refuse to provide futile treatment. Fletcher also testified that repeatedly placing Stephanie on a mechanical ventilator was excessive and was in fact harming her through the recurring infliction of invasive but pointless treatment.[25]

In response, Robert M. Veatch, director of the Kennedy Institute of Ethics at Georgetown University, testified as an ethics expert on behalf of the mother.[26] As with Fletcher's testimony, Veatch's opinion was informed by his own writing on the subject of medical futility. Fundamentally, he asserted that no moral principle justified the physicians' judgment overriding the mother's wishes regarding her daughter's treatment. More specifically, he disputed that physicians had an ethical right to refuse treatment that they deemed futile on a normative, rather than physiological, basis. In short, although the physicians might as a normative matter believe that repeated resuscitations had no point because they simply prolonged a non-cognitive and hopelessly doomed life, that belief did not permit them to refuse to provide the resuscitation, which was physiologically successful in extending a life that Contrenia highly valued.

In the meantime, while the litigation was pending, Stephanie was weaned from the ventilator, transferred back to the nursing home, returned to the hospital for ventilator support when she again developed difficulty breathing, and again transferred back to the nursing home. During her readmission to the hospital in March, physicians (with Contrenia's consent) surgically inserted a breathing tube in Stephanie's trachea in order to facilitate her breathing. During this period, as throughout Stephanie's life, Contrenia visited her daughter every day. She continued to believe that God might work a miracle by healing her daughter's incomplete brain and that it was up to God, and not her or the doctors, to decide when her baby should die.

While it was not the precise miracle that she prayed for, Contrenia received good news on July 1, 1993, when Stephanie was nearly eight months old. On that day, Judge Hilton decided that the hospital was legally obligated under EMTALA, the Rehabilitation Act, and the ADA to provide Stephanie the requested ventilator treatment.[27] The court found that EMTALA, which requires hospitals receiving Medicare payments to provide stabilizing treatment to an individual who comes to their emergency room with an emergency medical condition, would require the hospital to provide ventilator support to Stephanie if she were brought to the hospital suffering respiratory distress. In addition to rejecting the hospital's contention that EMTALA should be read not to require the provision of futile treatment, the court emphasized that it did not view the ventilator as futile in relieving Stephanie's respiratory distress, which the court considered to be the emergency condition bringing Stephanie to the hospital. Focusing on the slippery slope, the court highlighted the potential implications of the hospital's position for treatment of other patients under EMTALA: "To hold otherwise would allow hospitals to deny emergency treatment to numerous classes of patients, such as accident victims who have terminal cancer or AIDS, on the grounds that they eventually will die anyway from those diseases and that emergency care for them would therefore be 'futile.'"[28]

The court's discussion of the applicability of the Rehabilitation Act and the ADA, both of which prohibit discrimination on the basis of disability, was brief. With each, the court found that the hospital's refusal to provide emergency ventilator support to an infant with anencephaly, when it regularly provided such support to other infants suffering breathing difficulty, would violate the statute's antidiscrimination mandates. Addressing an issue that the hospital had not pled in its complaint, the court also cited the constitutionally protected right of parents (absent abuse or neglect) to bring up their children as they see fit as encompassing Contrenia's decision to continue seeking life-prolonging care for her baby. The court noted the "relative noninvolvement" of Stephanie's father in finding her mother to be the appropriate decisionmaker.

The hospital appealed the district court's decision to the United States Court of Appeals for the Fourth Circuit, but met with no more success there. Interpreting the statute's language literally, two of the judges on the Fourth Circuit three-judge panel found that EMTALA's requirement that hospitals provide stabilizing treatment for emergency medical conditions was not bounded by implicit exceptions for treatments deemed futile or beyond accepted standards of medical care.[29] The majority's opinion, written by Judge William W. Wilkins, explicitly distanced itself from any attempt to address the moral and ethical issues the case posed and instead contented itself to interpret the plain language of EMTALA. By contrast, Senior Circuit Judge James M. Sprouse, who dissented, could not bring himself to apply a statute designed to keep hospitals from "dumping" uninsured emergency room patients to "the sensitive decision-making process between family and physicians at the bedside of a helpless and terminally ill patient under the circumstances of this case."[30] Thus, he would have found no EMTALA violation if the hospital failed to provide further respiratory support for Stephanie.

As in *In re T.A.C.P.*, the litigation over Stephanie Keene's fate generated substantial media coverage once it became public. The decisions of the district court and of the Fourth Circuit triggered stories in major newspapers, including the *New York Times* and *USA Today*, and a column by nationally syndicated columnist Ellen Goodman.[31] Once again, Americans heard a story about doctors and parents disputing how to respond to the birth of a baby with an extreme condition with which most Americans had no familiarity. Once again, much of the coverage consisted of sound bites from physicians or medical ethicists reacting to the court decisions, and many of these reactions were critical. Reverend John J. Paris, a professor of bioethics at Boston College, stated that "for a judge to insist on a treatment that is contrary to all established standards of care is to destroy medicine as a profession and turn physicians into servants of the fantasies of families."[32] Arthur Caplan, a regular commentator on cases involving bioethical issues (and a key figure in another story in this volume, the death of Jesse Gelsinger), called the Fourth Circuit's reasoning "simply nuts. . . . Even on a bad day, Congress would not try to compel doctors to use all of their skills in hopeless causes."[33]

One aspect of the case that the hospital had sought to downplay for public relations purposes was the cost of the care that Stephanie was receiving. Yet much of the media's coverage focused on this very point, linking rapidly mounting health care costs to the apparent inability to contain families' voracious appetites for medical technology. (One commentator estimated that the hospital and nursing home care provided to Stephanie amounted to approximately $300,000.[34]) Although neither court treated resource issues as germane to its analysis, since the hospital had stipulated that a lack of resources had nothing to do with its proposed denial of care, newspapers rapidly made the connection. For some experts consulted by journalists, the ability to control costs was at the heart of the debate over medical futility. Linda Greenhouse wrote in the *New York Times* that hospital administrators and medical ethicists had "little hope for holding down health care costs if family members have a legal right to insist on treatments that doctors consider inappropriate."[35]

Performing what proved to be its own exercise in futility, the hospital requested first that the Fourth Circuit panel rehear the case, then that the Fourth Circuit rehear the case en banc, and finally — with the support of several national medical groups — that the U.S. Supreme Court hear the case. Each of these attempts at further review of the case was unsuccessful.

Meanwhile, despite the doctors who sought to block her efforts and the commentators who could not fathom her desire to prolong the existence of an infant they viewed as already lifeless, Contrenia continued to visit her unconscious daughter at the nursing home every day. When Stephanie turned two (less than two weeks after the Supreme Court denied the hospital's petition for review), her mother threw a birthday party for the child who for two years had seen and heard nothing, had thought nothing, and had never made a conscious movement. She said, "Some thought she would die in a few hours, a few days, a few months. God's proven them wrong."[36] Like other mothers, Contrenia carried photos of her daughter dressed in classic little girl clothing — lacy dresses and black patent leather shoes — along with the less typical colorful hats to hide the fact that the little girl had no skull. (According to one doctor, she had been looking for an orthopedic surgeon willing to build a skull to cover the brainless head.[37]) Contrenia expressed a conviction that her daughter "will eventually grow up and play like other children."

On April 2, 1995, Stephanie Keene's life ended where it started, at Fairfax Hospital. She died there of cardiac arrest, notwithstanding resuscitation efforts by physicians.

F. Post Mortems

One of the challenges in reading *In re T.A.C.P.* and *In the matter of Baby K.* is to remember — as the courts analyze the law's application to anencephalic infants — that the infants' parents are the real players in these dramas, the ones trying to push the envelope. Once the reader shifts her focus to the parents, the challenge then lies in resisting the temptation to understand the parents as caricatures, whether that means seeing Teresa Ann's parents purely as noble altruists and Stephanie's mother as deluded, or seeing Justin Pearson and Laura Campo as would-be instrumentalist killers and Contrenia Harrell as an exemplar of unconditional parental love. It is worth avoiding this temptation, though, for on some level the choices made by the parents in both cases — while far from typical — are understandable, respectable, and even predictable.

The typical reaction of parents who discover through prenatal diagnosis that a fetus has anencephaly is to terminate the pregnancy. If the pregnancy is carried to term, many of the resulting births will be stillbirths. And when an anencephalic infant is born alive, almost all parents will follow the advice of their physicians and simply provide warmth, nutrition, and hydration for the short time until the infant dies.

So how do we understand what was going on in the minds and hearts of the parents in these two cases? Justin Pearson and Laura Campo's efforts do appear as an altruistic attempt to snatch life for other children from the jaws of their baby's death, especially given the widespread media coverage of the shortage of transplantable pediatric organs and the possible use of anencephalic infants to address that shortage. Their efforts equally suggest an attempt to find for themselves a sense of meaning and source of comfort for their own loss. While not typical, they were not alone in desiring to donate organs from their infant. News stories also portrayed other parents with little patience for the "academic mumbo jumbo" of slippery slope concerns in light of the potential that their child's too-short life might be given some meaning.[38]

But what about Contrenia Harrell? How should we view a woman who demands that doctors provide aggressive care that they believe inappropriate in order to maintain the functioning of an infant who medical science says has no hope of ever having a sentient life or human relationships? One explanation begins with religious beliefs regarding the sanctity of life and concludes that life-prolonging medical care is mandatory. This reasoning is consistent with Contrenia's explanation that God should determine the time of her baby's death. (As Arthur Caplan pointed out in an editorial, however, arguably it was federal court judges who decided when her daughter would die.[39]) Parental bonding also may have played a powerful role. The fact that medical science would view that bonding as deluded, if not pitiful, does not change the experience of a woman who holds in her arms an infant who opens her eyes, as if looking about. Is it really so hard to believe that Contrenia simply, if irrationally, loved this infant, even though Stephanie never responded to her, and could not bear the thought that doctors were telling her Stephanie should die? Some readers may find it quite difficult to comprehend Contrenia's decision, but her choices display how difficult it can be to reconcile human emotion and religious faith with the rationalism that is deeply ingrained in medical and legal professional cultures.

So on one level, both these cases are the stories of parents driven by common human emotions in an uncommon situation. But these stories about parents do raise important legal and ethical questions about how far parents should be empowered to go in making medical decisions for their children. As the district court in *Baby K.* recognized, government intrusion on a mother's medical decision for her baby implicates constitutionally protected family privacy and parental autonomy. And even in cases where a private actor tries to compel or deny medical treatment over a parent's objection, legal and ethical principles generally find that the "stranger's" wishes must yield to the parents.

Both cases challenged that general principle. The Florida Supreme Court effectively found that parental autonomy did not extend to a decision to take vital organs from one living child to be used for the benefit of another. Fairfax Hospital and its physicians tried, but failed, to convince the federal courts that parental autonomy (and federal statutes that served to support the exercise of that autonomy) did not extend to compelling physicians to provide care they thought was futile and unethical. In probing the limits of parental autonomy regarding medical decisions, these cases revisited questions that a decade before had captured the public's attention in the "Baby Doe" case,[40] in which an infant with Down syndrome died after its parents refused to authorize surgery that would have saved his life. The Baby Doe controversy elicited widespread public condemnation and resulted in federal responses to limit parental autonomy. The federal government first sought to prohibit discrimination against disabled newborns by regulation. The courts struck down these regulations because antidiscrimination laws did not apply to private, family decisions; therefore, the administrative record evidenced no need for the regulation. The federal government then cast selective nontreatment of disabled infants as a form of medical neglect permitting state intervention into family privacy.

Of course, applying the label of "family privacy" to *T.A.C.P.* and *Baby K.* may seem ludicrous in light of the extensive attention both cases received from the press. One might wonder: Why did these private, family tragedies become so terribly public? Neither case established an important new way of viewing an issue or otherwise served as broadly influential precedent. It seems counterintuitive that a condition as rare as anencephaly should capture the public's attention so thoroughly. Did they touch on some raw nerve in the collective psyche or illuminate a rift in public sentiment? The next section offers a few suggestions about why we still care about these cases.

G. Postludes to the Cases

First, a brief examination of the subsequent unfolding of the bioethical issues on which these cases centered (using anencephalic infants as organ sources and medical futility) suggests that one might view *T.A.C.P.* and *Baby K.* — despite their many differences — as having in common something deeper than anencephaly and a challenge to parental autonomy. While in the public eye, each case offered the possibility that the law might provide a vehicle for advancing and establishing positions advocated by some in the medical and bioethical communities. The passage of time has shown, however, that no position pushed in these cases has been clearly accepted by the law.

1. Organs from Anencephalic Infants

Immediately after Teresa Ann's death, a representative of the major organ transplantation organization in the United States, the United Network for Organ Sharing (UNOS), indicated that it would not pursue the cause of allowing organ retrieval from living anencephalic infants. The group reasoned that the number of transplantable organs at stake did not warrant taking on the significant moral and legal barriers to retrieval that existed.[41] Within just a few years, though, the American Medical Association's (AMA's) Council on Ethical and Judicial Affairs (Council) issued an opinion finding it ethically acceptable to retrieve organs for transplant from an anencephalic infant prior to its death, as long as the parents consented to the retrieval and certain other safeguards were followed.[42] This opinion, which was issued in June 1994 (just months after the Fourth Circuit rebuffed Fairfax Hospital's attempts to refuse life-sustaining care to Stephanie Keene), represented a change in position by the Council, which previously had concluded that organs could not be removed ethically from an anencephalic newborn until death.

The Council justified this shift in part by asserting the controversial claim that a majority of medical and ethical experts on the issue had concluded that pre-death organ retrieval was "intrinsically moral." A year later, in May 1995, the Council published a report explaining its reasoning in hopes of developing a public consensus — and spurring legal reform — about letting parents choose to donate organs before their anencephalic newborn died. Rather than smoothing the way towards consensus, the report provoked strong reactions from many quarters and thus resurrected the controversy surrounding the question. One major paper characterized the Council as wading into "an ethical minefield that blurs the distinction between life and death . . . revealing no more consensus today than a decade ago when the issue was first debated."[43] The negative reaction from within the medical profession was so strong that, half a year later, the Council "temporarily suspended" the opinion approving pre-death removal of organs from anencephalic newborns.[44] Although the purpose of the "temporary" suspension was to give researchers time to study anencephalic infants' brain function to assess whether they hold any potential for developing consciousness, the Council has not subsequently returned to the question.

The policies of most transplant centers mirrored this retreat. By 1996, as a result of the controversy over using organs from anencephalic newborns and in recognition of the limited supply of high quality organs, only one hospital in the United States would accept anencephalic infants as potential sources for organs, and then only under very limited conditions.[45]

Underlying the moral issues surrounding the use of anencephalic infants as organ donors is a pragmatic question: Will any retreat from the established "dead donor rule"[46] corrode the public's trust that the lives of extremely ill or disabled individuals will not be prematurely sacrificed to save others? If this occurs, any resulting increase in the number of retrievable organs may be more than offset by a diminished willingness to sign donor cards. Although debates continue in the medical and ethical literature about the wisdom of maintaining the "dead donor rule," news accounts of allegedly over-anxious transplant surgeons seeking to hasten the deaths of organ donors continue to stir public fears and in one case prompted criminal charges.[47] Proponents of organ retrieval from anencephalic infants asserted that those infants' position was unique, but members of the public may not have been prepared to draw those distinctions. More than fifteen years after Teresa Ann Campo Pearson died, it seems that her parents' efforts to persuade lawmakers to permit organ retrieval from anencephalic infants have produced no fruit.

2. Checking the Provision of Futile Care

When the federal courts in *Baby K.* cited EMTALA in rejecting Fairfax Hospital's request to refuse to provide care based on medical futility, some commentators proclaimed the sky would fall.[48] Notwithstanding dire predictions that emergency departments would find themselves defenseless against the demands of the families of comatose patients for extraordinary life-prolonging care, other more pressing issues facing emergency departments have crowded out this concern. Nor have discussions about medical futility and physicians' ability to refuse to provide care deemed futile loomed large in the medical literature in recent years. Although disputes have occasionally generated news stories and even litigation, they have produced no clear-cut answer to the question of whether patients, or their families, legally can compel care that providers object to as futile.

Admittedly, a number of states have passed statutes empowering physicians to refuse to provide requested care that the physician believes would provide no significant benefit to the patient.[49] Physicians may be reluctant, however, to assert that right for fear of lawsuits. Instead, a means for addressing futility disputes has unfolded at the institutional level. In 1997, the AMA recommended that hospitals develop futility policies that would permit the ending of aggressive life-extending measures deemed futile by physicians, and today most hospitals have some kind of futility policy. Although the policies vary widely, they typically incorporate extensive procedures, including second opinions and the involvement of ethics and interdisciplinary panels. These processes are all aimed at increasing communication to produce a resolution to the patient-provider dispute.[50] Perhaps having learned from *Baby K.* that the courts are not reliable champions of physician autonomy, hospitals and physicians today may be more inclined to balance physician integrity against patient autonomy through a mediated dialogue.

3. People with Disabilities and Slippery Slopes

Lurking behind both of the issues just discussed are concerns about medical treatment decisions for persons with disabilities. Both the parents' efforts to donate organs in *T.A.C.P.* and the hospital's and physicians' attempts to deny treatment on futility grounds in *Baby K.* sought to value the existence of an anencephalic infant differently from other human existence. The parents of Teresa Ann Campo Pearson argued to the Florida courts that, with only a brain stem to regulate her nervous system, her existence should be deemed the legal equivalent of death. The physicians at Fairfax Hospital argued to the federal courts that a medical intervention that prolonged Stephanie Keene's existence was pointless, or futile.

In each case, proponents of judicial action focused on the inability of the anencephalic infant ever to experience conscious life, along with the infant's projected short life span. Those who backed organ retrieval or the physicians' right to withhold treatment emphasized that anencephaly, by the very extremity of its impact, should not even be understood as a disability. As one commentator put it, Stephanie was not disabled, but should instead be considered "unabled."[51] Advocates for people with disabilities did not find persuasive these attempts to completely distinguish anencephalic infants from the broader universe of people with disabilities. These advocates instead highlighted the dangerously slippery slope that society would step onto if it accepted on quality-of-life grounds the sacrifice of one individual for another, or permitted physicians to refuse treatment to sustain a life that the physicians deemed of no value.[52]

The district court in *Baby K.* found that the physicians' refusal to provide ventilator treatment to Stephanie would constitute disability discrimination in violation of federal statutes. Curiously, though, the Fourth Circuit's opinion, while affirming the district court's EMTALA holding, did not address the disability discrimination claim. Although the judges did not explain this omission (other than to state that a duty to treat under EMTALA rendered resolution of the disability discrimination claim unnecessary), perhaps they sought to avoid the question because they recognized just how tricky it was.[53] What does a prohibition of disability discrimination mean in this context, when a physician recommends what medical treatment an individual with a disability should receive? The idea of a "disability-blind" (and thus nondiscriminatory) medical treatment decision may be inconsistent with both the patient's best medical interests and professional standards of practice. But saying that physicians can freely take a patient's disability into account may also permit stereotypes to influence medical judgments and devalue the lives of persons with disabilities. This conundrum remains unresolved.

H. Conclusion

More than fifteen years have passed since the births of two anencephalic infants gave rise to separate lawsuits that briefly captured the nation's attention. In those cases, proponents for two different causes sought to obtain judicial resolutions of deeply divisive medical and ethical questions — about how to define death for organ retrieval purposes and the limits on physicians' obligations to provide requested treatment. As this chapter shows, neither case produced the hoped-for resolution. Indeed, the broader debates underlying these two cases still smolder and, on occasion, are fanned again into flames, as the *Schiavo* case (described in Chapter 3 of this volume) illustrates. Apparently, the common threads that appeared in *In re T.A.C.P.* and *In the matter of Baby K.* — our uncertainty about the moral and legal significance attached to the functioning of our minds and bodies and our difficulty in conceptualizing the moral and legal status of beings with whose existence we are entirely incapable of empathizing — remain very much a part of our communal fabric.

ENDNOTES

1. The information in this paragraph comes from The Medical Task Force on Anencephaly, *The Infant with Anencephaly*, 322 New Eng. J. Med. 669 (1990).

2. Except as otherwise indicated, the facts in the following section are drawn from the Florida Supreme Court's opinion, In re T.A.C.P., 609 So. 2d 588 (1992); Cindy Schreuder, *AMA Takes Walk in an Ethical Minefield*, Chi. Trib., May 28, 1995, at 1; Gina Kolata, *Baby's Low Brain Function Raises Ethical, Legal Issues*, Albany Times Union, Apr. 5, 1992, at B6; *Baby Without Viable Brain Dies, But Legal Struggle Will Continue*, N.Y. Times, Mar. 31, 1992, at A14; E. Clary, *Courts Deny Donation of Live Infant's Organs*, L.A. Times, Mar. 28, 1992, at 1; Linda Kanamine, *A Tiny Heart Blurs Life, Death; Brainless Tot's Fate in Court*, USA Today, Mar. 30, 1992, at 3A.

3. Schreuder, *supra* note 2.

4. Clary, *supra* note 2.

5. *Id.*

6. Reena Shah & Barbara Hijek, *Redefining the Line Between Life and Death*, St. Petersburg Times, Mar. 28, 1992, at 1A.

7. In re T.A.C.P., 609 So. 2d 588 (1992).

8. Fla. Stat. §382.009(4) (1987).

9. Unif. Determination of Death Act §1, 12 U.L.A. 340 (Supp. 1991).

10. 609 So. 2d at 595.

11. Except as otherwise indicated, the discussion in this section is drawn from Robert D. Truog, *Anencephalic Newborns: A Source of Transplantable Organs?*, 5 J. Intensive Care Med. 82 (1990), and J. C. Wilke & Dave Andrusko, *Personhood Redux*, Hastings Center Rep., Oct./Nov. 1988, at 30.

12. Shah & Hijek, *supra* note 6.

13. The discussion in this and the following paragraph is drawn largely from Truog, *supra* note 11.

14. This successful transplantation was not the first time that Loma Linda had made the news for what one commentator called "creative alternative approaches." In 1984, surgeons there transplanted a baboon heart into a newborn suffering from a congenital heart problem, an ultimately unsuccessful effort immortalized by singer Paul Simon's reference to "the baby with the baboon heart" in his song *The Boy in the Bubble*.

15. Christine Gorman, *A Balancing Act of Life and Death: New Uses of Fetuses and Brain-Absent Babies Trouble Doctors*, Time (Feb. 1, 1988) at 49.

16. Truog, *supra* note 11; Wilke & Andrusko, *supra* note 11.

17. Truog, *supra* note 11, at 84.

18. See, e.g., Wilke & Andrusko, *supra* note 11; Larry R. Churchill & Rosa Lynn B. Pinkus, *The Use of Anencephalic Organs: Historical and Ethical Dimensions*, 68 Milbank Q. 147 (1990).

19. Sabra Chartrand, *Legal Definition of Death is Questioned in Florida Infant Case*, N.Y. Times, Mar. 29, 1992, at 112 (quoting Dr. Robert J. Levine, a professor of medical ethics at Yale University).

20. Shah & Hijek, *supra* note 6 (quoting Burke Balch, state legislative director of the National Right to Life Committee).

21. The discussion of medical futility that follows is drawn from Mary Crossley, *Medical Futility and Disability Discrimination*, 81 Iowa L. Rev. 179 (1995).

22. Except as otherwise indicated, the facts in the following section are drawn from the district court's findings of fact, In the matter of Baby K., 832 F. Supp. 1022 (E.D. Va. 1993); Ellen J. Flannery, *One Advocate's Viewpoint: Conflicts and Tensions in the Baby K Case*, 23 J. L. Med. & Ethics 7 (1995); John C. Fletcher, *Bioethics in a Legal Forum: Confessions of an "Expert" Witness*, 22 J. Med. & Phil. 297 (1997); Carol J. Castaneda, *Baby K—Now Stephanie—Turns 2*, USA Today, Oct. 13, 1994, at 3A; Arthur Caplan, *U.S. Court Usurps Doctors' Role in Anencephalic Baby Case*, St. Paul Pioneer Press, Feb. 21, 1994, at 7A; Karen R. Long, *Whose Life Is It, Anyway?*, Clev. Plain Dealer, Oct. 9, 1994, at 1A.

23. 42 U.S.C. §5102 (1996).

24. Emergency Medical Treatment and Active Labor Act, 42 U.S.C. §1395dd (2003); Rehabilitation Act of 1973, 29 U.S.C. §794 (2002); Americans with Disabilities Act, 42 U.S.C. §§12101 et seq. (1990); Child Abuse Amendments of 1984, *supra* note 23; Virginia Medical Malpractice Act, Va. Code Ann. §§8.01-581.1 et seq. (2008).

25. Fletcher, *supra* note 22, at 307.

26. *Id.*; Linda Greenhouse, *Court Order to Treat Baby with Partial Brain Prompts Debate on Costs and Ethics*, N.Y. Times, Feb. 20, 1994, at 120.

27. The court declined to rule on the legality of the hospital's proposed action under either the Child Abuse Amendments of 1984 or the Virginia Medical Malpractice Act. 832 F. Supp. at 1031.

28. *Id.* at 1027.

29. In the Matter of Baby K., 16 F.3d 590, 596 (4th Cir.).

30. *Id.* at 598–99.

31. Greenhouse, *supra* note 26; Castaneda, *supra* note 22; Ellen Goodman, *The Shift from Dr. Partner to Dr. Provider*, Boston Globe, Oct. 24, 1993.

32. Linda Greenhouse, *Hospital Appeals Ruling on Treating Baby Born with Most of Brain Gone*, N.Y. Times, Sept. 24, 1993, at A10.

33. Caplan, *supra* note 22.

34. Long, *supra* note 22 (quoting Dr. Steven Miles).

35. Greenhouse, *supra* note 26.

36. Castaneda, *supra* note 22.

37. Long, *supra* note 22 (quoting Dr. Steven Miles).

38. Schreuder, *supra* note 2.

39. Caplan, *supra* note 22.

40. *See* Bowen v. American Hospital Association, 476 U.S. 610, 617 (1986) (plurality opinion) (describing the *Baby Doe* case).

41. *Baby Without Viable Brain Dies, But Legal Struggle Will Continue*, N.Y. Times, Mar. 31, 1992, at A14.

42. See AMA Council on Ethical and Judicial Affairs, *The Use of Anencephalic Neonates as Organ Donors*, 273 JAMA 1614 (1995); *AMA Rejects Harvest of Organs from Infants with Brain Stems Only*, Hous. Chron., Jan. 7, 1996, at A5.

43. Schreuder, *supra* note 2.

44. *AMA Rejects Harvest of Organs from Infants with Brain Stems Only*, supra note 42.

45. Jeff Goldberg, *Should Dying Babies Be Organ Donors?*, 187 Redbook 132 (Sept. 1996).

46. *See* Norman Fost, *Reconsidering the Dead Donor Rule: Is It Important That Organ Donors Be Dead?*, 14 Kennedy Inst. Ethics J. 249 (2004).

47. Rob Stein, *New Zeal in Organ Procurement Raises Fears*, Wash. Post, Sept. 13, 2007, at A1.

48. *See* David G. Savage, *Requiring Aid for Hopelessly Comatose Upheld*, L.A. Times, Oct. 4, 1994, at 1 (quoting Fairfax Hospital's attorneys as saying that the case would have "sweeping and unintended implications for clinical medicine . . . [and] profound implications for the financing of medical care in this country").

49. *See* Thaddeus M. Pope, *Medical Futility Statutes: No Safe Harbor to Unilaterally Refuse Life-Sustaining Treatment*, 75 Tenn. L. Rev. 1–81 (2007).

50. David B. Caruso, *More Hospitals Create Policy to Cut Care for Dying Patients*, Hous. Chron., Dec. 15, 2002, at A50.

51. Arthur Caplan, *Anencephaly Case: No Cure, Just Prolonging of Death*, St. Paul Pioneer Press, Oct. 4, 1993, at 7A.

52. Historical precedent for the slipperiness of this slope can be found in the Nazis' progression from compelled sterilization of persons with disabilities, on eugenics grounds, to their forced euthanization. *See* Robert Jay Lifton, The Nazi Doctors: Medical Killing and the Psychology of Genocide 22–79 (2000).

53. The application of disability discrimination law to medical treatment decisions is explored in Mary A. Crossley, *Of Diagnoses and Discrimination: Discriminatory Nontreatment of Infants with HIV Infection*, 93 Colum. L. Rev. 1581 (1993).

Chapter 7

NEWMAN
v.
SATHYAVAGLSWARAN

Unbundling Property in the Dead

Michele Goodwin*

Recently, marketing the dead has become an international trafficking issue. Often, organ demand consumes the airwaves and public service announcements. Considerable profits are rendered from selling body parts, such as corneas, heart valves, bone, and even tendons. The human tissue market is a multi-billion dollar international enterprise with significant ties, if not origins, in the

Henry Reid, UCLA Director of Cadaver Procurement, caught stealing body parts

Ernest Nelson, modern-day grave robber and body-part middleman

---

* Michele Goodwin is the Everett Fraser Professor of Law at the University of Minnesota, where she holds joint appointments in the Medical School and School of Public Health.

United States. Most recently, Ernest Nelson, a body-part broker, and Henry Reid, the former head of cadaver procurement for the University of California at Los Angeles (UCLA), were caught in a highly profitable scheme that involved selling body parts donated to the UCLA Medical School. Reid and Nelson raked in hundreds of thousands of dollars in this scheme, which implicated even a Fortune 500 company. Prior to *Newman v. Sathyavaglswaran*,[1] a seminal decision in the U.S. Court of Appeals for the Ninth Circuit, families harmed by their scheme might have been left without a civil remedy.

A. Introduction: Los Angeles Stories

1. Kenneth

Six years after Kenneth Obarski's death, his mother, Barbara Obarski, received a chilling phone call from an attorney asking if she knew that her son's corneas had been stolen by the Los Angeles coroner. According to his mother, Kenneth Obarski looked like John F. Kennedy. He also had JFK's stature: accomplished, outgoing, caring, and very handsome.[2] He had "such beautiful blue eyes," she remembered. Why, asked his mother, would the coroner want to take his corneas? In fact, one of Kenneth's corneas had been damaged when he was a child, from an accident when he and his sister were playing in the backyard: "He was hit in the eye with a handle," recalled Mrs. Obarski, and that had damaged a cornea. Who would want a damaged cornea? All Mrs. Obarski knew about his death was that Kenneth's girlfriend found him dead on the sofa shortly after dinner.[3]

Kenneth Obarski was a young, gifted doctor in his early 30s and "his patients loved him."[4] He died unexpectedly — something related to his heart? Maybe he choked on food? His mother remains unsure of the exact cause of his death; the coroner's phone call explaining Kenneth's death raised more questions than it answered. She remembers thinking that the caller seemed "uncouth," providing "gory" but inconclusive details about Kenneth's death.

What haunts Mrs. Obarski the most is what happened *after* Kenneth's death, just over ten years ago. Kenneth's corneas were harvested without her consent by the Los Angeles coroner and later sold to a profitable biotech company. That company later resold Kenneth's corneas and those from other dead bodies at the morgue for a 1400 percent markup. Mrs. Obarski is unsure that she will ever find closure from this horrific episode in her life. She wonders why the coroner never asked permission; after all, they spoke over the phone, she was easy to reach, and she was sensitive to organ and tissue transplant issues because Kenneth's brother had had two kidney transplants.

Mrs. Obarski is now a widow and both sons are dead. When she thinks about Kenneth, sometimes she "wonder[s] what else they took," because she found "wires at the back of his head" when she prepared his body for burial.[5]

2. Carlos

Carlos M. Gudino appeared twice in the *Los Angeles Times*.[6] The first time was a kind of turning point or rebirth. He was only nineteen years old when he worked on a mural with Jesse Rojas, another young, aspiring artist, trying desperately to move beyond the reach of Los Angeles gang life.[7] Their story, one of possible triumph, or at least of hope, was captured by a bold headline: "Praise for His Art Keeps Young Muralist from Being Walled in by Harsh Gang Life."[8] A photograph memorialized Carlos' gaze as Jesse applied the final touches to the mural of the Madonna that Carlos helped to create.[9]

Five years later, almost to the very day, in November 1997, Carlos again appeared in the same daily newspaper that captured him gazing at the mural of the Madonna.[10] Ironically, his violent death, which had occurred earlier in the year, was not the focus of the second article. Instead, the article exposed the surreptitious harvesting of corneas at the local coroner's office without prior consent from deceased "donors" or their relatives.[11] The article raised questions about the roles of race, socioeconomic status, and consent in this controversial process known as presumed or legislative consent.[12] Reporters from the *Los Angeles Times* contacted the Gudino family as part of a study being conducted to determine whether the Los Angeles coroner sought consent before harvesting and selling corneas from homicide victims.

In November 1997, after reviewing nearly 600 cases of body harvesting at the coroner's office, Ralph Frammolino reported the story to local and national readers. Like Barbara Obarski, the Gudinos were unaware that cornea extraction had taken place.[13] The Los Angeles coroner harvested Carlos' corneas without his family's consent.[14] The families were alarmed by the way in which the Los Angeles coroner's office operated. Their frustration did not abate after learning that the coroner had the *authority* to operate in what some have called a "clandestine" manner, referring to the legislatively approved process which presumes that one is willing to be a donor unless a prior refusal has been recorded or relatives have objected.[15] In their case, the fact that money was exchanged for Carlos' corneas was all the more offensive, heightening sensitivities and paranoia about racial profiling, manipulation, and economic justice.

What made the Gudinos' situation a bit different from Mrs. Obarski's and other victims, as Carlos' sister Maria pointed out in an interview with Frammolino, was the fact that the family had registered their objection to any organ or tissue donation the morning after Carlos' death.[16] In fact, their objection, dutifully noted by an investigator from the coroner's office in a supplemental report, was quite specific: "Family is profoundly against ANY organ or tissue donation."[17]

However, the family's objection was too late; three hours earlier, Carlos' corneas had been harvested by the Doheny Eye and Tissue Bank under authorization of the coroner.[18] Doheny and the coroner's office had an arrangement whereby corneas were harvested and the coroner's office was paid "an average of about $250 for a set of corneas, which [were] then sold to transplant institutions for a 'processing fee' of $3,400."[19] Carlos' family learned the details of this transaction from reporter Frammolino nearly eight months after his death.[20]

Ralph Frammolino, the lead investigative reporter, and his colleagues uncovered an unsettling business in body part selling conducted through the coroner's office. Relatives of victims suggested that the Los Angeles coroner's office was essentially operating the equivalent of a "chop shop" — only with human bodies instead of cars. Reporters and critics referred to the scandal as a "virtual cornea mill" that had netted the coroner's office more than $1,000,000 over a five-year period.[21] After a year-long investigation, *Los Angeles Times* staff reported the rather gruesome details: the coroner's office had a clandestine practice of non-consensually removing corneas from people like Kenneth and Carlos, homicide victims, people who had died in car crashes, and deaths by other circumstances that triggered the coroner's jurisdiction for forensic autopsy. The coroner and accomplices sold those tissues to companies that would later resell the corneas for thousands of dollars.

The case Frammolino cracked seemed more fitting for a Stephen King novel or Hollywood script: a greedy coroner, suspicious employees, falsification of medical reports, diseased tissues being passed off as healthy, grieving relatives, and a company recycling human body parts and selling them to unwitting patients. The case became defined by a series of chilling headlines and led to investigative reports in surrounding communities and states. It resulted in legislative action, and ultimately culminated in *Newman v. Sathyavaglswaran*, a Ninth Circuit appellate opinion in a lawsuit brought by Mrs. Obarski and Richard Newman (another parent whose son's corneas were harvested and sold) against the Los Angeles coroner over property rights to the dead.

The case against the coroner was initiated by Bill Colovos, an attorney from Southgate, Michigan. Colovos contacted Mrs. Obarski and Richard Newman years after their sons' deaths about pursuing litigation against the Los Angeles' coroner's office. Mrs. Obarski observed that she never met Colovos, and was a bit surprised by his phone call, but was all the more dismayed by the nonconsensual harvesting of her son's corneas. She agreed to allow Colovos to represent her. The case, according to the plaintiffs, was straightforward: the coroner violated their constitutionally protected interests to dispose and bury their children, and that right to bury amounted to a property interest.

As the plaintiffs had hoped, the court in *Newman* determined that principles of property, including ownership, donation, and possession, are appropriately applied to the human body, and that this bundle of interests provided a basis for relief on Richard's and Barbara's claim. The case can be credited for two advancements in health care law jurisprudence. First, *Newman* clarifies the meaning of the traditional "quasi property" interests in dead bodies. Disagreement among courts as to the meaning of these interests reflected the struggle over time to define the contours of this quasi right, which was largely borne out of a public health responsibility. Second, the case elevates the weaker "quasi property" interests to a robust declaration that relatives have a constitutionally protected interest — a property right — in their dead relatives' bodies, protecting the intimacy and autonomy of the family in this regard.

On the other hand, the defense articulated a different perspective on the importance of the court's ruling and its potential negative impact. According to the defendant, "[t]he issue is particularly important because investing next-of-kin with a property interest of constitutional dimension in their relatives' dead bodies will have a deleterious impact on organ and tissue donation by undermining the immunity provisions of organ and tissue donation statutes enacted on the state level nationwide."[22] In fact, the speedy recovery of human tissues had conformed (in part) to a state statute that "expressly authorized the coroner to remove corneal eye tissue if the coroner had no knowledge of any objection to the removal."[23] This statute, as discussed later in this chapter, was enacted to address a significant public health concern, basically the "shortage of corneal eye tissue for transplantation."[24] Presumed consent proponents argue that the policy is the best way to ease the tissue and organ crisis. To them, it would be so easy to respond to demand for body parts if we only presumed everyone was a donor. The California statute did not "require the coroner to seek out the decedent's relatives or obtain their express consent to the removal of the corneal eye tissue,"[25] which became the nexus for challenge at the appellate court level.

The appropriate handling and disposal of dead bodies "has been regulated by law from earliest times, on the continent of Europe by the canon law, and in England by the ecclesiastical law."[26] *Newman* joined a debate among the courts as to whether the "national common law, that next of kin have the exclusive right to possess the bodies of their deceased family members creates a property interest, the deprivation of which must be accorded due process of law under the Fourteenth Amendment of the United States Constitution."[27] In a split decision, the Ninth Circuit Court of Appeals held that next of kin have a property interest in the deceased and that Richard and Barbara properly stated claims for relief under §1983.[28] The U.S. Supreme Court's refusal to hear the case effectively settled the matter, at least for the Ninth Circuit.

This chapter unpacks the *Newman* case, revealing the complicated story behind the litigation. First, it describes early case law in the domain of the dead. The story begins nearly three centuries before the deaths of Richard Newman and Kenneth Obarski, with the grave robbing scandals of the 18th century and ironically the emergence of public policy aimed at promoting sanitary and dignified interment of cadavers. Second, this chapter discusses the Uniform Anatomical Gift Act (UAGA), which established the first comprehensive guidelines on organ and tissue donation in the United States. Finally, this chapter analyzes what the case portends for future transplant conflicts.

B. From the Grave

> [I]t was an offense at common law to dig up the bodies of those who had been buried, for the purpose of dissection. It is an outrage upon the public feelings, and torturing to the afflicted relatives of the deceased. If it be a crime thus to disturb the ashes of the dead, it must also be a crime to deprive them of a decent burial, by a disgraceful exposure, or disposal of the body contrary to usages so long sanctioned, and which are so grateful to the wounded hearts of friends and mourners.[29]

Centuries ago, training hospitals and medical schools created demand for human tissues, bones, and other body parts, and zealously pursued their procurement.[30] Grave robbing was spurred in Europe and the United States by competing motivations, including greed, reputation, desperation, ambition, but also seemingly altruistic motivations to develop knowledge, technology, and skills to save lives. The reputations of elite medical schools and hospitals were built on cadaver supply. Cadavers were necessary for medical research, but procurement was problematic and not well organized. As a result, training hospitals, doctors, and their medical students, particularly those engaged in anatomy research, undertook radical means to obtain cadavers — they stole them.[31]

Grave robbing was popular not only in Europe, but also was common in the United States. Some of the more famous American medical institutions engaged in body purchasing from a variety of sources, including African American cemeteries, plantations, and even carnivals and circuses.[32] In a forthcoming book, Ray Madoff, a law professor at Boston College Law School, argues that Harvard Medical School was purposefully located in Boston — away from the Cambridge campus — specifically to be near poor houses where it could more easily obtain dead bodies for anatomy research.[33] Eerie clues to that forgotten era emerge from time to time. Nearly four hundred cadavers were found in the basement of the University of Georgia Medical School during a recent renovation. Most of those bodies, according to journalist Harriet Washington, were former slaves.[34] They were obtained from cemeteries or sold by former owners.

The practice — widely known as "body snatching" — became popular in England during the 18th and 19th centuries, although the earliest legal cases date back to the 17th century.[35] British surgeons first relied on an inconsistent supply of bodies from the gallows or poor houses.[36] Cadavers from the poor houses sprinkled throughout England provided a meager supply, which underserved the growing demand for corpses for medical research and anatomy classes. Consequently, medical students "desperate to advance their knowledge of anatomy" harvested their own cadavers from local cemeteries.[37] Thus began the process of grave robbing, not for treasure buried with the deceased, but for the corpse itself.

Consider the notorious case of Burke and Hare. William Burke and William Hare committed a series of murders and subsequently sold the victims' dead bodies to doctors and medical students.[38] They, however, played a very small role in the supply of cadavers to medical institutions. In 1828, William Burke's trial began in Edinburgh, Scotland, for the murder of more than a dozen people who were later sold to Doctor Robert Knox and his student.[39] Burke's companion, Mr. Hare, avoided trial by testifying against Burke, who was hanged on January 28, 1829.[40]

Contemporary scholars reexamining the exploits of Burke and Hare suggest that the two were never really grave robbers or "body snatchers" as commonly understood.[41] Rather, they were brazen murderers. The pair murdered Hare's lodgers, tourists, prostitutes, couples, a mother and child, and a distant relative of Burke's girlfriend.[42] It is hard to know exactly what motivated Burke and Hare. Did the financial incentives offered for procuring cadavers give rise to their murders? Were they simply motivated to kill, and selling bodies to medical institutions was a means of easy disposal? These questions may never be answered, but it is clear that the infamous two were not the first to supply human bodies to medical schools for dissection and research. Grave robbing remained popular in Great Britain even after the hanging of Burke.[43] The demand for cadavers, fueled by medical research, experimentation, and technology was so great that cemetery administrators built tall walls and watchtowers at graveyards in Edinburgh.[44]

In 1832, the passage of the Anatomy Act coincided with philosopher Jeremy Bentham boldly declaring his body in part to medical research upon his death, and otherwise to be on full display.[45] Bentham bequeathed his body to his dear friend, Dr. Southwood Smith, who was charged with preparing the corpse for dissection and permanent public exposition. His wishes fulfilled, Bentham's corpse remains on display at the University College of London (UCL) in a structure similar to that of a telephone booth. His head, which was damaged during the operation, and later by student pranks, remains in a hatbox on the UCL campus. A wax head and period clothing adorn his body. According to one commentator, "this was a final gesture of his utilitarian view of seeking to promote the greatest good for the greatest public."[46] Subsequently, laws were enacted that created two permissible or legal streams of cadaver procurement.[47] The first was through altruistic donations in the spirit of Bentham.[48] The second was through unclaimed corpses, a process that may be viewed as a precursor to the California law that presumed the consent of Newman and Obarski.

A discourse on property interests in dead bodies emerged during this era, and ironically it had little to do with grave robbing. Instead, one could say that quasi property interests in the dead evolved in response to concerns regarding public health and human dignity.

C. Public Health and Quasi Property Interests in Dead Bodies

> The problem with dealing with the California law [is] what does it mean to have a quasi property interest? I think we have to recognize that it is more of a religious or social mores type of recognition. It's a gray area.
> — Cheryl Orr, Defense Attorney in Newman v. Sathyavaglswaran[49]

Prior to *Newman*, dead bodies were not considered property in a traditional sense. The traditions of Roman, canon, and English ecclesiastic law adopted in the U.S. posited that although dead bodies are not property in a strict construction of common law, they are quasi property "over which the relatives of the deceased have rights which the courts will protect."[50] These rights could more appropriately be framed as a responsibility, indeed a duty, to appropriately bury the dead or preserve its bodily tissues.[51] Indeed, early thinking on appropriate burial of the dead emanated from the belief that even after death, the human body deserved dignified treatment. Equally compelling, however, were public health concerns that the poor or frugal might cremate their relatives in furnaces or fireplaces, creating foul stenches in their neighborhoods, or bury the bodies in shallow graves behind their homes, or simply dump decaying bodies in public spaces. The dual concerns about human dignity and public health fueled the common law development of "quasi property rights." Typical violations or interference of this right included illegal possession of a corpse, wrongful burial or autopsy, and even mutilation or destruction of a corpse.

A quasi property "right" vests in the next of kin — husbands, wives, children, and parents — for purposes of burial or other legal disposition.[52] Early iterations of this right were counterintuitive, however, as it had little if anything to do with an individual's ownership or property interest in their own body, but rather was an interest vested in familial third parties. Such rights were not equal among relatives; rather, the marital right trumped that of the next of kin.[53] This logic — a ranking system — became the foundation for organ donation policy a century later and was codified in the Uniform Anatomical Gift Act (UAGA).[54]

As courts continued to craft this new hybrid right/responsibility, its contours were not always clear nor consistently applied. For example, there was confusion as to whether the right in question is one of a right to bury and choose the disposition of the body, or a quasi right to possess the body. A Tennessee court framed the answer in the following way, "[t]his 'quasi-property right' is '*the right to the possession of a dead body* for the purposes of decent [disposition]'" which vests in the decedent's next-of-kin."[55] Similarly, in Kansas, courts emphasized that the right in such cases is not of "property" in the traditional sense, but instead a right of possession.[56]

Georgia courts articulated the quasi property right slightly and relevantly differently. In *In re Tri-State Crematory Litigation*, the court expressed that "Georgia recognizes a *quasi property* right *in* the deceased body of a relative,"[57] a subtle but important linguistic and legal distinction that steps beyond a legal duty to bury, but implies a right for aggrieved or harmed relatives. It would also appear that rights "in" the body are not confined to burial, but extend beyond disposition. In Illinois, the quasi property right has been explained through a rugged line of precedent as a procedural right, rather than an actual property right.

The United States District Court in Northern Illinois observed in *Wells v. Nuwayhid* that in Illinois the "state quasi-property right in the disposition of a dead body by the next of kin qualifies as a property interest for procedural due process purposes."[58] This means that state actors, such as coroners or state employees acting in their official capacity, must at least provide notice and an opportunity for relatives to be heard — and in many instances refuse state intervention with their dead relative. In *Wells,* the wife gave birth to a still-born baby, and without the parents' consent, hospital personnel caused the baby's body to be incinerated, after which the parents filed a lawsuit.[59]

Finally, consider the infamous case of *State v. Bradbury,*[60] where the defendant was convicted for the common-law offense of burning a body in an indecent manner that would evoke public outrage and disgust. In that case, Frank E. Bradbury, the defendant, built a hot fire in the basement furnace of the house he shared with Harriet, his sister. Both Bradbury and Harriet were elderly, and the day after her death, Bradbury "tied a rope around the legs of his sister's body, dragged it down the cellar stairs, shoved it into the furnace and burned it,"[61] thereby causing a heavy dark smoke with a disagreeable odor to pour from the house.[62] More disagreeable to police was the glib manner in which Bradbury spoke of his disposition process. When police asked Bradbury to take them to his sister, he took them to the basement, opened the furnace and shoveled out the ashes, and offered "if you want to see her, there she is."[63] Bradbury's quasi property interest in his sister's body was really a duty to properly dispose of her corpse.

In framing the holding, the court made an effort to distinguish burning of a corpse for cremation purposes from that which caused shock and outrage in a community. Judge Thaxter admonished, "in the case before us the essence of the offense charged and proved is, not that the body was burned, but that it was indecently burned, in such a manner that, when the facts should in the natural course of events become known, the feelings and natural sentiments of the public would be outraged."[64] Yet there is an economic tension not addressed by the court. For the economically disenfranchised, burials were expensive and cost prohibitive. As a result, some poor people were likely to employ methods for disposition that were most expedient and economically efficient; means that could be considered "outrageous." Common necessities, such as life insurance, were generally not an option, as it was considered morally repugnant to associate a financial interest with dead bodies. Thus, "proper" burial was as much an economic question as legal duty for poor families.

It could be said that the common law establishment and enforcement of burial duties and rights in next of kin effectively resolved the public health concerns about bodies being abandoned in public spaces or relatives inappropriately disposing of their deceased loved ones. Over time, however, the failure to properly dispose was not regarded as a simple a breach of stewardship in the dead, but also a public offense to members of the community, including neighbors. Thus, the duty to bury properly was intensified and policed within communities by neighbors. In similar fashion to the *Bradbury* decision, courts in Michigan,[65]

Indiana,[66] Tennessee,[67] Virginia,[68] Georgia,[69] Illinois,[70] and other states extended the application of quasi property right theory in their jurisdictions. Furthermore, as the message in cases like *Bradbury* gained traction, more claims concerning commercial interests in dead bodies arose.

D. Shifts and Trends Paving the Common Law for *Newman*

Two shifts defined the "body as property" jurisprudence in the 20th century, which led to *Newman* and the controversy over its holding. The first shift was from individual culpability for failure to properly execute the duty to bury to a smattering of cases involving funeral home negligence or crematorium malfeasance. In those cases, the issues before courts involved malfeasance and negligence when crematoria substituted the ashes of humans for dust and animal remains and cemeteries negligently disposed of dead bodies. The line of cases emerging in the 20th century confirming familial rights to the dead are a logical response to relatives' contracting with commercial facilities for appropriate burial and cremation.

The second shift is one of public policy implicated by the law of supply and demand for organs for transplantation. By the mid-20th century, the debate about the proper use of bodies morphed into a public policy plea for organ and tissue donation. Technology provided the means to recycle human body parts to save lives. The language of burial also morphed, with burial associated with wasting the body — as organ and tissue donation became elevated with charity, generosity, and giving life. In part, this period is characterized by biotechnology outpacing legislative action and judicial rule making. The era preceding *Newman* is defined by the universal adoption of state statutes based on the Uniform Anatomical Gift Act (UAGA), and the enactment of the National Organ Transplant Act (NOTA).

1. The Uniform Anatomical Gift Act (1968)

The Uniform Anatomical Gift Act (UAGA) was a progressive response to a new and potentially revolutionary technology — organ transplantation. The National Conference of Commissioners on Uniform State Laws (NCCUSL) drafted the UAGA during the summer of 1968,[71] shortly after the first successful liver transplant in 1967, and subsequent heart and pancreas transplants in 1968. The Act regulates the retrieval of organs from cadavers and establishes legal guidelines for organ procurement, including a ranking of persons with authority to consent. This ranking followed patterns of the common law quasi property right, beginning with rights belonging to the spouse and then, in order, the adult children, parents, siblings, guardians, and others authorized or obligated to dispose of the body. In essence, family members were ranked in order by what might be called "greater rights." In ranking order, they were vested with the power to donate organs, such as kidneys, a heart, liver, or other body parts from their deceased relative.

By 1973, the UAGA in its original or modified version was adopted in each state and the District of Columbia. The more significant provisions provided for express authorization of donation for educational, research, and medical purposes. Thus, a body or part could be donated to: a) any hospital, surgeon, or physician for dental or medical research; b) any medical or dental school; c) any storage facility or "bank" for research purposes; and lastly, d) for any specified individual for therapy or transplant. Perhaps the drafters were prophetic or were aware at that time that doctors, medical schools, and tissue banks had greater demand for body parts than did patients seeking transplants. Doctors and medical schools needed organs in the 1960s more than sick patients did, or at least they could make better use of them, because cyclosporine, the leading immunosuppressant medication, had not yet been discovered, and transplantation resulted in very high rejection rates. Thus, the demand may not have been for transplants as much as for medical research.

Twenty years later, the UAGA was revised. The 1987 UAGA was a direct, state-level response to the federal National Organ Transplant Act (NOTA) of 1984. In an effort to comply with NOTA, the UAGA drafters clarified important issues, including banning payments for organs and whether relatives could cancel or revoke the donor's pre-mortem expression of gift. The 1987 Act also introduced two new concepts to donation: required request (mandating that hospitals inquire about organ donation from families of dying patients), and presumed consent — the process at issue in *Newman*.

2. Presumed Consent

Newman addresses a fundamental question: can the state compel an individual to donate his or her organs or tissues? In a presumed consent framework, the state acknowledges that the body has value as a source of transplantable goods. However, that value is gifted to the state absent notification to the state that the gift is revoked.[72] First enacted in Maryland,[73] presumed consent legislation authorizes medical examiners, coroners, and their designated personnel to extract corneas, heart valves, and other tissues from cadavers without first obtaining consent from the person previously alive, or from the person authorized to make donation decisions if the person is deceased.[74] Presumed consent laws had an opt-out clause, which allowed an individual or relative to decline donation.

The 1987 UAGA claimed to have an opt-out provision for those who would otherwise refuse to donate under the presumed consent rubric. However, that may have been a more illusory concept given information shortfalls. In other words, individuals could not decline donating tissues and corneas if they were not informed about the possibility of choosing to donate. This illusory opt-out provision veiled the fact that presumed consent laws are more like conscription measures and less like an option or "choice." Where, after all, was Barbara Obarski to opt out? By what means do the dead opt out? How can the uninformed relative opt out? Indeed, studies show that most people, even local legislators such as aldermen and city council members, are relatively ignorant about presumed consent (in their own states) and have no idea of what the term means or what the law authorizes.[75]

Cornea harvesting may be perceived as less invasive than removal of other tissue or organs: it is hard to notice after funeral preparations when the eyes are closed, and the evidence of cornea extraction is untraceable after bodies are cremated. Cornea extraction does not leave signs easily noticeable to lay people; there are no bruises on the face and no scratches on the eye lids.[76] Thus, if the deceased is prepared for burial, particularly with her eyes closed, her family would be completely unaware of the medical intrusion.[77] For this reason, critics of presumed consent measures regard these laws as surreptitious and unethical while proponents argue that statutory consent measures are creative efforts to procure corneas, reflecting what they believe most people would do.[78] Proponents also argue that compulsory donations require so little and that families hardly notice.[79] That the deceased can be laid to rest with the appearance of "wholeness" is persuasive if appearances are the only impediment to broader support of presumed consent measures.

Courts are divided on this issue, with disagreement evident among courts in the same state, and the Ninth Circuit's split opinion in *Newman* reflects that tension. In *Georgia Lions Eye Bank v. Lavant,*[80] the young parents of a dead infant filed a civil suit against the eye bank that was authorized by the state medical examiner to remove their son's corneas. Like Mrs. Obarski, the grieving parents were not consulted prior to the extraction and therefore had not authorized cornea harvesting. Essentially, they were denied the opportunity to object to the extraction.[81] The trial court held in favor of the parents, ruling that the presumed consent statute violated due process in that it deprived the parents of a property right in the corpse of their son and failed to provide constitutionally required notice and an opportunity to object.[82] On appeal, however, and despite Georgia common law precedent, the Georgia Supreme Court reversed, ruling that parents have no constitutionally protected interest in the body of their dead child.[83]

Paradoxically, an earlier Georgia appellate case, *Pollard v. Phelps*, recognized that "the courts of civilized and Christian countries regard respect for the dead as not only a virtue but a duty, and hold that, in the absence of testamentary disposition, a quasi property right belongs to the husband or wife, and, if neither, to the next of kin."[84] Quasi property rights are meaningless unless they can be protected from the tyranny of the state. The *Georgia Lions* court's assertion that statutory enactments naturally trump common law rules is correct only in instances when the statute itself does not violate constitutional protections even in a utilitarian scheme designed to protect health and safety or to benefit a public purpose.

Consider then, the Sixth Circuit's response to the question of presumed consent and property interests in the human body. In *Brotherton v. Cleveland*, a widow and her children brought a civil rights complaint after a coroner caused the removal of her husband's corneas, despite a refusal to donate listed on his medical chart.[85] According to the Sixth Circuit, the widow satisfied the necessary prerequisites to assert a valid due process claim. First, she proved that she was deprived of property under color of state law. Further, the court observed, the "only governmental interest enhanced by the removal of the corneas is the interest in implementing the organ/tissue donation program; this interest is not substantial enough to allow the state to consciously disregard those property rights which it has granted." The burden of notice here, the court noted, would be a "minimal burden to its interest."[86]

An additional problem posed by legislation enabling this type of body part conscription is that nonconsensual removal is authorized only in cases of mandatory autopsy.[87] Thus, the only bodies to which presumed consent applies are victims of homicide or catastrophic deaths requiring a medical investigation, as was the case for Carlos Gudino, Richard Newman, and Kenneth Obarski. Frammolino's investigation confirmed the suspicions of physicians like Clive

Callender, that blacks and Latinos are the overwhelming majority of the presumed consent donors.[88] The *Los Angeles Times* investigation revealed that 80 percent of presumed consent donors were black and Latino.[89] The overwhelming majority of those individuals were homicide victims.

E. *Newman* and Its Legacy

The *Newman* court answered questions about duty, notice, appeal, and due process. The court made clear that the aggrieved parents had exclusive and legitimate claims of entitlement to possess, control, dispose of, and prevent the violation to, the corneas and other parts of their deceased children's bodies. These discrete rights created a property interest in their children's bodies, which cannot be taken without due process of law.

But the court was split in its ruling. Judge Fernandez rejected the majority's analysis in *Newman*,[90] arguing instead that the body has no property status, and therefore, conversion is not an appropriate cause of action in relation to the body.[91] Fernandez attempted to revitalize the traditional approach of a quasi property theory, and it is worth considering how his contemporary approach to an age-old question might work. He argues that if any property right exists, it is a right only to possess the body for purposes of burial and disposal.[92] Judge Fernandez rationalized that "this so-called right is actually in the nature of a duty and expense designed to assure that the remains will not simply be left about, but will be quickly interred."[93] He refers to this special set of responsibilities as "something like a table of intestate succession for the purpose of assuring that the right and duty land firmly on a defined group."[94] Fernandez describes this right as being grounded in pragmatism, although he offers no further explanation.[95] Fernandez is concerned about morality toward corpses and the responsibility of relatives to act with due haste and decency to assure that bodies are properly interred.

Possessory rights may also seem like empty vessels because there are no causes of action for which courts may grant a remedy, even in instances where the right to possess is interfered with at death. In other words, interfering with one's right to bury may be reprehensible, but courts may not have a remedy. Thus, an additional element to be developed in this theory is how to decide whether the state or relatives have the controlling interest at death. As it stands, the outcome of possessory rights according to the Fernandez approach will differ from state to state, offering no clear guidance for plaintiffs.

Unlike Fernandez's approach, the majority in *Newman* describes rights and duties as being jural correlatives, meaning that they are different aspects emerging from the same or similar legal relation.[96] At issue is whether possession and control arise to the level of a constitutionally protected property interest. Property, for the majority in *Newman*, is a "group of rights inhering in the citizen's relation to the physical thing, as the right to possess, use and dispose of it."[97] The court makes clear that to have a property right or interest, one must have more than an abstract notion of a thing, but rather, a "legitimate claim of entitlement to it."[98]

The U.S. Supreme Court has yet to address whether the bundled property rights to control, donate, possess, and even destroy one's body are property interests and thus "protected" by the Due Process Clause. The Supreme Court denied certiorari to the *Newman* defendants who attempted to appeal the Ninth Circuit's ruling. Nor has the Supreme Court addressed what due process protections are applicable to the rights of next of kin to possess and control the bodies of their deceased relatives.[99] However, constitutionally protected property rights extend "beyond actual ownership of real estate, chattels, or money."[100] As expressed by the Supreme Court in *Board of Regents v. Roth,* a property interest can be extended to the realms of the social and economic.[101] These realms include interactions between an individual and state that involve fundamental rights, employment contexts, and in this case, the human body. Accordingly, these rights "are not created by the constitution . . . they are created and their dimensions are defined by existing rules or understandings."[102]

Thus far, only two circuits, the Ninth and Sixth, have recognized that the body remains property independent of obligations and rights relating to burial. What does this recognition mean for future cases? A few scholars, like Professors Lori Andrews and Arthur Caplan caution against being too swift in naming the body as property, lest we fail to fully comprehend the socioeconomic, cultural, and political ramifications of such judicial or legislative intervention. In a brilliant book co-authored with Dorothy Nelkin, Andrews wisely challenges the reader to think about the praxis and pitfalls of granting property status to cells, organs, and conceivably all other parts that have recently been subject to market forces, including brains, bones, and limbs.[103] To the extent that property rights are recognized in body parts, plaintiffs may have greater access to courts for interference with their control of their own bodies. On the other hand, it could be true that recognition of property interests in the body may push us closer to commodification. You could imagine, for example, joint ventures between patients and their physicians, buying kidneys, or bartering for organs. It is also conceivable that individuals might strive to invest in the products derived from their bodies. But, of course, commodification of the human body is hardly a new space, particularly in the era of assisted reproduction and tissue banking.

A determination of whether the body is property might influence the outcome of future cases or those in dockets now, including whether heart valves and tissues used for donation are products, whether universities have a property claim or proprietary interest in research subjects' DNA and tissues, the constitutionality of body part conscription laws, and whether causes of action can be sustained for wrongful implantation, directed implantation, and likely a host of other foreseeable problems. These questions have been at the center of recent litigation, including *Miller v. Hartford Hospital,*[104] a case involving the implantation of contaminated heart valve tissue in Connecticut,[105] and *Martin v. Young Kim,*[106] in Indiana, and likely many more.

Property proponents, such as the majorities in *Newman, Brotherton,* and *Martin,* argue that "the right of every individual to the possession and control of his own person, free from all restraint or interference of others" is a well established principle, recognized by the U.S. Supreme Court.[107] This right, according to *Newman,* is deeply rooted in the conscience, traditions, and culture of Americans.[108] It is "to be ranked as one of the fundamental liberties protected by the 'substantive' component of the Due Process Clause."[109] Quoting *Schmerber v. California,* the *Newman* court asserted "the integrity of an individual's person is a cherished value of our society."[110] One can even read *Newman* as extending the notion of property interest to the decisions that affect end-of-life decision-making. The case evokes the right to die cases, starting with *Cruzan v. Missouri,*[111] to draw parallels with the contemporary biotech cases, and particularly the compelled donation/presumed consent laws. The majority opinion in *Newman* quotes Justice Brennan's dissent in *Cruzan* in which he declared that a right to die with dignity emanates from "the right to determine what shall be done with one's own body [which] is deeply rooted in this Nation's traditions . . . and is securely grounded in the earliest common law."[112]

F. Closing Thoughts

Cheryl Orr's observations provide a compelling perspective on the unresolved tensions and ambiguities involved in presumed consent and the *Newman* holding. Orr questions the validity of allowing recovery for parents who are not in close contact with their adult children. A concern she had, "is that relatives are far flung; some of the people who were victims were not in touch with their kids [who were the subject of litigation]."[113] For her, the Ninth Circuit opinion is at best a cloth with holes. Why, for example, emphasize a familial relationship "and not a personal relationship"?[114] You could imagine the complicated ways in which the scenarios might play out: a same-sex partner could not recover although a cousin could, or a mother's interest might be given greater consideration than a domestic partner.

Perhaps more important to Orr is the growing demand for organ and tissue transplants. As she pointed out, the presumed consent legislation was enacted because of pressing need, and it is also true that organs and tissues must be harvested before their viability diminishes. According to Orr, "that is what precipitated the law being before the legislature."[115] Ms. Orr emphasized that even with the *Newman* holding, this is a "grey area."[116] Indeed, it is not unusual that a medical examiner will remove, and even store, human remains as part of an ongoing investigation or to determine the cause of death. So, Ms. Orr is correct when she observes that there are competing and conflicting interests. However, presumed consent as part of the UAGA is now a bygone era. As drafters convened to revise the Act between 2004 and 2006,[117] the controversies involving Mrs. Obarski's son and other persons subjected to state tissue conscription proved persuasive to commissioners, advisers, and observers. The state entitlement was deleted from the new version of the Act, as California had already done after the *Los Angeles Times* revelations.[118]

The cases of Newman and Obarski and others tracked in Frammolino's investigation are troubling for a few reasons, however. First, families were deceived and felt betrayed by the state and its agents. In some instances families had refused to donate, and their preferences were noted on medical charts but were ignored. Equally frustrating for families — even those sympathetic to donation — is that presumed consent practices emphasize secretiveness lest individuals refuse to donate. Thus, the state incentivizes surreptitious behavior on the part of those responsible for harvesting body parts. In a robust biotech economy, those instances become ripe for fraud and coercion. Second, as a matter of public health policy, social histories should be obtained with all human donations, but were not in these cases — as that information would have required interviews and conversations with relatives. Social histories are important because of what doctors learn about the health status of the deceased, independent of medical evaluation and tests. For example, relatives may know whether the "donor" had a criminal history, was a drug user or addict, had AIDS, was a prostitute, or was exposed to cattle in certain European communities (mad cow disease) or fowl in plagued cities (bird flu), and in each instance donations are to be refused for public health concerns. In Mrs. Obarski's case, she could have informed doctors about the damage to Kenneth's cornea had she been asked. Third, the corneas were mostly harvested from blacks and Latinos. They made up over 80 percent of the population whose tissues were nonconsensually removed. Their deaths, caused by homicides and gang and drug violence in the late 1990s, provided a more reliable pool of cornea and other tissue, which could have been captured through a more transparent donation process rather than the ignoble, surreptitious manner in which the coroner's office operated.

But more, the compulsory aspect of the presumed consent regulations makes these donations problematic. Forced use of nonconsenting individuals' tissues is justifiable only if the donation is viewed as a form of civic duty or our bodies are property of the state. Donation as a civic duty is a laudable concept, though not supported by social custom or an American legal tradition. Our common law tradition resists the duty to rescue doctrine, and more pointedly warns "rescue at your own risk." That our bodies belong in service to the state cannot be justified by the ways in which we organize labor, medicine, our system of justice, or even the military. Marx's concept of a communitarian society operating for the common good of man and woman, no matter how laudable, is not a philosophy that constitutional framers or the subsequent generations of electorate adopted, nor it appears, the Ninth Circuit.

ENDNOTES

1. 287 F.3d 786 (9th Cir. 2002).
2. Telephone interview with Barbara Obarski, Feb. 28, 2008.
3. *Id.*
4. *Id.*
5. *Id.*
6. Lisa Richardson, *Praise for His Art Keeps Young Muralist from Being Walled in by Harsh Gang Life*, L.A. Times, Nov. 27, 1992, at B1; Ralph Frammolino, *Harvest of Corneas at Morgue Questioned*, L.A. Times, Nov. 2, 1997, at A1.
7. Richardson, *supra* note 5.
8. *Id.*
9. *Id.* Richardson notes that "amid the gangbanging and hard living, looking down upon the frustrations of the jobless young men hungry for recognition, is a just-painted red, yellow, and green mural of the Virgin Mary." *Id.*
10. Frammolino, *Harvest of Corneas, supra* note 5.
11. *Id.*
12. *Id.*
13. *Id.* Frammolino comments in his article that all the families "were shocked that they had not been asked or told." *Id.*
14. *Id.*
15. Cal. Gov. Code §27491.47 (West 1988) (amended 1998).
16. Frammolino, *supra* note 5. Carlos, then aged 24, died shortly before nine o'clock in the evening on March 26, 1997, from head and chest wounds. The next day his sister called the morgue. She recalls, "my parents told me to let them know they didn't want any organs donated or anything." *Id.*
17. *Id.*
18. *Id.*
19. *Id.*
20. *Id.* Carlos Gudino died March 26, 1997. However, it was not until Frammolino contacted the family in the course of his investigation later that year that they became aware of the nonconsensual cornea removal. *Id.*

21. Ralph Frammolino, *Reforms on Cornea Harvesting OK'd*, L.A. Times, Oct. 1, 1998, at A3.

22. Petition for Rehearing at 6, Newman v. Sathyavaglswaran, 287 F.3d 786 (9th Cir. 2002) (No. 00-55504).

23. *Id.*

24. *Id.*

25. *Id.*

26. State v. Bradbury, 136 Me. 347, 349 (1939).

27. *Newman*, 287 F.3d at 788.

28. *Id.*

29. Kanavan's Case, 1 Me. 226, 227 (1821).

30. *See* Christopher Hudson, *Theatres of Horror; Baying Crowds, Stolen Bodies and Surgeons Feted Like Film Stars*, Daily Mail, Nov. 23, 2002, at 44 (detailing famous cases of grave robbing and subsequent public body dissections at London theatres).

31. *See* Charles Seabrook, *The Body Snatchers of Augusta: Bought as a Slave to Rob Black Graves*, Atl. J. & Const., Mar. 8, 1998, at C4 (chronicling the life of Grandison Harris, the Medical College of Georgia's most invaluable grave robber or "resurrection man").

32. *See* Charles Seabrook, *The Body Snatchers of Augusta: Medical Faculty of a Century Ago Needed Corpses for Dissection and Raided African-American Graves*, Atl. J. & Const., Mar. 8, 1998, at C1 (chronicling the discovery of thousands of African-American bones at the old medical college site of Georgia State University and examining the macabre history of body snatching in the United States to supply professors and students with corpses to dissect); Stanley M. Aronson, *History and Its Grave Violations*, Providence J.-Bull. July 14, 1997, at B5 (noting that many early medical schools in the United States were "attacked and ransacked" by the public protesting the dissection of cadavers and the "very frequent and wanton trespasses" of burial grounds).

33. Ray D. Madoff, Immortality and the Law (forthcoming).

34. Harriet A. Washington, Medical Apartheid: The Dark Side of Medical Experimentation on Black Americans from Colonial Times to Present (2007).

35. The first body snatching reported in a British legal case, according to author Norman Adams, involved a child who had been murdered along with his family and buried in a shallow grave. The next morning his body was reported missing. A contemporary account of the case speculates that the child had been "snatched." Adams suggests that this indicates "that the practice was well known at the time." In that case four members of a Romani family known as the Shaws were prosecuted and hanged for murdering a man and his pregnant wife. The Shaws were buried in a shallow grave, which was disturbed the very next morning. The youngest of the clan had been "snatched," according to reports. The use of the term at the time gives some indication that as early as 1678 grave robbery was in practice. *See* Jennifer Veitch, *Unearthing the City's Original Body-snatchers*, Edinburgh Evening News, June 21, 2002, at 20.

36. *Id.*

37. *Id.*

38. *See* Hudson, *supra* note 30, at 44 (chronicling the voyeurism and fascination associated with early dissection); Brian Bailey, Burke and Hare: The Year of the Ghouls (2005); Norman Adams, Scottish Bodysnatchers — True Accounts (2002) (exploring the widespread practice of bodysnatching and murder-for-profit to supply physicians with corpses, and acknowledging that this practice only dissipated after the passing of the Anatomy Act of 1832, which enabled the medical community to acquire corpses legally).

39. *See* Tom Kyle, *In Search of a Body to Kill For*, Daily Mail, Aug. 30, 2002, at 60.

40. *See* Veitch, *supra* note 35, at 20.

41. *Id.* Arguably, the profitability of human body sales appealed to the prurient character in both Burke and Hare. According to scholarly accounts, their first victim of sale was not someone whom they murdered, but rather a tenant at Hare's lodging house who died with an outstanding bill. According to Adams, the two men bound the corpse and hauled it to the home of Dr. Robert Knox, at Surgeons Square. The two were paid a handsome fee for the corpse and later returned with fifteen bodies during an eleven-month period.

42. *Id.*

43. Grave robbing flourished around medical schools in Edinburgh, Glasgow, and Aberdeen, in Scotland. Undoubtedly, Edinburgh's formidable international reputation at that time could partially be attributed to the advances discovered through anatomy research, which increased surgical knowledge. *Id.*

44. *Id.*

45. *See* John Zen Jackson, *When It Comes to Transplant Organs, Demand Far Exceeds Supply: American Medical Association Renews the Debate on Financial Incentives to Obtain Organs for Transplant*, 170 N.J.L.J. 910 (2002).

46. *Id.* (commenting on the American Medical Association House of Delegation vote to encourage organ procurement agencies to study the use of financial incentives).

47. *Id.*

48. *Id.*

49. Interview with Cheryl Orr, Esq., Feb. 21, 2008.

50. Pierce v. Proprietors of Swan Point Cemetery, 10 R.I. 227 (R.I. 1872).

51. *See, e.g.*, Spiegel v. Evergreen Cemetery Co., 117 N.J.L. 90, 93 (N.J. Sup. 1936).

52. In re Johnson, 94 N.M. 491, 494 (N.M. 1980) (acknowledging "a quasi-property right in a dead body which vests in the nearest relative of the deceased").

53. The *Pierce* court gives meaning to a ranking order as regarding burial and disposition, including recognizing that what is now called first person consent should be controlling in cases where disputes arise regarding interment.

54. Unif. Anatomical Gift Act §2 (1968).

55. Trinity Universal Ins. Co. v. Turner Funeral Home, No. 1:02-cv-231, No. 1:02-cv-298, No. 1:03-cv-083, 2003 U.S. Dist. LEXIS 27205, at *30 (E.D. Tenn. Dec. 12, 2003) (quoting Hill v. Travelers Ins. Co., 154 Tenn. 295, 298, 294 S.W. 1097, 1098 (1927)) (emphasis added).

56. Perry v. Saint Francis Hosp. & Med. Ctr., 886 F. Supp. 1551, 1563 (D. Kan. 1995).

57. In re Tri-State Crematory Litig., 215 F.R.D. 660, 697 (N.D. Ga. 2007) (emphasis added).

58. Wells v. Nuwayhid, No. 96 C 4456, 1996 U.S. Dist. LEXIS 17541, at *7 (N.D. Ill. Nov. 13, 1996).

59. *Id.* The parents were unsuccessful in their litigation because the doctor in question was sued in his individual capacity — and not as an actor of the state. *Id.*

60. State v. Bradbury, 136 Me. 347 (Me. 1939).

61. *Id.* at 348.

62. *Id.*

63. *Id.*

64. *Id.* at 351.

65. Whaley v. County of Tuscola, 58 F.3d 1111 (6th Cir. 1995).

66. Martin v. Kim, No. 2:03-cv-536, 2005 U.S. Dist. LEXIS 20595 (N.D. Ind. Sept. 19, 2005).

67. Hill v. Travelers Ins. Co., 154 Tenn. 295, 298, 294 S.W. 1097, 1098 (Tenn. 1927).

68. Siver v. Rockingham Mem. Hosp., 48 F. Supp. 2d 608 (W.D. Va. 1999).

69. Sweigart v. Heritage Mem. Funeral Home, Inc., 5:06-cv-221 (CAR), 2007 U.S. Dist. LEXIS 61507 (M.D. Ga. Aug. 16, 2007).

70. Palenzke v. Bruning, 98 Ill. App. 644 (1901); Wells v. Nuwayhid, No. 96 C 4456, 1996 U.S. Dist. LEXIS 17541 (N.D. Ill. Nov. 13, 1996).

71. *See, e.g.* Unif. Anatomical Gift Act §5(b), 8A U.L.A. 47 (amended 1987).

72. Unif. Anatomical Gift Act §4 (1987).

73. *See* Md. Code Ann., Est. & Trusts §4-509.1 (West 2005)

74. Unif. Anatomical Gift Act §4 (stating "[t]he [coroner] [medical examiner] may release and permit the removal of a part from a body within that official's custody . . .").

75. *See e.g.*, Michele Goodwin, Black Markets: The Supply and Demand of Body Parts (2006).

76. *See, e.g.*, Frammolino, *supra* note 5 (noting that the lack of noticeable physical differences is how coroners have managed to remove corneas without the knowledge of relatives); S. Gregory Boyd, Comment, *Considering a Market in Human Organs*, 4 N.C. J.L. & Tech. 417, 441 (2003) (discussing a Florida court's characterization of corneal removal as a small instrusion).

77. *See, e.g.*, Frammolino, *supra* note 5; Boyd, *supra* note 76.

78. Marie-Andree Jacob, *On Silencing and Slicing: Presumed Consent to Post-Mortem Organ "Donation" in Diversified Societies*, 11 Tul. J. Comp. & Int'l L. 239, 254–55 (2003) (describing the criticism that presumed consent is unethical); Maryellen Liddy, *The "New Body Snatchers": Analyzing the Effect of Presumed Consent Organ Donation Laws on Privacy, Autonomy, and Liberty*, 28 Fordham Urb. L.J. 815, 819 (2001) (describing that many supporters believe presumed consent will increase the supply of organs available for transplant).

79. Linda C. Fentiman, *Organ Donation as National Service: A Proposed Federal Organ Donation Law*, 27 Suffolk U. L. Rev. 1593 (1993); Boyd, *supra* note 76; Theodore Silver, *The Case for a Post-Mortem Organ Draft and a Proposed Model Organ Draft Act*, 68 B.U. L. Rev. 681 (1988).

80. Georgia Lions Eye Bank v. Lavant, 335 S.E.2d 127 (Ga. 1985).

81. *Id.* at 128.

82. *Id.*

83. *Id.*

84. Pollard v. Phelps, 193 S.E. 102, 106 (Ga. Ct. App. 1937).

85. Brotherton v. Cleveland, 923 F.2d 477 (6th Cir. 1991).

86. Id. at 482.

87. *See, e.g.,* Fred H. Cate, Symposium: Organ Donation, *Human Organ Transplantation: The Role of Law,* 20 J. Corp. L. 69, 84 (1995) (presumed consent "laws generally provide that a coroner or medical examiner may remove the corneas from a cadaver in the course of a legally-required autopsy . . .").

88. *See* Gabriel Escobar, *Deaths Pose Continuing D.C. Mystery; City Carries Hundreds of Undetermined Cases, Muddying Vital Statistics,* Wash. Post, Dec. 22, 1997, at A1 (commenting on the rise in urban violence in the 1980s and remarking that many of the deaths of black urban Americans from that era remain unsolved).

89. Frammolino, supra note 5, at A1; *see also The Late Edition: Crime in the U.S. Is Discussed* (CNN television broadcast Oct. 24, 1993) (Transcript #4-2); Eric Lichtblau, *Reporter's Notebook: Going Beyond Line Scores of Gang Carnage,* L.A. Times, Nov. 25, 1990, at B3 (noting that during a one-month time span there were over 300 gang-related killings in Los Angeles County).

90. Newman v. Sathyavaglswaran, 287 F.3d 786, 800 (9th Cir. 2002) (Fernandez, J., dissenting).

91. *Id.* (declaring that states can, when conferring a duty to dispose of decedent's body, limit property rights to mere possessory interests).

92. *Id.*

93. *Id.*

94. *Id.*

95. *Id.*

96. *Id.* at 790 n.5.

97. *Id.* at 795 (quoting United States v. Gen. Motors Corp, 323 U.S. 373, 378 (1945)).

98. *Id.* (quoting Bd. of Regents v. Roth, 408 U.S. 564, 577 (1072)).

99. *Id.* at 789–90.

100. *Id.* at 790 (quoting Bd. of Regents v. Roth, 408 U.S. 564, 571–72 (1972)).

101. Bd. of Regents v. Roth, 408 U.S. 564 (1972).

102. *Id.* at 577.

103. *See* Lori Andrews & Dorothy Nelkin, Body Bazaar: The Market for Human Tissue in the Biotechnological Age (2001) (warning of an inevitable devaluation of human life resulting from business interests in harvesting human tissues). *See also* Arthur L. Caplan, If I Were a Rich Man Could I Buy a Pancreas? and Other Essays on the Ethics of Health Care 158 (1992).

104. Miller v. Hartford Hosp., 40 Conn. L. Rptr. 508 (Conn. Super. Ct. 2005).

105. *See, e.g., Human Aorta Valve May Qualify as Product,* Ct. Law Trib., Jan 9, 2006.

106. *See* Martin v. Young Kim, No. 2:03-cv-536, 2005 U.S. Dist. LEXIS 20595 (N.D. Ind. Sept. 19, 2005) (where a young man was killed and the parents wished to have his kidney donated to his uncle, but were denied because the coroner determined an autopsy would be necessary, thus rendering the kidneys unavailable, the court held the claim survived summary judgment because Indiana case law supported a property right in a deceased family member).

107. Newman v. Sathyavaglswaran, 287 F.3d at 789; *see also* Brotherton v. Cleveland, 923 F.2d 477, 481 (6th Cir. 1991) (extending rights in oneself to "quasi-property" rights in decedent's next of kin); *Martin,* No. 2:03-cv-536, 2005 U.S. Dist. LEXIS 20595 (applying *Brotherton* reasoning to a refusal to allow a kidney transplant from decedent to decedent's cousin due to a mandatory autopsy law for homicide victims).

108. 287 F.3d at 789.

109. *Id.*

110. *Id.* at 789.

111. Cruzan v. Missouri Dep't of Health, 497 U.S. 261 (1990).

112. *Id.* at 305 (1990) (Brennan, J., dissenting), as quoted in *Newman,* 287 F.3d at 789.

113. Orr interview, *supra* note 49.

114. *Id.*

115. *Id.*

116. *Id.*

117. Unif. Anatomical Gift Act (2006) (Refs. & Annos.).

118. S.B. 1403 Gen. Assem., Reg. Sess. (Ca. 1998).

Part V

PUBLIC HEALTH

Chapter 8

JACOBSON

v.

MASSACHUSETTS

The Police Power and Civil Liberties in Tension[1]

LAWRENCE O. GOSTIN* and KATRINA A. PAGONIS**

The contention that compulsory vaccination is an infraction of personal liberty and an unconstitutional interference with the right of the individual to have the smallpox if he wants it, and to communicate it to others, has been ended [by the U.S. Supreme Court]. . . . [This] should end the useful life of the societies of cranks formed to resist the operation of laws relative to vaccination. Their occupation is gone.

New York Times, February 22, 1905[2]

Vaccination may bother you a little, but smallpox would interfere much more seriously with your business.

Boston Daily Globe, November 19, 1901[3]

Jacobson v. Massachusetts,[4] the 1905 U.S. Supreme Court case upholding the power of states to compel vaccination, is generally viewed as the foundational judicial decision in public health law.[5] The case arose out of efforts to control Boston's last smallpox epidemic, an outbreak that, from 1901 to 1903, resulted in 1,596 cases and 270 deaths.[6] In the winter of 1902, the Cambridge Board of Health, acting under Massachusetts' compulsory vaccination law, ordered the vaccination and re-vaccination of all Cambridge residents above the age of twenty-one.[7] On July 17, 1902, a complaint was issued against Henning Jacobson, and he was summoned along with Albert M. Pear and Frank Cone to appear in district court.[8] Thus began perhaps the most important Supreme Court case in the history of American public health.

---

* Associate Dean (Research and Academic Programs), the Linda D. and Timothy J. O'Neill Professor of Global Health Law, and Faculty Director of the O'Neill Institute for National and Global Health Law, Georgetown University; Professor of Public Health, the Johns Hopkins University; Fellow, Oxford University, Center for SocioLegal Studies.
** Fellow, O'Neill Institute for National and Global Health Law, Georgetown University.

The impact of *Jacobson* on modern public health jurisprudence is more than evident from an examination of the seventy Supreme Court decisions that have cited *Jacobson* over the past century (see Table 8.1 on page 178). These decisions range from the famous to the infamous; they include *Roe v. Wade*[9] (abortion) and *Buck v. Bell*[10] (compulsory sterilization). A central question is why is *Jacobson* so foundational in modern public health law? Is it because of the Supreme Court's deference to public health decision making? Is it because the Court enunciated a framework for the protection of individual liberties that persists today? Perhaps it is because *Jacobson* was decided during the same term as *Lochner v. New York*[11] — the most infamous Supreme Court case of its era. If *Lochner* was judicial activism at its extreme for striking down reasonable economic regulation, then *Jacobson* was judicial recognition of the police power, the most important aspect of state sovereignty. A further question deserves attention: would *Jacobson* be decided the same way today? It is fitting, given the modern emphasis on biosecurity and public health, to reexamine the case's historical context and to consider the importance and enduring meaning of the most famous decision in the realm of public health law.

A. The 1901–1903 Smallpox Epidemic

In the years leading up to the Boston epidemic, scattered cases of smallpox developed among towns to the north of Boston. Twelve miles outside of Boston, in the city of Swampscott, a case of smallpox was reported in May 1899. Over the summer, there were cases in Everett and in Charlestown, which is just across the Charles River from Boston.[12] Cases continued to be reported through 1901, and, in the summer of 1901, dozens of cases appeared in the Roxbury neighborhood of Boston.[13] By the fall, numerous cases were reported throughout the city.[14] The epidemic peaked in December of 1901, and from November through January, over 200 smallpox cases emerged each month in Boston.[15]

With the proliferation of cases came a surge in voluntary vaccination. The city offered free vaccination stations, which residents widely used. The *Boston Daily Globe* opined, "There is a greater demand for vaccination in Boston than there is for salvation, even though both are free."[16] Boston's Board of Health estimated that by mid-December, 400,000 persons in the city underwent vaccination or revaccination.[17]

But this initial surge in voluntary vaccination did not result in complete coverage. According to the city's Board of Health, Boston was "practically a hot-bed of the anti-vaccine heresy."[18] And, on December 27, 1901, the Boston Board of Health ordered the vaccination or revaccination of all Boston residents who had not been successfully vaccinated since 1897.[19] Two months later, the Cambridge Board of Health followed suit and issued a similar vaccination order:

> Whereas, smallpox has been prevalent to some extent in the city of Cambridge and still continues to increase; and whereas, it is necessary for the speedy extermination of the disease, that all persons not protected by vaccination should be vaccinated; and whereas, in the opinion of the board, the public health and safety require the vaccination or re-vaccination of all the inhabitants of Cambridge; be it ordered that all the inhabitants of the city who have not been successfully vaccinated since March 1, 1897, be vaccinated or re-vaccinated.[20]

It was the enforcement of this order that led to Jacobson's arrest, conviction, and famed appeal.

Boston's vaccination efforts mainly targeted the working class and poor and were at times coercive. In January 1902, the Board of Health deployed 125 physicians to vaccinate those in the working-class neighborhood of East Boston. The doctors went door-to-door on a Sunday, hoping to catch families spending their day off at home.[21] Workers were also the target of a Board of Health circular, which recommended that employers require certificates of vaccination or revaccination from all employees to protect the "health, comfort and business interests" of the city.[22] The city physician in Lynn, Massachusetts went a step further — he approached an employer who had recently hired cutters to break a strike and demanded that all the cutters show evidence of recent vaccination or be vaccinated on the spot. "Some objected, but the physician declared they must consent or be arrested."[23]

Vaccination among the poor was far more coercive and, at times, involved outright violence. In November 1901, a month before Boston's vaccination order came into effect, the Board of Health undertook forcible vaccinations targeting the city's homeless. The city organized a "compulsory vaccination squad," which, according to local newspaper reports, was to "visit the cheap lodging houses and vaccinate all the men they find there, whether the lodgers are yearning for free vaccination or not."[24] The vaccination campaign involved a plan where

> one policeman should stand guard at the outer door of the lodging house after the vaccinating party had entered, prepared to bar the egress of any tramp who wanted to get away, while the three other policemen were to go with the doctors from cot to cot, and where resistance was offered, hold down the objector until he had been operated upon.[25]

The press observed an officer club in the head one man who resisted: "The tramp went down in a heap on the floor, and then the policeman jumped on him, and the vigor with which the doctor, who had been wait[ing] with his vaccine point in hand, jumped forward and jabbed the virus into his arm made the tramp shout."[26] The doctor then gave the man stitches where his skin had split from the blow. When anecdotal evidence of a similar event was discussed at the meeting of state boards of health in January 1902, Dr. W. T. Sedgwick, Professor of Biology and Public Health at the Massachusetts Institute of Technology, asserted, "[Cases] must be decided on the basis of the greatest good to the greatest number. A man would not be allowed to go through the subway with a stick of dynamite."[27]

In the end, 485,000 people in Boston were vaccinated (some voluntarily, others by coercion or outright force) by early 1902. Between 1901 and 1903, there were 1,596 cases of smallpox and 270 deaths. The overall case fatality rate during the epidemic was seventeen percent, but the case fatality rate was lower at eleven percent among those who had previously been vaccinated. Individuals who had never been vaccinated experienced a higher case fatality rate of twenty-two percent.[28]

B. Cambridge's Vaccination Order and Jacobson's Resistance

On March 15, 1902, less than a month after the passage of Cambridge's vaccination order, the chairman of the Board of Health, E. Edwin Spencer, visited the Reverend Henning Jacobson, who refused to be vaccinated.[29] That same day, Dr. Felix McGirr, who had been retained by the Board of Health to aid enforcement, called upon Albert M. Pear and "informed him that if he refused to be vaccinated he would incur the penalty of five dollars provided by the vaccination law, and would be prosecuted therefor and then and there offered to vaccinate [Pear] without any expense to him; but [Pear] then and there absolutely refused to be vaccinated."[30] In July 1902, Pear and Jacobson were arraigned along with Frank Cone.

Both Pear and Cone worked for the city of Cambridge — Pear was an assistant city clerk and Cone was employed in the city water office.[31] Pear was the most well known of the three men, described as "one of the most strenuous antivaccinationists" in Cambridge. In an interview after his arraignment, the thirty-two-year-old Pear claimed that he was taking "powders" from his physician to prevent smallpox infection and that he would not submit to vaccination before exploring his legal rights. He declared, "I do not propose that the board of health shall dictate to me what medicine I shall put into my system."[32] Jacobson, Cone, and Pear were tried at the same time as Ephraim and Maggie Gould and Paul Morse. Morse was found innocent upon proof of vaccination. Only Jacobson and Pear appealed their convictions.[33]

Little is known about the life of Henning Jacobson. He was born in Yllestad, Västergötland, Sweden on September 15, 1856. At thirteen, Jacobson left Sweden for Rockford, Illinois, where he "experienced a thorough conversion" during a general "spiritual awakening" in the area. He studied at Augustana College in Rock Island, Illinois, and then worked as a student pastor in Illinois, Iowa, and Connecticut, spending some time at Yale Divinity School along the way. In 1882, he married Hattie C. Anderson, and they had five children together. In 1892, Rev. Jacobson was ordained and began his service as pastor in Cambridge, Massachusetts. There, he oversaw the building and dedication of Augustana Church in 1909. He delivered his last sermon at Augustana Church on October 12, 1930, and died the following night at seventy-four years of age.[34]

Pastor Henning Jacobson
1892 - 1930

The Reverend Henning Jacobson, at sixty-six years of age, twenty years after he refused to obey the Cambridge vaccination order and became the subject of the most important Supreme Court decision in public health law. Photo courtesy of the Archives of the Evangelical Lutheran Church in America.

The historical record contains mere suggestions as to why Jacobson steadfastly defied the Cambridge vaccination order. Some have suggested that his religious beliefs played a role; he practiced a form of pietism in which spirituality was infused into daily life.[35] Resistance to vaccination was also generally strong among recent immigrants from northern Europe like Jacobson.[36] But it appears to have been his personal experiences that made Jacobson especially wary of vaccination. According to Jacobson's filings in the Massachusetts courts:

> [He] refused to submit to vaccination for the reason that he had, when a child, been caused great and extreme suffering, for a long period, by a disease produced by his vaccination at that time.
>
> [He] had witnessed a similar result of vaccination in the case of his own son, and . . . [Jacobson's] refusal was prompted by his knowledge of the danger and his dread of the terrible consequence of vaccination.[37]

It is not clear what, if any, adverse reaction Jacobson or his son suffered. Jacobson was predeceased by his son Joseph Henning,[38] but there is no evidence that Joseph's death was related to his vaccination or even that it was Joseph rather than one of Jacobson's two other sons that suffered the alleged adverse reaction.

Beyond Jacobson's legal appeals, there is little documentation of his participation in any antivaccinationist activities. In November 1902, Jacobson did participate in a meeting of the Massachusetts Anticompulsory Vaccination Society. He attended the meeting along with his attorney J. W. Pickering. At the meeting, Pickering briefed the group on Jacobson's and Pear's pending appeals, and Jacobson "told of the terrible experience of himself and [his] children from vaccination, and of his own knowledge of the uselessness of the practice."[39] This is the only known evidence of Jacobson's participation in antivaccinationist activities.[40] His obituaries make no mention of the vaccination controversy or his involvement in the landmark case.[41]

After Jacobson and Pear were found guilty in the third district court of Eastern Middlesex, they secured Pickering's representation. At Jacobson's jury trial on February 27, 1903, the court refused to admit Jacobson's evidence disputing the safety and efficacy of vaccination and the jury returned a guilty verdict. Pear and Jacobson appealed their cases, and on April 2, 1903, the Supreme Judicial Court of Massachusetts affirmed their convictions, holding that the compulsory vaccination law was constitutional and that the exclusion of Jacobson's evidence was proper.[42] Jacobson, now represented by the prominent lawyer and politician George Fred Williams[43] and James A. Halloran, appealed his case to the U.S. Supreme Court. Oral arguments were heard December 6, 1904. By a 7-to-2 decision,[44] handed down on February 20, 1905, the Supreme Court affirmed Jacobson's conviction.

C. The Immunization Debates and Jacobson's Fourteen "Facts"

The Boston epidemic generally reignited the smallpox immunization debate, and there was plenty of hyperbole on both sides. Antivaccinationists launched a "scathing attack":[45] compulsory vaccination is "the greatest crime of the age"; it "slaughter[s] tens of thousands of innocent children;" and "is more important than the slavery question, because it is debilitating the whole human race."[46] The antivaccinationists gave notice that compulsory powers "will cause a riot."[47]

Their influence was noticeable, on both sides of the Atlantic. Antivaccinationist efforts successfully secured the insertion of a "conscience clause" in Britain's vaccination laws, exempting any parent who can "satisfy Justices in petty sessions that he conscientiously believes that vaccination would be prejudicial to the health of the child."[48]

The response of the mainstream press was equally shrill, characterizing the debate as "a conflict between intelligence and ignorance, civilization and barbarism."[49] The *New York Times* remarked that "No enemy of vaccination could ask better than to have England's compulsory vaccination law nullified by that [conscience] clause"; the paper referred to antivaccinationists as a "familiar species of crank," whose arguments are "absurdly fallacious."[50] The mainstream media continued its campaign against the "jabberings" of "hopeless cranks" for years,[51] joined by the medical media, which depicted antivaccinationists as "ignorant" and "deficient in the power to judge [science]."[52]

In the Massachusetts courts, Jacobson's arguments frequently mirrored that of prominent antivaccinationists. In support of his claim that the vaccination order violated the United States and Massachusetts constitutions, Jacobson offered to prove fourteen "facts" relating to vaccination, some of which were common antivaccinationist contentions of the day. For example, Jacobson charged that vaccination is ineffective and actually spreads smallpox, offering to prove:

> that vaccination does not prevent the spread or contagion of smallpox; . . . that in fact all the beneficial results in combating smallpox are fairly attributable to [sanitation, isolation, and disinfection], and in no part to vaccination; that on the contrary, vaccination is a positive means of disseminating and spreading smallpox in the community.[53]

Antivaccinationist literature similarly argued that the decline in smallpox was actually "a necessary consequence of improved sanitary conditions of life among people"[54] and that vaccination is a "plague" generating increased mortality.[55] Jacobson also echoed popular antivaccinationist beliefs when he offered to show that the vaccine virus "is not analagous [sic] to smallpox, but to greatpox, or syphilis, whence the syphilitic nature of the sores and symptoms of the sores produced."[56]

Amidst these extreme claims in Jacobson's fourteen "facts," however, are some legitimate concerns regarding the safety of smallpox vaccination and the appropriateness of compulsory vaccination. In particular, nine of Jacobson's "facts" focus on the risk of adverse reactions and a tenth addresses the risks associated with contaminated vaccine serum. Evidence in support of these facts, however, was excluded at trial as immaterial[57] because such evidence would only have invited a judicial balancing of the risks and benefits of the compulsory vaccination policy. As the Supreme Judicial Court of Massachusetts noted, "[If] a statute purports to be enacted to promote the general welfare of the people, and is not at variance with any provision of the Constitution, the question whether it will be for the good of the community is a legislative, and not a judicial, question."[58] Jacobson's offers of proof, "in effect, invited the court and jury to go over the whole ground gone over by the legislature when it enacted the statute in question."[59] Instead, United States Supreme Court Justice Harlan asserted, the balancing of vaccination risks and benefits was properly left to the legislative rather than the judicial branch. To find for Jacobson on the basis of his purported facts "would practically strip the legislative department of its function to care for the public health and the public safety when endangered by disease."[60]

Nonetheless, Jacobson's claims warrant discussion because they capture much of the substantive critique of compulsory vaccination at the time. Nine of Jacobson's points touch on the health effects and risks of smallpox vaccination and his apprehension of these risks. He offered to prove:

1. Vaccination often results in injury to health.
2. Vaccination occasionally causes death.
3. Vaccination causes loathsome diseases.
4. The result of vaccination cannot be foretold in any case.
5. Vaccination results in incapacitating sickness, more or less prolonged.
6. Impure condition of the blood makes vaccination dangerous.
7. Danger from impurity of the blood cannot be tested.
   . . .
13. Defendant refused vaccination because he had previously suffered from it.
14. Defendant's son had suffered severely and defendant feared serious consequences.[61]

Taken together, these points assert that smallpox vaccination is dangerous, that it is impossible to tell who will experience an adverse reaction from vaccination, and that Jacobson feared an adverse reaction based on his personal experiences.

After vaccination, patients typically experience a variety of symptoms, and, in some cases, life-threatening adverse reactions. In a modern smallpox vaccination study, every vaccinee reported one or more of the following vaccine-associated symptoms: fatigue (50%), headache (40%), muscle aches and chills (20%), nausea (20%), and fever (10%). A ten-state survey in 1968 found that there were 953.3 serious but non-life-threatening adverse reactions per million vaccinees; these generally consisted of severe rashes. Life-threatening reactions (e.g., postvaccinial central nervous system disease, which is associated with brain lesions, altered mental status, lethargy, seizures, and coma) occurred in 52.3 patients per million vaccinees. A little over one vaccinee per million suffered an adverse reaction resulting in death. With the eradication of smallpox in the United States in the 1940s, vaccination risks soon outweighed the risk of smallpox; accordingly, the United States Public Health Service recommended in 1971 that routine smallpox vaccination be discontinued.[62] But, during a smallpox epidemic, such as the one experienced by Boston in 1901–1903, the calculation of risks was quite different. According to Marcus P. Knowlton, Chief Justice of the Massachusetts Supreme Judicial Court, medical experts at the time "generally . . . considered the risk of such an injury too small to be seriously weighed as against the benefits coming from the discreet and proper use of [vaccination]."[63] Jacobson's alleged "facts" focused on contesting this popularly accepted balance of risks concerning vaccination.

Some modern commentators read Jacobson's thirteenth and fourteenth facts as challenging more than the underlying medical science; they understand him to be arguing that he was uniquely susceptible to an adverse reactions based on his past experiences and that of his son. One scholar has gone so far as to characterize the failure to allow Jacobson to introduce evidence on this point as "truly embarrassing" to modern eyes.[64] The U.S. Supreme Court, however, did not treat Jacobson's appeal as raising such a challenge. Justice Harlan, writing for the majority, says:

> It is easy, for instance, to suppose the case of an adult who is embraced by the mere words of the act, but yet to subject [him] to vaccination in [light of] a particular condition of his health or body would be cruel and inhuman to the last degree. We are not to be understood as holding that the statute was intended to be applied in such a case or, if it was so intended, that the judiciary would not be competent to interfere and protect the health and life of the individual concerned. . . . No such case is here presented.[65]

Rather, Jacobson was "in perfect health and a fit subject of vaccination."[66] Justice Harlan at one point explicitly notes, "[T]he defendant did not offer to prove that, by reason of his then condition, he was in fact not a fit subject of vaccination."[67] The Court's understanding of Jacobson's argument is not at odds with his fourteen facts. Taken as a whole Jacobson's offers of proof do not amount to an argument that he was unusually susceptible to an adverse reaction; rather, they focus more on the general risk of adverse reactions. In fact, his fourth and seventh allegations assert that one cannot determine whether a particular individual has a heightened risk of an adverse reaction because the result of vaccination "cannot be foretold in any case" and impurity of the blood, which makes vaccination dangerous, "cannot be tested."[68] Read in the context of Jacobson's fourteen facts, it appears that Jacobson's allegations concerning his and his son's past experiences were offered as anecdotal support of his larger argument that adverse reactions often result from vaccination. Had Jacobson's offers of proof focused on a unique susceptibility to an adverse reaction, instead of demonstrating the "theoretical possibility"[69] of an adverse reaction, a very different case might have been presented.

Jacobson's fourteen "facts" also addressed the risk posed by "spurious vaccine points." In the eighth of his fourteen "facts," Jacobson sought to prove that the

> vaccine matter, or points, that is used for the purpose of vaccination, as manufactured and sold for use, quite often is impure and in a condition unfit and dangerous to be so used, and that there is no known practical test [by which an ordinary physician could determine whether the vaccine is impure and] a source of danger.[70]

Concerns regarding spurious vaccine matter — serum that is ineffective or dangerous because of contamination or otherwise — date back to Edward Jenner's original discovery of the smallpox vaccine.[71] But, despite over a century of reports on spurious vaccines and the prevalence of compulsory vaccination laws and regulations at the turn of the century, the safety of smallpox vaccine supplies was not uniformly assured in 1902. Before 1902, the federal government did not regulate the production or sale of vaccines.[72] Some states undertook responsibility for providing safe vaccine. For example, New York boards of health were responsible under state law for supplying safe vaccines.[73] But, many other states, including Massachusetts, did not have adequate legislation in 1902. After the epidemic and Jacobson's arrest, Massachusetts enacted legislation providing for the state-sponsored production of the smallpox vaccine.[74]

Bacterial contamination was a documented problem with unregulated vaccine points. In 1895, Dr. Walter Reed, a surgeon in the U.S. Army, undertook an evaluation of the purity of vaccine points from six vaccine companies.

Averages of 383 to 73,300 colonies of bacteria were found per vaccine point for the different companies.[75]

At the turn of the century, the scientific community's understanding of how to prevent bacterial contamination was at a relatively nascent stage. In 1891, Sydney Arthur Monckton Copeman demonstrated that the addition of glycerin in distilled water to calf lymph vaccine reduced the risk of bacterial contamination. Public health departments in England began public distribution of glycerinated vaccine in 1899. The New York Department of Health also began using glycerinated vaccine in the late 1890s after sending representatives to observe the practice in Europe's most noted vaccine laboratories. But excessive bacterial contamination of smallpox vaccine supplies remained a problem until the mid-twentieth century.[76] Interestingly, much of the modern controversies over vaccine safety have centered on another preservative, thimerosal, which was added to some vaccines to prevent bacterial and fungal contamination. (See further discussion of the thimerosal controversy below.)

In a competitive but unregulated market, the various vaccine manufacturers were free to make unevaluated claims about the relative safety and purity of their products. An article in the *Medical Times and Register*, a medical journal, described the situation as follows:

> [T]here are various brands of vaccine virus — some of them cheaper than others, some that are not tested with the same care, some that produce more apparent signs of having proved effective while in reality they have done nothing towards rendering the patient immune against smallpox, but have only caused a septic sore.[77]

A November 18, 1901, editorial in the *New York Times* called for regulation of vaccine production. The article described the open market of vaccine production and the "tempting[ ] profit[s]" of the vaccine business: "Vaccine and serum farms are springing up all over the country, without adequate supervision and in many cases under the direction of ignorant and irresponsible managers."[78] The editors concluded:

> It is not enough to place [vaccine producers] under the perfunctory oversight of State Boards of health, to be looked after when complaints are received or injury has been inflicted. No one should be permitted anywhere to begin or continue the business without a permit issued after his premises have been critically inspected by a qualified expert, and certified in correct in every detail, and such permit should remain operative only so long as he maintains standards which . . . are beyond criticism.[79]

These recommendations were largely adopted the next summer when Congress passed the Biologics Control Act of 1902, which banned the importation or interstate shipment of vaccine virus not produced at federally licensed facilities.[80] While the Act was passed a few weeks before Jacobson's arraignment, it did not take effect until months after his trial.

But while Jacobson's "facts" regarding spurious vaccines may have been politically salient, they were not legally significant. Even if the entirety of Jacobson's claims regarding spurious vaccine were true and could be proven by competent evidence, the legal result would have remained the same. The courts in Massachusetts and the District of Columbia were firm in asserting the overarching principle of legislative deference.[81]

D. The Many Faces of *Jacobson*: Personal Freedom and the Common Good

It was within this historical context that the U.S. Supreme Court decided *Jacobson v. Massachusetts*. Justice Harlan's opinion had many faces and was, at some points, in tension. Relying on social compact theory, Harlan displayed strong deference to public health agencies. Relying on a theory of limited government, Harlan set standards to safeguard individual freedoms. This was a classic case of reconciling individual interests in bodily integrity with collective interests in health and safety. In the more than 100 years since *Jacobson*, the case has been cited in 70 Supreme Court cases — most in support of the police power and a minority in support of individual freedom (see Table 8.1).

1. Social Compact Theory: The Police Power and Public Health Deference

In early American jurisprudence, before *Jacobson*, the judiciary staunchly defended the police powers, which Chief Justice Marshall in *Gibbons v. Ogden* (1824) described as "that immense mass of legislation, [including] . . . inspection laws, quarantine laws, [and] health laws of every description."[82] To Justice Miller in *The Slaughter-House Cases* (1873), the police power was preeminent for "upon it depends the security of social order, the life and health of the citizen, the comfort of an existence in a thickly populated community, the enjoyment of private and social life, and the beneficial use of property."[83] The judiciary even periodically suggested that public health regulation was immune from constitutional review, expressing the notion that "where the police power is set in motion in its proper sphere, the courts have no jurisdiction to stay the arm of the legislative branch."[84] The core issue, of course, was to understand what was meant by the "proper legislative sphere," for it was not supposed, at least since the enactment of the Fourteenth Amendment in 1868, that government could act in an arbitrary manner free from judicial control.[85]

The *Jacobson* Court's use of social compact theory to support this expansive understanding of police powers was unmistakable. Justice Harlan preferred a community-oriented philosophy where citizens have duties to one another and to society as a whole:

> [T]he liberty secured by the Constitution . . . does not import an absolute right in each person to be . . . wholly freed from restraint. . . . On any other basis organized society could not exist with safety to its members. . . . [The Massachusetts Constitution] laid down as a fundamental . . . social compact that the whole people covenants with each citizen, and each citizen with the whole people, that all shall be governed by certain laws for the "common good," and that government is instituted "for the protection, safety, prosperity and happiness of the people, and not for the profit, honor or private interests of any one man. . . ."[86]

The Court's opinion is filled with examples ranging from sanitary laws and animal control to quarantine, demonstrating the breadth of police powers. Justice Harlan granted considerable leeway to the elected branch of government, displaying an almost unquestioning acceptance of legislative findings of scientific fact. He was also a federalist, asserting the primacy of state over federal authority in public health. The distinct tenor of the opinion was deferential to agency action.[87]

A primary legacy of *Jacobson*, then, surely is its defense of social welfare philosophy and police power regulation. Although the progressive era appeal to collective interests no longer has currency, most of the 70 Supreme Court cases citing *Jacobson* do so in defense of the police power (see Table 8.1). Post-*Jacobson* decisions affirm the state's authority to regulate individuals and businesses for public health and safety (8); limit liberty to achieve common goods (34); permit legislatures to delegate broad powers to public health agencies (5); and defer to the judgment of legislatures and agencies in the exercise of their powers (14).

2. Theory of Limited Government: Safeguarding Individual Liberty

Jacobson's social compact theory was in tension with its theory of limited government. Beyond its passive acceptance of state discretion in matters of public health was the Court's first systematic statement of the constitutional limitations imposed on government. *Jacobson* established a floor of constitutional protection consisting of four overlapping standards: necessity, reasonable means, proportionality, and harm avoidance. These standards, while permissive of public health intervention, nevertheless required a deliberative governmental process to safeguard liberty.[88]

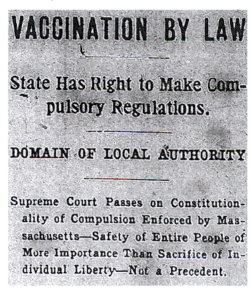

A report on the Supreme Court's decision in *Jacobson* was featured on the front page of the *Washington Post* on February 21, 1905. Copyright 1905 The Washington Post Co.

Necessity. Justice Harlan, writing for the Court, insisted that police powers must be based on the "necessity of the case" and could not be exercised in "an arbitrary, unreasonable manner" or go "beyond what was reasonably required for the safety of the public."[89] The state must act only in the face of a demonstrable health threat. Necessity requires, at a minimum, that the subject of the compulsory intervention must pose a threat to the community.

Reasonable Means. Although government may act under conditions of necessity, its methods must be reasonably designed to prevent or ameliorate the threat. *Jacobson* adopted a means/ends test that required a reasonable relationship between the public health intervention and the achievement of a legitimate public health objective. Even though the objective of the legislature may be valid and beneficent, the methods adopted must have a "real or substantial relation" to protection of the public health, and cannot be "a plain, palpable invasion of rights."[90]

Proportionality. Even under conditions of necessity and with reasonable means, a public health regulation is unconstitutional if the human burden imposed is wholly disproportionate to the expected benefit. "[T]he police power of a State," said Justice Harlan, "may be exerted in such circumstances or by regulations so arbitrary and oppressive in particular cases as to justify the interference of the courts to prevent wrong, . . . and oppression."[91] Public health authorities have a constitutional responsibility not to overreach in ways that unnecessarily invade personal spheres of autonomy. This suggests a requirement for a reasonable balance between the public good to be achieved and the degree of personal invasion. If the intervention is gratuitously onerous or unfair it may overstep constitutional boundaries.

Harm Avoidance. Those who pose a risk to the community can be required to submit to compulsory measures for the common good. The control measure itself, however, should not pose a health risk to its subject. Justice Harlan emphasized that Henning Jacobson was a "fit person" for smallpox vaccination, but asserted that requiring a person to be immunized who would be harmed is "cruel and inhuman in the last degree."[92] If there had been evidence that the vaccination would seriously impair Jacobson's health, he may have prevailed in this historic case (see the discussion of Jacobson's fourteen "facts," *supra*). *Jacobson*-era cases reiterate the theme that public health actions must not harm subjects. Notably, courts required safe and habitable environments for persons subject to isolation or quarantine on the grounds that public health powers are designed to promote well-being, and not to punish the individual.[93]

The facts in *Jacobson* did not require the court to enunciate a standard of fairness under the Equal Protection clause of the Fourteenth Amendment because the vaccination requirement was generally applicable to all inhabitants of Cambridge. Nevertheless, the federal courts had already created such a standard in *Jew Ho v. Williamson* in 1900. In that case, a federal district court reviewed a quarantine for bubonic plague in San Francisco that operated exclusively against Chinese Americans. In striking down the quarantine, the court said that health authorities had acted with an "evil eye and an unequal hand."[94]

Several of these standards for protecting liberty have been discernable in U.S. Supreme Court cases citing *Jacobson* from 1905 through 2008 (see Table 8.1). Some cases cite *Jacobson* for the simple, albeit important, proposition that bodily integrity is a constitutionally protected liberty interest (6); others do so to require the state to have an important interest (real and substantial (6), compelling (1), or fairly balanced with individual interests (4)); and still others cite *Jacobson* to prevent the state from acting arbitrarily or unreasonably (7). Federalism is also used as a tool to rein in the national government, with one decision stating, probably incorrectly, that the federal government lacks the police power.

E. *Lochner v. New York*: The Antithesis of Good Judicial Governance

Jacobson was decided during the same term as *Lochner v. New York*, the beginning of the so-called *Lochner* era in constitutional law — from 1905 to 1937.

In *Lochner*, the Supreme Court held that a limitation on the hours that bakers could work violated the Due Process Clause of the Fourteenth Amendment. The Court perceived a limitation on bakers' hours as an interference with the freedom of contract, rather than as a legitimate police regulation. Yet Justice Harlan, in a powerful dissent, professed that the New York statute was expressly for the public's health. Quoting standard health treatises, Harlan observed that "[d]uring periods of epidemic diseases the bakers are generally the first to succumb to disease, and the number swept away during such periods far exceeds the number of other crafts."[95]

The *Lochner* era posed deep concerns for those who realized that much of what public health does interferes with economic freedoms involving contracts, business relationships, the use of property, and the practice of trades and professions. *Lochner*, in the words of Justice Harlan, in dissent, "would seriously cripple the inherent power of the states to care for the lives, health, and well-being of their citizens."[96] So it was. For in the next three decades, the Supreme Court struck down important health and social legislation protecting trades unions, setting minimum wages, protecting consumers from risky products, and regulating businesses.[97] By the time of the New Deal, those who believed that individuals do not have unfettered contractual freedom and that economic transactions were naturally constrained by unequal wealth and power relationships, challenged the laissez-faire philosophy that undergirded Lochnerism. This was also a time when people looked toward government to pursue actively the values of welfare, health, and greater socioeconomic equity. It was within this political context that the Supreme Court repudiated the principles of *Lochner*: "What is this freedom? The Constitution does not speak of freedom of contract."[98] The post-New Deal period led to a resurgence of a permissive judicial approach to public health regulation, irrespective of its effects on commercial and business affairs.

Why have legal historians viewed *Jacobson* so favorably and *Lochner* so unfavorably? *Lochner* represented an unwarranted judicial interference with democratic control over the economy to safeguard public health and the environment. *Lochner* was a form of judicial activism that was unreceptive to protective and redistributive regulation. The *Lochner* Court mistakenly saw market ordering as a state of nature rather than a legal construct.[99] *Jacobson* was the antithesis of *Lochner*, granting democratically elected officials discretion to pursue innovative solutions to hard social problems. Justice Harlan made no distinction between health and economic regulation, provided the government's objectives were legitimate and the interventions were measured.

F. *Jacobson* and Its Enduring Meaning

Supreme Court jurisprudence has progressed markedly from the deferential tone of *Jacobson* and its Progressive Era embrace of the social compact. The Warren Court, within the context of the civil rights movement, transformed constitutional law. The Court developed its "tiered" approach to due process and equal protection that placed a constitutional premium on the protection of liberty interests. Would *Jacobson* be decided the same way if it were presented to the Court today? The answer is indisputably "yes," even if the style and reasoning would differ. Indeed, if anything, the Roberts Court would be more likely to defer to the state's claims of scientific expertise and the public health imperatives of immunization.

The validity of *Jacobson* as a sound modern precedent seems, at first sight, almost too obvious. The federal and state courts, including the U.S. Supreme Court, have repeatedly affirmed its holding and reasoning, describing them as "settled" doctrine.[100] Developments in constitutional law and our understanding of the liberty interests protected under the Constitution have not diminished *Jacobson*'s precedential value. During the last several decades, the Supreme Court has recognized a constitutionally protected "liberty interest" in refusing unwanted medical treatment.[101] The Court accepted the principle of bodily integrity in cases involving the rights of persons with terminal illness and mental disability.[102] Outside the context of reproductive freedoms,[103] however, the Court has not viewed liberty interests in bodily integrity as "fundamental." Instead of heightened scrutiny, the Supreme Court balances a person's liberty against state interests. In fact, where it adopts a balancing test, the Court usually sides with the state.[104] The Court has held that health authorities may impose serious forms of treatment, such as anti-psychotic medication, if the person poses a danger to himself or others.[105] The lower courts, using a similar harm prevention theory, have upheld compulsory physical examination and treatment of persons with infectious diseases.[106]

The enduring value of *Jacobson* is also evident in lower courts' decisions on compulsory vaccination statutes, which have upheld compulsory vaccination on numerous occasions.[107] Even the rare judicial reservations about compulsory vaccination focus on religious exemptions and do not query the state's authority to create a generally applicable immunization requirement. For example, in 2001, a number of parents challenged the Arkansas compulsory vaccination statute in the federal courts. They argued that the school vaccination statute violated the Equal Protection and Due Process clauses of the Fourteenth Amendment and the Establishment and Free Exercise clauses of the First Amendment. The religious exemption provision of the vaccination statute, which only exempted members of recognized religious sects, was found to be unconstitutional but severable from the remainder of the compulsory vaccination statute.[108] Therefore, the compulsory vaccination statute, which was found to be constitutional, remained in force, untempered by an exemption provision. While consolidated appeals before the Eighth Circuit were pending, the appellants successfully lobbied the Arkansas legislature to rewrite the statute to allow philosophical as well as religious exemptions.

While *Jacobson* may now be settled law, many of the controversies that fueled the antivaccinationist movement at the turn of the twentieth century continue to animate vaccination debates at the turn of the twenty-first century. In particular, vaccine safety concerns still drive much of the public dialogue on vaccination. In the late 1990s, asthma, autism, diabetes, and multiple sclerosis were each claimed to be linked with vaccinations.[109] Claimed correlations between autism and the measles-mumps-rubella (MMR) vaccine and thimerosal-containing vaccines proved particularly salient as autism rates appeared to be rapidly climbing in the United States.[110]

Andrew Wakefield, a British physician, co-authored a 1998 article in *The Lancet* hypothesizing that twelve cases of severe intestinal abnormalities and autism were associated with the MMR vaccine given to the children years earlier.

Ten of the thirteen doctors involved in the study later retracted their support for the hypothesized correlation between the MMR vaccine and autism after the journal disclosed assertions of ethical improprieties, including the allegation that Dr. Wakefield was gathering evidence for a potential lawsuit on MMR-related autism at the time of the study.[111]

On the heels of the Wakefield study came a 1999 review by the Food and Drug Administration that found the use of thimerosal as a preservative in some vaccines may have resulted in children being exposed to cumulative levels of mercury over the first six months of life that exceed a federal guideline on methyl mercury. Thimerosal was being used as a preservative, particularly in vaccines sold in multidose preparations, because it is effective in preventing bacterial contamination. In a joint statement, the American Academy of Pediatrics and the U.S. Public Health Service recommended the removal of thimerosal from vaccines; as of this writing, all routine childhood vaccines, other than inactivated influenza vaccine, are thimerosal-free or contain only trace amounts of thimerosal.[112] Further study revealed no evidence of a causal relationship between thimerosal exposure in vaccines and neurodevelopmental disorders, including autism.[113]

As the thimerosal controversy erupted, safety concerns surrounded another vaccine; 15 cases of intussusception (a potentially fatal intestine blockage) were reported among children receiving the vaccine against rotavirus (one of the most common causes of severe diarrhea and serious infections in children).[114] The vaccine was pulled from the market within months. Some argued that the incident evidenced the dangers of vaccines, but others pointed to the swift reporting and response as demonstrating the effectiveness of the government's vaccine safety-monitoring system.[115]

In the wake of these highly publicized episodes, vaccine safety became a prominent issue, spurring congressional hearings and wide media coverage. Some parents, fearing adverse vaccination events, refused to vaccinate their children, resulting in an estimated 42,937 children remaining underimmunized in 2001 because of safety concerns.[116] Antivaccinationist attitudes among parents were fueled by an explosion of antivaccinationist literature on the Internet. These websites blended safety concerns with traditional libertarian critiques of childhood vaccination laws. One antivaccinationist website featured the following quote on its home page: "If the State can tag, track down and force citizens against their will to be injected with biologicals of unknown toxicity today, there will be no limit on what individual freedoms the state can take away in the name of the greater good tomorrow."[117]

Jacobson only began a debate about the appropriate boundaries of the police power that is still evolving today. Americans strongly support civil liberties, but they equally demand state protection of public health and safety. The compulsory immunization controversy still swirls, with flare-ups ranging from childhood and school vaccinations to counter-bioterror vaccinations for anthrax and small-pox.[118] Despite all the discordance in public opinion, *Jacobson* endures as a reasoned formulation of the boundaries between individual and collective interests in public health.

Table 8.1. U.S. Supreme Court Decisions Citing *Jacobson v. Massachusetts*: February 1905 - July 2008

Context of Citation to *Jacobson*	Assertion Cited to *Jacobson*	Majority Opinions	Concurring Opinions	Dissenting Opinions	Total Cases*
Public Health Deference: *Social Compact Theory*	State Can Regulate Individuals and Businesses to Protect Public Health and Safety[a]	8	1	—	8
	Liberty Interests Can Be Limited by the State[b]	22	7	9	34
	Questions of Policy and Science Are for the Legislature, Not the Courts[c]	13	—	1	14
	State Can Delegate Police Powers to Agencies[d]	5	—	—	5
Individual Rights: *Theory of Governmental Restraint*	Liberty Interests Safeguarded by the Constitution[e]	4	2	—	6
	Police Power Regulation Must Have Real and Substantial Relationship to State Interest[f]	5	1	—	6
	State Must Demonstrate Compelling State Interest in Exercise of Police Power[g]	1	—	—	1
	Evaluate Exercise of Police Power by Balancing State Interest against Implicated Individual Interest[h]	4	—	—	4
	Police Power Cannot Be Exercised in an Unreasonable or Arbitrary Manner[i]	6	—	1	7
	Federal Government Lacks the Police Power[j]	1	—	—	1
Statutory Construction	Courts Should Avoid Absurd Results in Interpreting Statutes[k]	2	—	—	2
Total*		**59**	**7**	**8**	**70**

* *Jacobson* was cited in a total of 78 Supreme Court cases, but citations in Supreme Court memoranda (8) were excluded from this analysis. *Jacobson* was sometimes cited for more than one assertion in a case or was cited in the majority opinion as well as concurring or dissenting opinions. Where *Jacobson* was cited for more than one assertion in a case or was cited in a concurring or dissenting opinion as well as the majority opinion, each reference was indicated separately on the table, but the case was only counted once in the total cases and total opinions.

Case Examples:

(a) German Alliance Insurance Co. v. Hale cites *Jacobson* when asserting that "all corporations, associations, and individuals . . . are subject to such regulations, in respect of their relative rights and duties, as the state may, in the exercise of its police power, . . . prescribe for the public convenience and the general good." 219 U.S. 307, 317 (1911).

(b) Williams v. Arkansas quotes *Jacobson* as saying: "the liberty secured by the Constitution . . . does not import an absolute right in each person to be at all times, and in all circumstances, wholly freed from restraint." 217 U.S. 79, 88 (1910).

(c) South Carolina State Highway Department v. Barnwell Bros. cites *Jacobson* when saying that where legislative action is "within the scope of the police power, fairly debatable questions as to its reasonableness, wisdom, and propriety are not for the determination of courts, but for the legislative body." 303 U.S. 177, 191 (1938).

(d) Plymouth Coal Co. v. Pennsylvania cites *Jacobson* when saying "it has become entirely settled that [police powers] may be delegated to administrative bodies." 232 U.S. 531, 543 (1914).

(e) Roe v. Wade notes, "As stated in *Jacobson* . . . 'There is, of course, a sphere within which the individual may assert the supremacy of his own will.'" 410 U.S. 179, 213–14 (1973) (Douglas, J., concurring).

(f) California Reduction Co. v. Sanitary Reduction Works cites *Jacobson* when saying courts will not strike down a regulation for the protection of the public health that "has a real, substantial relation to that object." 199 U.S. 306, 318-19 (1905).

(g) Bates v. City of Little Rock cites *Jacobson* when asserting that the state interest must be "compelling" for a "significant encroachment on personal liberty" to stand. 361 U.S. 516, 524 (1960).

(h) Cruzan v. Director, Missouri Dept. of Health notes that in *Jacobson* "the Court balanced an individual's liberty interest in declining an unwanted smallpox vaccine against the State's interest in preventing disease." 497 U.S. 261, 278 (1990).

(i) Price v. Illinois cites *Jacobson* when saying that unless a prohibition "is palpably unreasonable and arbitrary we are not at liberty to say it passes beyond the limits of the state's protective authority." 238 U.S. 446, 452 (1915).

(j) Carter v. Carter Coal Co. notes that the federal government lacks the broad police power of the states. 298 U.S. 238, 292 (1936).

(k) Sorrells v. United States cites *Jacobson* in asserting that courts should read statutes so as to avoid unreasonable or absurd results. 287 U.S. 435 (1932).

ENDNOTES

1. This chapter is an extended version of a previously published article, Lawrence O. Gostin, *Jacobson v. Massachusetts at 100 Years: Police Power and Civil Liberties in Tension*, 95 Am. J. Public Health 576 (2005).

2. *Editorial*, N.Y. Times, Feb. 22, 1905, at 6.

3. *Editorial Points*, Boston Daily Globe, Nov. 19, 1901, at 6.

4. 197 U.S. 11 (1905).

5. James A. Tobey, Public Health Law 355 (2d ed. 1939) ("This famous decision is reproduced here in its entirety . . . because it is a noteworthy statement of the constitutional principles underlying public health administration."); Lawrence O. Gostin, Public Health Law: Power, Duty, Restraint 66 (2000) ("The beginning point, as in all discourse on public health law, is . . . the foundational Supreme Court case of Jacobson v. Massachusetts."); James Colgrove & Ronald Bayer, *Manifold Restraints: Liberty, Public Health, and the Legacy of* Jacobson v. Massachusetts, 95 Am. J. Pub. Health 571, 571 (2005) (referring to *Jacobson* as "one of the most important pieces of public health jurisprudence.").

6. Michael R. Albert et al., *The Last Smallpox Epidemic in Boston and the Vaccination Controversy, 1901–1903*, 344 New Eng. J. Med. 375, 344 (2001).

7. Transcript of Record at 10, Jacobson v. Massachusetts, 197 U.S. 11 (1905) (No. 70). Massachusetts' general vaccination law authorized town and city officials to "enforce re-vaccination whenever they shall judge the public health requires the same." Mass. Rev. Laws ch. 75, §137 (1902).

8. Transcript of Record, *supra* note 7, at 9; *Won't Submit*, Boston Daily Globe, July 18, 1902, at 12.

9. 410 U.S. 113, 154 (1973).

10. 274 U.S. 200, 207 (1927).

11. 198 U.S. 45 (1905).

12. *Smallpox at Swampscott*, Boston Daily Globe, May 19, 1899, at 4; *Case of Smallpox in Everett*, Boston Daily Globe, Aug. 6, 1899, at 2; *Dread Disease*, Boston Daily Globe, Sept. 25, 1899, at 4 (Everett cases); *More Small Pox Cases*, Boston Daily Globe, Apr. 26, 1899, at 12 (Charlestown cases). In response to the first case in Everett, the city Board of Health quarantined the house and ordered all of Everett to be vaccinated within 48 hours. The order was derided in the Boston Daily

Globe as extreme: "All this because a single case of smallpox was discovered at 103 Broadway last Friday." *Bogie at First*, Boston Daily Globe, Aug. 11, 1899.

13. *Total of 27 Smallpox Cases*, Boston Daily Globe, Sept. 7, 1901, at 12 (cases in Roxbury); *Smallpox in Somerville*, Boston Daily Globe, Mar. 4, 1901, at 8; *Smallpox at Malden*, Boston Daily Globe, Jan. 16, 1900, at 8.

14. *See, e.g.*, *Durgin's Advice*, Boston Daily Globe, Nov. 10, 1901, at 9 (indicating that there were thirty-six cases of smallpox in the hospital at the time); *Six More Smallpox Cases*, Boston Daily Globe, Nov. 12, 1901, at 4 (listing six new cases of smallpox in Boston); *Smallpox Case in East Boston*, Boston Daily Globe, Nov. 5, 1901, at 14 (reporting a case of smallpox in a fifty-year-old man in East Boston).

15. Albert et al., *supra* note 6, at 376 fig.1 (based on the annual reports of the Boston Health Department).

16. *Editorial Points, supra* note 3; *see also Durgin's Advice, supra* note 14; *Smallpox Case in East Boston, supra* note 14.

17. *Smallpox Decreasing*, Boston Daily Globe, Dec. 27, 1901, at 7.

18. Albert et al., *supra* note 6, at 376 (quoting the Boston Board of Health).

19. *Smallpox Decreasing, supra* note 17.

20. Transcript of Record, *supra* note 7, at 10.

21. *To East Boston*, Boston Daily Globe, Jan. 27, 1902, at 1.

22. *Smallpox Circular*, Boston Daily Globe, Nov. 23, 1902, at 9.

23. *Lynn Crowds Obey Police*, Boston Daily Globe, Jan. 22, 1903, at 2.

24. *Virus Squad Out*, Boston Daily Globe, Nov. 18, 1901, at 7.

25. *Id.*

26. *Id.*

27. *Smallpox Talk*, Boston Daily Globe, Jan. 31, 1902, at 2.

28. Albert et al., *supra* note 6, at 376 fig.1. The eleven percent case-fatality rate was among those who showed evidence of previous vaccination (e.g., vaccination scars). This population would include those who had recently been vaccinated or revaccinated as well as those who had been vaccinated decades earlier.

29. Defendant's Exceptions at 2, Commonwealth v. Jacobson, 66 N.E. 719 (Mass. 1903) (No. 2287).

30. Defendant's Exceptions at 2, Commonwealth v. Pear, 66 N.E. 719 (Mass. 1903) (No. 2286).

31. *Fined Them $5 Each*, Boston Daily Globe, July 24, 1902, at 12.

32. *Id.*

33. *Id.*

34. S.G. Hägglund, *Henning Jacobson*, 17 My Church 160, 160 (1931); Obituary — *The Rev. Henning Jacobson*, N.Y. Times, Oct. 15, 1930, at 17.

35. Wendy E. Parmet et al., *Individual Rights versus the Public's Health — 100 Years after Jacobson v. Massachusetts*, 352 New Eng. J. Med. 652, 653 (2005). His brief before the Massachusetts Supreme Judicial Court, written by attorneys Henry Ballard and James W. Pickering, was replete with religious rhetoric; it concludes by asking, "Can the free citizen of Massachusetts, who is not yet a pagan, nor an idolator, be compelled to undergo this rite and to participate in this new — no, revived — form of worship of the Sacred Cow?" *Id.* at 654. (The smallpox vaccine is derived from a bovine form of the virus — cowpox — a fact many antivaccinationists found disturbing.)

36. Alan Hyde, Bodies of Law 243 (1997); *see* Parmet et al., *supra* note 35, at 653.

37. Transcript of Record, *supra* note 7, at 7.

38. Hägglund, *supra* note 34, at 160.

39. *Discuss Vaccination*, Boston Daily Globe, Nov. 4, 1902, at 7. The news report refers to Jacobson as "Rev. Henry Jacobson" of Cambridge.

40. Previously, it was assumed that Jacobson did not participate in such activities. *See, e.g.*, James Colgrove, State of Immunity 40 (2006) ("it is unclear whether he ever participated in any organized antivaccination activities").

41. Hägglund, *supra* note 34, at 160; Obituary, *supra* note 34, at 17.

42. Commonwealth v. Pear, 66 N.E. 719 (Mass. 1903), *aff'd*, 197 U.S. 11 (1905).

43. Colgrove, *supra* note 40, at 41.

44. Justices David Brewer and Rufus Peckham dissented, but they did not issue a minority opinion.

45. *Vaccine is Attacked: English Lecturer Denounces Inoculation for Smallpox*, Washington Post, Feb. 25, 1909, at 3.

46. *Vaccination a Crime: Porter Cope, of Philadelphia, Claims It Is the Only Cause of Smallpox*, Washington Post, July 29, 1905, at F7 (discussing Porter F. Cope, who devoted his life to fighting the "delusion").

47. *Editorial*, N.Y. Times, Sept. 26, 1885, at 4.

48. *The Anti-Vaccinationists' Triumph*, N. Y. Times, Aug. 18, 1898, at 6.

49. *Editorial, supra* note 47, at 4. Times, Sept. 26, 1885, at 4.

50. *The Anti-Vaccinationists' Triumph, supra* note 48, at 6.

51. *Topic of the Times*, N.Y. Times, June 19, 1901, at 6.

52. *General Acceptance of Vaccination*, The Lancet, *reprinted in Smallpox: Vaccination and Tetanus*, 32 Current Literature 484, 485 (1902).

53. Transcript of Record, *supra* note 7, at 7.

54. Alfred E. Giles, The Iniquity of Compulsory Vaccination, and the Unconstitutionality of its Statutes 3 (1882); *see, e.g.*, Matilda Morehouse, *Compulsory Vaccination and its Errors*, 13 Medico-Legal J. 303, 305 (1895) ("The only protective power against human small pox is true Sanitation, perfect health and a little old-fashioned remedy of cream of tartar taken once or twice a day"); *Repeal Wanted*, Boston Daily Globe, Jan. 30, 1902 (noting the antivaccinationist argument for focusing on sanitation instead of vaccination).

55. Montague R. Leverson, *Vaccination: Should It Be Enforced by Law?* (pt. 2), 14 Medico-Legal J. 421, 438 (1897); *see, e.g.*, Giles, *supra* note 54, at 4 (setting forth statistics purporting to show an increase in smallpox morbidity and mortality associated with vaccination); *Repeal Wanted, supra* note 54 (noting a doctor's assertion that smallpox had increased proportionately with vaccination); *Vaccination a Crime, supra* note 46, at F7 (quoting the antivaccinationist Porter Cope as saying vaccination is the cause of smallpox).

56. Transcript of Record, *supra* note 7, at 7. Antivaccinationists argued that the cowpox virus, the key component of smallpox vaccinations, produces a form of syphilis in humans. *See, e.g.*, Leverson, *supra* note 55, at 426–29 (comparing smallpox, cowpox, and syphilis and purporting to show that cowpox is more closely analogous to syphilis); Morehouse, *supra* note 54, at 305 ("Cow pox may be regarded as the same type of disease as syphilis in the human body").

57. Defendant's Exceptions, *supra* note 29, at 4. The historical record contains no indication as either the content of the excluded evidence or its form. In his appeal to the Supreme Judicial Court of Massachusetts, Jacobson merely says that he offered to prove his fourteen facts through "competent evidence." *Id.* at 2. Presumably, expert testimony would have been central in proving the fourteen facts.

58. Commonwealth v. Pear, 66 N.E. 719, 721 (Mass. 1903).

59. Jacobson v. Massachusetts, 197 U.S. 11, 36 (1905).

60. *Id.* at 37.

61. Brief of Plaintiff-in-Error at 2, Jacobson v. Massachusetts, 197 U.S. 11 (1905) (No. 70). A more detailed list, which was submitted in the Massachusetts courts, can be found in the transcript of record for the Supreme Court. Transcript of Record, *supra* note 7, at 7–8.

62. Centers for Disease Control and Prevention (CDC), *Smallpox Vaccination and Adverse Reactions: Guidance for Clinicians*, 52 Morbidity & Mortality Wkly. Rep. 4–5 (2003), *available at* http://www.cdc.gov/mmwr/PDF/rr/rr5204.pdf; CDC, *Smallpox Vaccine: Adverse Events Rates, 1968, available at* http://www.bt.cdc.gov/agent/smallpox/vaccine-safety/pdf/adverse-events-chart.pdf.

63. Commonwealth v. Pear, 66 N.E. 719, 721 (Mass. 1903).

64. Hyde, *supra* note 36, at 244; see also Colgrove, *supra* note 40, at 42–43.

65. Jacobson v. Massachusetts, 197 U.S. at 38–39.

66. *Id.*

67. *Id.* at 36.

68. Brief of Plaintiff-in-Error, *supra* note 61, at 2.

69. Commonwealth v. Pear, 66 N.E. 719, 722 (Mass. 1903).

70. Transcript of Record, *supra* note 7, at 6.

71. Edward Jenner, An Inquiry into the Causes and Effects of the Variœ Vaccinæ, a Disease Discovered in Some of the Western Counties of England, Particularly Goucestershire, and Known by the Name of the Cow Pox (1798). Jenner's second book focuses almost wholly on spurious vaccine virus. Edward Jenner, Further Observations on the Variœ Vaccinæ (1799); *see also* Samuel Scofield, Practical Treatise on Vaccina or Cowpock 63–72 (1810) (devoting an entire section of his treatise to a "Description of the Spurious Cowpock").

72. From 1813–1822, however, the federal government did make vaccine virus centrally available through a vaccine agent. The 1813 Act to Encourage Vaccination, ch. 37, 806 Stat. 806, provided for the appointment of a national vaccine agent, "to preserve the genuine vaccine matter, and to furnish the same" to citizens as needed. The Act was repealed in 1822. An Act to Repeal, ch. 50, 3 Stat. 677 (1822). The federal government was not again involved in securing the vaccine virus supply until 1902. The Biologics Control Act of 1902, Pub. L. No. 57-244, ch. 1378, 32 Stat. 728.

73. 1893 N.Y. Laws, ch. 661, art. 2, §24 ("Every such local board of health . . . shall provide . . . a suitable supply of vaccine virus of a quality and from a source approved by the state board of health.").

74. Albert et al., *supra* note 6, at 375 (citing the thirty-seventh annual report of the State Board of Health of Massachusetts (1906)).

75. Leverson, *supra* note 55, at 431–32 (quoting Dr. Walter Reed).

76. Donald R. Hopkins, The Greatest Killer: Smallpox in History 301 (2002). The history of Dr. Copeman's discovery is set forth in works by Arthur Salusbury MacNalty, *The Prevention of Smallpox: From Edward Jenner to Monckton Copeman*, 12 Medical Hist. 1, 12 (1968), and Donald R. Hopkins, The Greatest Killer: Smallpox in History 95 (2002). *See also Glycerinated Calf Vaccine Lymph*, The Lancet, January 1, 1898, at 45 (noting Dr. Copeman's finding that the addition of glycerin "did not affect [the vaccine's] efficacy whilst tending to destroy other organisms").

Soon after Dr. Copeman's discovery, the Vaccine Act of 1898 came into effect in England. The Act provided for the free distribution of glycerinated calf lymph to public vaccinators. MacNalty, *supra*, at 13. At this time, New York began using glycerinated vaccine as well. *New York. Vaccine Virus of the Health Department of New York*, The Lancet, January 8, 1898, at 131. Today, smallpox vaccine still contains glycerin; in addition, it is processed with a combination of antibiotics to minimize the risk of bacterial contamination. Product Label for Dryvax® Smallpox Vaccine: Dried, Calf Lymph Type, *available at* http://www.fda.gov/CBER/label/dryvaxLB.pdf.

77. W. R. Inge Dalton, *The Responsibility for the Recent Deaths from the Use of Impure Antitoxins and Vaccine Virus*, 40 Med. Times & Reg. 3, 6 (1902); *see also The Production of Vaccine Lymph*, 146 Boston Med. & Surgical J. 22–25 (1902) (noting the employment of "unscrupulous methods" of vaccine production among some manufacturers); W. R. Inge Dalton, *Vaccine, Antitoxins, and the Health Board*, N.Y. Times, Nov. 23, 1901, at 5.

78. *Commercial Virus and Antitoxin*, N.Y. Times, Nov. 18, 1901, at 6.

79. *Id.*

80. Pub. L. No. 57-244, ch. 1378, 32 Stat. 728 (1902). Violations were made punishable by a fine not exceeding five hundred dollars and/or by imprisonment not exceeding one year. *Id.* at §7. The Act, passed on July 1, 1902, did not take effect until February 21, 1903, when the first implementing regulations were promulgated by the Public Health and Marine Hospital Service. James A. Tobey, Public Health Law: A Manual of Law for Sanitarians 45 (1st ed. 1926). Once in effect, the law was largely successful in ensuring a safe vaccine supply. Henry Bixby Hemenway, Legal Principles of Public Health Administration 25 (1914).

81. Jacobson v. Massachusetts, 197 U.S. 11, 36 (1905) ("These offers, in effect, invited the court and jury to go over the whole ground gone over by the legislature when it enacted the statute in question"); Commonwealth v. Pear, 66 N.E. 719, 721 (Mass. 1903) ("the question whether [a policy] will be for the good of the community is a legislative, and not a judicial, question").

82. Gibbons v. Ogden, 22 U.S. 1, 203 (1824).

83. The Slaughter-House Cases, 83 U.S. 36, 62 (1873).

84. State *ex rel.* Conway v. Southern Pac. Co., 145 P.2d 530, 532 (Wash. 1943), *quoting* State *ex rel.* McBride v. Superior Court, 174 P. 973, 976 (Wash. 1918); *see* Leroy Parker & Robert H. Worthington, The Law of Public Health and Safety and the Powers and Duties of Boards of Health 5 (1892) ("[T]he legislature has a discretion which will not be reviewed by the courts; for it is not a part of the judicial functions to criticize the propriety of legislative action in matters which are within the authority of the legislative body.").

85. Wendy E. Parmet, *From Slaughter-House to Lochner: The Rise and Fall of the Constitutionalization of Public Health*, 40 Am. J. Legal Hist. 476 (1996).

86. 197 U.S. 11, 26–27 (1905).

87. Harlan's deference to the democratic branches and local governments can be seen throughout the opinion. *E.g.*, *id.* at 34 ("the legislature has the right to pass laws which, according to the common belief of the people, are adapted to prevent the spread of contagious diseases"); *id.* at 38 ("it is of last importance, [that the judiciary] should not invade the domain of local authority except when it is plainly necessary"). State courts that had broached the issue of compulsory vaccination prior to *Jacobson* were markedly deferential as well. An article summarizing compulsory vaccination case law in 1901 noted: "Whether vaccination is or is not efficacious in the prevention of smallpox is a question with which the courts declare they have no concern." *Compulsory Vaccination*, 1901 N.Y. Law Notes 224; *see also* Blue v. Beach. 56 N.E. 89, 91 (Ind. 1900) ("The question is one which the legislature or boards of health . . . must in the first instance determine, as the law affords no means for the question to be subjected to a judicial inquiry or determination.").

88. State courts considering compulsory vaccination laws prior to *Jacobson* rarely imposed limits on the exercise of the police power. They routinely found vaccination laws constitutional. *E.g.*, Bissell v. Davison, 32 A. 348 (Conn. 1894); Abeel v. Clark, 24 P. 383 (Cal. 1890). Some courts did, however, make reference to a requirement of necessity; in Morris v. City of Columbus, the Supreme Court of Georgia noted that "the right to enforce vaccination . . . is derived from necessity" and found that the requirement was met where smallpox was prevalent in nearby towns. Morris v.

City of Columbus, 30 S.E. 850, 851–52 (Ga. 1898). In most cases where compulsory vaccination orders were found to be unlawful, the operative limit on the board of health's authority to compel vaccination did not derive from constitutional provisions; rather, the courts grounded such limits in administrative law. *E.g.*, Potts v. Breen, 47 N.E. 81 (Ill. 1897) (noting that, where the board of health's duties under the authorizing statute were "purely ministerial," it lacked the delegated authority to compel school vaccinations absent an emergency).

89. 197 U.S. at 28.

90. *Id.* at 31.

91. *Id.* at 38–39.

92. *Id.* at 39. In Blue v. Beach, the Indiana Supreme Court upheld a school vaccination order, emphasizing, as Harlan later did in *Jacobson*, that the plaintiff was "well and healthy" and that vaccination was not medically contraindicated. 56 N.E. 89 (Ind. 1900).

93. *See* Jew Ho v. Williamson, 103 F. 10, 22 (C.C.N.D. Cal. 1900) (large-scale quarantine may spread disease); Kirk v. Wyman, 65 S.E. 387, 391 (S.C. 1909) (isolation in a pesthouse might be a "serious affliction and peril to an elderly lady").

94. 103 F. at 22.

95. Lochner v. New York, 198 U.S. 45, 71 (1905) (Harlan, J., dissenting).

96. *Id.* at 73 (Harlan, J., dissenting).

97. *See* Coppage v. Kansas, 236 U.S. 1 (1915) (invalidating federal and state legislation forbidding employers to require employees to agree not to join a union); Adkins v. Children's Hosp., 261 U.S. 525 (1923) (invalidating a law establishing minimum wages for women); Weaver v. Palmer Bros. Co., 270 U.S. 402 (1926) (striking down a public health law that prohibited use of rags and debris in mattresses); New State Ice Co. v. Liebmann, 285 U.S. 262 (1932) (striking down a statute forbidding a state commission to license the sale of ice except on proof of necessity).

98. West Coast Hotel Co. v. Parrish, 300 U.S. 379, 391 (1937) (upholding a minimum wage law for women).

99. Cass R. Sunstein, *Lochner's Legacy*, 87 Colum. L. Rev. 873 (1987).

100. Zucht v. King, 260 U.S. 174, 176 (1922) ("Jacobson v. Massachusetts had settled that it is within the police power of the State to provide for compulsory vaccination.").

101. Cruzan v. Dir. Mo. Dep't of Health, 497 U.S. 261 (1990).

102. Washington v. Glucksberg, 521 U.S. 702 (1997) (terminal illness); Washington v. Harper, 494 U.S. 210 (1990) (mental disability).

103. Planned Parenthood of Southeastern Pennsylvania v. Casey, 505 U.S. 833 (1992). The Supreme Court has invoked *Jacobson* in judicial opinions upholding reproductive freedoms and those allowing restraints on such freedoms. In *Casey*, the Court cited *Jacobson* to support the proposition that "a State's interest in the protection of life falls short of justifying any plenary override of individual liberty claims." *Id.* at 857. Recently, the Court upheld a federal ban on partial birth abortion, citing *Jacobson* to support the assertion that "state and federal legislatures [have] wide discretion to pass legislation in areas where there is medical and scientific uncertainty." Gonzales v. Carhart, 127 S.Ct. 1610, 1636 (2007). In its most extreme restriction on reproductive freedom, the Court permitted the involuntary sterilization of an allegedly mentally incompetent woman, concluding that "[t]he principle that sustains compulsory vaccination is broad enough to cover cutting the Fallopian tubes." Buck v. Bell, 274 U.S. 200, 207 (1927).

104. Cruzan v. Dir. Mo. Dep't of Health, 497 U.S. 261 (1990).

105. Washington v. Harper, 494 U.S. 210 (1990). However, the treatment must be medically appropriate. Sell v. U.S., 539 U.S. 166 (2003).

106. Reynolds v. McNichols, 488 F.2d 1378 (10th Cir. 1973) (examination); City of New York v. Antoinette R., 630 N.Y.S.2d 1008 (N.Y. Sup. Ct. 1995) (treatment).

107. Steve P. Calandrillo, after reviewing federal and state vaccination cases, concludes, "[c]ompulsory vaccination laws . . . enjoy broad judicial and constitutional support." *Vanishing Vaccinations: Why are so Many Americans Opting Out of Vaccinating Their Children?* 37 U. Mich. J.L. Reform 353, 388 (2004).

108. McCarthy v. Boozman, 212 F. Supp. 2d 945, 949-50 (W.D. Ark. 2002); Boone v. Boozman, 217 F. Supp. 2d 938, 953 (E.D. Ark. 2002) (on the free exercise question, the court noted that the immunization statute, as a neutral law of general applicability, is not subjected to heightened scrutiny "even though compulsory immunization may burden plaintiff's right to free exercise"). These cases were consolidated on appeal and dismissed as moot. McCarthy v. Ozark School Dist., 359 F.3d 1029 (8th Cir. 2004).

109. Robert T. Chen, *Vaccine Risks: Real, Perceived and Unknown*, 17 Vaccine S41, S41 (1999).

110. Sarah K. Parker et al., *Thimerosal-Containing Vaccines and Autistic Spectrum Disorder: A Critical Review of Published Original Data*, 114 Pediatrics 793, 793 (2004); *see* Colgrove, *supra* note 40, at 230 (discussing media attention given to reports of a 300 percent increase in autism in

California between 1987 and 1999). Reports of the increasing prevalence of autism, however, were not necessarily a result of an increase in autism in the population. As the Institute of Medicine observed, "it is difficult to discern how much of the observed increase is real or possibly due to other factors, such as the adoption of a broader diagnostic concept of autism, improved recognition of autism, or variations in the precision of the studies." Institute of Medicine, Immunization Safety Review: Vaccines and Autism 4 (2004) [hereinafter Vaccines and Autism].

111. Colgrove, *supra* note 40, at 249; Andrew J. Wakefield et al., *Ideal-Lymphoid-Nodular Hyperplasia, Non-Specific Colitis, and Pervasive Developmental Disorder in Children*, 351 Lancet 637 (1998).

112. *Notice to Readers: Thimerosal in Vaccines: A Joint Statement of the American Academy of Pediatrics and the Public Health Service*, 48 Morbidity & Mortality Wkly. Rep. 563 (July 9, 1999); Food and Drug Administration, *Thimerosal in Vaccines, available at* http://www.fda.gov/cber/vaccine/thimerosal.htm.

113. Vaccines and Autism, *supra* note 110, at 7; Institute of Medicine, Immunization Safety Review: Thimerosal-Containing Vaccines and Neurodevelopmental Disorders 5 (Kathleen Stratton et al. eds., 2001) [hereinafter Thimerosal-Containing Vaccines].

114. Colgrove, *supra* note 40, at 233.

115. *Id.*

116. Deborah A. Gust et al., *Underimmunization Among Children: Effects of Vaccine Safety Concerns on Immunization Status*, 114 Pediatrics e16, e21 (2004).

117. Colgrove, *supra* note 40, at 239. In one study, 43 percent of the first ten results of a search for "vaccination" and "immunization" on web-based search engines pointed readers to antivaccinationist websites. P. Davies et al., *Antivaccination Activists on the World Wide Web*, 87 Archives of Diseases in Child. 22 (2002).

118. *See, e.g.*, Thimerosal-Containing Vaccines, *supra* note 113 (childhood vaccinations); Thomas May & Ross D. Silverman, *"Clustering of Exemptions" as a Collective Action Threat to Herd Immunity*, 21 Vaccine 1048 (2003) (school vaccinations); Doe v. Rumsfeld, 297 F. Supp. 2d 200 (D.D.C. 2004) (anthrax vaccinations); Board of Health Promotion and Disease Prevention, Institute of Medicine, The Smallpox Vaccination Program: Public Health in an Age of Terrorism (2005); Board of Health Promotion and Disease Prevention, Institute of Medicine, Review of the Centers for Disease Control and Prevention's Smallpox Vaccination Program Implementation: Letter Reports #1-6 (2003–04).

Part VI

REGULATORY, ORGANIZATIONAL, AND BUSINESS ISSUES

Chapter 9

UNITED STATES

v.

KRIZEK

Rough Justice Under the Civil False Claims Act

THOMAS L. GREANEY* and JOAN H. KRAUSE**

> The Government's pursuit of Dr. Krizek is reminiscent of Inspector Javert's quest to capture Jean Valjean in Victor Hugo's *Les Miserables*. While the Government's vigor in pursuing violators of the law is to be commended, there comes a point when a civilized society must say enough is enough. That point has been reached in this case.[1]

On January 11, 1993, the United States Attorney for the District of Columbia filed suit against Dr. George Krizek and his wife Blanka for submitting fraudulent Medicare and Medicaid billings. On August 21, 2002, the Krizeks paid a total of $315,537.28. In between those dates — indeed, ever since the investigation began in 1988 — there has been virtually no agreement among the parties as to what occurred. The Krizeks say what happened to them was "a blatant injustice" perpetrated against a dedicated foreign-born practitioner, motivated by prejudice, politics, and misunderstandings about a psychiatric practice serving the poorest and sickest of patients. Prosecutors, on the other hand, maintain that the Krizeks failed to comply with the most rudimentary of Medicare and Medicaid billing requirements, generating bills for more care than Dr. Krizek humanly could have provided.

The Krizeks' story would make a compelling screenplay: a renowned psychiatrist who escaped from the Communist regime in Czechoslovakia, ultimately

---

  * Chester A. Myers Professor of Law and Director of the Center for Health Law Studies at Saint Louis University School of Law.
 ** George Butler Research Professor of Law and Co-Director, Health Law & Policy Institute, University of Houston Law Center. I would like to thank Michael Smith and Peter Egler for their invaluable research assistance with this chapter, and Richard Saver for his boundless supply of insight, patience, and good humor. The authors are grateful to Dr. George and Mrs. Blanka Krizek, as well as to the attorneys and others who shared with us their experiences concerning this case.

G.O. Krizek (left) with the President of the Czech Republic, Vaclav Klaus (2007)

becoming the doctor of last resort for the elderly and indigent psychiatric patients of Washington, D.C.; prosecutors dedicated to rooting out health care fraud; and a judge steeped in a family judicial tradition, determined to "do justice" in what he considered a "tragic case beyond belief." While best known for setting precedent regarding the types of claims that are actionable under the civil False Claims Act (FCA) — and for Judge Stanley Sporkin's colorful criticism of the government's zealous pursuit of the suit — the case offers a rich illustration of the legal and human complexities of health care fraud litigation. Complicated by a number of unforeseeable coincidences, *Krizek* ultimately stands as a cautionary tale for doctors, prosecutors, and defense attorneys alike.

A. Background of the Dispute

Dr. George O. Krizek was born in Prague, Czechoslovakia, in 1932. He received his medical degree summa cum laude in 1957 from Charles University School of Medicine, Central Europe's oldest medical school. He taught psychiatry and neurology, and served as Chief Psychiatrist at the Charles University Psychiatric Outpatient Clinic. After being pressured to conduct politically motivated psychiatric evaluations for the Communist party, Dr. Krizek defected alone to Austria in 1966, in an escape that his wife, Blanka, told Congress "was dramatic enough for a movie."[2] Dr. Krizek obtained a second medical degree from the University of Vienna Medical School, and was reunited with Blanka and their daughter, Monika. In 1968, following the invasion of Czechoslovakia by Warsaw Pact forces, the Krizeks emigrated to the United States. Dr. Krizek completed a second residency specializing in substance abuse disorders at Beth Israel Medical Center in New York, and the Krizeks settled in Washington, D.C.

Dr. Krizek became an attending physician at the 800-bed Washington Hospital Center (WHC) in 1972, becoming Senior Attending Psychiatrist in 1977. Believing "he had an obligation to his newly adopted country to serve the poorest and sickest of people in society when others would not,"[3] Dr. Krizek primarily treated the urban poor and elderly. Many of his patients received benefits through Medicare or Medicaid; others were uninsured, and Dr. Krizek treated many of them for free. He often covered for colleagues with young children, sometimes serving as WHC's sole psychiatrist on weekends and holidays. The Krizeks purchased a burned-out rooming house on the edge of the Kalorama neighborhood for $200,000, within walking distance of the hospital. Blanka spent the next decade restoring the house, finishing Dr. Krizek's home office before their living quarters. Blanka's hobby led to the renovation of at least three additional properties — assets held in her name, later cited by prosecutors as proof that the Krizeks could afford a multimillion dollar judgment.

Dr. Krizek became a Medicare and Medicaid participating provider in 1973. As a participating provider, he was required to submit bills on HCFA 1500 claim forms and to follow billing and documentation requirements established by federal law, as well as by the local carrier, Pennsylvania Blue Shield (PBS). When Dr. Krizek opened a private outpatient office in his home, Blanka took on the role of office manager in addition to her real estate ventures. Blanka billed for the patients Dr. Krizek admitted to WHC, as well as those seen in his office. Blanka consulted with other doctors' secretaries, as well as with Mrs. Anderson, a professional billing agent who handled the accounts of other WHC doctors (and prepared the bills when Dr. Krizek covered for those doctors). Blanka also attended PBS seminars and called Medicare with questions, although she admitted at trial that she did not review every coding instruction and manual. Blanka prepared the bills based on information received from Dr. Krizek, often on scraps of paper. Although Dr. Krizek's failure to oversee the billing process became a key issue in the case, PBS had never notified him of any prior billing problems.

How the Krizeks became the subject of a federal investigation remains a point of contention. Blanka claims to have received documents indicating that Dr. Krizek was targeted personally for investigation,[4] while prosecutors maintain that he was identified through an audit of psychiatric coding practices. According to the trial testimony of PBS representatives, the Department of Health and Human Services (HHS) Office of Audit did a review in 1988-1989 of Common Procedure Terminology (CPT) code 90844, used to bill for a 45–50 minute psychotherapy session.[5] Dr. Krizek's use of the code stood out, prompting a more in-depth review of his bills. That review came to the startling conclusion that approximately *81 percent* of Dr. Krizek's bills from 1986-1991 were 90844s, compared to an average of 37 percent for other D.C. psychiatrists. Moreover, the physicians who billed more 90844 codes primarily saw outpatients, for whom 50-minute sessions are common. In contrast, Dr. Krizek stood out because of the unexpectedly high rate of 90844 bills for his *inpatient* hospital practice.

The Krizeks maintain that the first they learned of the investigation was when three HHS Office of the Inspector General (OIG) agents arrived at their home on December 12, 1989. What happened on that day remains something of a mystery, and the parties' diametrically opposed accounts reflect a divide that continues to this day. The agents, led by recently trained Special Agent Matthew Kochanski, called Dr. Krizek's office to ask whether someone could accept a "delivery" — actually a subpoena, which they did not identify out of concern that documents might be destroyed or altered before they arrived.[6] The agents went to the office, apparently unaware that it was also the Krizeks' home. Kochanski testified that the agents introduced themselves and were invited in by Blanka; that the conversation was polite; and that the house was under heavy construction, with many workers present. The agents say they did not serve the subpoena or photocopy any documents because Blanka did not have any patient records in the house that day, presumably due to the construction. The agents testified that Blanka made a number of incriminating statements, including admitting that she had told her husband "for years that they were going to be in trouble" for their billing practices and that she felt "desperately uneasy" about not knowing what was going on with the billing.[7] Most damningly, the agents testified that when they first identified themselves, Blanka stated, "I'm not surprised you're here. I'm just surprised it took you so long."[8]

The Krizeks paint an entirely different picture of the visit. Blanka testified that the agents specifically asked whether she would be home to receive a "Christmas delivery," and that she in fact was expecting a poinsettia. She claims she was home alone, that the agents offered no official identification when they arrived, and that they basically pushed their way into the house. For the next several hours, even after Dr. Krizek returned home, Blanka said the agents "behaved like animals" — screaming, threatening, laughing at the Krizeks' foreign accents, and disparagingly referring to Dr. Krizek as a "psychologist."[9] Contrary to the agents' assertions that there were no patient records on the premises during the construction, Blanka claimed she went to the built-in file cabinets in Dr. Krizek's office and produced records for all patients the agents mentioned.

After the visit, the Krizeks heard nothing more from the government for three years. In 1991, PBS requested records for a 25-patient sample from Dr. Krizek and WHC. Rather than explaining that the records were part of a fraud investigation, however, the letter sent to Dr. Krizek merely requested documents for "utilization review." PBS personnel testified that this was a common practice in fraud investigations, given the concern that a targeted physician might try to alter or destroy records.[10] Although PBS never followed up with Dr. Krizek regarding the records he provided, those records were eventually sent for outside review by a consultant, whose conclusions formed the basis for the government's case. Investigators initially viewed this as a criminal case, but the U.S. Attorney's Office declined criminal prosecution and the case ultimately was pursued by the Civil Division.

Three years after the OIG visit, on Christmas Eve 1992, the Krizeks received a certified demand letter stating that the government was prepared to file suit against them for submitting 8,002 false Medicare and Medicaid claims. The Krizeks met with Assistant U.S. Attorney (AUSA) John Munich in early January 1993, and miscommunications were evident from the start. Although Munich repeatedly warned Blanka that they should be represented by counsel, the Krizeks came alone; Munich vividly recalls that Blanka wore a full-length fur coat. Believing the letter was a mistake, the Krizeks demanded an explanation, much to Munich's surprise.[11] Despite having a golden opportunity to avoid litigation, neither side seemed to perceive any real possibility of settlement. With no negotiations or requests for delay, the government filed the case four days later.

The Krizeks soon realized they needed an attorney. An acquaintance suggested Marsha Swiss, whose office was located nearby and who was married to a psychiatrist. Swiss in turn hired Brian Shaughnessy, known for his trial expertise. Initially it appeared the dispute could be settled within a few months, although that would not prove to be the case.[12] As the months dragged on, with most of their money tied up in Blanka's real estate ventures, the Krizeks say they became increasingly concerned about legal fees. Blanka suggested that their daughter Monika, an attorney for the Federal Reserve in New York, become involved both as a way to save money and as an opportunity for her to learn about the field of health law — a decision that would have major repercussions for both the litigation and the Krizek family.[13]

By February of 1994, less than two weeks before trial, Swiss and Shaughnessy concluded that they could no longer adequately represent the Krizeks. The attorneys referred to a "philosophical difference" in approaches, noting that the Krizeks "see their daughter as the only person . . . in whom they repose trust and confidence," which made it difficult to communicate with them. Monika responded that while it had not been her intention to replace the attorneys, she believed Swiss "ha[d] not done everything possible to settle" the case.[14] Judge Sporkin initially declined to accept the withdrawal, instead referring the parties to Magistrate Judge Alan Kay for settlement discussions. But by mid-February it was clear that settlement efforts had failed, and Swiss and Shaughnessy were permitted to withdraw. Judge Sporkin expressed skepticism about Monika's intention to try the case herself. In a particularly telling moment, Monika explained that her parents could not afford to hire an outside lawyer because "I have been informed that it would be quite expensive to have qualified counsel try this case" — to which Sporkin quipped, "So we get unqualified counsel?"[15] Despite his misgivings, the judge rescheduled the trial for March 21 and reopened discovery for 30 days, during which time Monika was able to obtain informal assistance from the law firm of Crowell & Moring.[16]

B. The Litigation

The *Krizek* case is best known for its interpretation of the FCA, a Civil War-era statute that has become a key component of the federal government's fight against health care fraud. Under the FCA, liability arises when a defendant: (1) presents, or causes to be presented, a claim for payment or approval; (2) the claim is false or fraudulent; and (3) the acts are undertaken "knowingly," which includes not only actual knowledge, but also deliberate ignorance and reckless disregard of the truth or falsity of the claim.[17] A "claim" includes "any request or demand . . . for money or property" if the federal government provides any portion thereof, making the law clearly applicable to the Medicare and Medicaid programs. The act also prohibits knowingly making or using false records or statements to get false or fraudulent claims paid, as well as conspiracies to defraud the government. Violators are subject to a civil penalty of $5,500 to $11,000 per claim, plus treble damages.[18]

According to the Complaint, between January 1986 and March 1992, the Krizeks submitted approximately 8,002 "improper, false, and/or unlawful claims" for psychiatric services totaling $245,392.[19] Prosecutors alleged that Dr. Krizek engaged in "a pattern of 'billing steropy,' meaning that the vast and inordinate majority of patients he [saw were] billed for a 50-minute" psychotherapy session when a shorter session was appropriate. The government contended that at least 24 percent of the inappropriately coded 50-minute sessions should have been billed as 25-minute sessions, 33 percent should have been billed as "minimal psychotherapy" sessions (such as brief visits or telephone calls), and 41 percent of these sessions "should not have been performed at all in that they were not medically necessary." The Complaint asserted violations of the false claims, false records, and conspiracy provisions of the FCA, as well as the common law theories of unjust enrichment and payment under mistake of fact. Prosecutors sought treble damages and civil penalties of the then-maximum $10,000 for each of the 8,002 claims, plus interest and costs, totaling more than $80 million. In the alternative, prosecutors sought $245,392 as the amount mistakenly paid to Dr. Krizek or by which he was unjustly enriched.

The magnitude of the case posed problems from the start. Prosecutors originally subpoenaed the Krizeks' office records from 1986 through 1992; the Krizeks moved to quash the subpoena, concerned that a response would require them to breach patient confidentiality — a particular danger for patients with sensitive psychiatric conditions. Apparently at the suggestion of defense attorney Marsha Swiss, Judge Sporkin resolved the issue by determining that the trial would proceed on the basis of 200 representative claims for seven sample patients, with the resulting error rate to be applied to all 8,000 claims.[20]

By the time Judge Sporkin issued his initial opinion in the case, after a three-week bench trial in Spring 1994, the allegations had crystallized under two theories of liability: (1) Dr. Krizek had "upcoded" by using a billing code for longer therapy sessions (and a higher level of reimbursement) than he provided; and (2) Dr. Krizek had performed services that were not "medically necessary" and thus not reimbursable by Medicare and Medicaid.[21] Running through both theories was the common thread of Dr. Krizek's failure to maintain adequate documentation to support the level of services he claimed. The lack of documentation — and the corollary question of which party bore the burden of reconstructing what happened during the sessions — became a key issue in the litigation.

The medical necessity claims had been contentious throughout the pre-trial period. Because of the decision to limit discovery to a small group of representative patients — as well as practical concerns regarding the mental state of patients who might be called as witnesses — the government had not engaged in extensive discovery on the issue. Indeed, on the first day of trial there was some confusion regarding whether the government was expected to try the issue at all, with Judge Sporkin clarifying that he would leave the issue "open."[22]

The medical necessity case focused on the testimony of the PBS consultant who had reviewed Dr. Krizek's records, Dr. Harvey Resnik. Resnik testified that Dr. Krizek's documentation did not support the level of care provided, let alone his "unfailing, unchanging use of" 45-minute therapy sessions.[23] According to Resnik, some patients did not require hospitalization at all, while others were ready to go home several days before discharge; for example, Dr. Krizek appeared to tie one patient's discharge to the end of his *wife's* unrelated hospitalization. Moreover, the records contained multiple undated entries, without any intervening notes from other hospital staff, which suggested that the notes had all been written on the same day despite indicating multiple dates of treatment.[24] Judge Sporkin stopped this line of questioning, however, stating that it was first necessary to hear Dr. Krizek's explanation of the care provided.

Dr. Krizek countered with a detailed description of the patients, providing a primer on their medical and psychiatric conditions. He also tried to cast doubt on

Resnik's qualifications, noting that the expert did not treat a similar patient population and had admitted that he was unfamiliar with one particular diagnosis in the records, yet did not bother to look it up before opining on whether Dr. Krizek's treatment was proper. Prosecutors, however, used Dr. Krizek's cross-examination to bolster their allegations about whether his records supported his recollections. One particularly contentious example — which prosecutor Bruce Hegyi recalls to this day — involved a patient whom Dr. Krizek had described as lying in a fetal position. Prosecutors argued that because she was basically catatonic, Dr. Krizek could not in fact have engaged her in the type of conversation necessary to justify an extensive therapy session.[25]

Despite having initially indicated that the medical necessity issue would be left open for further development, Judge Sporkin found that the government had not made its case — and likely would not be able to do so without direct testimony from patients, which prosecutors conceded they could not obtain. Sporkin clearly was swayed by the defendant's account and dissatisfied with what he described as Resnik's "cold review of Dr. Krizek's notes for each patient."[26] Although the facts were contested, Judge Sporkin clearly accepted the defense's characterization of Dr. Krizek as "a capable and competent physician" who "worked long hours on behalf of his patients," many of whom "were afflicted with horribly severe psychiatric disorders and often suffered simultaneously from other serious medical conditions."[27] Likening the medical necessity argument to "gross malpractice," the judge made clear that he did not see this as the essence of the government's case.

The upcoding allegations focused on Dr. Krizek's use of billing code 90844 rather than the codes for shorter treatment sessions. Dr. Krizek maintained that the 45–50 minute time frame was a guideline designed to include not only "face to face" interaction with the patient but also time spent preparing for the session, doing further research, and following up on the patient's care. The government's key witness was Dr. Barton McCann, the Executive Medical Officer in the Health Care Financing Administration's (HCFA) Office of Payment Policy and a member of the AMA's CPT Editorial Panel. McCann testified that the codes had been developed by taking into account the average time spent before, during, and after a patient session; because reimbursement for the other activities was built into the code, the physician should bill only for the time spent face-to-face with the patient.[28] Dr. Krizek responded not only with his own understanding of the billing rules, but also by presenting the testimony of several other psychiatrists — who also had served in CPT advisory capacities — stating that it was common for hospital psychiatrists to "bundle" the "floor time" spent on patient-related tasks when choosing an appropriate CPT code.[29] To complicate matters, the face-to-face requirement did not appear in the code definitions until a new resource-based billing system utilizing "evaluation and management codes" was introduced in 1992, after the time period at issue in the case.

Rejecting the government's contentions, Judge Sporkin refused to "impose False Claims Act liability based on such a strained interpretation of the CPT codes."[30] The judge not only credited the defense's testimony regarding common billing practices, but also criticized what he saw as the inherent illogic of the government's position: witnesses had testified that a telephone call to another physician made in the patient's presence would count as part of the session, while the same call made in the hallway would not. Echoing a theme that ran throughout the trial — that the Medicare and Medicaid reimbursement rules were both unclear and unfair — Judge Sporkin concluded that the government's position was "not rational and . . . applied in an unfair manner to the medical community, which for the most part is made up of honorable and dedicated professionals."[31]

Having found against the government on both the face-to-face billing and medical necessity theories, Judge Sporkin turned to an issue that lay at the core of the government's case, although it had not been argued explicitly: the "irregularities" that permeated the Krizeks' billing system. The Krizeks admitted that the billing was handled by Blanka and Mrs. Anderson, with little involvement by Dr. Krizek. In Blanka's words, although Dr. Krizek would hand her scraps of paper with information about patients, "My husband didn't make any decision. He was never involved in billing. . . . My husband was relying in all practical matters in life on me. I am sorry to say that I . . . married a brilliant doctor, but he was absolutely impossible in practical things."[32] Dr. Krizek testified that the standard practice was for Blanka to bill for code 90844 unless he said otherwise.[33] Finding that Blanka and Mrs. Anderson used the 90844 code by default for each patient unless explicitly told to bill a shorter therapy session, Judge Sporkin concluded that this system generated bills for services that could not have been performed as claimed, including bills for more than 24 hours of patient care in a single day. Thus, Sporkin found the Krizeks had acted with "reckless disregard" under the FCA.

Translating this holding into actual damages and penalties, however, was a difficult task. During a post-trial status call the parties agreed to use a nine-hour "benchmark," with the Krizeks "presumed liable" for any claims in excess of nine patient-service hours in a 24-hour period (the equivalent of twelve 45–50 minute 90844 sessions) unless they could prove the time had been devoted to patient care.[34] Judge Sporkin referred the case to Special Master William H. Briggs, Jr. to calculate the damages caused by this "nonsystem" of billing.[35] In carrying out his duties, the Special Master confronted a difficult problem: because Dr. Krizek's records did not indicate the length or time of each session, it was impossible to determine with any certainty how long he had spent with a patient. Moreover, because even the government's witnesses admitted that each code encompassed a range of times, there was no easy way to divide a day into defined time slots. To resolve this problem, the Special Master relied on a declaration prepared by Agent Kochanski setting forth the minimum number of minutes that the government would accept under each billing code. By multiplying these times by the number of bills submitted for each code, the Special Master could recreate an approximation of the number of patient care hours Dr. Krizek claimed to have performed on a given day.

Although an innovative way to address the lack of time records, this methodology raised numerous problems. The Krizeks argued that the methodology was pure conjecture: not only was the government unable to prove how much time was spent with each patient, the fact that the codes mandated no specific time frames meant there was no basis for holding Dr. Krizek liable for any time-related misrepresentations.[36] Instead, they argued that the suggested times merely illustrated the *intensity* of the services provided.

The Krizeks also argued that on some weekends and holidays when he was the only psychiatrist on call, Dr. Krizek did in fact work around the clock — and that care rendered close to midnight could easily be billed to the wrong day. While Judge Sporkin instructed the Special Master to take into account any proof that Dr. Krizek actually provided the services claimed on a given day, it appears no such proof was introduced. Instead, the Krizeks' rebuttal evidence consisted of declarations from 39 of Dr. Krizek's colleagues attesting to his dedication and long hours at the hospital. Noting that such declarations could not prove the duration of patient care rendered on any particular day, prosecutors countered with voluminous deposition and hearing testimony (including from defense witnesses) in which colleagues referred to Dr. Krizek as "a morning person" who "tends not to be here at night."[37]

This debate raised an issue that continues to anger the Krizeks to this day: who bears the burden of proving (or disproving) "reckless disregard"? Noting that the government must prove FCA liability by a preponderance of the evidence, the Krizeks argued that the fact that the records failed to specify the exact duration/content of care could not be used to infer that such care wasn't provided; rather, the government had to affirmatively prove it *wasn't* done.[38] The Krizeks made impassioned (and at times quite convincing) arguments that the government could not prove that even one claim was submitted for a longer time period than the session warranted. This argument is significantly undercut, however, by the fact that the government need not prove *actual* falsity under the FCA, but merely recklessness. Moreover, the reason the government lacked proof of the duration of the services rendered was because such information was *missing* from Dr. Krizek's records. Rather than altering the legal burden of proof under the FCA, Judge Sporkin merely reiterated the government's position that it is the *provider's* duty to keep records supporting the level of care billed.

The Special Master identified 264 days on which the Krizeks submitted 1,149 claims for more than nine hours' worth of care, for a total of $47,105.39. Judge Sporkin accepted the Special Master's findings and ruled that the Krizeks would have to repay that sum to the government. With regard to the FCA, however, Sporkin set a higher benchmark so there could be no question about the impropriety of the bills: he imposed the then-maximum $10,000 FCA penalty only for the 11 claims made on three days on which the Krizeks billed in excess of *24 hours*.[39] Sporkin also enjoined Dr. Krizek from participating in Medicare and Medicaid until he could demonstrate that his billing practices had been corrected.[40]

Both parties appealed, and in May 1997 the D.C. Circuit affirmed in part and reversed in part.[41] The appellate court affirmed the basic liability decision, as well as the Special Master's findings, the use of the seven-patient trial sample, and Judge Sporkin's definition of reckless disregard as "an extension of gross negligence."[42] However, the court found that Sporkin had erred when he imposed FCA liability on the basis of the 24-hour (rather than the nine-hour) benchmark without giving the government the opportunity to offer additional evidence. The court also held that each HCFA 1500 billing *form* — rather than each *service* listed on the form — constituted a single FCA "claim." To the extent the government could identify only a single bill for a patient, regardless of how many services were included on it, only one false claim could be alleged.[43]

On remand, the government requested discovery for an additional 25 dates, and again requested information about Dr. Krizek's private-pay patients. Judge Sporkin limited discovery to ten additional days, although the Krizeks responded for all 25 days — a search that yielded only two additional days of billings for more that 24 hours. Sporkin appeared to balk at subjecting the Krizeks to significant additional damages, noting that the Special Master's methodology could not establish whether these claims had been billed to Medicare/Medicaid or to private patients. Finding that the government was required to identify specifically which fraudulent billings were for Medicare/Medicaid patients, and applying the rule that each HCFA 1500 form constituted one claim (and so multiple false claims on a single form had to be eliminated), the court found that at least *one* false claim had been submitted on three additional days — constituting only three additional FCA violations.[44]

On a second appeal the D.C. Circuit disagreed, noting that it had explicitly ordered additional discovery regarding the Krizeks' private pay patients. Because the FCA merely required the government to prove by a preponderance of the evidence that the defendants acted in *reckless disregard*, the court held that prosecutors were not required to prove that the excess claims were for Medicare/Medicaid services. Rather, the court held that the government's burden of establishing recklessness could be "satisfied when any patient is seen beyond the twenty-fourth hour."[45] The court remanded the case yet again, explicitly instructing Sporkin to calculate the number of false claims by eliminating any overlap after the 24th hour on each of the days at issue. The opinion concluded:

> This prosecution of a single doctor has now spanned over six years. . . . The five days on which the false claims were made occurred over twelve years ago. According to defense counsel, Dr. Krizek no longer practices medicine and is dying of cancer. . . . It is time for the parties to stop refighting battles long-ago lost and for the district court to bring this prosecution to an expeditious conclusion. . . . We fully expect that these simple steps will bring this prosecution to a long-deserved end.[46]

Sadly, that would not be the case.

In January 2000, Judge Sporkin returned to private practice and the case was transferred to Judge James Robertson. Robertson entered judgment against the Krizeks in August of 2000. Despite the D.C. Circuit's admonition, the case continued for another three years, with two summary appellate affirmances and an unsuccessful certiorari petition to the U.S. Supreme Court.[47] In August 2002, the Krizeks satisfied the judgment by paying a total of $315,537.28 — a significant sum, but far below the amount originally sought by the government.[48]

Yet the true costs of the case went far beyond the monetary damages, and began to accrue long before the litigation ended. The trial was cut short to permit the Krizeks to visit Dr. Krizek's ill mother in Prague, but she died before they arrived. By October 1995, Blanka described Dr. Krizek as "totally disabled" and under treatment for major depression and hypertension.[49] Dr. Krizek was diagnosed with thyroid cancer in 1996, and later prostate cancer; Blanka's health similarly deteriorated. While the injunction was only temporary, Dr. Krizek appears to have made the decision to stop practicing medicine even before the trial was over. During his testimony, he described being "anxious, depressed, and hav[ing] the feeling I am fighting for my life now, and for the life of my relatives, and family, and reputation."[50] In a letter to Judge Sporkin in April 1995, Dr. Krizek stated, "I don't believe that I will ever treat patients again."[51] By July 1998, Judge Sporkin described him as "a broken and sick man."[52] When he reluctantly agreed to be interviewed for this project in September 2007, Dr. Krizek explained that "my only interest is to die in peace."[53] The Krizeks now live a quiet life, relying on Blanka's rental properties for income. Slowly, they have rebuilt their relationship with their daughter, Monika, and her family. Dr. Krizek remains an avid butterfly enthusiast, taking photographs and publishing articles on entomology.

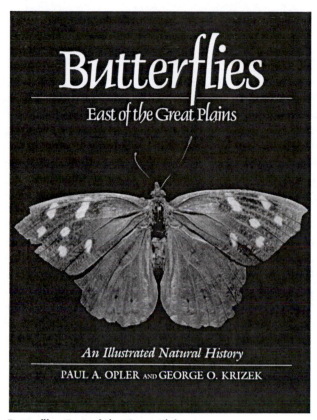

Butterflies East of the Great Plains
(Johns Hopkins University Press, 1984)

C. The Lessons Learned

For a generation of health law students, prosecutors, defense attorneys, and their physician clients, the *Krizek* case has become something of a landmark. Besides its doctrinal significance in elucidating the boundaries of intent under the FCA, it also serves as a cautionary tale about the risks of ignoring or dealing cavalierly with the government's billing and recordkeeping requirements. Yet on closer examination, the litigation itself should be seen as a failure and the end result a tragedy. Its shortcomings are readily documented by the years spent on investigating (five) and litigating the case (seven), the number of appeals (five), the cost to the government ($600,000 to $1 million), its toll on the lives of the defendants, and the ultimate result (payment of $315,537, essentially what the case could have been settled for ten years earlier). Moreover, *Krizek* serves to expose some of the severe problems plaguing government financing of health care, including the complexities of the process and the inevitable temptations for abuse.

Whether framed as a Greek tragedy or a prisoners' dilemma, the *Krizek* litigation seemed to ensnare the parties in a litigation net that defied escape. Few would dispute that the case should have been settled at an early stage. The inability of the parties to come together to reach a mutually agreeable solution (and the failure of the legal system to help forge one) offers an opportunity to consider the dynamics that prolong litigation. A substantial academic literature has developed concerning why cases go to trial. Economic analysis suggests that parties will reach agreement whenever they agree on the expected value of a trial, and that trials occur when one or both parties miscalculate the likely outcome.[54] These models, generally applicable to private civil litigation, also have some saliency with regard to government civil actions. Other approaches examine the bargaining context in which settlements are negotiated, and conclude that settlements fail when the parties' bargaining strategies lead to impasse. While most of these models assume that the disputants are rational actors, recent scholarship has focused on the psychological factors that may impel parties to reject settlement even when there is no error in evaluating likely outcomes, and no bargaining strategies that preclude settlement.[55] The background story of the *Krizek* case offers some anecdotal insights into these extra-legal factors that shape the course of litigation.

While many lessons might be drawn from the case, we discuss three that serve to help understand the events and illustrate some of the idiosyncrasies of fraud litigation involving health care providers. First, we explore how the strong personalities involved in the case established an atmosphere conducive to conflict and inhospitable to settlement. Next we discuss the ways in which myriad misunderstandings plagued the process and blocked possible outcomes that would have both satisfied the interests of the litigants and served the ends of justice. Finally, we consider how the applicable law, specifically the FCA and Medicare billing regulations, interacted to place the parties in positions in which conflict escalated and amicable resolution became all but impossible.

1. Failures of Understanding: The Human Element

The *Krizek* case offers an object lesson on the ways in which the personalities of the participants affect the course of litigation. The confluence of a number of factors — stubborn defendants who believed they were once again the victims of government persecution; zealous prosecutors eager to send a message about false claims; a pragmatic, bottom-line oriented trial judge; and legal representation that fell short of the ideal — all conspired to produce an outcome that could not have been predicted.

The government's team was led by aggressive investigators who, from the outset, appear to have adopted an FBI/criminal investigation approach. Because the case was one of the first health care fraud investigations brought in the District of Columbia, the government investigators were necessarily on unfamiliar ground. The Krizeks loudly complained throughout the litigation that the investigators' ruse of a "Christmas delivery" and conduct in the first interview was abusive and designed to intimidate. Regardless of which version of the events one credits, at a minimum it appears that the investigators came to the Krizeks' house without notice and acted in a manner which the Krizeks (and later Judge Sporkin) viewed as an attempt to intimidate. Although there was extensive and hotly disputed testimony at trial concerning the alleged abusive treatment, it was never cited by the district or appellate court. Nevertheless, these actions had a major impact on the case, as the conduct seems to have reinforced Judge Sporkin's view that the doctor was a "little guy" fighting against the "overreaching" government.[56] In addition, these actions likely fueled an already antagonistic atmosphere and hardened the defendants' resistance to settlement. Further contributing to these perceptions was the fact that the investigation stretched on for almost three years before the Krizeks received any follow-up, which came in the form of a demand letter threatening prosecution. This extraordinary delay in bringing the case not only stoked the frustration of the defendants, but contributed to the court's impression that the underlying claims were stale.

The *Krizek* case was one of the first brought by a new fraud unit in the office of the U.S. Attorney for the District of Columbia to combat health care fraud. Besides reflecting a growing interest among politicians concerning the problems of fraud in federal health programs, the new office may have been a response to the highly visible actions of other U.S. Attorneys Offices, such as the work of Jim Sheehan in Philadelphia, which were gaining considerable publicity in pursing these cases. Perhaps owing to the D.C. office's desire to begin with a flourish, the case received considerable notoriety from the beginning. On January 11, 1993, U.S. Attorney Jay Stevens announced "a major enforcement initiative targeting health care fraud and abuse," describing the *Krizek* case (along with another colorful investigation) at a press conference as involving "fraudulent multiple billings for patients' psychoanalytic sessions."[57] Not surprisingly, the announcement received considerable media attention, including a local television report that included a photograph of the Krizeks' home. The case elicited strong reactions from provider groups, and the publicity it received — along with the extraordinary recovery sought by the government — soon established *Krizek* as a showcase for the government's war on health care fraud.

The case was originally handled by John Munich, an experienced AUSA. Munich handed the case over soon after it was filed to Bruce Heygi, who served as the government's primary attorney for almost the entirety of the litigation. Heygi, a former police officer, had been a medical malpractice litigator in private practice but had limited trial experience. Heygi's background in malpractice litigation seems to have influenced his approach to the case. In particular, he saw the medical necessity claim as akin to a medical malpractice case in that support from expert witnesses could provide sufficient evidence to prove that Dr. Krizek's practices were not in accord with accepted medical standards. Perhaps owing to the staleness of the evidence and the doctor's reputation, however, from the outset Judge Sporkin had little use for this theory or for the government's proffered proof. While the government should not be faulted for litigating vigorously, its strategy may have not been well suited to the personality of the judge it drew at trial.

For their part, the Krizeks are a study in cultural dissonance. Both reflect the strong influence of their years first in Nazi and then Communist Czechoslovakia, and their resistance to governmental interference with Dr. Krizek's practice. Yet in many respects this background worked to undermine the portrait the Krizeks attempted to present in their defense. The trial record and depositions are replete with Blanka's claims — some expressed in extravagant terms[58] — that the government's conduct was reminiscent of the communist regime they fled. If not undermining her credibility, the excessiveness of her claims may have had the unintended effect of reinforcing the government's allegation that Blanka acted recklessly.

Cultural factors also detracted from Blanka's ability to present a coherent picture of her understanding of the law and her role in the doctor's office. Unfamiliar with the details of practice administration, Blanka undertook to handle the office billing with no training or experience with the government's requirements. Although claiming at trial that she sought clarification from HHS and consulted a billing professional for help, it is apparent that Mrs. Krizek had little patience with the niceties of Medicare and Medicaid billing rules.[59] In some respects her naiveté may have underscored the appearance of wrongdoing. Her repeated insistence that she thought she would be contacted if the carrier uncovered any problems with her billing, together with the alleged out-of-court admission to investigators that she expected to see them some day, tended to support the inference that she undertook a "let's see what happens" approach.

Dr. Krizek, a scholarly gentleman whose avocation is the study of butterflies, exuded both disinterest and impatience with the billing issues raised by the case. At trial and in his deposition, he indicated that he had little understanding of the meaning of the 90844 CPT code and had undertaken little effort to familiarize himself with the government regulations. The impression left by the Krizeks (and strongly endorsed by Judge Sporkin) was of a hard-working doctor, intensely devoted to his patients, but having an intense dislike for the business aspects of practice. Given these predilections, and his wife's dominant personality and control over family finances, Dr. Krizek was content to leave all billing matters to Blanka, exercising little if any supervision. Likewise, his distain for the bureaucratic side of medicine appears to have spilled over into a disregard of Medicare recordkeeping norms. The government consistently stressed the absence of the required records and at times suggested that Dr. Krizek never kept contemporaneous billing records at all, instead going back every few months to recreate them.

Blanka Krizek projects a quite different personality. Extremely outspoken and given to hyperbole (one party described her as "histrionic"),[60] Mrs. Krizek played the dominant role in making decisions about the course of the couple's joint defense. Her characterization of the prosecutors and impugning of the government's motives continue to this day.[61] She took full control of Dr. Krizek's billing, seemingly predisposed to taking a fast and loose approach. More than one observer has speculated the case would likely have settled at an early stage if Dr. Krizek was calling the shots. Moreover, as suggested above, her tendency to sensationalize probably lessened her overall credibility, strengthened inferences that she was reckless in her billing practices, and affected prosecutors' attitudes toward settlement.

An important turning point in the case was the Krizeks' change of counsel before trial, replacing well-regarded attorneys Swiss and Shaughnessy with their daughter, Monika. Although Blanka claimed the change was based on concerns about the mounting attorneys' fees and a desire to give Monika a chance to gain legal experience, her attorneys' motions for withdrawal cited "irreconcilable differences . . . [and] very major conflicts."[62] While the specifics are not known, strong personal conflicts appear to have been the underlying causes in the change of counsel.[63] Moreover, in handing the case to their daughter, the Krizeks chose to rely on counsel whose inexperience was evident at trial, and whom other participants felt as a family member was "too close to the case" — lacking the objectivity needed to assess the best course for her parents. Perhaps the most telling indication of the problem of the Krizeks' legal representation is the fact that at one point Judge Sporkin appears to have contacted counsel at a law firm to obtain assistance for Monika on appeal.

Finally, Judge Stanley Sporkin, a well-known figure in Washington D.C., presided over the initial trial. Judge Sporkin served in the 1970s as Director of the Bureau of Enforcement of the Securities and Exchange Commission, where he earned a reputation for vigorous prosecution of white collar crime.[64] Sporkin subsequently served as general counsel to the Central Intelligence Agency, and was appointed to the bench in 1985. Judge Sporkin was strongly influenced by his father, a judge in Philadelphia, whom he relates always talked about "doing justice." Judge

Sporkin takes a rough justice approach, acknowledging that he is tough on enforcement but always seeking to be fair. In his words, "fairness permeates my whole background."[65] Yet he wasn't so regarded by all. On the bench he earned a reputation for being tough on government prosecutors (indeed, prosecutors sometimes referred to unfavorable rulings in his court as "being Sporked"). On the other hand, he also gained notoriety for receiving a sharp rebuke from the Court of Appeals for his apparent bias against Microsoft in his handling of the consent decree in the government's early antitrust litigation against the company.[66]

Judge Sporkin expressed skepticism about the government's fraud allegations in the first pretrial meeting (when he characteristically conducted what attorneys referred to as a "mini-trial"), and was unreceptive to prosecutors' efforts to establish a pattern of practice and behaviors indicating that the Krizeks' "upcoding" activities were intentional. In addition, his comments from the bench showed a desire to steer the case away from an inquiry into medical necessity or questions about the doctor's medical judgment. Finally, Sporkin's pragmatic, no-nonsense approach to litigation was manifest throughout the trial. He repeatedly chastised the government for attempting to establish issues that would prolong the trial and often cut short lines of testimony with dismissive comments. In one startling move, after becoming extremely upset with a witness from PBS who refused to provide certain evidence to the defense, Sporkin stated that the case was dismissed "for failure to turn over information to this Court." Upon the announcement, the Krizeks cried out in joy, hugged each other and began celebrating — but moments later the judge reinstated the case, with instructions to the witness to obtain the evidence during the lunch break.[67] Likewise, the judge did not conceal his impatience with Monika, whose lack of trial experience was evident throughout the trial; on many occasions, the judge took over the questioning of witnesses or short-circuited lines of inquiry. Finally, using every technique available, including expressions of exasperation, exhortation and threat, and employment of the services of an experienced Magistrate Judge, the court tried valiantly to get the parties to settle the case. Despite his commanding presence, Judge Sporkin met with no success.

2. Failures of Communication

The record of the *Krizek* case is replete with failures to communicate. Misunderstandings about the law and the motives of the other side had a powerful influence on the participants' conduct throughout the case. These misunderstandings, which to some extent are a byproduct of the personalities and predilections previously discussed, ultimately stood in the way of settlement and shaped the course of the litigation.

One readily apparent source of confusion was the complexity of the billing rules for Medicare patients. As noted above, at the time of the *Krizek* case the text of the government's descriptors of the CPT codes employed for psychiatric services lacked a clear explanation of the critical parameter of whether face-to-face contact was required for the specified times. Although the government introduced credible evidence that clarification was readily available, such information was less than transparent — as evidenced by the testimony of doctors who asserted that the codes did in fact permit some of the Krizeks' billing practices. Given that a fee-for-service billing system relies on the ability of physicians to report their services using administratively determined categories, it is obviously critical that those categories be readily understood by physicians and their staffs. The testimony offered a compelling example of the confusion that the billing regulations could sow.

The government's conduct also caused misunderstanding. At several key junctures the government took steps that conveyed a message that undermined its position in court and produced unintended consequences: missteps at the investigative stage, in framing the case, and the extraordinary delay in bringing the case portrayed the government in an unfavorable light and inhibited frank communications with defendants. Most prominently, the aggressive tactics of the investigators sent a signal that the Krizeks interpreted as evidence that they would not be treated fairly by the government, and likely reduced the chances of settlement. Likewise, the incident seems to have contributed to the Judge's determination that the government was "overreaching."[68]

In addition, several of the government's tactical choices may have been ill-suited to communicate effectively with Judge Sporkin. For example, framing the case as an $81 million fraud prosecution struck a discordant note from the outset, given Dr. Krizek's background and modest practice serving indigent patients in a busy hospital setting. In addition, pursuing the medical necessity theory in the face of Judge Sporkin's expressed skepticism also contributed to the unfavorable image the government presented at trial. Perhaps owing to his background in medical malpractice litigation, Hegyi insisted on trying to establish that Dr. Krizek provided services that were not medically needed or appropriate. Besides the almost insuperable evidentiary difficulties this approach presented, it clearly was not the most direct way to prove a violation of the FCA.

From the very beginning, the Krizeks did not appear to grasp the significance of the charges or comprehend the need for competent legal advice to help them navigate the legal proceedings that lay ahead. Following their receipt of the demand letter apprising them of the suspected violations, the Krizeks insisted on meeting with Munich without counsel present. Rather than discuss the possibility of settlement or ask for any delay in filing the case, the Krizeks chose to use the meeting to vent their frustrations and to demand that the government provide them with an explanation, rather than vice versa. Blanka did almost all of the talking, taking a very combative, accusatory approach and comparing the dispute to her family's experiences in Czechoslovakia. According to Munich, at no time did she discuss or appear willing to enter into any kind of settlement agreement or negotiate in any way.[69]

Moreover, the withdrawal of counsel dramatically impacted the dynamic of the litigation. In handing the case to their daughter, the Krizeks relied upon someone who apparently lacked two characteristics essential to effective representation: experience and detachment. Despite Judge Sporkin's efforts, opportunities for amicable settlement were squandered. In addition, by virtue of being too close to the case, Monika may have been unable to speak with the objectivity and authority needed to convey the sound advice her parents needed. Whether more experienced counsel could have produced a different result is, of course, impossible to know. However, as evidenced by their confused and hyperbolic testimony and continued misunderstanding of the legal issues confronting them, it is fair to say that the Krizeks likely would have benefited had they had access to consistent advice from experienced counsel.

Ultimately, the *Krizek* case became a cause celebre for groups highly critical of the government's prosecution of physicians for billing irregularities. The

Association of American Physicians and Surgeons (AAPS), a long-standing opponent of government health care, offered the Krizeks support and legal advice during the litigation. In 1998, the House Judiciary Committee held a hearing on "Administrative Crimes and Quasi-Crimes," responding to anecdotal evidence of government agencies abusing their administrative enforcement powers. The Krizeks were invited to testify; because of Dr. Krizek's ongoing treatment for thyroid cancer, Blanka delivered their prepared testimony. Most recently, the Krizeks' story was featured in a book on "The Criminalization of Medicine: America's War on Doctors."[70] While contributing to the notoriety of the case, these advocacy efforts did little to assuage the Krizeks' pain and anger. To this day, the Krizeks believe that they were singled out, that they were treated unfairly by the legal system, and that they in fact did nothing legally or ethically improper. The persistence of these beliefs evidences the most palpable communication breakdown in this case: the utter failure of the legal system to communicate the boundaries of the law to the defendants.

3. Failures of Law

The *Krizek* case also reflects tensions inherent not only in the fraud provisions, but also in the structure of Medicare and Medicaid reimbursement. Part of the problem is due to the fact that fraudulent conduct can be pursued under a variety of criminal, civil, and administrative provisions, and it is rarely certain at the outset how a case will end up. Thus, Agent Kochanski advised the Krizeks during the 1989 visit that the investigation was a criminal one, yet the U.S. Attorney's office ultimately chose to pursue civil sanctions; in contrast, the Krizeks insist that the billing issues should have been handled administratively by PBS.

Moreover, the FCA is a powerful but blunt tool. The law was designed to address the problem of military fraud, and the very features that make the law useful against the defense industry are problematic as applied to health care. Recall that the FCA currently imposes treble damages plus a per-claim statutory penalty of $5,500 to $11,000. Because defense contractors often submit a few extremely large invoices each year, treble damages may be extremely large while per-claim penalties are negligible. Particularly for physicians, the reverse is true: because physicians submit a bill for each patient, they may submit thousands of small claims per year. In such cases treble damages may be reasonable, but the statutory penalties can be enormous — leading to the somewhat counterintuitive result that FCA liability is often greatest for providers who submit the largest *number* of claims, even if the financial harm to the government is small. As a result, providers have an enormous incentive to settle FCA allegations even if they might have a reasonable chance of success at trial.[71]

In this case, while the alleged 8,002 false claims would have resulted in the Krizeks paying treble damages of less than $1 million, the $10,000 per-claim penalty resulted in a demand for almost $81 million dollars. Prosecutors have stated that this amount would have been "draconian" — and that the Krizeks knew it was never really on the table even though the U.S. Attorney publicized it in announcing the case — yet that is nonetheless the result reached under the statute. Ironically, this appears to have worked *against* the government, as it added to Judge Sporkin's concerns that the government's actions were unjustifiably heavy-handed.

These difficulties are magnified when combined with the extreme complexity of the Medicare and Medicaid reimbursement systems. Clearly, a uniform coding system cannot capture the nuances of the services provided to individual patients. The Krizeks argued this was particularly true in the context of psychiatry, where most treatment consists of patient interaction rather than discrete medical procedures, and where patients may also suffer from severe physical conditions. The complexity is compounded by periodic changes to the codes, requiring that physicians and their billing agents frequently check the rules. As even one of the prosecution's witnesses lamented, "doctors are asked to spend more time managing paper than they are patients. And it seems to me that the patients deserve the priority and not the paper."[72]

Moreover, mental health services have long been subject to reimbursement limitations that do not apply to physical illnesses. Medicare Part B pays only 62.5 percent of covered treatment expenses; this amount is further subject to the beneficiary's twenty percent coinsurance requirements, meaning that Medicare will only reimburse the physician for 80 percent of 62.5 percent of covered expenses (and, in effect, that the patient is responsible for 50 percent of the cost).[73] This struck a chord with Judge Sporkin, who worried that the reimbursement was "far below the norm for charges reimbursed by non-governmental insurance carriers."[74] Inpatient psychiatric treatment poses additional problems. Hospital psychiatrists frequently are pulled away for consultations and other tasks — one of the key reasons auditors thought Dr. Krizek's reliance on the standard 45–50 minute session code was aberrant. A variety of codes are available for use in the hospital setting, some with clearer time specifications than others. Moreover, hospital psychiatrists may provide a variety of both medical and psychiatric services. While prosecutors argued that Medicare and Medicaid require all services to be coded separately, rather than "bundled" as Dr. Krizek tried to do, the doctor may not be reimbursed for each one.[75] Clearly, Judge Sporkin was troubled by this, noting that "[w]hen Medicare dictates that a physician must report each service rendered as a separate code item, the physician is entitled to believe that he will be reimbursed for each of the services rendered."[76] While it is clear that Judge Sporkin was unwilling to countenance the Krizeks' billing system, it is equally clear he believed the government bore some level of responsibility for the problem.

Finally, *Krizek* illustrates how complex health care litigation strategies, such as a liability trial based on a small sample of representative patients, may create a host of new problems. In part this is because such strategies necessarily foster some degree of inaccuracy: there is simply no way to know whether the seven-patient sample truly represented Dr. Krizek's overall patient load, or whether the Special Master's time estimates bore any resemblance to the actual care provided. Without such strategies it would be impossible to try a fraud case involving more than a handful of claims. Yet what we gain in convenience we may lose in accuracy — a questionable trade-off given the coercive effects of the FCA.

Indeed, focusing on the failures of law apparent in the *Krizek* case suggests that Judge Sporkin, in fact, may have gotten it right. True, he did not follow the letter of the law in awarding damages and penalties, he refused to fully consider the medical necessity allegations, and he adopted a perhaps unnecessarily complex damages methodology. But Sporkin nonetheless had an intuitive sense of the dispute: a dedicated doctor with a grossly deficient billing system. By crafting the recovery accordingly, he may have come as close as anyone could to a fair result.

D. Conclusion

The *Krizek* litigation is best known for setting precedent under the FCA. Yet the case also stands as a stark reminder of the human side of health care fraud: the emotional aspects of the litigation process, the ways in which the parties' backgrounds can interfere with dispassionate legal analysis, and the devastating personal impact of such cases.

Was justice served by the prosecution of the Krizeks? No one who cares about the solvency of the federal health care programs can countenance blatant disregard for billing rules, but at what cost? None of the attorneys involved have expressed satisfaction with the result. Prosecutors have said that it was never their intention to drive Dr. Krizek out of medical practice (or Monika out of legal practice), yet that is precisely what occurred. The Krizeks were crushed by what they saw as unfair treatment at the hands of their adopted country, and still do not understand exactly what they did wrong. As Blanka explained with her characteristic bluntness, "KGB interrogations and my imprisonment in Prague were easier."[77] In the end, prosecutors received far less than they expected, the Krizeks lost their careers and their health, and the poor and elderly psychiatric patients of Washington, D.C., lost a caring physician. Justice, indeed. Rough justice, in every sense.

ENDNOTES

1. United States v. Krizek, 7 F. Supp. 2d 56, 60 (D.D.C. 1998).

2. Administrative Crimes and Quasi-Crimes: Hearing Before the Subcomm. on Commercial and Administrative Law of the H. Comm. on the Judiciary, 105th Cong. 43 (1998), *available at* http://commdocs.house.gov/committees/judiciary/hju59925.000/hju59925_0.htm [hereinafter *Krizek Congressional Testimony*] (testimony of George O. Krizek, M.D., and Blanka H. Krizek). Blanka herself had an eventful youth, spending several years in hospitals with a severe case of tuberculosis as well as being interrogated and imprisoned by the KGB.

3. Ronald T. Libby, The Criminalization of Medicine 86 (2008).

4. *Krizek Congressional Testimony, supra* note 2, at 47.

5. Transcript of Bench Trial, vol. II, at 20–23, 54–56, 74–76, United States v. Krizek, 859 F. Supp. 5 (D.D.C. 1994) (Civ. A. No. 96-54). Medicare and Medicaid billing codes are largely based on the CPT system, designed by the American Medical Association (AMA) as a uniform nomenclature for physician services. *See* 42 U.S.C. §1395w-4(c) (2006) (requiring Secretary of HHS to develop uniform procedure coding system); American Soc. of Dermatology v. Shalala, 962 F. Supp. 141, 144 (D.D.C. 1996) (describing agreement permitting HHS to use AMA CPT codes).

6. Transcript of Bench Trial, vol. IV, at 100 et seq., *Krizek*, 859 F. Supp. 5 (Civ. A. No. 96-54).

7. *Id.* at 108–17.

8. Transcript of Bench Trial, vol. V, at 95, *Krizek*, 859 F. Supp. 5 (Civ. A. No. 96-54) (testimony of Special Agent Hillary Mullen). All three agents testified that they distinctly remembered this comment.

9. *See, e.g., Krizek Congressional Testimony, supra* note 2, at 43, 58. According to Dr. Krizek, the agents' allegations changed during the course of the visit: first they claimed he billed for nonexistent patients, then they claimed he billed for patients on days he did not see them, and finally they claimed he saw the patients but billed in the wrong way.

10. Transcript of Bench Trial, vol. II, *supra* note 5, at 100–12. The Krizeks argued that any concerns over their billing should have been addressed in the first instance by PBS. *See Krizek Congressional Testimony, supra* note 2, at 49. PBS took the somewhat circular position that Dr. Krizek was not offered education initially because no problems were identified prior to the audit; yet after the audit, education was inappropriate because it was now a suspected fraud case. Transcript of Bench Trial, vol. II, *supra* note 5, at 111–13.

11. Interview with John Munich, in St. Louis, Missouri (Sept. 7, 2007).

12. It is unclear what settlement range may have been under discussion. One source thought a $250,000 offer initially was on the table, although prosecutors recall the range as being closer to $300,000–400,000.

13. In retrospect, Blanka says that the decision "changed a lot of things in [the] family," none of them for the better. Telephone Interview with Blanka Krizek (July 16, 2007). The experience apparently proved so disheartening that Monika stopped practicing law.

14. Transcript of Status Call, Feb. 3, 1994, at 2-6, 10, *Krizek*, 859 F. Supp. 5 (Civ. A. No. 96-54).

15. *Id.* at 5–6.

16. The extent of Crowell & Moring's involvement in the case remains unclear. At trial, Monika confirmed that they were assisting with her legal analysis but had not entered an appearance. Transcript of Bench Trial, vol. II, *supra* note 5, at 85–86. Joseph Onek of Crowell & Moring later entered an appearance after trial, when he helped craft the judge's order for relief. Transcript of Status Call, April 14, 1994, at 19, *Krizek*, 859 F. Supp. 5 (Civ. A. No. 96-54).

17. 31 U.S.C. §3729(a)(1), (b) (2006).

18. *Id.* §3729(a); 28 C.F.R. §85.3(a)(9) (2006). The FCA also prohibits several other types of fraud that are less common in the health care industry. 31 U.S.C. §3729(a)(4)-(7).

19. Complaint at 7–9, *Krizek*, 859 F. Supp. 5 (Civ. A. No. 96-54).

20. Protective Order, United States v. Krizek, No. 93-54 (D.D.C. Mar. 9, 1994). When the Krizeks later challenged this ruling, the D.C. Circuit noted that their attorney had "not only agreed to, but proffered, the idea." United States v. Krizek, 111 F.3d 934, 940 (D.C. Cir. 1997).

21. United States v. Krizek, 859 F. Supp. 5 (D.D.C. 1994).

22. Transcript of Bench Trial, vol. I, at 4, *Krizek*, 859 F. Supp. 5 (Civ. A. No. 96-54).

23. Transcript of Bench Trial, vol. III, at 20, *Krizek*, 859 F. Supp. 5 (Civ. A. No. 96-54).

24. *Id.* at 53, 58. Because Medicare generally paid for only one psychiatric service per patient per day, prosecutors alleged that Dr. Krizek "backdated" claims so that he could bill for multiple services performed on a single day. Memorandum of Points and Authorities in Support of Plaintiff's Cross-Motion for Partial Summary Judgment on Liability Issues at 23–24, *Krizek*, 859 F. Supp. 5 (Civ. A. No. 96-54).

25. Telephone Interview with Bruce Hegyi (Oct. 5, 2007); Transcript of Bench Trial, vol. X, at 91–95, *Krizek*, 859 F. Supp. 5 (Civ. A. No. 96-54). Dr. Krizek insisted that the patient had always been communicative, although delusional. Transcript of Bench Trial, vol. X, *supra*, at 95–96.

26. *Krizek*, 859 F. Supp. at 8.

27. *Id.* The prosecutors have criticized Sporkin's treatment of this issue, noting that the propriety of medical treatment is often established by chart review rather than by direct patient evidence (such as in medical malpractice suits). But rather than ruling that medical necessity must be proven *by law* through direct testimony, Judge Sporkin's comments likely reflected his view of the *factual credibility* of the evidence offered on the issue.

28. Transcript of Bench Trial, vol. II, *supra* note 5, at 6. McCann testified, to a somewhat incredulous Judge Sporkin, that "I don't believe that it really needs to say 'face-to-face,' it's been so understood for many years . . . and this has never been an issue." Transcript of Bench Trial, vol. XI, at 85, *Krizek*, 859 F. Supp. 5 (Civ. A. No. 96-54).

29. Transcript of Bench Trial, vol. IV, *supra* note 6, at 22–33 (testimony of Dr. Tracy Gordy); Transcript of Bench Trial, vol. VI, at 5–38, *Krizek*, 859 F. Supp. 5 (Civ. A. No. 96-54) (testimony of Dr. Chester Schmidt).

30. *Krizek*, 859 F. Supp. at 10. Judge Sporkin further remarked, "I think you've got . . . an epidemic out there, quite frankly. And I think part of it is because you've got a ridiculous system." Transcript of Bench Trial, vol. XI, *supra* note 28, at 130–31.

31. 859 F. Supp. at 10.

32. Transcript of Bench Trial, vol. XI, *supra* note 28, at 51–52. This testimony also bolstered the prosecution's argument that Blanka was jointly and severally liable for the harm, a theory that allowed the prosecution to reach the real estate assets held in her name.

33. Transcript of Bench Trial, vol. X, *supra* note 25, at 35. Moreover, neither Dr. nor Mrs. Krizek reviewed the bills prepared by Mrs. Anderson.

34. 859 F. Supp. at 12; Transcript of Status Call, April 14, 1994, *supra* note 16, at 23–26. The nine-hour benchmark was based on the testimony of Dr. Norman Wilson, former Chairman of the WHC Psychiatry Department, who testified that he could not recall billing more than twelve 90844 sessions on a single day. Dr. Wilson later submitted a declaration clarifying that his testimony described the average hours worked in his office practice, not the duties of a hospital psychiatrist on call during weekends and holidays. The Washington Psychiatric Association intervened in order to file a memorandum objecting to the nine-hour "presumption," leading Judge Sporkin to clarify that the benchmark applied only in this case. Memorandum Opinion and Order, United States v. Krizek, Civ. A. No. 93-0054 (D.D.C. Jan. 9, 1995). Rather than viewing this as a compromise devised to address deficiencies in their billing procedures, to this day the Krizeks take offense at what they view as a ruling that Dr. Krizek was not permitted *by law* to work more than nine hours a day. Moreover, they argued that the benchmark was agreed to by Joseph Onek, an attorney they did not know, during a post-trial status call in which they could not participate because they were in Prague attending to

Dr. Krizek's dying mother (although Monika was present and did not object). Transcript of Status Call, April 14, 1994, *supra*, at 23–26. The Krizeks further question Onek's involvement in the case because he served as counsel to the American Psychiatric Association, which they believe not only failed to support Dr. Krizek but also may have played a role in targeting him. Additional Declaration of Co-Defendant Blanka H. Krizek in Support of Motion to Dismiss at 12–13, Krizek, 909 F. Supp. 32 (D.D.C. 1995).

35. Order, United States v. Krizek, Civ. A. No. 93-0054 (D.D.C. Apr. 6, 1995).

36. With the support of the Association of American Physicians and Surgeons (AAPS), the Krizeks also argued that the CPT codes did not have the force of law because they had not been adopted through notice-and-comment procedures pursuant to the Administrative Procedure Act. The District Court for the District of Columbia later held that the Social Security Act precluded judicial review of the HHS-AMA agreement. *See* American Soc. of Dermatology v. Shalala, 962 F. Supp. 141 (D.D.C. 1996) (finding court had no jurisdiction to review the way in which HHS adopted the coding system).

37. Plaintiff's Motion for Entry of Judgment in Conformity with the Findings of the Special Master and Memorandum of Points and Authorities in Support Thereof and Plaintiff's Response to Defendants' Objections to the Findings and Recommendations of the Special Master at 11–16, Krizek, 909 F. Supp. 32 (D.D.C. 1995) (Civ. A. No. 93-0054).

38. Dr. Krizek went so far as to testify that the fact that his signature was missing from the notes of a multi-disciplinary team conference (one of the patient-related activities he sought to bundle into the time code) "doesn't mean I was not present." Transcript of Bench Trial, vol. X, supra note 25, at 40. When the prosecutor responded, "But it surely doesn't support that you were present, does it?," Dr. Krizek shot back, "That's a legal terminology." *Id.*

39. United States v. Krizek, 909 F. Supp. 32, 33–34 (D.D.C. 1995). Although understandable, Sporkin's decision to use a different benchmark for the FCA and unjust enrichment theories led to a curious result: he imposed *no* damages under the FCA at all, merely imposing $10,000 per-claim civil penalties in addition to the damages found under the common law causes of action (which the Krizeks unsuccessfully argued on appeal meant that no violations of the FCA had been found).

40. *Krizek*, 859 F. Supp. at 14. In April 1995, the court imposed a freeze on the Krizeks' real estate assets, prompting an outraged Dr. Krizek to write to Judge Sporkin, "Doesn't Mr. Hegyi know that since the first HHS investigation in 1989 we had ample time to sell everything and run?" Letter from George O. Krizek, M.D., to Hon. Judge Stanley Sporkin (Apr. 3, 1995) [hereinafter *Krizek Letter*].

41. United States v. Krizek, 111 F.3d 934 (D.C. Cir. 1997).

42. *Id.* at 942.

43. Responding to the government's objection that this approach permitted a defendant to control his exposure under the law, the court noted "Precisely so. It is the conduct of the medical practitioner, not the disposition of the claims by the government, that creates FCA liability." *Id.* at 940.

44. United States v. Krizek, 7 F. Supp.2d 56 (D.D.C. 1998).

45. United States v. Krizek, 192 F.3d 1024, 1029 (D.C. Cir. 1999).

46. *Id.* at 1031.

47. The appeals primarily sought to raise due process and excessive fines arguments, which the D.C. Circuit found the Krizeks had failed to raise below. Order, United States v. Krizek, No. 005385 (D.C. Cir. Apr. 17, 2001); Order, United States v. Krizek, No. 01-5452, 02-5119 (D.C. Cir. May 9, 2002). In the unsuccessful petition for certiorari, the Krizeks argued that the government lacked standing to sue under the FCA because there was no proof of actual damages, that the requisite government injury could not be satisfied by incorrect use of CPT codes, and that an unjust enrichment award was not available to the government as it fell outside the comprehensive statutory scheme. Petition for Writ of Certiorari, Krizek v. United States (No. 01-646), *cert. denied*, 534 U.S. 1067 (2001).

48. It is unclear who actually paid. The Krizeks refer to having to sell off rental properties, paying the government, and owing money "to the bank." Letter from Blanka H. Krizek to Professor Joan H. Krause (Oct. 3, 2007). However, another author states that Monika "mortgaged her home and used her savings to settle the case." Libby, *supra* note 3, at 93.

49. Additional Declaration of Co-Defendant Blanka H. Krizek, *supra* note 34, at 6.

50. Transcript of Bench Trial, vol. IX, at 43, *Krizek*, 859 F. Supp. 5 (Civ. A. No. 96-54).

51. *Krizek Letter*, *supra* note 40, at 4.

52. *Krizek*, 7 F. Supp.2d at 60.

53. Interview with Dr. George and Mrs. Blanka Krizek, in Washington, D.C. (Sept. 16, 2007).

54. George L. Priest & Benjamin Klein, *The Selection of Disputes for Litigation*, 13 J. Legal Stud. 1 (1984).

55. Russell Korobkin & Chris Guthrie, *Psychological Barriers to Litigation Settlement: An Experimental Approach*, 93 Mich. Law Rev. 107 (1994).

56. At one point, Judge Sporkin expressed his reaction to the government's conduct:

> You got real problems because of what you did in this case. . . . You don't go and mislead somebody and say we got a delivery to make and you inveigle yourself into somebody's house. You probably violated the Privacy Act by doing that. . . . [T]he SEC never did that. . . . That's a gumshoe operation at its worst. . . . [T]his is not the way . . . a legitimate agency of the United States government conducts an investigation.

Transcript of Status Call, April 14, 1994, *supra* note 16, at 41–43, 48.

57. 2 Health L. Rep. (BNA) 14 (Jan. 14, 1993).

58. As Blanka characterized the government's approach to the case:

> It was impossible to prove that Dr. Krizek caused the collapse of Medicare. So why don't we make him homeless. . . . Who cares that he had seen 25 patients on Christmas Day while his family was home alone. . . . After all he is foreign and we don't like immigrants any more . . . we have chosen a sort of psychological war to kill him gently, slowly. His tragedy will scare to death many doctors who treat the poor, and they will choose to run away from Medicare and Medicaid and thus save lots of money to the Government.

Additional Declaration of Co-Defendant Blanka H. Krizek, *supra* note 34, at 14.

59. Moreover, the Krizeks and their counsel seemingly were unaware of the slippery slope this argument posed: the government used her assertions that she sought out assistance to bolster their claims that she acted "knowingly" within the meaning of the FCA. *See* Memorandum of Points and Authorities, *supra* note 24, at 4–5.

60. *See* Plaintiff's Response to Defendants' "Additional Declaration of Co-Defendant Blanka H. Krizek in Support of Motion to Dismiss" at 1, *Krizek*, 909 F. Supp. 32 (D.D.C. 1995) (referring to "Mrs. Krizek's pseudo-histrionic accusations").

61. Mrs. Krizek made note on several occasions of the fact that Mr. Hegyi's ancestry was Hungarian (a nation with a long history of conflict with Czechoslovakia). In a newsletter published in 1999, after Hegyi was replaced on the case, she wrote, "He was obviously not cruel enough, and he was replaced by a woman. It was said in the Nazi camps that women were more effective." AAPS Newsletter, Members' Page, vol. 55, no. 1 (Jan. 1999), *available at* http://www.aapsonline.org/newsletters/jan99.htm.

62. Judge Sporkin expressed incredulity at the Krizeks' decision to replace counsel on the eve of trial, asking "I mean is trial counsel going to drop from the ceiling? Where is trial counsel going to come from? . . . Folks this is beyond belief. I'll tell you in all my years, I've never been faced with anything like this." Transcript of Status Call, Feb. 3, 1994, *supra* note 14, at 7.

63. Swiss characterized the problems as follows:

> The fact of the matter is, Dr. and Mrs. Krizek have had a very strong attitude of lack of confidence and distrust in me and in Mr. Shaughnessy since November of 1993. We have had no discussions of any productive sort. . . . They have no belief in my qualities and capacities to act as their trial attorney. And I cannot handle a case where I can't event talk to my own clients."

Id. at 9–11.

64. The New York Times referred to Sporkin as "one of the most aggressive enforcement directors in S.E.C. history." Steve Labaton, *Head of Insider Inquiry Leaving the SEC*, N.Y. Times, May 11, 1989.

65. Interview with Hon. Stanley Sporkin, in Washington, D.C. (Sept. 17, 2007).

66. In reversing Judge Sporkin's finding that the proposed consent decree was not in the public interest, the Court of Appeals for the District of Columbia took the unusual step of removing him from the case on remand, noting it was "deeply troubled by several aspects of the proceedings in district court," particularly the appearance of bias. United States v. Microsoft, 56 F.3d 1448 (1995).

67. Transcript of Bench Trial, vol. II, *supra* note 5, at 63–66. One prosecutor noted that "on a human level, it just broke your heart" to see the Krizeks' reaction to the dismissal, only to have the judge withdraw his comments. Telephone Interview with Bruce Hegyi (Jan. 8, 2008).

68. One prosecutor conceded that the judge felt the incident was "horrible." Telephone Interview with Bruce Hegyi, *supra* note 25.

69. Interview with John Munich, *supra* note 11.

70. Copies of some of the Krizek litigation materials are available on the AAPS web site, and the case has been cited repeatedly by the organization as an example of government abuse. *See* U.S. v. Krizek, *available at* http://www.aapsonline.org/judicial/krizek.htm; *see also* Administrative Crimes and Quasi-Crimes, *supra* note 2; Libby, *supra* note 3, at 86–93.

71. For a discussion of this and other issues surrounding the use of the FCA in health care, see Joan H. Krause, *"Promises to Keep": Health Care Providers and the Civil False Claims Act*, 23 Cardozo L. Rev. 1363 *(2002);* Joan H. Krause, *Health Care Providers and the Public Fisc: Paradigms of Government Harm Under the Civil False Claims Act*, 36 Ga. L. Rev. 121 (2001).

72. Transcript of Bench Trial, vol. IX, *supra* note 50, at 28 (testimony of Dr. Barry Gold). In fact, during this time period Medicare created an entirely new Resource-Based Relative Value Scale (RBRVS) methodology for reimbursing most physician services, which significantly revised the psychotherapy codes at issue in the case. *See* HCFA, Medicare Program; Fee Schedule for Physicians' Services, 56 Fed. Reg. 59,502 (Nov. 25, 1991). This system incorporates the use of "evaluation and management" (E/M) services to determine the complexity of clinical interactions; the psychotherapy codes are broken down not only by the length of a session, but also by whether it takes place in an inpatient or outpatient setting. *See, e.g.*, Centers for Medicare and Medicaid Services, Medicare Program; Revisions to Payment Policies Under the Physician Fee Schedule and Other Revisions to Part B for FY 2009; and Revisions to the Amendment of the E-Prescribing Exemption for Computer Generated Facsimile Transmissions; Proposed Rule, 73 Fed. Reg. 38,502, 38,792-38,793 (July 7, 2008) (listing psychiatric codes); 1997 Documentation Guidelines for Evaluation and Management Services at 4-13, 39–40, www.cms.hhs.gov/MLNProducts/Downloads/MASTER1.pdf (setting forth guidance for general and psychiatric E/M services).

73. *See* 42 C.F.R. §410.155 (2005).

74. *Krizek*, 859 F. Supp. at 14.

75. *See, e.g.*, Transcript of Bench Trial, vol. I, *supra* note 22, at 122–24 (testimony of Dr. Brent O'Connell).

76. 859 F. Supp. at 14.

77. Letter from Blanka H. Krizek to Professor Joan H. Krause, *supra* note 48, at 2.

Chapter 10

UTAH COUNTY
v.
INTERMOUNTAIN HEALTH CARE

*Reconsidering the Charitable Status of
Nonprofit Hospitals*

JOHN D. COLOMBO*

A. Introduction

Before the mid-1980s, nonprofit hospitals routinely qualified for both federal income tax exemption and state property tax exemption. The rationale for granting tax exemption, however, had always been somewhat murky. In general, hospitals are not specifically enumerated as tax-exempt entities under either federal or state law; rather, qualification for tax exemption either at the federal or state level requires that the hospital prove it is a "charity" under common law principles.[1] But what, exactly, defines a "charity" in these circumstances? At the federal level, the Internal Revenue Service (IRS) prior to 1969 had insisted that nonprofit hospitals provide substantial free care for the poor in order to be classified as a charity under Internal Revenue Code Section 501(c)(3).[2] In 1969, however, the IRS jettisoned the free care standard in favor of a broader "community benefit" approach, declaring that providing health care for the general benefit of the community was itself a charitable purpose, and nonprofit hospitals governed by a community board that treated all patients who could pay for services (including Medicare and Medicaid patients) qualified even without providing charity care.[3] More recent federal case law has interpreted the community benefit test as "health care plus" — that is, a nonprofit hospital claiming exemption must provide health care services for the general community and must also provide some significant "plus" such as free care for the poor, medical research, or health education. Free care for the poor, however, is still not *required* in order for a nonprofit hospital to receive federal exemption.

---

* Albert E. Jenner, Jr. Professor, University of Illinois College of Law.

State standards for exemption through the 1970s generally were less well-defined than federal standards. Often, states had recognized the charitable status of nonprofit hospitals in very early decisions that lacked much analysis[4] or by statutory mandate.[5] By the mid-1980s, property tax exemptions for nonprofit hospitals seemed a settled fact.[6] Then in 1985 a legal cataclysm occurred. That year the Utah Supreme Court shocked the hospital industry by denying property tax exemption to two nonprofit hospitals operated by the successor to the Church of Latter Day Saints in *Utah County v. Intermountain Health Care*,[7] a case that is now an obligatory part of virtually every casebook and legal treatise on the nonprofit form in health care. The arguments made by the parties in *Utah County* continue to remain the issues still at the heart of the nonprofit hospital tax-exemption debate: is charity care a requirement of exemption or should we grant exemption to nonprofit hospitals because they provide a necessary public service (health care) for the general community? If charity care is required, how much is necessary? Do "bad debts," contractual discounts, and Medicare/Medicaid shortfalls count? The *Utah County* case, therefore, is timeless in its discussion of the core issue: when is an organization operating very much like a for-profit business considered a "charity" for tax exemption purposes?

B. Forces Colliding: The Changing Face of the Nonprofit Hospital, For-Profit Competition, and Local Revenue Needs

The *Utah County* case probably was inevitable; if not 1985 or not Utah, then it would have come about somewhere sooner or later. The reason for the inevitability was the collision of three forces: the changing nature of the nonprofit hospital, for-profit competition in health services generally and the acute-care hospital sector in particular, and the revenue needs of local governments resulting in escalating property tax assessments.

The changing nature of the nonprofit hospital has been well documented elsewhere.[8] Simply put, the operations of most nonprofit hospitals in the early 1980s bore virtually no resemblance to the institutions that had been routinely granted exemption throughout the first two-thirds of the twentieth century. Until World War I, hospitals were more like homeless shelters than the modern institutions we know today. They generally were staffed by volunteers, were often affiliated with particular churches, and a significant part of their mission was to treat the poor.[9] Classifying these institutions as charities for tax purposes was easy; whatever else one may throw into the charitable hopper, helping the poor has been a central facet of the definition of charity for centuries.[10]

Even after the professionalization of medical care in the first half of the twentieth century, hospitals retained a core mission of service to the poor, helped in large part by generous reimbursement rates from private insurers and, until the 1980s, the federal government via the Medicare and Medicaid programs. By the early 1980s, however, the health care landscape had changed dramatically. Spiraling health care costs led to the rise of managed care, particularly in the form of the health maintenance organization (HMO) in which individuals paid a flat monthly fee for access to a core package of health services. These managed-care vehicles replaced a large segment of the traditional fee-for-service system that supported the stand-alone hospital and individual (or small-group practice) physician. By 1994, nearly 20 percent of the United States population received health care via an HMO.[11] The move toward managed care, moreover, almost invariably meant a move toward large vertically integrated health systems that could provide a full array of hospital and doctor services in both inpatient and outpatient settings.[12] The truly independent community hospital rapidly became an anachronism.[13] At the same time, both the federal government (through the Prospective Payment System, introduced in 1983 for the Medicare program) and private insurers had taken steps to "ratchet down" reimbursement rates, making it ever harder for hospitals to use "profits" on government or private insurance cases to pay for the costs of serving the poor. The combination of integration resulting from managed care and the "ratcheting down" of reimbursements in turn led hospitals to reduce free services for the poor and become more "businesslike" in their operations, stressing the importance of positive margins — "no margin, no mission" became the phrase of the day.[14]

This general description of the changing hospital enterprise fit the hospitals operated by the Church of Latter Day Saints (LDS) to a "T." Although Utah's first hospital, St. Mark's, was built by the Episcopalian Church in 1872, by the turn of the century LDS had established their own permanent hospital facilities, LDS Hospital and Primary Children's Hospital in Salt Lake City.[15] By the early 1970s, LDS operated fifteen hospitals in Utah, Idaho, and Wyoming.[16] In 1970, LDS formed LDS Health Services Corporation to integrate the administration of the hospital system, and by 1973, the system had become one of the largest hospital systems in the nation, with over 2000 beds.[17] Then in September 1974, facing the need for capital to expand its worldwide missionary program, an estimated $100 million cost of upgrading now-old hospital facilities, and ever-increasing federal regulation of medical care (including a concern that the recent *Roe v. Wade* decision by the U. S. Supreme Court would require LDS to offer abortion services at its hospitals), the LDS Church announced that it would "spin off" its hospital operations by donating them to a new nondenominational nonprofit corporation, Intermountain Health Care (IHC or Intermountain).[18]

Intermountain immediately instituted or accelerated significant changes in the financial operation of the hospitals aimed at cost cutting and efficiency, including centralizing a number of services, entering into joint purchasing arrangements with other hospitals, centralizing budgeting, eliminating duplicate services at facilities, and adopting "a cost-saving program to save on insurance and risk management."[19] In 1978, *Business Week* ran a feature on Intermountain, touting it as the "survival formula" for nonprofit hospitals.[20] Indeed, the Intermountain "formula" was successful in saving some community hospitals headed for financial disaster. For example, Valley View Medical Center had operated at a loss for 12 years prior to joining the Intermountain group in 1976 and had lost its accreditation with the Joint Commission on Accreditation of Hospitals;[21] by 1978, the hospital generated over $200,000 in net revenues.[22] But the Intermountain formula also meant de-emphasizing free care for the uninsured poor. While Intermountain management steadfastly maintained that their hospitals did not deny treatment to any person based on inability to pay, officers of Intermountain freely admitted that Intermountain did not publicize its free care policies because of the potential for a "deluge of people that say [they] can't pay."[23] "Everyone wants charity care, and they all consider them as good cases for charity," stated William Jones, the Chairman of Intermountain.[24]

While the nonprofit hospital was undergoing significant structural change, the early 1980s also saw the rise of for-profit acute-care hospital chains such as Hospital Corporation of America (HCA) and Humana.[25] Both HCA and Humana operated hospitals in Utah in the late 1970s and 1980s; HCA's Mountain View Hospital in Payson, Utah, was a direct competitor of IHC's Utah Valley Regional Medical Center in Provo, one of the hospitals involved in the *Utah County* case.[26] The rise of these for-profit competitors not only influenced the behavior of nonprofit hospitals (Stewart Kirkpatrick of Intermountain was quoted in 1981 saying "If the nonprofits don't start behaving like those run for a profit, they'll be pushed out of the industry"[27]), it also provided a source of opposition to tax exemptions for the nonprofit providers that had not existed previously. For example, press reports leading up to the *Utah County* decision often quoted officials from HCA to the effect that the only difference between HCA and Intermountain was that HCA paid taxes.[28] Pathology Associates Laboratories, a for-profit medical lab in Salt Lake City, got involved in the litigation more directly, filing an amicus brief in the case that accused Intermountain of unfair competition.[29] Indeed, Alan Sullivan, legal counsel for Intermountain at the time of the *Utah County* case, cited the rise of for-profit hospitals as a key factor in the litigation.[30]

The final force leading to *Utah County* was the economic climate that resulted in greater demands on local tax dollars, resulting in rising property tax rates, property valuation assessments, and accompanying taxpayer anger. The most visible result of pressure on local property taxes in the late 1970s and early 1980s was California's famous Proposition 13, passed in 1978, which strictly limited local governments in raising both tax assessments and assessed valuations. California was hardly alone, however: within two years, Arizona and Massachusetts had also passed property tax limitations, and since then some 26 other states have adopted some form of property tax limitation.[31] The role of tax exemptions in pressuring the local tax base did not go unnoticed, moreover. A six-part investigative report conducted in the early 1990s on the operation of charities in Philadelphia and nearby communities became a book that highlighted the wealth of charities that paid no property taxes.[32] Boston and Philadelphia were pioneers in using "payments in lieu of taxes" (PILOTS) to extract tax-like payments from nonprofit organizations that otherwise enjoyed property tax exemptions.[33]

The collision of these three forces — the changing nature of the nonprofit hospital, for-profit competition, and the struggle over local property tax revenues — can be seen clearly in various facets of the *Utah County* case. But given that these were nationwide trends, a case like *Utah County* was almost certain to occur sooner, rather than later, somewhere.

C. The Intermountain Litigation and Decision

Bill Thomas Peters was not a crusader out to change the way nonprofit hospitals treated the poor. But he was concerned about the increasing tax burden on property owners in Salt Lake County and on ensuring that tax exemptions were strictly limited to those authorized by the Utah Constitution. Peters first became involved in property tax disputes when Salt Lake County hired him in 1971 to represent it in a dispute with Friendship Manor, a nonprofit corporation that provided housing to the elderly and disabled.[34] In this case,[35] Peters honed some of the arguments that would later appear in *Utah County*. Though designed for the elderly, Friendship Manor did not accept tenants unless they were ambulatory and fully able to pay rent. It did not provide nursing services or tend to the poor in any way. Peters concluded that the provision of the Utah Constitution exempting from property taxes property "used exclusively . . . for charitable purposes" did not encompass what essentially was a retirement home.

The fact that Friendship Manor enjoyed exemption under federal law was irrelevant to the Utah determination. "Charitable purposes" under Utah law, Peters argued, was a sort of "quid-pro-quo" in which the government gave up taxes because it would derive benefits from the charity that were of at least equivalent value; charity required some sort of gift to the community. The Utah Supreme Court agreed, and in a comment that foreshadowed *Utah County,* noted that Friendship Manor did not operate any differently from Newhouse Hotel, a for-profit residence for senior citizens.[36]

Utah Valley Hospital from around the time of the tax exemption litigation

After the successful challenge to property tax exemption for Friendship Manor, the county commissioners in various Utah counties hired Peters to review charitable tax exemptions in their jurisdictions. Peters mailed a questionnaire to organizations with exempt property, inquiring about their services, their beneficiaries, the use of the property, and so forth. Based on the responses, Peters concluded that many other parcels of property, including those

American Fork Hospital from around the time of the tax exemption litigation

of hospitals run by IHC, also did not qualify for exemption. Two of these hospitals were in Utah County: Utah Valley Hospital and American Fork Hospital. In 1980, the Utah County Tax Assessor put the property owned by these two hospitals back on the tax rolls, but these two hospitals were hardly singled out for attention. Shortly after Utah County pulled exemption from Utah Valley and American Fork, Salt Lake County revoked exemption for five hospitals in and around Salt Lake City.[37] By dint of being first, however, the *Utah County* case became the test; after the county assessor put Utah Valley and American Fork back on the tax rolls, Intermountain filed an application for exemption with the Utah County Board of Equalization. The Board denied this application on July 14, 1980. Intermountain then appealed to the Utah State Tax Commission, which held an administrative hearing on January 15, 1981, and reversed the Utah County Board of Equalization and granted exemption.

The reversal was part of an ongoing "cat and mouse" game between the Utah Legislature and local property tax officials over property tax exemptions for charities. Like most states, Utah's property tax exemption provisions flow from the state constitution, which at the time stated that "lots with buildings thereon used exclusively for either religious worship or charitable purposes . . . shall be exempt from taxation."[38] The Utah Legislature then passed enabling statutes governing the actual property tax collection processes which generally followed the constitutional exemption mandate. After cases like *Friendship Manor*, however, the Utah Legislature in 1973 passed an amendment to the enabling statutes, declaring that property used exclusively for "religious, hospital, educational, employee representation, or welfare purposes" would be deemed used for charitable purposes within the Utah constitutional provision.[39]

Believing these provisions unconstitutionally expanded the scope of charitable exemption as set forth in the Utah Constitution, Peters and Salt Lake County Tax Assessor Earl W. Baker filed appeals in some 96 different exemption cases during the 1970s, challenging the validity of the legislative changes.[40] As a result of these challenges (and some hints by the Utah Supreme Court in resulting cases that the provisions exceeded constitutional authority),[41] the Utah Legislature proposed a constitutional amendment to the property tax exemption provision in 1980, but it failed in a public referendum.[42] The Utah Supreme Court, however, had never definitively ruled whether the 1973 legislation in fact was constitutional. Accordingly, at the time Utah County denied exemption to IHC's two hospitals in Provo, the 1973 legislation was still "on the books." The State Tax Commission, in turn, felt bound by the 1973 legislative changes and held that since the legislation clearly provided a presumption of charitable use for nonprofit hospitals, the Utah County Board of Equalization had exceeded its authority by denying exemption to Utah Valley and American Fork hospitals. Utah County then appealed the Tax Commission's ruling to the Utah Supreme Court, and the groundwork was laid for the landmark court decision three years later.[43]

Utah County's attack on the exemptions for Utah Valley and American Fork was two-fold. The county first had to convince the Utah Supreme Court to rule definitively that the 1973 legislative changes to the exemption enabling statutes were unconstitutional, a part of the opinion almost always edited out of the versions presented in health law casebooks. The county's argument on this front was straightforward: the 1973 changes to the enabling legislation in effect created automatic exemption for certain property, whether that property was in fact used for charitable purposes under the common law view of charity. Accordingly, the legislation expanded the scope of exemption beyond what was permitted by the Utah Constitution, and therefore was invalid.[44] IHC, predictably, argued that the legislative changes merely clarified a vague constitutional provision (e.g., what constituted a "charitable" use) and therefore were constitutional.[45] In fact, in what in retrospect probably was a strategic mistake, IHC's brief spent the bulk of its page allotment arguing that the 1973 legislation was not unconstitutional and that the Utah Supreme Court was required to give considerable deference to the legislature in this case.[46]

The second prong of Utah County's argument is the famous one. Assuming the court agreed that the 1973 statutory changes providing a presumption of charitable use for hospitals were invalid, the county argued that IHC's hospitals did not meet the traditional requirements of Utah law regarding charitable use.

Utah County's brief in the case first reminded the court that federal exemption under Section 501(c)(3) of the Internal Revenue Code was irrelevant to the determination of charity under Utah law. Second, the county stressed that simply being organized as a nonprofit corporation did not entitle the hospitals to exemption; rather it was the underlying use of the property that was the key issue.

On this key point, the county argued that "charity" under Utah law required some gift to the community, generally in the form of help for the poor. "Without this element of giving, the so-called charity is just another business in competition with other businesses."[47] The county argued that the hospitals in question charged "competitive commercial rates" designed to generate positive margins between five to seven percent, and quoted testimony from William Jones, IHC's Chairman, that IHC did not advertise charity care because "everyone wants charity care, and they all consider them as good cases for charity."[48] Failure to publicize charity care policies, the county argued, meant that the poor effectively went without medical care.[49] The county then presented data showing that from 1978 through 1980, less than 1 percent of the gross revenues of each of the two hospitals under consideration were used for charity care — in some cases, the number was as small as .07 percent.[50] In making these calculations, Utah County specifically excluded the amounts of bad debt, discounts from charges negotiated with insurers, and "shortfalls" from Medicare and Medicaid. The county noted that charity should include only amounts of care rendered without expectation of payment; bad debts and other discounts were common to for-profit hospitals and therefore should not be counted.[51]

Boiled down to its essentials, the Utah County argument was that substantial charity care was a necessary part of defining a "charitable" hospital for Utah state law; that charity care should include only the value of services rendered without expectation of payment; that contractual discounts and program shortfalls should not count as charity care; and that less than one percent of gross revenues dedicated to charity care under this definition was simply too little for the hospitals to qualify as charities under state law.

IHC, of course, countered each of these points. It first argued that health services delivered via nonprofit form were historically considered charitable, even if the number of patients served without charge was small. Citing IRS Revenue Ruling 69-545 and decisions from several states, IHC argued that the legal trend was "away from definitions of 'charity' that would restrict tax exempt status to those hospitals, supported by philanthropy, which serve only the poor. Such hospitals simply do not exist any more."[52] Echoing the rationale that led the IRS to adopt the community benefit standard in 1969 (see introduction above), IHC claimed "the universal availability of health insurance, workmen's compensation, and government health care subsidies make distinctions between rich and poor practically unnecessary."[53] Utah County's definition of charity, according to IHC, was "antiquated."[54] IHC also disputed Utah County's calculation of the amount of free care the hospitals offered, claiming that one should include unreimbursed charges for Medicaid/Medicare patients and bad debts. When these amounts were added, Utah Valley Hospital provided some $5 million in "uncompensated care" over the period 1978–80, rather than the roughly $175,000 cited by Utah County.[55] Finally, IHC noted that its hospitals indeed had an "open door policy" and treated all patients requiring care, even those who could not pay. Citing the testimony of Chairman Jones and the administrators of Utah Valley and American Fork, IHC asserted, "[n]one of these officials was aware of any instance in which a patient had been denied care at an IHC hospital on the basis of his inability to pay."[56]

Though the case was argued in 1982, the Utah Supreme Court did not issue its opinion until 1985. The final decision was a close one, with a three-judge majority holding sway over two dissenters. The majority essentially bought Utah County's arguments lock, stock and barrel. On the rarely excerpted constitutional issue, the Court held that the statute was unconstitutional to the extent that it provided an automatic tax exemption for nonprofit hospitals.[57] Instead, according to the court, a nonprofit hospital would be exempt only if it could show that it met a six-factor test, which Utah Valley and American Fork hospitals mostly failed:

> (1) whether the stated purpose of the entity is to provide a significant service to others without immediate expectation of material reward; (2) whether the entity is supported, and to what extent, by donations and gifts; (3) whether the recipients of the "charity" are required to pay for the assistance received, in whole or in part; (4) whether the income received from all sources (gifts, donations, and payment from recipients) produces a "profit" to the entity in the sense that the income exceeds operating and long-term maintenance expenses; (5) whether the beneficiaries of the "charity" are restricted or unrestricted and, if restricted, whether the restriction bears a reasonable relationship to the entity's charitable objectives; and (6) whether dividends or some other form of financial benefit, or assets upon dissolution, are available to private interests, and whether the entity is organized and operated so that any commercial activities are subordinate or incidental to charitable ones.[58]

The majority's detailed discussion of the nature of the modern nonprofit hospital, which is the part of the opinion excerpted in most casebooks, highlighted the impact on its decision of each of the three precipitating forces discussed earlier: the changing nature of the nonprofit hospital; for-profit competition in health services; and escalating property tax assessments. The court began its opinion with the last of these issues, affirming the traditional doctrine that exemptions should be very strictly construed in order to protect the tax base. Quoting from a student note in the *Minnesota Law Review*, the court stated, "A liberal construction of exemption provisions results in the loss of a major source of municipal revenue and places a greater burden on nonexempt taxpayers . . . ."[59]

The court majority then turned to the changing nature of the nonprofit hospital with a three-printed-page history of the changes in hospital operations, quoting liberally from Paul Starr's book, *The Social Transformation of American Medicine*, and other academic work on the structure of modern nonprofit hospitals. In this discussion, the court noted that nonprofit hospitals traditionally had received tax exemption because they provided custodial care for the poor, but that "traditional assumptions bear little relationship to the economics of the medical-industrial complex of the 1980s."[60] Hospitals of the 1980s "were redefined from social welfare to medical treatment institutions; their charitable foundation was replaced by a business basis; and their orientation shifted to 'professionals and their patients,' away from 'patrons and the poor.'"[61] The court criticized the "polycorporate" model of modern health care in which hospitals increasingly were owned by holding companies with a mix of for-profit and nonprofit subsidiaries.

Finally, the majority also noted the rise of for-profit hospitals and their similarity to IHC: "For-profit hospitals provide many of the same primary care services as do those hospitals organized as nonprofit entities. They do so at similar rates as those charged by defendants."[62] In short, modern nonprofit hospitals were businesses first; if they were to be categorized as charities, it would be only because they made a substantial gift to the community in the form of free care for the poor. By the end of the opinion, the court majority's rejection of the "community benefit" approach to exemption embodied in the federal exemption standard under Revenue Ruling 69-545 was complete: "[W]e believe that the defendants in this case confuse the element of gift to the community, which an entity must demonstrate in order to qualify as a charity under our Constitution, with the concept of community benefit, which any of countless private enterprises might provide."[63]

The two dissenters, in contrast, strongly supported the "community benefit" formula for tax exemption. Justice Stewart, whose dissent is sometimes excerpted along with the majority opinion, characterized the majority's holding as "without precedent either in Utah or elsewhere in the United States."[64] He stressed that the common law definition of charity was and always had been extremely broad and had never been limited strictly to relief of the poor.[65] The dedication of nonprofit hospital facilities to the public good coupled with an "open door" policy that treated all patients regardless of ability to pay satisfied the common-law tests of charity. The hospitals in question did, in fact, embody a substantial gift to the community: by virtue of their nonprofit form, all their facilities and net revenues were in essence owned by the public in perpetuity. Justice Stewart also took IHC's side in calculating the value of free services rendered by the two hospitals, including in that calculation bad debts and "shortfalls" from Medicare and Medicaid and adopting the same $5 million final number that IHC argued for in its brief.[66] Finally, Stewart opined that there is a basic difference in services provided by nonprofit hospitals versus their for-profit counterparts: "The record indicates that for-profit hospitals in Utah have invested to a limited extent in high-volume, low-cost services such as pediatric, psychiatric, and obstetrical-gynecological services, but not in higher-cost, lower-volume kinds of services."[67]

Despite the clear rejection of a "community benefit" approach to exemption by the *Utah County* majority, a point that is often overlooked in the litigation is that the Utah Supreme Court held only that *automatic* exemptions for nonprofit hospitals were unconstitutional. The court left open the possibility that the two hospitals involved in the case might meet the six-factor test in the future. "[W]e make no judgment as to the ability of these hospitals or any others to demonstrate their eligibility for constitutionally permissible tax exemptions in the future. . . . It may be that adjustments in accounting practices and other policies will enable these defendants and other hospitals to qualify in the future for the constitutional exemption."[68] Indeed, as noted below, a peculiar twist to the *Utah County* litigation was that the Utah County Board of Equalization ultimately granted tax exemption to both Utah Valley and American Fork hospitals in a reconsideration of their cases after the *Utah County* opinion.

D. Aftermath

The immediate response to the *Utah County* decision was shock in the nonprofit hospital community and a petition for rehearing by both the Utah State Tax Commission and IHC. Many critics complained that the six-factor test used by the Utah Supreme Court would leave local tax assessors without firm guidelines for determining when hospitals were tax-exempt.[69] Shortly after the release of the Utah County opinion, the Provo Herald quoted Carolyn Ecklund, the senior vice president of the Utah Hospital Association, stating that 26 additional nonprofit hospitals in Utah would face loss of exempt status unless the Utah Supreme Court clarified its opinion in *Utah County*.[70] The Utah State Tax Commission echoed this view in its Petition for Rehearing, expressing concern over the number of potential tax appeals and the "voluminous records" that would be required to apply the *Utah County* six-factor test.[71]

IHC's Petition for Rehearing attacked the opinion on more substantive grounds. It claimed that the court's opinion essentially would require a hospital to become self-liquidating: "Never before has this or any other court disqualified a nonprofit hospital from exempt status for failing to prove an imbalance between current revenues and current expenses."[72] IHC argued that the requisite "gift to the community" was inherent in the nonprofit form, since that form guaranteed that all of the hospitals' assets and earnings were dedicated to the public in perpetuity. For the first time, moreover, IHC argued that the services provided by its nonprofit hospitals differed substantially from those provided by the for-profit sector. "For-profit hospitals in Utah provide remunerative services like obstetrics and pediatrics but do not provide costly tertiary or acute care for serious trauma, burns, neonatal complications . . . or the like."[73] IHC, however, steadfastly maintained that free care was not the key to exempt status. "[A] requirement that tax-exempt hospitals give away a certain quantity of free care, or give away more free care than non-exempt hospitals, misses the more important distinctions that justify exemption. The consideration for the tax exemption is not a certain percentage of care to indigents, but is rather the nonprofit hospital's donation of capital and net revenues to the public good."[74] The arguments did not persuade the Utah Supreme Court, which denied rehearing on September 26, 1985.

The Utah Legislature then sprang into action once again. It repealed the 1973 versions of the enabling legislation that the Utah Supreme Court had ruled unconstitutional in Utah County, and then proposed yet another amendment to the Utah Constitution that explicitly would grant exempt status to nonprofit hospitals. Proposition 1, as it became known, was placed on the 1986 election ballot, but was very narrowly defeated.[75] Not surprisingly, the major force in favor of Proposition 1 was Citizens Against the Sick Tax (CAST), a group organized by Intermountain and other nonprofit hospitals. CAST used an extensive advertising campaign to argue that without Proposition 1, hospitals would have to pay property taxes in Utah, and those costs would be passed on to all paying patients.[76] Interestingly, the main opposition to Proposition 1 turned out not to be the for-profit hospitals, but rather a coalition of activists organized by a doctor from Utah County.[77]

Nevertheless, the six-factor test set forth by the Utah Supreme Court did prove unwieldy in practice, as the early critics had predicted. By March 1, 1988, three years after the *Utah County* decision, all Utah counties with nonprofit hospitals had completed their assessment hearings on hospital-owned property. In a bizarre turn of events, the Utah County Board of Equalization reversed course and granted exemption to the two hospitals that were defendants in the *Utah County* litigation.[78] Other Utah counties followed suit, exempting nonprofit hospitals in their jurisdictions. Salt Lake County, however, held its ground and denied exemption to four nonprofit hospitals and several other health facilities.[79] As a result of these conflicting decisions, the state tax commissioner halted all tax appeals involving nonprofit hospitals until the Utah State Tax Commission could develop guidelines for the application of the six-factor test in *Utah County*.[80]

The State Tax Commission issued these guidelines in 1990, and practically eviscerated the *Utah County* holding. For example, in interpreting the key requirement of "gift to the community," the standards count "the reasonable value of the hospital's unreimbursed care" measured by "discounted" standard charges (that is, standard charges less "average of reductions afforded to all patients who are not covered by government entitlement programs), plus expenses directly associated with special indigent clinics," as well as the difference between Medicare and Medicaid reimbursements and discounted standard charges.[81] In effect, the standards include bad debts along with Medicare/Medicaid shortfalls, all measured from "discounted" standard charges instead of average costs. Under the standards, the "gift to the community" also includes the expenses of community education programs, donations of time and money to the hospital, and the operation of tertiary care units or other "critical services or programs" whether or not the value of such programs is "precisely quantifiable." In short, the standards basically incorporated everything that IHC and the nonprofit hospital community counted as "community benefit."[82] Nevertheless, the Utah Supreme Court upheld the standards in a subsequent case.[83]

E. Epilogue

In an article about *Utah County* written in 1989, Phelon Rammel and Robert Parsons opined that "it is unlikely that *Utah County* will have much impact on the decision of other jurisdictions and on the development of the law of charitable hospitals . . . ."[84] This statement surely should go in the top-ten list of reasons to avoid making predictions about the development of the law, because just the opposite has proven true: *Utah County* opened the floodgates to reconsidering the basis for tax-exemption for nonprofit hospitals, and the flow has only grown stronger in the two decades since the opinion.

At about the same time that Utah County was decided, the Pennsylvania Supreme Court decided *Hospital Utilization Project v. Commonwealth*,[85] which set forth a five-factor test for property-tax exemption under Pennsylvania law. One of these factors was that an exempt organization "must donate or render gratuitously a substantial portion of its services."[86] Local Pennsylvania taxing authorities interpreted this decision as requiring some substantial charity care by nonprofit hospitals in order to be eligible for tax exemption. The local tax commissions in Pennsylvania, however, turned out to be less generous in dealing with nonprofit hospitals after the *Hospital Utilization Project* case than did the Utah tax commissions after *Utah County*: one academic paper stated that by

1996, Pennsylvania tax assessors had challenged the exemptions of 175 of Pennsylvania's 220 nonprofit hospitals.[87]

In the decade after *Utah County* and *Hospital Utilization Project* were decided, at least ten other state supreme courts also heard cases challenging the property tax exemption for nonprofit hospitals.[88] While most of these cases held in favor of the hospitals on a "community benefit" theory, at least one held that a minimum amount of charity care was necessary to justify exemption.[89] In two states, Pennsylvania and Texas, state legislatures intervened to clarify exemption standards.[90] In Pennsylvania, this intervention was intended to bring closure to the spate of exemption challenges fostered by *Hospital Utilization Project*;[91] in Texas, legislative action came at the behest of the state Attorney General.[92] Congress also got into the act: in 1991, two separate bills were introduced in the House of Representatives to alter exemption standards for nonprofit hospitals. While differing in details, each bill would have significantly tightened the existing federal exemption standards under Internal Revenue Code Section 501(c)(3) by requiring hospitals in effect to "earn" their exemption through charity care or other subsidized health services.[93] Though neither federal bill became law, the ill-fated Clinton health care reform proposals released in 1993 also addressed the issue of tax exemption for nonprofit hospitals. This time the federal government headed in the opposite direction, essentially proposing to codify a broad community benefit standard for exemption.[94]

Despite the flurry of activity in the decade after *Utah County*, the issues raised by the opinion have yet to be resolved. Although most commentators now agree that charity care should be measured by average costs, not charges,[95] other issues, including the central question whether charity care is required for exemption (and if so, how much) remain hotly debated. In a case eerily reminiscent of *Utah County*, in 2004 the Champaign County Board of Review recommended to the Illinois Department of Revenue that it revoke property tax exemption for Provena-Covenant Hospital in Urbana, Illinois,[96] and in 2005 the Board made a similar recommendation regarding Carle Hospital in Urbana.[97] In each case, the Board of Review found that the hospitals failed their charity-care obligations to the population by billing all patients, including the uninsured poor, for services and then pursuing aggressive debt collection techniques against them,[98] just as Utah County's Board of Equalization complained 20 years earlier about the charity-care and billing practices of Intermountain. Echoing the criticism of the "medical-industrial complex" of the *Utah County* majority, the Board of Review found that each hospital had entered into complex joint venture and contractual arrangements with for-profit doctor groups and other entities, violating the "exclusive use" requirement of Illinois law.[99] After a lengthy internal appeals process, the Illinois Department of Revenue issued a final opinion in the *Provena* case on September 29, 2006, upholding revocation of Provena's tax exemption.[100]

The arguments made in *Provena* were virtual copies of those in *Utah County*. Provena argued that it provided over $25 million in charity care and other community benefits, valuing charity care at customary charges and including bad debts, Medicare/Medicaid "shortfalls," and contractual discounts. The Director of the Illinois Department of Revenue, Brian Hamer, rejected these arguments, however. Hamer valued charity care at average costs and excluded bad debts, contractual discounts, and government program shortfalls. As a result, Hamer found that Provena provided only $832,000 in charity care on revenues of

$113,000,000, or about seven-tenths of one percent (0.7%) of revenues.[101] Like the majority in *Utah County*, Hamer criticized the multitude of services Provena provided via contracts with for-profit subsidiaries and outside providers. In a statement that easily could have been written by Justice Durham of the Utah Supreme Court, Hamer concluded his opinion by squarely rejecting the community benefit theory of exemption: "No one disputes the fact that a hospital and the services it offers may improve the well being of the community within which it operates. But that general proposition holds true for for-profit hospitals as well not-for-profit ones. Property tax exemptions do not turn on these generalities."[102]

Meanwhile, potential legislative action continues to bubble. In January 2006, Illinois Attorney General Lisa Madigan proposed legislation that would have imposed a strict charity care standard on exempt hospitals in Illinois.[103] The proposal was later withdrawn pending discussions with Illinois hospitals, though officials at the Attorney General's office maintain that the idea is still alive. Other state legislatures and attorneys general are also considering tightening exemption standards.[104] At the federal level, both the House Ways and Means Committee and Senate Finance Committee have held recent hearings on hospital tax exemption. In July 2007, the minority staff of the Senate Finance Committee released a discussion draft of proposals for changing federal exemption rules, including a specific charity care requirement.[105] Even the IRS has made exemption for hospitals a priority: its revised Form 990,[106] the annual informational return that exempt organizations file with the IRS, includes for the first time a separate schedule that requires exempt hospitals to report in detail their charity care and other community benefit expenditures.[107]

The central question of *Utah County* regarding what makes a modern nonprofit hospital a "charity" for tax exemption purposes may never be resolved as long as the debate pits a strict charity care view against a broad community benefit view. There are many policy reasons to avoid both these approaches.[108] "Community benefit" indeed is something that "countless for-profit entities provide" and does little to insure accountability from the nonprofit sector; yet tying exemption solely to charity care for the poor is probably bad health policy and ignores the possibility that nonprofit hospitals provide services unavailable from the for-profit market. Instead, perhaps a focus on how (or whether) a nonprofit hospital enhances access to health services (such as providing care for underserved populations or providing expensive, unprofitable services such as a burn unit or level-three trauma center) would provide a manageable middle ground in this debate.[109] Without such a paradigm shift, it is likely that the issues raised by *Utah County* that still dominate exemption debate 25 years after the case was argued will remain the core disagreement when the opinion reaches its fiftieth birthday.

ENDNOTES

1. See Rev. Rul. 69-545, 1969-2 C.B. 117 ("To qualify for exemption under section 501(c)(3) of the Code, a nonprofit hospital must be organized and operated exclusively in furtherance of some purpose considered 'charitable' in the generally accepted legal sense of that term . . ."); Janne Gallagher, *The Legal Structure of the Property Tax Exemption*, 28 State Tax Notes 451, 452 (2003).

2. Rev. Rul. 56-185, 1956-1 C.B. 202. *See generally* John D. Colombo, *The Failure of Community Benefit*, 15 Health Matrix 29, 30–32 (2005).

3. Rev. Rul. 69-545, 1969-2 C.B. 117; for an extended discussion and critique of this ruling, see Daniel M. Fox & Daniel C. Schaffer, *Tax Administration as Health Policy: Hospitals, the Internal Revenue Service and the Courts*, 16 J. Health Pol. Pol'y & L. 251 (1991).

4. Illinois, for example, approved exemption for hospitals in a series of cases decided in 1907–08. *See* John D. Colombo, *Federal and State Tax Exemption Policy, Medical Debt and Healthcare for the Poor*, 51 St. Louis U. L.J. 433, 440 n.51 (2007).

5. *See* Mark A. Hall & John D. Colombo, *The Charitable Status of Nonprofit Hospitals: Toward a Donative Theory of Tax Exemption*, 66 Wash. L. Rev. 307, 318 n.33 (1991).

6. *Id.* at 323–24. *See* Gallagher, *supra* note 1.

7. Utah County v. Intermountain Health Care, 709 P.2d 265 (Utah 1985).

8. *E.g.*, Charles E. Rosenberg, The Care of Strangers: The Rise of America's Hospital System (1987); Paul Starr, The Social Transformation of American Medicine (1982); Rosemary Stevens, In Sickness and in Wealth: American Hospitals in the Twentieth Century (1989).

9. Hall & Colombo, *supra* note 5, at 319.

10. Trusts for the relief of "aged, impotent and poor people" were recognized as charitable in the preamble to the Elizabethan Statute of Charitable Uses, which is generally considered the headwaters of the common law of charitable trusts. The official citation to the statute is *An Act To Redress the Mis-Employment of Lands, Goods and Stocks of Money Heretofore Given to Certain Charitable Uses*, 1601, 43 Eliz., ch. 4, *reprinted in* 7 Stat. At Large 43 (Eng. 1763). The federal tax laws have recognized relief of the poor as a charitable purpose since the first comprehensive income tax was passed in 1913; prior to new regulations passed in 1959, in fact, the IRS viewed relief of the poor as the predominant feature of charity. *See* Fox & Schaffer, *supra* note 3, at 255-56.

11. Michele M. Garvin, *Health Maintenance Organizations* in Health Care Corporate Law: Managed Care (Mark A. Hall & William S. Brewbaker III eds., 1999) at §1.2.

12. Mark A. Hall, *Managed Competition and Integrated Health Care Delivery Systems*, 29 Wake Forest L. Rev. 1, 4-6 (1999).

13. *See* Starr, *supra* note 8, at 429-36.

14. *See, e.g.*, Steven D. Pearson, James E. Sabin & Ezekiel J. Emanuel, No Margins, No Mission: Health Care Organizations and the Quest for Ethical Excellence (2003).

15. David M. Walden, *Intermountain Health Care, Inc.*, in 27 International Directory of Company Histories 237 (2006).

16. *Id.*

17. David M. Walden, *Utah's Health Care Revolution: Pluralism and Professionalization Since World War II* 48 (1989)(unpublished thesis).

18. *Id.* at 49-50.

19. *The Chain: A Survival Formula for Hospitals*, Business Week, January 16, 1978, at 113.

20. *Id.*

21. Walden, *supra* note 17, at 56.

22. *Medicine and Profits: Unhealthy Mixture?* U.S. News and World Report, Aug. 17, 1981, at 50.

23. Brief for Appellant at 16, Utah County v. Intermountain Health Care, 709 P.2d 265 (Utah 1985)(No. 17699)(*quoting* William Jones, Chairman of Intermountain Health Care).

24. *Id.*

25. *See* Starr, *supra* note 8, at 430; *Medicine and Profits*, *supra* note 22.

26. Walden, *supra* note 17, at 63.

27. *Medicine and Profits*, *supra* note 22, at 50.

28. *See, e.g.*, Rose Gilchrist & Anne Wilson, *Hospitals Ask Reversal of Loss of Tax-Exempt Status*, Salt Lake Tribune, Sept. 21, 1983, at 2B (quoting John Wagner, a spokesman for HCA, stating "My personal interpretation is that the difference [between HCA and Intermountain] is basically the tax base. We pay more taxes.").

29. Brief of Amicus Curiae Pathology Associates Laboratories at 1–4, Utah County v. Intermountain Health Care, 709 P.2d 265 (Utah 1985)(No. 17699).

30. E-mail from Alan Sullivan, Administrative Partner of Snell & Willmer, LLP (March 24, 2007) (on file with author).

31. Dick Netzer, *Local Government Finance and the Economics of Property-Tax Exemption*, in Property Tax Exemption for Charities 47 (Evelyn Brody ed., 2002); Barry Poulson, *Property Tax Revolts and Tax and Spending Limits*, available at http://www.americansforprosperity.org/index.php?id=1941.

32. Gilbert M. Gaul and Neill A. Borowski, Free Ride: The Tax Exempt Economy (1993).

33. *See* Pamela Leland, *PILOTs: The Large City Experience*, in Property Tax Exemption for Charities, *supra* note 31, at 193.

34. Telephone Interview with Bill Thomas Peters (July 16, 2007).

35. Friendship Manor Corp. v. Tax Comm'n, 487 P.2d 1272 (Utah 1971).

36. *Id.* at 1280.

37. Jack Fenton, *Commissioners Put 5 Hospitals on Tax Rolls*, Salt Lake Tribune, June 19, 1983, at B1.

38. Utah Const., art. XIII, §2, *quoted in* Utah County v. Intermountain Health Care, 709 P.2d 265, 267–68 (Utah 1985).

39. Utah Code Ann. §59-2-30, 59-2-31 (1973), *quoted in* Utah County v. Intermountain Health Care, 709 P.2d 265, 267 n.1 (Utah 1985).

40. *See* Richard Andrews & Chris Allen, *Claims for Proposition No. 1 Are Challenged*, Salt Lake Tribune, Nov. 2, 1986, at 18A.

41. *See, e.g.*, Salt Lake County v. Good Shepard Lutheran Church, 548 P.2d 630, 631 (Utah 1976).

42. Andrews & Allen, *supra* note 40.

43. An interesting side note is that during the time the appeal was pending, Utah Valley and American Fork refused to pay the assessed property taxes; this led to speculation that Utah County would sell the hospitals in a tax sale for the unpaid back taxes. The county and the two hospitals, however, avoided this prospect with an agreement that the hospitals would pay the back taxes with interest if the case ultimately was decided against them. *See, e.g.*, J.J. Jackson, *Utah County, Hospital Reach Agreement on Overdue Taxes*, The Daily Herald, March 19, 1985, at 1; J.J. Jackson, *Hospitals Miss Sale List for Tax Auction in May*, The Daily Herald, April 14, 1985, at 3.

44. Brief of Petitioner Utah County at 8-12, Utah County v. Intermountain Health Care, 709 P.2d 265 (Utah 1985)(No. 17699) [hereinafter *Utah County Brief*].

45. Brief of Respondent Intermountain Health Care at 8–9, Utah County v. Intermountain Health Care 709 P.2d 265 (Utah 1985)(No. 17699) [hereinafter *IHC Brief*].

46. The "Argument" section of IHC's brief was 22 double-spaced pages long; its arguments regarding the constitutionality of the 1973 legislation used 17 of those 22 pages; only 5 pages were directed specifically to the argument that IHC's hospitals met common law tests of charity.

47. *Utah County Brief, supra* note 44, at 16.

48. *Id.* at 16-17.

49. *Id.*

50. *Id.* at 18.

51. *Id.* at 18-19.

52. *IHC Brief, supra* note 45, at 27.

53. *Id.*

54. *Id.* at 28.

55. *Id.* at 6.

56. *Id.* at 5.

57. Utah County v. Intermountain Health Care, 709 P.2d 265, 278-89 (Utah 1985).

58. *Id.* at 269. For an extended discussion of the factors and their application in the *Utah County* case, see Phelon S. Rammell & Robert J. Parsons, *Utah County v. Intermountain Health Care: Utah's Unique Method for Determining Charitable Property Tax Exemptions—A Review of Its Mandate and Impact*, 22 J. Health L. 73 (1989).

59. *Id.* at 268 (citing Comment, *Real Estate Tax Exemption for Federally Subsidized Housing Corporations*, 64 Minn. L. Rev. 1094, 1096–97 (1980)).

60. *Id.* at 270.

61. *Id.*

62. *Id.* at 274.

63. *Id.* at 276.

64. *Id.* at 279.

65. *Id.* at 280–82.

66. *Id.* at 284.

67. *Id.* at 290.

68. *Id.* at 279.

69. Rammell & Parsons, *supra* note 58, at n.170.

70. J. J. Jackson, *One Hospital to Get Exemption*, The Daily Herald, August 18, 1985, at 23.

71. Petition for Rehearing, Brief of Utah State Tax Commission at 5, Utah County v. Intermountain Health Care, 709 P.2d 265 (Utah 1985)(No. 17699).

72. Petition for Rehearing, Brief of Intermountain Health Care at 4, Utah County v. Intermountain Health Care, 709 P.2d 265 (Utah 1985)(No. 17699).

73. *Id.* at 10.

74. *Id.* at 12–13.

75. The proposition lost by about 2000 votes or about .5% of the total votes cast. Rammell & Parsons, *supra* note 58, at n.49.

76. *Id.*

77. *Id.*

78. *Id.* at n.170.

79. *Id.* at nn.171-79. The four hospitals denied exemption were Cottonwood Hospital, Alta View Hospital, St. Marks Hospital (the first hospital built in Utah), and Jordan Valley Hospital. Cottonwood and Alta View were both owned by IHC; St. Mark's was operated by the Episcopal Church, and Jordan Valley by Holy Cross Health System. *Id.*

80. Alice A. Noble, Andrew L. Hyams & Nancy M. Kane, *Charitable Hospital Accountability: A Review and Analysis of Legal and Policy Initiatives*, 26 J.L. Med. & Ethics 116, 121 (1998).

81. Utah State Tax Commission, Property Tax Division, *Property Tax Exemption Standards of Practice*, app. at 2-35 (rev. 2007), *available at* http://propertytax.utah.gov/standards/standard02.pdf.

82. Noble, Hyams and Kane note that the standards were promulgated in "an extremely political process" and were virtually identical to those suggested by the hospital industry. *See* Noble et al., *supra* note 80, at 121.

83. Howell v. County Bd., 881 P.2d 880 (Utah 1994).

84. Rammell & Parsons, *supra* note 58, at n.164.

85. 487 A.2d 1306 (Pa. 1985).

86. *Id.* at 1317.

87. *See* Noble et al., *supra* note 80, at 121.

88. These states included Alabama, Arkansas, California, Georgia, Illinois, Minnesota, Missouri, Tennessee, Vermont and Wisconsin. *See generally*, Noble et al., *supra* note 80, at 120-129. In many of these cases, the state taxing authorities cited specifically the decisions in *Utah County* and/or *Hospital Utilization Project*. *See, e.g.*, Med. Ctr. Hosp. of Vt., Inc. v. City of Burlington, 566 A.2d 1352 (Vt. 1989) (citing, and disagreeing with, *Hospital Utilization Project*); Downtown Hospital Ass'n v. Bd. of Equalization, 760 S.W.2d 954, 957 (Tenn. Ct. App. 1988) (extended discussion of *Utah County*).

89. *See, e.g.*, Highland Park Hosp. v. Dep't of Revenue, 507 N.E.2d 1331, 1336-37 (Ill. App. Ct. 1987) (all patients were billed and some collection efforts were made for all bills; since bad debt is not the equivalent of charity care, facility failed to "dispense charity to all those who need or apply for it.") Two further Illinois cases after *Highland Park Hospital* reinforced significant charity care as a requirement for exemption in Illinois. *See* Alivio Med. Ctr. v. Dep't of Revenue, 702 N.E.2d 189, 190 (Ill. App. Ct. 1998); Riverside Med. Ctr. v. Dep't of Revenue, 795 N.E.2d 361 (Ill. App. Ct. 2003). For a discussion of these cases and the pending Provena-Covenant case in Illinois, see John D. Colombo, *The Provena Tax Exemption Case: the Demise of Community Benefit?* 55 Exempt Org. Tax Rev. 175 (2007).

90. *See* Noble et al., *supra* note 80, at 121-22, 129-30. Four other states (Florida, Connecticut, Wisconsin and Colorado) apparently considered taxing hospitals or imposing strict charity care requirements. *Id.* at 123.

91. *Id.* at 121.

92. *Id.* at 123.

93. *See* John D. Colombo & Mark A. Hall, *The Future of Tax-Exemption for Nonprofit Hospitals and Other Health Care Providers*, 2 Health Matrix 1 (1992). The two bills were introduced respectively by Representative Edward R. Roybal, then the chair of the House Select Committee on Aging, and Representative Brian Donnelly. Each reflected a hybrid compromise between community benefit proponents and a strict charity care standard for exemption. The Roybal bill would have created a sort of tax credit for charity care and community benefit services, while the Donnelly bill provided five different tests for exemption, including devoting 5% of gross revenues to charity care or 10% of gross revenues to specific community health services. *See id.* at 11-13.

94. *See generally* John D. Colombo, *Health Care Reform and Federal Tax Exemption: Rethinking the Issues*, 29 Wake Forest L. Rev. 215, 264-65 (1994).

95. See Healthcare Financial Management Association, P&P Board Statement 15: Valuation and Financial Statement Presentation of Charity Care and Bad Debts by Institutional Healthcare Providers (as revised and approved November 7, 2006).

96. Champaign County Board of Review, Notes on Exempt Applications 6-7 (2004), *available at* http://www.co.champaign.il.us/BOR/PROVENA.pdf [hereinafter Provena Filing].

97. Champaign County Board of Review, Notes on Exempt Applications 8-9 (2005), *available at* http://www.co.champaign.il.us/BOR/CARLE2004.pdf [hereinafter Carle Filing].

98. Carle Filing, *supra* note 97, at 9-10; Provena Filing, *supra* note 96, at 5.

99. Carle Filing, *supra* note 97, at 4-6; Provena Filing, *supra* note 96, at 2-4.

100. Ill. Dep't of Revenue v. Provena Covenant Med. Ctr., No. 04-PT-0014, Sept. 29, 2006 [hereinafter *Provena Opinion I*]. The opinion is available from the Department of Revenue web site at: http://www.revenue.state.il.us/legalinformation/hearings/pt/pt06-26.pdf. Provena appealed the

Department of Revenue decision, and in August 2007 a state trial judge reinstated Provena's tax exemption. Provena Covenant Med. Ctr. v. Dep't of Revenue, Ill. Cir. Ct., No. 2006-MR-597 (Aug. 8, 2007). In an opinion released on August 26, 2008, the Illinois 4th District Court of Appeals reversed the trial court and upheld the Department of Revenue's revocation of Provena's tax exemption. Provena-Covenant Medical Center v. Dept. of Revenue, Case No. 4-07-0763 (Aug. 26, 2008). Observers expect the case to end up before the Illinois Supreme Court.

101. *Provena Opinion I, supra* note 100, at 14.

102. *Id.* at 16–17.

103. The title of the proposed legislation was the Tax-Exempt Hospital Responsibility Act, H.B. 5000, 94th Gen. Assembly, 2006. The bill would have required exempt hospitals in Illinois to spend a minimum of 8% of their operating costs on charity care, measured by average costs. For a discussion of the legislation, see Colombo, *supra* note 4, at 444–45.

104. *See* Nancy M. Kane, *Tax Exempt Hospitals: What Is Their Charitable Responsibility and How Should It Be Defined and Reported?*, 51 St. Louis U. L.J. 459, 460–61 (2007).

105. Senate Committee on Finance — Minority, *Tax Exempt Hospitals: Discussion Draft* (released July 18, 2007), *available at* http://grassley.senate.gov/releases/2007/07182007.pdf. The discussion draft would impose a requirement that exempt hospitals spend at least 5% of revenues or expenses (whichever is greater) on charity care, as defined.

106. Even if an organization is exempt from federal income taxes, it generally is required to file an annual informational return with the IRS. This return is filed using Form 990, which requires the organization to provide extensive information about its sources of revenue, expenditures and other matters. The IRS substantially revised Form 990 in 2007, effective for tax years beginning in 2008 (filings due in 2009).

107. *See* Internal Revenue Service, Form 990 Schedule H 2008 (draft of December 19, 2007), *available at* http://www.irs.gov/pub/irs-tege/f990rschh.pdf (effective for tax year 2008; for filing in 2009).

108. For an extended discussion of these policy issues, see Colombo, *supra* note 4, at 446–55.

109. *See, e.g.*, John D. Colombo, *The Role of Access in Charitable Tax Exemption*, 82 Wash. U. L.Q. 343, 375–79 (2004).

Chapter 11

Estate of Gelsinger
$v.$
Trustees of University of Pennsylvania

Money, Prestige, and Conflicts of Interest
in Human Subjects Research

ROBIN FRETWELL WILSON*

A. Introduction

Jesse Gelsinger was an adult by the narrowest of margins, merely three months past his 18th birthday, when he died on September 17, 1999. Jesse was the first person reported to die in a human gene-therapy trial, although sadly not the last.[1]

The Food and Drug Administration (FDA) charged that a cascade of mistakes culminated in Jesse's death. The consent forms Jesse signed failed to disclose both the death of monkeys in an earlier animal study using higher dosages of the viruses infused into Jesse's liver and "significant adverse events" experienced by other subjects in the same trial — "important evidence," the FDA said, "of increased risk."[2] The researchers failed to adequately alert the FDA about the adverse events, denying the agency the opportunity to stop the study well before Jesse's infusion.[3] The researchers infused Jesse even though his liver was not functioning within the study's limits 24 hours prior to infusion.[4] Less than four days later, Jesse died, apparently because the viruses "triggered an

* Law Alumni Faculty Fellow and Professor of Law, Washington & Lee University School of Law. I am indebted to Paul Gelsinger and Alan Milstein for access to documents collected in the captioned suit and to Louis Girifalco for permission to reprint his letters. Thanks also to David Hoffman, William Kelley, Carol Grande, and James Wilson's attorney, Michael Waitzkin, for their insights and to Ann Bartow, Nathan Crystal, Tim Jost, Pamela Melton, Caroline Osborne, Joan Shaughnessy, Rod Smolla, Sally Wiant, and anonymous reviewers for their advice. I am grateful for the diligent and thorough research assistance I received from Dinah Danforth, George Davis, Stephanie Hager, Joseph Mercer, Richard Schlauch, and Erin Willoughby. James Wilson, Mark Batshaw, Steve Raper, and Art Caplan each declined interviews. I have been retained as an expert by Milstein's firm in connection with the death of a participant in a subsequent gene-therapy trial, Jolee Mohr.

overwhelming inflammatory reaction — in essence, an 'immune-system revolt' that ended in 'multiple-organ-system failure.'"[5]

In the months following Jesse's death, the University of Pennsylvania's (Penn) Institute for Human Gene Therapy (IHGT), a sponsor of the trial, acknowledged mistakes but vigorously disputed whether they affected the outcome for Jesse. IHGT conceded that elevated liver-function tests for earlier participants "should have been sent [to the FDA] in October and November of 1998 — and . . . discussed . . . with FDA before proceeding."[6] Nonetheless, IHGT contended that the "FDA had . . . comprehensive reports in its possession for over six months when in August, 1999, it expressly approved" continued testing.[7] IHGT also acknowledged that it was slow to report "the deaths of two monkeys" in a concurrent animal study. It countered, however, that "these deaths did not have significant implications for the safety" of Jesse's trial. The monkeys received 17 times the dosage Jesse received and "were infused with a first- and second-generation vector," not the third-generation vector Jesse received.[8] In response to the FDA's charge that the "consent process was not well documented," IHGT affirmed that "[e]ach and every patient . . . gave clear and unambiguous consent."[9] Finally, IHGT defended the decision to infuse Jesse despite his elevated ammonia levels the day before. Jesse tested "well within the protocol inclusion criteria" when screened three months before and "the protocol did not require that [qualifying levels] exist immediately before infusion."[10] "[T]he investigators," IHGT maintained, "reasonably interpreted the protocol to allow the exercise of clinical judgment in deciding whether to proceed."[11] Because ammonia levels "change appreciably even during [a] 45-minute period," the researchers concluded that Jesse's level represented a "transiently heightened" amount that "did not warrant terminating [Jesse's] participation."[12]

In the early days following Jesse's death, his father, Paul Gelsinger, publicly defended the researchers. He told the *Tucson Citizen*, "I still have a lot of faith in these guys. They could not have foreseen what was about to happen."[13] He told the *Washington Post* that the researchers are "very ethical men."[14] On December 8, 1999, the day that the FDA released its preliminary findings on Jesse's death, Paul still maintained that "[t]hese guys didn't do anything wrong."[15]

All that changed as news emerged of one researcher's, Dr. James Wilson's, financial interests in the trial. One year and one day after Jesse died, Paul Gelsinger filed suit in the Court of Common Pleas in Philadelphia County against Wilson, a co-investigator and a sponsor of Jesse's trial; Drs. Mark Batshaw and Steve Raper, the trial's two principal investigators; Penn, which approved and sponsored the research through IHGT, employed Wilson and Raper, and owned the hospital where the trial was conducted; Genovo, the gene-therapy company that partially funded IHGT and in which Wilson had shares; William Kelley, the Dean of Penn's medical school; Arthur Caplan, Penn's world famous medical ethicist who had advised the researchers to test the virus on relatively healthy adults rather than dying infants; Children's Hospital of Philadelphia, the hospital that approved the protocol; and Children's National Medical Center (CNMC), Batshaw's employer.[16]

The suit broke new ground, both in terms of the defendants named and the legal theories advanced.[17] It sought compensatory and punitive damages for using an adenovirus that was "unreasonably dangerous," a product liability claim; intentional assault and battery; breach of the duty to secure informed consent; intentional infliction of emotional distress; fraud and intentional misrepresentation; and fraud on the FDA.[18] While any litigator knows there is a huge chasm between what is alleged and what can be proven, the Complaint must have grabbed the defendants' attention, not to mention the attention of their insurers.

In one sense, the story of Jesse's case is easy to tell. The case settled quickly by litigation standards, with a settlement reached less than seven weeks later, before Penn even filed an answer to the Complaint.[19] It was no wonder. The FDA had suspended not only Jesse's trial but all the gene-therapy trials conducted at Penn. The FDA's Recombinant DNA Advisory Committee (RAC) and the United States Senate both held public hearings. The media placed Wilson's substantial financial stake and Penn's relationship with Genovo under a microscope. The reputations of the university and the researchers, once gleaming, became more tarnished with each passing day.[20]

But in another sense, Jesse's story, like Jesse's life, was prematurely cut short, buried with the parties' private settlement.[21] Unlike many of the cases in this book, no public court record exists anywhere of the mistakes made in Jesse's clinical trial. When the Gelsingers' suit settled, no one accepted responsibility for Jesse's death or apologized publicly to the Gelsinger family. When the government subsequently brought and settled a civil false claims suit against the researchers and sponsoring institutions, no one admitted any wrongdoing or apologized. No one grappled in detail with the substance of the FDA's original charges. Each defendant maintained that it acted lawfully at all times, even as Penn and CNMC together paid more than a million dollars and the government restricted the researchers' ability to do human experimentation — terms that arguably say as much about the crushing power of federal false claims investigations as they do about the underlying merits. Over Paul Gelsinger's expressed wish that the government would make public the documents it collected, they were not made public.[22]

The amount of publicity generated by Jesse's death cannot be understated. A quick Google search of "Jesse Gelsinger death" yields 21,500 entries.[23] The *New York Times* alone has devoted more than 25 stories to Jesse's death.[24] Despite all the publicity, almost nothing is known publicly about the nature of the researchers' interests in the outcome of Jesse's trial, Penn's review and ultimate approval of Wilson's financial interests, the nature of the disclosures made to Jesse, or the precise nature of the claims asserted by the Gelsingers and the federal government.

What remains of Jesse's story sat in document boxes crammed full by the Gelsingers' attorneys and set aside after the insurers, the parties, and the court signed off on the settlement. This chapter resurrects that story and fills in those missing pieces.

B. Jesse's Participation in the Clinical Trial

Jesse lived from birth with a harmful genetic condition affecting his liver. Because of a defect in the enzyme ornithine transcarbamylase (OTC), nitrogen that Jesse's liver would normally change to urea and excrete as urine turned instead into ammonia in his body.[25] When ammonia accumulates in the body, it poisons the central nervous system and can lead to coma and even death.[26] The treatment for OTC deficiency (OTCD) includes special diets and daily medications.[27]

Batshaw, the nation's premier researcher on OTCD and a principal investigator for the study, explained the prognosis for OTCD infants: "[H]alf of all boys with [OTCD] die in the first few weeks of birth and half of these survivors die before age five."[28] The majority of children who survive past five have severe disabilities. Jesse was the rare child to survive into adulthood and thrive.

Nonetheless, OTCD shaped Jesse's daily experience of the world. It dictated his diet and medications. At one point, Jesse took over 50 pills a day. When he followed his regimen, he functioned well. As Paul Gelsinger said, "he grew and developed normally, he passed all the grades in school. He was symptomatic of his disorder, but not too often." The three times when Jesse had elevated ammonia he wound up in the hospital. When he was three, "[h]e got pretty sick and was in a coma, but they had medication for it. . . . and he was placed upon that medication, a strict diet of low protein, and did well." Jesse was ten when the second episode struck. "[H]e was hospitalized for five or six days. He was blind. He could only see color. He couldn't stand. We had to help him with everything. But he pulled out of that fine with no apparent neurological damage."

Jesse "did fairly well from there until his later teens" when, like many teenagers, he revolted against the regimentation. "You wanted to strangle him half the time and hug him the other half, but he was a good kid." The December before the trial "Jesse almost died from his disorder. His nutrient reserves became so depleted, he started catabolizing — that's where your body starts feeding on itself in an uncontrolled fashion. He literally stopped breathing in my wife's and my arms, right after Christmas. He was coded blue and they intubated him. He was in the ICU [intensive care unit] for a couple of days." A new medication reversed Jesse's course and he sprang back "as if nothing had ever happened. It was a miracle drug for Jesse." As Paul Gelsinger would later learn, Batshaw developed Jesse's "miracle drug."[29]

The idea behind gene therapy was to release patients like Jesse from OTCD's hold. The researchers hoped to use a cousin of the common cold virus, an adenovirus, as a "taxi" or vector to deliver corrective genes to the liver.[30] The vector would be "changed in structure, so that it [would] not cause cold symptoms."[31] The researchers clipped out risky parts that cause viral pathogenesis — the process by which viruses lead to disease — and viral replication — how viruses make copies of themselves in host cells — until they arrived at the third-generation vector that Jesse received. "That vector should have been 'much safer' than the earlier models," Batshaw would later note.[32]

The structure of Jesse's trial involved escalating dosages, with cohorts of three and sometimes four subjects receiving increasing doses of the vector on each stair-step.[33] Participants included both women who carried the defective OTCD gene and men who suffered from partial OTCD, as Jesse did. As the study protocol explains, the study began on the lowest stair-step with a "starting dose" that was "5,000 fold below the toxic dose in animals (obtained using the more immunogenic first-generation [vector])," while the subjects on the highest stair-step received a dose that was "100 fold below the toxic dose in animals given the [first-generation vector]."[34] Documents filed by Batshaw with Penn in 1995 explained that "[t]he original dose will be lower than that *associated with toxicity in preclinical animal studies.* . . . The goal will be to identify a dose which will *not cause excessive toxicity*, but may be associated with detectable metabolic improvement."[35]

Identified in the trial as patient OTC.019, Jesse was the 18th patient in the trial (the first patient withdrew). He was also the second patient in the sixth cohort, which received the highest dosage of the vector.[36]

1. A Primer on Human Subjects Research and Its Regulation

All clinical trials are conducted in phases. A Phase 1 trial involves the initial introduction of a new investigational drug or therapy into humans.[37] These studies are closely monitored. While Phase 1 studies may be conducted with individuals suffering from the underlying problem or disease, they are usually conducted with healthy volunteers, who by definition cannot benefit from the drug or therapy being tested. A Phase 1 trial seeks to determine dosing, show how a drug is metabolized and excreted, identify acute side effects, and, if possible, to gain early evidence of effectiveness. Generally, the total number of participants in a Phase 1 study ranges from 20 to 80. Because a Phase 1 trial is the first trial of a drug or therapy in humans, the risks to humans are, by definition, unknown and can be great.[38]

Confusion sometimes results when a Phase 1 trial is conducted with individuals who suffer from the underlying disease or malady. Not surprisingly, participants who suffer from the underlying disease sometimes labor under a "therapeutic misconception" — the unspoken hope that they will receive a positive outcome despite explicit disclaimers of benefit and clear warnings of potential side effects.[39] This therapeutic misconception makes informed consent challenging in the best of circumstances, as the discussion below of the Consent Form that Jesse signed illustrates.

The results of the Phase 1 trial are ultimately used to design a well-controlled, scientifically valid Phase 2 study.[40] Phase 2 studies use "control" groups — that is, participants who do not receive the drug or therapy under investigation — as a baseline against which to measure the effectiveness of the drug or therapy being studied. Phase 2 studies seek to obtain preliminary data on the drug or therapy's effectiveness for patients with the disease or condition. Unlike Phase 1 trials, then, Phase 2 trials must include patients who suffer from the disease or condition under consideration. Phase 2 studies also help to determine the common short-term side effects and risks associated with a drug or therapy. Like Phase 1 studies, Phase 2 studies are closely monitored and conducted with a relatively small number of patients, usually several hundred.

Phase 3 studies consist of expanded controlled and uncontrolled trials.[41] Researchers perform Phase 3 studies after preliminary evidence suggesting effectiveness has been obtained in a Phase 2 trial. Phase 3 studies seek to gather additional information about effectiveness and safety in order to evaluate the overall benefit-risk relationship of the drug or therapy. Usually encompassing several hundred to several thousand participants, Phase 3 studies provide the basis for extrapolating results to the general population and transmitting that information through the drug's labeling.

All three phases must comply with a set of federal regulations known as the Common Rule if they are federally funded. The Common Rule requires that participants voluntarily consent to participating, that risks to subjects be minimized, that researchers select subjects equitably, and that anticipated benefits to subjects *and* society be in "reasonable relationship" to the risks.[42] Researchers must also monitor the results to protect patient safety and ensure participants' privacy.[43] As commentators have noted, "Due to the introduction of the 'benefits to society from knowledge' component, theoretically no matter how small the benefit to the subject, a large risk to the subject could be found acceptable if there were substantial enough benefits to society from learning something important."[44]

Although Jesse suffered from the disease under consideration, he participated in a Phase 1 trial. Arthur Caplan, the head of Penn's Center for Bioethics who is sometimes described as "America's best-known bioethicist,"[45] explains that a Phase 1 trial of the kind Jesse participated in does not seek to benefit participants. "Not only is it sad that [Jesse] died, there was never a chance that anybody would benefit from these experiments. They are safety studies. They are not therapeutic in goal. If I gave it to you, we would try to see if you died, too, or did OK. . . . If you cured anybody, you'd publish it in a religious journal. It would be a miracle. . . . All you're doing is you're saying, I've got this vector, I want to see if it can deliver some gene where I want it to go without killing or hurting or having side-effects."[46]

Of course, there is an element of hyperbole to Caplan's observation. While it is true that Phase I trials are intended to assess safety, researchers would never consider them unless they believe the treatment has *some* possibility in the future of conferring a medical benefit to patients. In other words, the Phase 1 "safety" trial is a prelude to later Phase 2 and Phase 3 trials of effectiveness.[47]

2. State of "Gene Therapy" Before Jesse's Trial

Hype can hardly begin to capture the excitement that gene therapy, "a burgeoning field of medicine, . . . seemed to hold . . . for treating and even curing dozens of diseases."[48] In the early 1990s, Barron's announced that "Gene Therapy Is Now Stuff of Dollars, Not Just Dreams," observing that "[i]n the wasteland that has been pharmaceutical and biotech stocks, green shoots are sprouting from a source that sometimes seems as much science fiction as science: gene therapy."[49] Barron's was not joking. Mind-boggling amounts of money poured in from industry. In one deal alone, Sandoz AG acquired Genetic Therapy Inc. for $295 million, making "a bold bet on the experimental field of gene therapy."[50]

Notwithstanding the hype, gene therapy was all promise and no results when Jesse's trial began. As one bioethicist, Ruth Macklin, bluntly put it, "Gene therapy is not yet therapy."[51] In a letter to be read at Jesse's funeral, the researchers themselves recognized gene therapy's rudimentary state: "This treatment approach is brand new. . . . [W]e are at the level that penicillin was in the beginning of World War II. It had just been discovered and no one knew the correct or safe dose. Ultimately [penicillin] saved millions of lives, but adverse effects also led to some deaths."[52]

3. The Decision to Test Relatively Healthy Adults

To their credit, Wilson and Batshaw approached Caplan early on for advice about who should participate. Caplan had joined Penn only months before Wilson, in 1994. Appointed as director of Penn's new Center for Bioethics and as Trustee Professor of Bioethics in the department soon to be chaired by Wilson, Caplan's duties involved giving ethical advice to IHGT. Wilson tapped Caplan to serve on IHGT's steering committee, a faculty advisory board, where Caplan envisioned his role as "internal cop."[53]

Originally, the researchers wanted to test the protocol on sick infants. Caplan stopped the idea in its tracks: "I said, 'You're nuts.'" Although sick infants have very little to lose, distraught parents grasping for their newborn's salvation could not give meaningful, voluntary consent. As Caplan explains, "The problem is that consent obtained under such circumstances would be coerced consent because parents traumatized by the birth of a [terminally ill] baby . . . could not be expected to think rationally."[54]

Caplan's advice to the researchers tracks standard bioethics wisdom — a trial cannot be ethically conducted unless the participant or a surrogate consents voluntarily. Ethicists are wary of permitting research on vulnerable populations in part because of the history of research abuses with vulnerable populations.[55] In the now-infamous Tuskegee Study, the United States Public Health Service studied the effects of untreated syphilis in a group of African-American men beginning in the 1950s and continuing into the early 1970s.[56] The researchers purported to treat the men, but never disclosed to them that they continued to suffer from syphilis, which penicillin could treat. A stream of other research "scandals" also contributed to society's robust appreciation for the special risks to vulnerable populations. These include the "injection of live cancer cells into Jewish old age home residents, intentionally infecting institutionalized children with hepatitis (on the rationale that they would have gotten infected anyway), military experiments involving soldiers unknowingly consuming LSD, and government experiments in which thousands of Americans were exposed to radiation."[57] This checkered history is one reason we take special care with research involving vulnerable populations, like prisoners or institutionalized persons — we rightfully worry that the subject cannot really say no.[58]

Caplan has drawn heat for his advice to test relatively healthy adults rather than dying infants. Some asked after Jesse's death whether relatively healthy individuals should ever be used to test drugs when they stand to gain nothing. One former FDA official, Henry Miller, commented: "Rather than stable adult patients, it would have been more prudent to treat [OTCD] babies who were in comas and had dire prognoses."[59] Claims that sick infants would have been better subjects strike Caplan as a "they-were-going-to-die-anyway excuse."[60] That logic, he said in an interview with *Inquirer Magazine*, "justified Nazi experiments on human[s]. . . . They said people in the camps were going to die anyway, so let's experiment on them[.]"[61] As Caplan aptly notes, "Every single medical intervention that we've got [started with a safety trial.] . . . At some point somebody is up first as a human being. Why would anybody do it if they aren't going benefit? The answer is altruism."

After Jesse's death, Caplan had to defend not only his advice, but his objectivity. The relationship between Caplan and IGHT was a complex, interwoven one. IHGT funded one-half of a junior-faculty position in Caplan's center, costing approximately $25,000 per year.[62] Caplan sat on the committee charged with examining the financial arrangements between Penn, Genovo, and Wilson, but "as a member of Dr. Wilson's department, was asked [by the committee] to recuse himself from discussions on the Genovo proposal . . . to avoid any perceptions of conflict."[63] Caplan had his tenured appointment in the department chaired by Wilson, although as he told *Inquirer Magazine* "I technically don't have to report to [Wilson]. And I don't get any money from him." Instead, Caplan reported to Kelley, the medical school dean. The internal commission that Penn established to review Jesse's death, the Danforth Commission, would later identify the need for independence between bioethicists and the researchers being advised.

4. The Oversight of Gene-Therapy Trials

The oversight of clinical trials largely occurs at the institutional level, with minimal review by National Institute of Health (NIH) and FDA, the agencies that primarily fund or approve the resulting therapies. An institutional review board (IRB), the entity that oversees research at the institutional level, must approve a study before it begins and is supposed to monitor its progress. Human gene-therapy research receives an added layer of review at a national level: approval from NIH's RAC.

With Jesse's trial, both processes seemed robust. Penn's IRB approved the protocol and Consent Form on October 6, 1995. The approval placed special importance on adverse events. Researchers must "immediately" report "any untoward incidents or adverse reactions." They must seek prior IRB approval before "chang[ing] any aspect of this study, such as procedures [or] consent forms."

At the RAC meeting that considered the OTCD study in December 1995, members peppered the researchers with safety-related questions. One member questioned whether delivering viruses by catheter into the liver "was too invasive and advised using a less-invasive method."[64] The researchers agreed to that change although the FDA ultimately overruled it. Another member advised further animal studies before human testing. One member warned against giving participants false hope of benefiting and cautioned that participants may be unable to weigh the risks wisely. This member also worried about liver damage. Yet another member said that the risks didn't justify the means and suggested using children with life-threatening OTCD instead. Wilson countered with Caplan's advice and, according to one member present, reportedly said, "You should let people be heroes if they want to be."[65]

While any approval by the RAC would seem to signify scientific agreement on the protocol and the study's need, RAC decisions at that time were more often unanimous than not. Of the five other proposals considered at the December 1995 meeting, four were approved unanimously by the members who voted.[66] In contrast, the RAC approved the OTCD study with certain changes to the protocol in a divided vote, with one dissent and four abstentions. As a member of the RAC explained after Jesse's death, Wilson's reputation, advocacy, and charisma ultimately prevailed.[67]

5. Disclosures Made to Jesse

Despite the power of the therapeutic misconception for many participants who suffer from the underlying disease, Paul Gelsinger says that Jesse clearly understood that he would not directly benefit from the study and that participating might preclude future beneficial treatments.[68] Indeed, as the researchers noted after Jesse's death, portions of the Consent Form state multiple times that participants "should expect no direct benefit from the study," which sought to "help others."[69]

Although the Consent Form disclaims benefit in some places, it muddies the question of possible benefit in other places. The name itself, "gene therapy," suggests a proven therapy.[70] The term appears numerous times in the Consent Form. More confusing, the Consent Form sprinkles references to clinical improvements among its many disclaimers of benefit. It says "We will also be testing whether the virus has a helpful effect[,]" and notes "We have evidence in animal models that gene therapy for OTC deficiency may be helpful."[71] The Consent Form also waffles on the question of benefit while flatly claiming to offer no benefit: "We are using very low doses of the virus for safety reasons, but this also means that *effectiveness will be reduced. Even if there is some metabolic improvement, it is unlikely to last more than three months.*"[72] While, as noted earlier, Jesse did not expect a benefit, the internal contradictions in the Consent Form are nevertheless problematic.[73]

Like the Consent Form, the researchers themselves muddied the line between therapeutic and non-therapeutic research in the weeks following Jesse's death. A letter they asked to be read at Jesse's funeral called gene therapy a new "treatment approach," the first step toward which "was to enroll people who were willing to test the 'medication.'"[74] In testimony before the U.S. Senate after Jesse's death, Paul Gelsinger charged that his conversations with Batshaw before Jesse enrolled in the trial also muddied this line: "Jesse and I were told in late July 1999 that a prior patient had shown a clinical improvement of 50 percent in her ability to eliminate ammonia from her system following gene therapy."[75]

The Consent Form also discusses risks. It has been widely reported that the Consent Form failed to disclose the death of several monkeys in a prior study using an earlier-generation vector. Disclosure forms approved by the FDA and Penn's IRB reportedly included the disclosure, but neither the agency nor the IRB could explain why it was subsequently dropped without their approval.[76]

The Consent Form disclosed the following about the animal studies:

> The animals have not shown toxic effects to the liver or other body organs at the dosage of virus that is needed to transport the gene in this study. We have also tested the safety of this virus in monkeys and have not found toxicity at the doses being used in this study. (Higher doses were associated with liver inflammation [hepatitis] in animals.)[77]

The Consent Form nowhere says that monkeys died in a previous trial using an earlier-generation vector, as media accounts say an early version of the Consent Form disclosed.

On the risks actually posed, the Consent Form warns of liver damage, hepatitis, and "increased ammonia levels" and explains:

> There are three major risks that you need to consider. (1) It is possible that the adenovirus itself can cause an inflammation of your liver. (2) It is also possible that the adenovirus may produce an immune response from your body which could damage the liver. (3) Finally, it is possible that receiving the virus now may prevent you from receiving a therapeutic dose of the virus in the future.[78]

The Consent Form then discusses steps taken to minimize these risks.[79]

The possibility of death is discussed three times in the eleven-page Consent Form. As the researchers note, patients were warned of the "potential risks, including the possibility of life-threatening liver failure."[80] Death is also listed as a possible outcome of the liver biopsy, although only a "very small risk (1 in 10,000)." Discussing long-term follow-up, the Consent Form alerts subjects that if they die, the researchers will request an autopsy "no matter what the cause."[81]

In place after place, the Consent Form promises to monitor problems with each cohort. As the RAC later summarized it, "if a single patient developed a grade [III] or higher toxicity, the study would be put on clinical hold pending an explication acceptable" to the FDA and Penn's IRB.[82] Section 4.3 of the study protocol explained that "If a single patient develops Grade III or higher toxicity, the study . . . will be halted."[83] The FDA conditioned its approval on the researchers' agreement to respect these clinical stop-signs.

The Consent Form promises to disclose new risks to participants:

> SIGNIFICANT NEW FINDINGS
> Any significant new findings developed during the course of the study that could affect your willingness to continue participating in the study will be provided, in writing, to you. You will be given a chance to ask questions about this new information before continuing in the study. In such circumstances, we would revise the informed consent document and offer you an opportunity to reconsider your participation.[84]

While standard fare in consent forms because of federal guidelines, the paragraph arguably makes a promise to participants that they will be kept in the loop. The Consent Form also says that "[i]n over twenty . . . patients tested, however, we have not seen problems with high blood ammonia[.]"[85] The researchers later explained that the Consent Form promised "each patient's eligibility to participate [would be] evaluated and documented in the patient's medical file prior to performing the [necessary] procedures."[86]

Finally, the Consent Form presents the financial ties between Wilson, Penn, Genovo, and the study's outcome in a single sentence:

> SPONSOR INFORMATION
> Please be aware that the University of Pennsylvania, Dr. James M. Wilson (the Director of the Institute for Human Gene Therapy), and Genovo, Inc., (a gene therapy company in which Dr. Wilson holds an interest) have a financial interest in a successful outcome from the research involved in this study.[87]

6. Jesse's Death

The disheartening facts of Jesse's death are best recounted by his father, Paul Gelsinger. Paul gave the following account at a Forum on Research Ethics at the University of South Carolina in 2001 at my invitation:

> Three months before Jesse's brush with death in December 1998, Paul and Jesse learned about a clinical trial for Jesse's disorder. The specialist who treated Jesse, Dr. Heidenreich, received a letter soliciting patients to participate in a Phase I clinical trial of gene therapy. Paul and Jesse were instantly interested. Jesse was not allowed to participate, however, because he was not an adult — he was only seventeen. Paul told the doctor, "Well maybe when he is eighteen, if it's still going on."
> At Jesse's check-up in April 1999, Heidenreich again raised the idea. Paul said, "Listen, we are going back East in June to see family. Jesse will be eighteen. Why don't you see if they are interested in testing him to see if he can participate?" Heidenreich made the initial connection and Paul followed up. The visit to Penn occurred on June 22. Jesse was eighteen years old and four days. He had just graduated from high school.
> When they arrived, "They weren't ready for us. That should have been my first clue," Paul explained. Jesse received a special isotope of ammonia, N15, to see if he was a candidate for the study. The isotope tests how well a patient's body processes ammonia. It takes about five hours. While they waited, Raper

presented the protocol and Consent Form to them. He "spent 45 minutes answering our questions. This was our first experience with a clinical trial. Jesse had never participated in anything like this before and neither had I." Raper indicated there were potential dangers: flu-like symptoms; hepatitis, which could damage Jesse's liver and require a transplant; and a needle biopsy that leads to death in about one-in-ten-thousand patients. "When I heard that, I told Jesse, 'You need to pay attention here, son. They are talking death. The risk is remote, but it's something you need to consider before you participate.'" They finished the consent process, went on to New York City, and returned home to Tucson.

Four weeks later they received a letter from Batshaw addressed to Paul and Jesse. It indicated that Jesse's efficiency level was six percent, making him a good study candidate. Batshaw called a week later and spoke to Paul. "Jesse deferred to me to understand this." The conversation "got around to whether this therapy worked. Dr. Batshaw said one patient had shown a 50 percent increase in her ability to excrete ammonia following gene transfer. I was excited. I said 'Wow, Mark, this really works. So with Jesse at only six percent efficiency you may know exactly how well it works.' Then he responded, 'that's our hope for these kids.'"

Jesse's motivations could not have been purer: "There was nothing in this for Jesse. If it worked in him, it would work for four-to-six weeks. He was going to get flu-like symptoms. If he ever went into hyperammonia later, they would not be able to use this exact therapy because he would have built up an immunity. But Jesse had a right heart. He set aside his personal life to do this. He took an unpaid leave of absence from his job."

On September 9, Paul saw Jesse off at the airport. Self-employed as a handyman, Paul would join Jesse later that week. Paul gave him a hug and told Jesse he was proud of him, that he was his hero for doing this. "I go to that often. I walked this boy right into this thing."

Jesse in front of the Rocky statue in Philadelphia. Photograph provided courtesy of Mickey Gelsinger.

Jesse arrived on Thursday evening. Prior to the infusion, the researchers tested Jesse for a few days. "On Sunday night, Jesse was scared. His ammonia level was up around 100, he was on intravenous medication. I tried to ease his ill feeling: 'Jesse, these are the world's experts and I trust them. They know what they are doing.'"

The following morning, they infused Jesse with "about an ounce of [virus]. The protocol was designed to treat the liver only. This thing got everywhere in this kid's body. He started having an adverse reaction that night. I talked to Jesse Monday night, the 13th of September. He was not feeling well, having flu-like symptoms. We had a very brief phone call. I got a chance to tell him I loved him. He gave it right back to me. 'I love you, too, Dad.'"

Raper called Paul the next morning, Tuesday. Jesse was jaundiced, a complication not seen before. "Wow," Paul said, "that's a liver function. That's not good." Raper said they were doing more tests. "I was alarmed, but this prestigious institution, Penn, these guys are the experts in this field. I was a little leery they had been in his liver." Batshaw called several hours later and said Jesse's ammonia level was rising, a real indicator he was in trouble. Batshaw told Paul to wait another hour-and-a-half for test results. "When he called me back, Jesse's ammonia had doubled and he was in a coma. I just told him 'Here's my number. I am getting on an airplane and I'll be there as soon as I can.'"

When Paul got there Wednesday morning, Jesse was in a coma, hyperventilating. They asked Paul for permission to deepen Jesse's coma to get his respiration under control. "It was affecting his blood pressure. They had a real battle on their hands to save this kid. I was scared. I cried. I called my wife, told her it was at least as bad as when he almost died the previous December. And all the time I thought, 'These guys have been in his liver.'" That afternoon things improved and everyone relaxed. Batshaw actually returned to Washington, D.C. Paul went to dinner with his brother.

When Paul came back from dinner, he found Jesse in another ward. Paul explains:

I sat there for about an hour and noted his oxygen content dropping. 98, 95, 90, they asked me to leave. Jesse was dead within two days. The adverse reaction took out his whole body. Every cell in his body was affected. Waves of anger would come over me while we were waiting to shut off life support. I would say nobody could have seen this. I told them that I would support them, I would never file a lawsuit. I demanded an autopsy. I wanted to know what happened. They said they would tell me everything. For the next few months I continued to support them. What I didn't realize is that their conflicts of interests were so great that they themselves were blind. Mark Batshaw's desire to come up with a therapy to save babies he had watched die. I discovered the financial conflict of interests that Jim Wilson had in this. All of it clouded their thinking. They took their eyes off what was important: the great heart Jesse had, that is what is missing from research.[88]

C. A Preventable Death?

Days after Jesse's death, Raper told the *Tucson Citizen*, "This is such a tragedy. . . . We would never have done this if we could have anticipated the outcome."[89] Wilson told the *Philadelphia Inquirer* that none of the animals studied before Jesse's trial showed reactions like Jesse's. The animals experienced liver inflammation and blood clotting, but not lung failure like Jesse did. Wilson remarked, "It's scary having no reliable animal models."[90] Years later, the three researchers labeled a discussion of Jesse's death in a review article "Unanticipated Clinical Sequelae."[91]

In the months following Jesse's death, a chorus of newspapers picked up this theme. The *Philadelphia Inquirer* announced, "Nothing had predicted the cascade of crises that killed Jesse Gelsinger."[92] The *Boston Globe* discussed an unexpected patient death.[93] The *Tucson Citizen* noted the "cause unknown" for "Gelsinger's unexpected and unexplained death."[94]

An esteemed panel of gene-therapy experts pored over the trial's protocol looking for "errors or warning signs."[95] French Anderson, widely hailed as the "father of gene therapy,"[96] said, "In retrospect, it was really difficult to find anything . . . that's the most frightening thing."[97] Inder Verma, who later served on the commission Penn established to review Jesse's death, the Danforth Commission, recalls how perplexing Jesse's death was: "After all another woman [a carrier] was given the same [dosage on the same stair-step of the trial and] did not show the toxicity seen by Jesse."[98]

Other scientists believe the results were predictable. Holmes Morton, a metabolic diseases expert, "said there had been enough evidence about the side-effects of adenovirus to raise serious doubts about the wisdom of giving it to someone with [OTCD]. . . . 'Any time a [OTCD patient] is stressed by illness, and . . . develop[s] a fever, their underlying disease becomes not only unstable but life-threatening. . . . That, in a sense, is a quite predictable problem.'"[99] A German scientist who found toxic responses in rabbits, Guenter Cichon, believes "[t]o give adenoviruses to patients like Gelsinger 'would never be justified. And I am not the only one who thinks this way. We do not understand why [researchers] are taking these risks.'"[100]

In the months preceding Jesse's death, a number of adverse events occurred in gene-therapy trials around the world, raising the question of risks to participants. In these studies, conducted at other institutions on other diseases using different delivery mechanisms, participants experienced serious side-effects, but recovered. For example, "two patients suffered serious stroke-like attacks" in a Schering-Plough study of dying cancer patients. When asked about these unpublished but "widely disseminated" studies presented at scientific meetings, Wilson said "he was only vaguely aware" of them.[101]

After Jesse's death, the researchers backtracked to animal studies to sort out precisely why he died. As Inder Verma notes, "the moment Jesse's system shut down, the researchers went into the trenches and worked very hard to sort out why."[102] In a review article the researchers reported: "[W]e undertook a series of additional preclinical studies in mice and non-human primates to better understand this phenomenon. . . . [W]e learned that the [viruses] selectively target antigen-presenting cells . . . of the liver and spleen leading to their immediate activation and production of proinflammatory cytokines."[103]

Because the two civil suits discussed below ultimately settled, claims that the researchers could have foreseen Jesse's death were not tested in the crucible of litigation. Neither have the researchers had the occasion that a trial offers to publicly defend the choice to move from the bench to the bedside. In the end, we may never know whether the researchers were reasonable in evaluating the likelihood and seriousness of the risks.

For all its disadvantages, a civil trial may have also hastened a frank discussion about whether a single death in a field of research signals a complete failure of the system or whether instead there is an inevitable or acceptable error rate in human subjects research.[104] While individual civil suits are ill-equipped to decide such larger systemic questions,[105] the researchers, and the research community, would have had a platform to air their own concerns about human subjects regulation. For example, researchers may worry that regulatory oversight operates on 20-20 hindsight so that after a bad outcome, regulators can always look back and find a breach of some rule. The extensive documentation on which the system relies — together with the indeterminacy of some standards applied, like the meaning of the term "minimal risk"[106] — means that no researcher can be assured that regulators will not find a violation after the fact. These concerns have merit since, as the next section explains, federal regulators came down on Penn and the researchers like a ton of bricks.

D. FDA Leaps into Action

On the heels of Jesse's death, federal regulators kicked into high gear. Although Penn "immediately and voluntarily" halted Jesse's trial,[107] the FDA slapped a hold on it too, and by January 2000, halted all the human gene-therapy research underway at Penn. Freezing unrelated trials has become the federal government's tactic of choice,[108] although some believe that it amounts to a strong-arm measure that may inhibit beneficial research.[109]

In a series of warning letters, preliminary findings, and notices after Jesse's death, the FDA cited the researchers for a host of errors: failing to disclose monkey deaths in the Consent Form, treating an ineligible subject, and failing to adequately alert the FDA and participants to numerous adverse events.[110]

The researchers vigorously disputed the charges at every step. Consider the question of Jesse's eligibility for the study on the date he was infused. The Consent Form says that "[y]ou will have passed screening and eligibility procedures prior to entering this study."[111] Read narrowly, this statement could mean that subjects will be eligible if the screening conducted months before shows them to be within limits. A reasonable person might conclude, however, that the safety trial would not proceed if the subject didn't meet the threshold requirements *immediately before* infusion. Yet, as noted above, IHGT urged the first reading.

Wilson argues that although Jesse's ammonia levels exceeded the protocol's limits on the infusion date, Jesse was indeed eligible to participate. In a brief statement issued after the FDA released its preliminary findings, Wilson said "'We remain fully comfortable with the clinical decision' to treat him."[112] Paul Gelsinger wonders why "[e]ven if the investigators thought they had reasons for ignoring these rules, . . . weren't we at least consulted?"[113]

At the same time that federal regulators placed Penn and the researchers under a miscroscope, they also examined how other researchers were complying with federal regulations. The NIH chided researchers nationwide to report adverse events. A flood of reports showed that U.S. researchers had reported a paltry 5.6 percent of adverse events — despite federal rules requiring researchers to report serious adverse events to NIH and FDA within specified timeframes.[114] The woeful disclosure rate underlined an important fact: the regulation of medical research rests on trust.

Eager to restore trust in its own researchers, Penn undertook a searching self-examination in the months following Jesse's death.

E. Penn's Self-Examination

Penn's President, Judith Rodin, convened an independent commission to review Jesse's death and offer recommendations. Chaired by Dr. William Danforth, the former chancellor of Washington University, the Commission presented its report on April 27, 2000. It urged Penn to:

- "evaluate the function of [Penn's] IRBs," which annually review approximately "three to four thousand protocols" generating "about 80 adverse events reported per one hundred protocols";
- "evaluate [Penn's] process of ethical decision making" as "[i]t is unwise to have bioethicists, involved in decision making, report directly to" researchers;
- "do everything possible to ensure that informed consent is properly obtained," guided not only by the "letter" of FDA regulations but their "spirit";
- consider whether studies using viruses warrant "additional training in [their] unique properties and potential toxicities"; and
- consider whether "the monitoring of clinical trials" could be better done outside Penn.

On the crucial question of conflicts of interest, the Commission urged Penn to "review its policies . . . especially with regards to clinical trials" since avoiding conflicts "that even remotely might detract from putting the needs of patients first becomes paramount."[115] The next section discusses extensively the breadth and nature of the conflicts of interest in Jesse's trial.

Penn also appointed an internal Committee on Research Using Humans. The Committee's Interim Report recommended a comprehensive review of Penn's IRB and "[f]ormal monitoring mechanisms for clinical trials," especially those "funded from sources that do not provide . . . external review and monitoring." Penn should also examine its "[c]onflict of [i]nterest [d]isclosure to [the] IRB." The IRB, the committee suggested, would "determine on a case-by-case basis whether disclosures in the patient consent document or other protections are required."[116]

On May 24, 2000, Penn announced a number of responsive measures:

- instituting a new method to "determine the level of monitoring [of clinical trials] for strict compliance with all applicable regulations";
- creating "a set of clear standards [to] guide the review and monitoring of all clinical trials"; and
- initiating a "full review of its policies on conflict of interest" by an "internal review committee."

These overhauls extended to all clinical research at Penn. Most striking, Penn announced that "IHGT will not serve as a sponsor of clinical trials."[117]

F. Penn's Review and Approval of Wilson's Deal

Wilson's financial ties to Genovo — at the center of the controversy over Jesse's death — predate Penn's full-court press to recruit Wilson years before Jesse's trial. The deal Penn ultimately authorized was complex and gave Wilson, and Penn, hefty stakes in Genovo. Wilson's financial interest triggered federal conflict-of-interest rules.[118] Under those rules, institutions have to eliminate or manage conflicts of interests that are expected to exceed $10,000 in payments when aggregated over twelve months or which represent more than a five percent equity interest in a company.[119]

As Figure 11.1 illustrates, Wilson would keep up to a 30 percent non-voting equity stake in Genovo, which he incorporated while at the University of Michigan. By the time Genovo was acquired by Targeted Genetics, Wilson's stake and his children's had shrunk to 15 percent.[120] The deal gave Penn a lot, too. It cemented Penn's relationship with Wilson, the gene-therapy superstar and Dean Kelley's former protégé. Penn also received $21 million in funding for IHGT over a five-year period and five percent of Genovo's stock in exchange for allowing Genovo to license technologies that Wilson developed. Genovo saw the deal as a win; it boasted that the relationship "not only provides . . . access to Wilson's discoveries, but also minimizes business risks, because [we] can wait until Wilson's lab tests new treatments on humans before deciding whether to invest."[121]

Figure 11.1

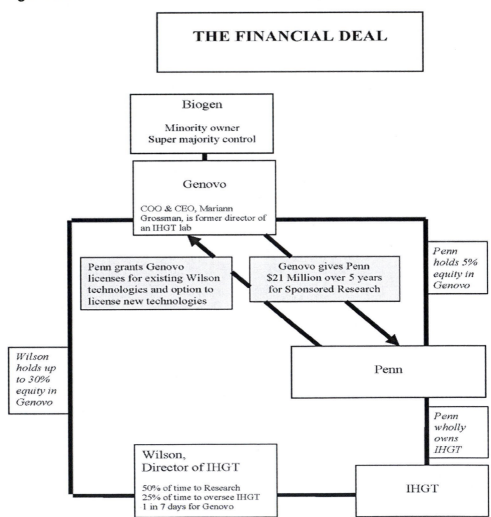

Although Wilson lacked management rights as a non-voting shareholder, Penn placed numerous restrictions on Wilson's arrangement with Genovo as a "strategy for management of the potential conflicts of interest."[122] Penn barred Wilson from serving as an executive or director of Genovo or Biogen and required him to forego monetary gains other Penn researchers receive in the technologies they develop.[123]

Penn had an elaborate process for evaluating potential conflicts of interests. The process originated with the Center for Technology Transfer (CTT), which referred cases to Penn's Conflict of Interest Standing Committee (CISC). Not a policing body, CISC only takes up cases referred by CTT.[124] Nine separate documents guided Penn's decisions, ranging from their Faculty Handbook to CISC's Procedures.[125] Penn's General Counsel sat on CISC, which prepared recommendations for the ultimate decision makers, Penn's Provost and President.

The deal raised eyebrows from the start. The proposal sparked vigorous discussions among CISC members about how rich Wilson's deal was and whether it would create conflicts of interests in his capacity as a researcher, Penn faculty member, or graduate-student mentor. Penn paid Hogan & Hartson, a leading health law firm, to advise it on the deal.[126] In CISC's meetings, committee members asked hard questions. On February 6, 1995, the committee asked what would happen if a death resulted from one of Wilson's trials.[127] Ironically, this question does not appear in the final minutes of the meeting.

Committee members grilled Wilson at CISC's March 13th meeting. Consider just one concern, raised by a member, Louis Girifalco of Penn's Materials Science department, who later resigned over the accuracy of CISC's minutes. Girifalco wondered whether the sponsored research arrangement would alter the relationship between Wilson and Penn. Girifalco asked "what mechanisms could be implemented to manage and avoid any possible distortions in academic and administrative objectives and decisions." The Chair, Neal Nathanson, suggested that this question be tabled until a later CISC meeting on institutional conflicts of interest. Throughout CISC's deliberations over several months, basic elements of Wilson's deal seemed unclear to some CISC members. For example, confusion arose about the extent to which Wilson would be involved in the design and evaluation of Genovo-sponsored trials.[128]

Shortly after CISC's meeting with Wilson, CISC decided that "unusual circumstances" would justify allowing Wilson to have such a substantial equity stake in Genovo.[129] Law School professor Seth Kreimer was "deputized" by CISC to draft a finding of unusual circumstances. He suggested that six considerations together "*may* constitute unusual circumstances [warranting] Dr. Wilson's entrepreneurial involvement." These included Wilson's "nascent technology . . . licence[d] to Genovo," the possibility of "medical advances," the need for a "timely" start on this cutting-edge technology given the "rapidly changing . . . scientific environment," the research's "likely success," and the inability to secure NIH funding. Kreimer nonetheless ends with the crucial question for CISC: "whether these findings are unusual enough to suggest that it is necessary for Dr. Wilson to get a large equity position and that Genovo be the corporate sponsor of the research . . . as opposed to simply justifying [direct funding] by Biogen?"

What CISC agreed upon, and whether it ever agreed at all, became a significant bone of contention. Girifalco repeatedly expressed frustration at the minutes' failure to reflect his reservations. On July 12, he wrote:

UNIVERSITY of PENNSYLVANIA

Louis A. Girifalco
University Professor of Materials Science
3231 Walnut Street
Philadelphia, PA 19104-6272
215-898-3448

July 12, 1995

Mr. Dale Lombardi
Director, Center for Technology Transfer
Suite 300 , 3700 Market Street

Dear Mr. Lombardi:

I will be unable to attend the meeting tomorrow, so I am asking you to clarify what I think are some errors in the minutes.

I am somewhat confused by the draft minutes of CISC for May 18, 1995 and June 15, 1995 that you just sent me. I am particularly concerned about the references to "unusual circumstances" in these minutes.

The minutes give the impression that our committee has carefully defined the term "unusual circumstances" and that this definition was applied to the Genova project. In fact, the May 18 minutes state that the committee voted to accept findings of "unusual circumstances" for this case.

This is not in accord with what transpired. The Committee did not generate any findings of "unusual circumstances", and my recollection of the vote is that it referred to process, not substance.

The minutes do not adequately reflect the concern some members of the Committee had with respect to the meaning of "unusual circumstances". I want to now repeat my statement that there was nothing in the discussion of the Genova case that led me to believe that the factors involved in the Genova case were very different from those involved in very many, if not all, high quality research programs. I believe that there were other members of the Committee that shared my views.

I hereby request that the minutes be amended accordingly.

Sincerely yours,

[signature]
Louis A. Girifalco

cc: Dr. N. Nathanson

When CISC failed to resolve his concerns, Girifalco resigned:

UNIVERSITY of PENNSYLVANIA

Louis A. Girifalco
University Professor of Materials Science
3231 Walnut Street
Philadelphia, PA 19104-6272
215-898-3448

July 18, 1995

RECEIVED
JUL 2 1 1995

Dr. Barry Cooperman
Vice Provost, Research
217 College Hall

Dear Dr. Cooperman:

This is to inform you that I hereby resign from the Conflict of Interest Standing Committee, effective immediately because I believe that I can no longer be an effective member of that committee.

If you will examine the Committee minutes, you will note that they state that the Committee voted to accept findings of "unusual circumstances" with respect to the proposed Genova arrangements. This was an error. The Committee did not vote on this. I wrote a letter to the Chairman and the Secretary of the Committee requesting that the minutes be corrected.

The minutes were not corrected; instead my letter was simply attached to the minutes. This can give the appearance that I was merely expressing a minority view that is open to interpretation and not that the minutes were in error.

In view of my inability to correct a simple question of fact, I cannot be of any further service on this Committee.

I hereby request that this resignation letter be made a part of the Committee record.

Sincerely yours,

[signature]

Louis A. Girifalco

LAG/ipc

cc: Dr. N. Nathanson
        Dr. D. Lombardi

It is difficult to know what to make of certain minutes of CISC's meetings. At the process' start, CISC's Chair discussed the need to appoint new members. In a fax dated January 4, 1995, to the Provost, Barry Cooperman, Nathanson said "I do not want to have further meetings . . . until we have beefed up [CISC's] membership. In view of the Jim Wilson case, pending, this is particularly important."[130] On March 16, 1995, two full months before CISC completed its work, Nathanson advised CISC's Secretary, Dale Lombardi, that he had "some outstanding concerns about the draft minutes from January and February meetings. I would like to get these 'cleaned up' ASAP." Similarly, Carol Grande, Director of Penn's Center for Venture and Industry Relationships, suggested that the May 26, 1996 minutes delete the words "and lack of adherence to" Penn's policies.[131] Grande also suggested that Kreimer's crucial question "be deleted."[132] These revisions may be nothing more than innocent wordsmithing intended to better reflect CISC's discussion, but they raise questions.

Other communications suggest that CISC's report was substantially done long before CISC completed its work. Consider Nathanson's March 16th fax to Lombardi, nearly three months before CISC finished its work on June 9, 1995. It said, "I have already completed a draft . . . report, based on our meeting yesterday. I will give you this draft [for] the committee [shortly]."[133]

At the end of CISC's vetting, reservations continued to arise. On May 31, one member persisted, "Is it possible that Biogen simply will not come in unless Wilson has a very strong stake?"[134] Penn's Associate General Counsel, Robert Terrell, annotated the "final" version of CISC's memorandum to Cooperman. Received too late to be incorporated, Terrell asked once more whether Wilson receives too juicy a deal.[135]

In the end, after CISC's in-depth review and the Provost's subsequent examination, the deal Penn ended up approving is substantially similar to the one with which their deliberations began.

G. The Gelsingers Finally Sue

Two disclosures precipitated the Gelsingers' suit. Despite promises that he "would be informed of everything," Paul Gelsinger "did not learn of the protocol violations and monkey deaths until . . . the FDA publicly accused the Penn researchers."[136] Just as damaging to his trust was news of Wilson's substantial financial ties to the trial. Weeks after Jesse's death, Wilson traveled to Paul Gelsinger's home to explain what they knew about Jesse's death; it was the first time they had met face to face. Paul says, "I pointedly asked [Wilson] what his financial interest was in the [study's] outcome . . . he stated that he was an unpaid consultant to [Genovo]. This conversation took place on my back porch in Tucson, Arizona."[137]

Later he learned that "Wilson had a 30% ownership of that company and received $13.5 million in stock from the company that bought him out."[138] Hence was born the Gelsingers' case.

The Gelsingers' suit was notable for pressing existing causes of action in new and creative ways. As an article in the Annals of Internal Medicine explained, the Gelsingers' suit:

> illustrate[d] even greater legal creativity in the drafting of claims [than previous suits arising out of human subjects research]. . . . The Gelsinger family coupled the usual informed consent claim with a product liability claim, and then went further: They alleged that the investigators had committed fraud by not revealing that previous subjects enrolled in the protocol had died and that the principal investigator had a financial relationship with the sponsoring biotechnology company.[139]

The litigation settled at lightning speed. Penn, CNMC, and the individual researchers never even filed answers. Only the Children's Hospital of Pennsylvania (CHOP) responded in any formal way, with preliminary objections. CHOP argued that existing Pennsylvania law did not support the novel theories advanced against it in the Complaint. On the lack of informed consent, CHOP said that "[i]n Pennsylvania, . . . such claims lie only against the physician . . ." and "Pennsylvania law does not impose 'upon hospitals the duty of obtaining informed consent.'" CHOP argued that "intentional infliction of emotional distress" had "not yet [been] adopted as part of Pennsylvania law" and even if it had, the facts did not show conduct "beyond all possible bounds of decency." Moreover, Pennsylvania's standard for "negligent infliction of emotional distress" required the "emotional distress [to be] 'accompanied by physical injury or physical impact' or . . . the plaintiff [must have been] 'in personal danger of physical impact . . . and [must have] fear[ed] the physical impact' of the alleged tortuous conduct" — none of which was asserted until the Amended Complaint.[140]

The Gelsingers' suit was notable not only for marshalling creative claims, but for whom it targeted. Caplan's advice earned him the dubious distinction of being the first bioethicist named in such a lawsuit.[141] In another unprecedented move, William Kelley, the dean of Penn's medical school, was also named. Both were ultimately dismissed as defendants, a condition, says the Gelsingers' attorney, Alan Milstein, for settlement.[142]

Given the nature of liability insurance, the researchers likely never paid anything out of their own pockets.[143] Any personal penalty came from having a patient die while in their care, the tarnishing of their reputations, and, later, being subjected to tight restrictions on their research.

When the suit settled, no one publicly apologized. Privately, Penn's President Judith Rodin sent a "handwritten note" to Paul Gelsinger — "more a note of condolence than . . . an apology."[144] Several years after the settlement, Paul traveled to Washington, D.C., for a meeting and met Batshaw in his hotel lobby. "I think Mark was looking for forgiveness, but when I pressed for an acknowledgement of wrongdoing, he insisted that while what happened to Jesse was wrong, . . . they could not have foreseen or prevented it. He didn't really apologize for anything and I really didn't accept what he had to say. We have not had any communication since."[145]

Because the suit settled, it is difficult to evaluate the likely success of its various claims. One difficulty for any tort suit is showing causation — that is, that a wrongful act or omission led proximately to the bad outcome. Several decisions in Jesse's trial plausibly constitute important links in the chain leading to Jesse's death. Tort law embodies the concept of "but for" cause — that is, whether "but for" the wrongful act the harm would have followed. Consider the infusion of the vector even though 24 hours earlier Jesse's liver was not functioning within the protocol's limits (although he tested within limits when screened months before).[146] Clearly, had the researchers excluded Jesse from the planned infusion because of the previous day's test result, Jesse would not have been infused and presumably would not have died four days later.

To show that the infusion proximately caused Jesse's death, however, is another matter. An act is the proximate cause of an injury "if the injury be one which might be reasonably anticipated or foreseen as a natural consequence of the wrongful act."[147] Legal liability requires the union of factual causation with the conclusion that the defendant's actions were wrong precisely because of their foreseeably harmful character. Thus, although many events are factual causes of an outcome, not every such cause constitutes a legally proximate cause. The determination of proximate cause generally requires considerable scientific evidence — of foreseeability, of the natural course of events, of whether another event may have intervened in a sequence and caused the outcome — evidence that was made unnecessary by the suit's settlement and that we may now never have.

What must be proven under the heading of "causation" varies with the nature of each claim. Thus, causation can be easier to demonstrate with some claims than others. To prove an informed consent claim in Pennsylvania, a plaintiff must show not only that the defendant should have disclosed omitted information but that a *prudent person* in the plaintiff's position would have considered it "material" — that is, relevant and significant to making an informed decision.[148] In Jesse's case, the question then becomes: Would information that monkeys had died when they received an earlier-generation vector administered at 17 times the dose planned for Jesse, if it had been disclosed, have affected a prudent person's decision to participate in the trial? Would greater detail about Wilson's and Penn's financial stakes have significantly informed a prudent person's decision to participate in the trial?

In some jurisdictions, whether Jesse would have changed *his own mind* about participating is relevant to these questions, although not always dispositive.[149] Yet, what Jesse would have done is something we will never know because he is deceased.

H. Every Conflict Is Not Alike

The mere presence of a conflict does not prove that the conflict distorted anyone's judgment, although it may create that appearance. Wilson sharply disputes whether financial interests ever mattered — as a sponsor, he sat high above the clinical fray. Wilson "went to great pains to ensure that his business interests would not influence his judgment during [Jesse's trial]. . . . [H]e gave Raper control over medical and patient care decisions."[150]

Publicly Wilson said, "To suggest that I acted or was influenced by money is really offensive to me. I don't think about how my doing this work is going to make me rich. It's about leadership and notoriety and accomplishment. Publishing in first-rate journals. That's what turns us on. You've got to be on the cutting edge and take risks if you're going to stay on top."[151] Of course, in academia, notoriety and publications translate directly into salaries, prestigious appointments, chairs, and other perks.

Just as the fact of a conflict does not prove an impact on judgment, neither does the fact of a conflict on the part of Wilson and Penn tell us whether better or different rules would have made a difference in Jesse's outcome.[152] The straightforward, unadorned disclosure in the Consent Form alerted Jesse to the fact of Penn's, Wilson's, and Genovo's "financial interest in a successful outcome from the research."[153] Whether that statement was sufficient to alert Jesse to the possibility that researchers may be blind to his best interests is the subject of intense debate.[154] Connecting the dots between the financial interest and later pivotal decisions is difficult, as well. A 2006 book on medical research, What the Doctor Did Not Say: The Hidden Truth about Medical Research, observes:

> There is little reason to think that the financial interests had anything to do with the specific "wrong things" that were considered to have taken place in [Jesse's] study. For example, some of the steps taken in enrolling Jesse in the study appeared to violate procedures required by the protocol. But there's no specific evidence linking these decisions to Dr. Wilson. More likely they were made by more junior members of the research team. . . .[155]

Because the civil suits settled, it is unclear what role, if any, Wilson played in evaluating research findings of Jesse's trial as they emerged, especially the presence of any grade III toxicities in earlier participants, as alleged by the FDA.[156] As noted earlier, the development of grade III toxicities served as a clinical stop-sign under the study protocol, which stated in Section 4.3 that "If a single patient develops Grade III or higher toxicity, the study . . . will be halted."[157]

Paul Gelsinger faults not only Wilson's financial stake but the blind spots that Batshaw's passion to cure children born with OTCD may have caused. Caplan echoes this idea — by focusing on Wilson's financial conflicts, the media overlooked Batshaw's motivations and the impact on his judgments. "Batshaw is the guy who is the [OTCD] specialist. He's the one who runs the Web site for people with this very rare, wacky, genetic liver disease. . . . [Batshaw] knew the patient groups, he knows the patients, he takes care of the kids. Jim's not a pediatrician. Jim never walks in a hospital. . . . Jim's a guy who makes industrial-strength delivery vehicles for gene therapy. He makes vectors. . . ."[158]

While the desires to cure and to profit both may cloud a person's judgment, there is a crucial difference. Batshaw's stake in the outcome — finding a cure for OTCD — is unavoidable in research. All investigators can be expected to want to influence their field by discovering newer, better treatments. By contrast, financial conflicts of interest:

> are distinct from other interests inherent in academic life that might impart bias or induce improper behavior, because financial interests are discretionary, and because the perception is widespread that they may entail special risks. . . . Financial interests . . . threaten scientific integrity when they foster real or apparent biases in study design, data collection and analysis, adverse event reporting, or the presentation and publication of research findings.[159]

Although some question whether there should ever be financial conflicts of interest,[160] Wilson's arrangement was not atypical. Indeed, financial conflicts of interest are endemic to modern research and medicine. For example, a meta-analysis of 37 studies published in the Journal of the American Medical Association in 2003 found that "approximately one fourth of investigators have industry affiliations, and roughly two thirds of academic institutions hold equity in start-ups that sponsor research at the same institutions."[161] Far from being an isolated instance, Penn's and Wilson's financial interests in Jesse's trial are part and parcel of a system rife with financial conflicts.[162]

Despite their widespread nature, it is not clear what can or should be done about financial conflicts of interest. Some academics believe that regulation of financial conflicts doesn't always lead to better protection, may chill necessary funding arrangements for innovative research, and may obscure equally troubling non-financial conflicts of interest.[163]

I. The Feds Settle

On February 9, 2005, the federal government concluded its own civil suits stemming from Jesse's trial. Predicated on the same errors alleged by the FDA early on, the government framed the errors as "false claims" under the federal False Claims Act. The government charged that "the study had produced toxicities in humans that should have resulted in termination," that reports "submitted to FDA, NIH and to [the institutional IRBs] . . . misrepresented the actual clinical findings," and that the Consent Form Jesse signed did not disclose the possible dangers to him.[164] Like the Gelsingers' civil suit, this suit also settled. As a result, these charges remain largely unanswered today.

Under the settlement, Penn agreed to pay $517,496 to the government, while CNMC agreed to pay $514,622. Both institutions agreed to additional safeguards in human subjects research.[165] The settlements with the three investigators placed "restrictive controls on their clinical research activities," with the toughest controls placed on Wilson.

The settlement bars Wilson, who had not been "involved with human research participants since January 2000," from sponsoring a FDA-regulated clinical trial or participating in human subjects research without restriction for a five-year period[166] — largely an empty penalty for Wilson, a bench scientist. Wilson further agreed to retraining and education on human subjects protections, after which he may conduct restricted clinical activity under supervision. If Wilson fails to complete the training and supervised research requirements, he will remain restricted.

The settlement also provides oversight by a Special Monitor of Wilson's animal research if the findings "could influence the safety of human research participants." Finally, Wilson agreed to author an article and lecture on "lessons of human research participants protections learned from" Jesse's trial. The agreement does not clearly state whether the "Lessons Learned" communications are a condition precedent to lifting Wilson's research restrictions. Milstein says that "[s]uch an article was supposed to be an express condition of the settlement of the claims. . . . At least this was the promise made by the United States Attorney to me and Mr. Gelsinger, a promise as yet still unfulfilled."[167] David Hoffman, who negotiated the settlement while he was the Assistant U.S. Attorney, says he cannot imagine Wilson's restrictions being lifted without meeting this requirement.[168]

Batshaw and Raper also agreed to restrictions on their human subjects research for three years, retraining and education on human subjects protections, and to supervised clinical research. No researcher or institution admitted any wrongdoing. Instead each "contend[s] that [their] conduct was at all times lawful and appropriate."[169] Some argue that by settling, "the parties are implicitly agreeing that Gelsinger's death was a by-product of their negligence."[170] Yet the crushing power of False Claims Act sanctions, illustrated in the chapter in this book on *United States v. Krizek*, belies the truth of the claim that by settling, the researchers or institutions admitted responsibility for Jesse's death.

The researchers and institutions welcomed the settlement. Wilson said, "Reaching this agreement means that I can continue to devote myself fully and without restriction to my laboratory research and that I may conduct clinical research when it would be appropriate for scientific advancement."[171] CNMC said that "although Batshaw has learned from the Gelsinger case, he and the hospital had committed no wrongdoing."[172]

Penn maintained that it acted in accordance with "government protocol. Jesse Gelsinger was properly enrolled in this study and . . . his death was not foreseeable based upon informed medical judgment and the best scientific information [then] available to Penn or the government."[173] Penn said it "would allow Wilson to return to human research."[174] Caplan said the settlement would have little impact: "People have already beefed up their oversight of gene therapy . . . have already come to grips with the tragedy."[175]

The terms disappointed Paul Gelsinger. "We wanted accountability. We wanted admission of responsibility for Jesse's death, apologies from all parties and open access to all documents. We received none of those things."[176] He also asked that the government archive "all the documents related to the trial so researchers and the media can try to learn what really happened."[177] Hoffman, the former Assistant U.S. Attorney, says that such public disclosures never occur.

J. Post-Script

1. Batshaw, Raper, and Wilson

Batshaw has risen to Chief Academic Officer at CNMC and chairs the Department of Pediatrics at George Washington University's medical school, where he is also the Associate Dean for Academic Affairs. Raper continues in the Department of Surgery at Penn as an Associate Professor. Wilson heads Penn's scaled-back "Gene Therapy Program." In the end, Wilson made money, but not nearly as much as the Wall Street Journal reported. In August 2000, Targeted Genetics Corp. acquired Genovo in a deal valued at $89.9 million, triggering "a windfall for James Wilson"; in exchange for his shares, Wilson received stock valued then "at about $13.5 million."[178] By the time he sold his shares, Wilson's tax liability may well have exceeded his gains.[179] For its part, Penn received $1.4 million in stock.[180] Targeted Genetics later sponsored another trial in which a relatively healthy patient, Jolee Mohr, died.[181] Milstein filed suit on her family's behalf.[182]

While some rightfully question the ultimate impact of Wilson's financial conflict of interest,[183] the conflict remains the primary criticism of Jesse's trial. In a scathing commentary, Marcia Angell, former editor of the *New England Journal of Medicine*, lamented that Penn "permitted Wilson to own a piece of Genovo, even while he was doing research on its products. Now, that is hardly surprising, given that Penn itself . . . will receive $1.4 million worth of stock. . . . Some watchdog."[184]

By the end of 2008, no "Lessons Learned" article had been published by Wilson, although he has lectured on the subject at elite institutions such as Duke.[185] In declining an invitation to be interviewed, Wilson indicated that he "anticipate[s] completing a paper related to the lessons learned from that experience in the near future."[186]

Wilson did circulate a draft article outline to Hoffman, who then sent it on to Paul Gelsinger.[187] In the draft, Wilson asks:

- Was the scientific basis for the study and its continuation justified?
- Did complexity of the trial complicate its implementation?

He also notes:

- Need to remember that [volunteers] are independent human beings with identities rather than research subjects.
- Best solution [to conflicts of interest] is avoidance.
- [C]omment [on] how this has affected me.[188]

Paul expressed frustration at Wilson's outline: "Any 'lessons learned' paper . . . without getting into the exact failures of following the protocol would be meaningless"; Wilson should instead "comment on how this has not only affected him but how the research has affected the participants, their immediate families, and . . . any damage done to [research's] integrity."[189]

Aside from this skeletal attempt at a "Lessons Learned" paper, Wilson co-authored an article with Batshaw, Raper, and others discussing Jesse's death. The article, Batshaw told Paul, "basically summarizes . . . the scientific lessons we learned. . . . These lessons include that one cannot always predict from [animal] studies the results of all human trials, . . . and that there can be significant variation from one individual to another in response to the same does [sic] of vector."[190]

It is perplexing why Wilson has not completed the pro-forma step of publishing the "Lessons Learned." As he said shortly after Jesse's death, "As a scientist it's very difficult to do the tests, because of what they might show. [Yet,] if a mistake was made, we've got to own up to it and learn from it. Ultimately, the tragedy of Jesse's death would be if we don't learn anything."[191]

2. Paul Gelsinger

Paul Gelsinger lives with the knowledge that "everyone failed to protect Jesse, even me. I didn't do enough to ensure that Jesse was safe in what he was doing and will always regret the way I encouraged him to participate. I am guilty of trusting a system that is not trustworthy, and I should have known better."[192] For five years after Jesse's death, Paul served as Vice-President of Citizens for Responsible Care and Research (CIRCARE), a patient advocacy group, and traveled to conferences "to try to get the system to fix itself."[193] He has since stopped: "[T]here was little more I could do to change things, [it's] now up to others to bring about the necessary changes." He manages a 100-year-old triplex rental property that he extensively remodeled and is building a house in the mountains north of Tucson.

3. Human Subjects Research

Jesse's death put the skids on gene-therapy researchers who wanted to move quickly from laboratory to bedside. His death prompted "researchers to delay gene-therapy experiments over concerns that 'there are things maybe we haven't anticipated in the animal data,'" said Katherine High, president of the American Society of Gene Therapy.[194] Jesse's death also prompted a renewed appreciation for protecting volunteers in clinical trials. "Gone are the days," said one NIH official, "of a lot of hype. Now there's a focus on careful monitoring and careful science."[195]

Jesse's death sparked a robust debate about the regulation of human subjects research.[196] Indeed, his death marks a divide between two sides in that debate. For some, Jesse's near-death experience the December before his trial shows why the system is important, albeit imperfect, and one that we should continue to try to improve. For others, Jesse's death reveals the system's weaknesses: the tremendous reliance on paperwork; its conflation of paperwork completion with ethics and compliance; and the possibility of harshly punishing individual researchers after the fact through multiple proceedings brought by participants and independent regulators.

But more than anything, Jesse's death has come to stand for the pervasive influence of financial interests in human subjects research.[197]

ENDNOTES

1. Jim Smith, *Hospitals, Docs Settle with Feds in Gene-Therapy Death*, Phila. Daily News, Feb. 10, 2005, at 24.

At least one other death has resulted in a gene-therapy trial. In 1998, researchers in Paris began gene-therapy trials on 11 children suffering from X-linked Severe Combined Immunodeficiency (X-SCID) or the "bubble boy" disease, a rare immune system disorder caused by a single gene defect. Four of the 11 children developed T-cell leukemia, one of whom died in October 2004. Rick Weiss, *Boy's Cancer Prompts FDA to Halt Gene Therapy*, Wash. Post, March 4, 2005, at A2. "There is no doubt, in the Paris cases," the BBC reported, "that the leukemia was caused by the gene therapy, where the introduced gene was implanted next to, and switched on, an oncogene (a cancer causing gene)." *Q&A: Gene Therapy Cancer Case*, BBC News, December 18, 2007, *available at* http://news.bbc.co.uk/2/hi/health/7149460.stm (last visited October 23, 2008).

2. Letter from Steven A. Masiello, Dir., Office of Compliance & Biologics Quality, F.D.A. Ctr. for Biologics Evaluation & Research to Mark L. Batshaw, Children's Nat'l Med. Ctr. 7 (Nov. 30, 2000) (Warning Letter), *available at* www.fda.gov/foi/nidpoe/n14l.pdf (last visited Aug. 6, 2008); *see also* Letter from Dennis E. Baker, Assoc. Comm'r for Regulatory Affairs, F.D.A. Ctr. for Biologics Evaluation & Research to James E. Wilson, M.D., Ph.D., Inst. for Human Gene Therapy, Univ. of Pa. Health Sys. (Feb. 8, 2002) (Notice of Opportunity for Hearing), *available at* www.fda.gov/foi/nooh/Wilson.htm (last visited Aug. 6, 2008).

3. *See* Letter from Steven A. Masiello, Dir., F.D.A. Office of Compliance & Biologics Quality, Ctr. for Biologics Evaluation & Research to James E. Wilson, M.D., Ph.D., Inst. for Human Gene Therapy, Univ. of Pa. Health Sys. (Nov. 30, 2000) (Notice of Initial Disqualification Proceeding & Opportunity to Explain), *available at* www.fda.gov/foi/nidpoe/n121.pdf (last visited Aug. 16, 2008).

4. *Id.*

5. Sheryl Gay Stolberg, *The Biotech Death of Jesse Gelsinger*, N.Y. Times Mag., Nov. 28, 1999, at 137 (quoting Steven E. Raper).

6. Inst. for Human Gene Therapy, Univ. of Pa., Summary of Responses to F.D.A. Inspectional Observations 4 (Feb. 14, 2000) [hereinafter *IHGT Responses*].

7. *Id.*

8. Inst. for Human Gene Therapy, Univ. of Pa., Responses to F.D.A. Form 483 Inspectional Observations 16 (Feb. 14, 2000).

9. *Id.* at 12.

10. *Id.* at 5–6.

11. *Id.* at 5.

12. *Id.* at 6.

13. Gabrielle Fimbres, *Tucsonan Who Sacrificed Life in Gene Study Called a Hero*, Tucson Citizen, Sept. 23, 1999, at A1.

14. Deborah Nelson & Rick Weiss, *Hasty Decisions in the Race to a Cure?: Gene Therapy Study Proceeded Despite Safety, Ethics Concerns*, Wash. Post, Nov. 21, 1999, at A1.

15. Sheryl Gay Stolberg, *F.D.A. Officials Fault Penn Team in Gene Therapy Death*, N.Y. Times, Dec. 9, 1999, at A22.

16. *See, e.g.*, Alexis Gilbert, *Penn Hit by Gene Therapy Lawsuit: Suit Calls Penn Negligent in Study that Led to Arizona Teen's Death Last Year*, Daily Pennsylvanian, Sept. 19, 2000, at News Section, *available at* http://media.www.dailypennsylvanian.com/media/storage/paper882/news/2000/09/19/News/Penn-Hit.By.Gene.Therapy.Lawsuit-2161264.shtml (last visited Aug. 6, 2008).

17. *See* Michelle M. Mello, David Studdert & Troyen A. Brennan, *The Rise of Litigation in Human Subjects Research*, 139 Ann. Int. Med. 40 (2003).

18. *See* Complaint, Estate of Gelsinger v. Trustees of the Univ. of Pa., No. 001885 (C.P. Phila. County, Oct. 16, 2000) *available at* www.sskrplaw.com/links/healthcare2.html (on file with author) (last visited Nov. 13, 2008).

19. Rick Weiss & Deborah Nelson, *Penn Settles Gene Therapy Suit; University Pays Undisclosed Sum to Family of Teen Who Died*, Wash. Post, Nov. 4, 2000, at A4.

20. Barbara Sibbald, *Death But One Unintended Consequence of Gene-Therapy Trial*, 164 Can. Med. Ass'n J. 1612 (2001).

21. Under the settlement agreement, the settlement amount remains confidential but the file was not sealed.

22. *See* David B. Caruso, *Feds Settle Suit over Death in Penn Gene Therapy Study*, AP Alert – Pa., Feb. 9, 2005.

23. I am indebted to an anonymous reviewer for the points in this paragraph. Results of Google search performed on October 14, 2008, at 2:05 P.M.

24. A Westlaw search in ALLNEWS of story abstracts performed on October 14, 2008, at 3:00 P.M. yielded 28 stories.

25. *See* Consent Agreement for Recombinant Adenovirus Gene Transfer in Adults with Partial Ornithine Transcarbamylase Deficiency at 2 (1999) (on file with author) [hereinafter *Consent Form*].

26. *Id.* at 2.

27. *Id.*

28. Letter from Mark Batshaw, Children's Nat'l Med. Ctr., Steven E. Raper, Assoc. Prof., Dep't of Surgery, Univ. of Pa., & James Wilson, M.D., Ph.D., Inst. for Human Gene Therapy, Univ. of Pa. Health Sys. (Sept. 23, 1999) (to be read at Jesse Gelsinger's funeral) (on file with author) [hereinafter *Funeral Letter*].

29. Information and quotes from this and the preceding paragraph are from Paul Gelsinger, Statement at the Forum on Research Ethics, Univ. of S.C. Sch. of Law, Apr. 5, 2001 (transcript on file with author) [hereinafter *Gelsinger Remarks*].

30. *Funeral Letter*, *supra* note 28.

31. *Consent Form*, *supra* note 25, at 3.

32. Paul Smaglik, *After Gene Therapy Death: Investigators Ponder What Went Wrong*, 13 The Scientist 1, 2 (1999), *available at* www.the-scientist.library.upenn.edu/yr1999/oct/smaglik_p1_991025.html (last visited Aug. 6, 2008).

33. University of Pennsylvania Health System Institute for Human Gene Therapy, Study OTC.6624, Recombinant Adenovirus Gene Transfer in Adults with Partial Ornithine Transcarbamylase Deficiency (OTCD), Protocol Version 4.0, November 1, 1998, at 4-3. [hereinafter *Protocol Version 4.0*].

34. *Id.*

35. University of Pennsylvania Registration Document for Recombinant DNA Research, Reg. No. 95–99 (on file with author).

36. Mark L. Batshaw, M.D., Steven E. Raper, M.D. & James M, Wilson, M.D., Ph.D., Study of Adenoviral Vector Mediated Gene Transfer in Liver in Adults with Partial Ornithine Transcarbamylase Deficiency (IND 6624): Review of Data, at Table 1.

37. FDA Center for Drug Evaluation and Research Handbook, *available at* http://www.fda.gov/cder/handbook/Phase1.htm (last visited Nov. 13, 2008).

38. I am indebted to an anonymous reviewer for several observations in this paragraph.

39. *See* Paul S. Appelbaum et al., *False Hopes and Best Data: Consent to Research and the Therapeutic Misconception*, 17 Hastings Center Rep. 20 (1987).

40. FDA Center for Drug Evaluation and Research Handbook, *available at* http://www.fda.gov/cder/handbook/Phase2.htm (last visited Nov. 13, 2008).

41. FDA Center for Drug Evaluation and Research Handbook, *available at* http://www.fda.gov/cder/handbook/Phase3.htm (last visited Nov. 13, 2008).

42. *See* 45 C.F.R §46.111. The Common Rule requires that "Risks to subjects are minimized: (i) By using procedures which are consistent with sound research design and which do not unnecessarily expose subjects to risk, and (ii) whenever appropriate, by using procedures already being performed on the subjects for diagnostic or treatment purposes." 45 C.F.R. §46.111(a). A second prong requires that "Risks to subjects are reasonable in relation to anticipated benefits, if any, to subjects, and the importance of the knowledge that may reasonably be expected to result." *Id.*

43. *See Id.*

44. Jerry Menikoff & Edward P. Richards, What the Doctor Didn't Say 56 (2006).

45. Michael Matza, *Lights, Camera, Ethics*, Inquirer Mag., May 14, 2000, at 9.

46. *Id.* at 9.

47. I am indebted to an anonymous reviewer for this observation.

48. Susan FitzGerald & Virginia A. Smith, *Penn to Pay $517,000 in Gene Therapy Death, Doctors Face Research Restrictions*, Phila. Inquirer, Feb. 10, 2005, at A1.

49. Lissa Morgenthaler, *Just What the Doctor Ordered—Is Now Stuff of Dollars, Not Just Dreams*, Barron's, Sept. 20, 1993 at 10.

50. Stephen D. Moore, *Sandoz AG Agrees to Acquire the Rest of Genetic Therapy for $295 Million*, Wall St. J., July 11, 1995, at B3.

51. Stolberg, *supra* note 5, at 138.

52. *Funeral Letter*, *supra* note 28.

53. Matza, *supra* note 45, at 11 (quoting Caplan). Facts and quotes from Caplan in this paragraph are taken from Matza, *supra* note 45.

54. Quotes from Caplan in this paragraph are taken from Matza, *supra* note 45.

55. I am indebted to an anonymous reviewer for this observation.

56. Menikoff & Richards, *supra* note 44, at 6.

57. *Id.*

58. *See* William Curran et al., Health Care Law & Ethics 261–62 (6th ed. 2003).

59. Henry I. Miller, *Gene Therapy on Trial*, 287 Science Mag. 591, 591 (2000).

60. Quotes from Caplan in this paragraph are taken from Matza, *supra* note 45.

61. *Id.*

62. Quotes from Caplan and facts in this paragraph are taken from Matza, *supra* note 45, unless otherwise noted. *See also* note 115 *infra* (describing Danforth Commission's view that "[i]t is unwise to have bioethicists, involved in decision making, report directly to" researchers).

63. CISC Draft Minutes of Mar. 15, 1995 meeting (Mar. 28, 1995) (on file with author).

64. Recombinant DNA Advisory Comm., Dep't of Health & Human Servs., N.I.H., Minutes of Meeting (Dec. 4–5, 1995), *available at* http://www4.od.nih.gov/oba/rac/minutes/124-5-95.pdf (last visited Aug. 6, 2008).

65. Nelson & Weiss, *supra* note 14 (quoting Robert Erickson, a RAC member at the time).

66. Recombinant DNA Advisory Comm., *supra* note 64. Three proposals passed unanimously; one passed by a vote of 14 in favor, 0 opposed, and 1 abstention; and one passed 11 in favor, 5 opposed, and no abstentions.

67. Nelson & Weiss, *supra* note 14.

68. *See Gelsinger Remarks*, *supra* note 29.

69. *IHGT Responses*, *supra* note 6, at 13.

70. Jeffery Kahn, *Commentary, Informed Consent in Human Gene Transfer Clinical Trials*, 19 Hum. Gene Therapy 7 (2008).

71. *Consent Form*, *supra* note 25, at 9.

72. *Id.* at 3, 4, 9 (emphasis added).

73. For example, one can easily imagine that the inconsistencies in the Consent Form could have confused *other* patients and opened the researchers up to claims of fraud or breach of the duty of informed consent. For this reason, the Consent Form makes a nice study of document drafting.

74. *Funeral Letter*, *supra* note 28.

75. *Gene Therapy: Is There Oversight for Patient Safety?: Hearing Before the Subcomm. on Pub. Health of the S. Comm. on Health, Educ., Labor, and Pensions*, 106th Cong. 6 (2000) (testimony of Paul Gelsinger).

76. *See, e.g.*, Nelson & Weiss, *supra* note 14.

77. *Id.* note 25, at 3.

78. *Id.* at 6–7.

79. *Id.* at 2, 6.

80. *IHGT Responses*, *supra* note 6.

81. *Consent Form*, *supra* note 25, at 6, 8.

82. Recombinant DNA Advisory Comm. Dep't of Health and Human Servs., N.I.H., Minutes of Symposium and Meeting (Dec. 8–10, 1999), *available at* www4.od.nih.gov/oba/rac/minutes/1299rac.pdf (last visited Aug. 6, 2008).

83. *Protocol Version 4.0*, *supra* note 33, at 4-3.

84. *Consent Form*, *supra* note 25, at 10–11.

85. *Id.* at 8.

86. *IHGT Responses*, *supra* note 6.

87. *Consent Form*, *supra* note 25, at 11.

88. All quotes in this and the preceding eleven paragraphs taken from *Gelsinger Remarks*, *supra* note 29.

89. Fimbres, *supra* note 13.

90. Donald C. Drake, *Penn Gene Therapy Destroyed Teen's Lungs*, Phila. Inquirer, Dec. 2, 1999, at A01.

91. Steven E. Raper et al., *Fatal Systemic Inflammatory Response Syndrome in a Ornithine Trasncarbamylase Deficient Patient Following Adenoviral Gene Transfer*, 80 Molecular Genetics & Metabolism 148, 155 (2003).

92. Donald C. Drake, *Nothing Had Predicted the Cascade of Crises That Killed Jesse Gelsinger*, Phila. Inquirer, Dec. 2, 1999, at Domestic News.

93. *See* Richard Saltus, *Gene Therapy Researcher Defends Trials*, Boston Globe, Feb. 8, 2000, at B1.

94. Fimbres, *supra* note 13.

95. Smaglik, *supra* note 32.

96. Jennifer Kahn, *Molest Conviction Unravels Gene Pioneer's Life*, 15 Wired Mag. *1, *1 (2007).

97. Smaglik, *supra* note 32.

98. E-mail from Inder Verma, Am. Cancer Soc. Prof. of Molecular Biology, Salk Inst., to author (July 16, 2008) (on file with author).

99. Stolberg, *supra* note 15.

100. Nelson & Weiss, *supra* note 14.

101. *Id.*

102. Interview with Inder Verma, Am. Cancer Soc. Prof. of Molecular Biology, Salk Inst., in Daleville, Va. (Aug. 8, 2008).

103. Raper et al., *supra* note 91.

104. I am indebted to an anonymous reviewer for the points in this paragraph.

105. David A. Hyman, *Institutional Review Boards: Is This the Least Worst We Can Do?*, 101 Nw. U. L. Rev. 749, 765 (discussing Grimes v. Kennedy Krieger, 782 A.2d 807 (Md. 2001)).

106. Menikoff & Richards, *supra* note 44, at 171 (observing that the term "minimal risk" is "extremely vague" and that "[t]here is virtually no guidance other than the definition provided in the regulations" to "clarify its meaning").

107. *IHGT Responses, supra* note 6, at 1.

108. *See* Richard S. Saver, *Medical Research Oversight from the Corporate Governance Perspective: Comparing IRBs and Corporate Boards*, 46 Wm. & Mary L. Rev. 619 n.18 (2004).

109. Miller, *supra* note 59.

110. *See, e.g.*, Letter from Dennis E. Baker to James M. Wilson, *supra* note 2.

111. *Consent Form, supra* note 25, at 8.

112. Stolberg, *supra* note 15.

113. Letter from Paul Gelsinger & Family to David Hoffman, Asst. U.S. Atty. (Nov. 4, 2004) (on file with author). *Compare supra* note 84 and accompanying text (discussing disclosure of new risks to participants in the trial).

114. *See Oversight of Gene Therapy Experiments*, Comtex Newswire, Feb. 18, 2000 (on file with author); Recombinant DNA Research: Proposed Actions Under the NIH Guidelines, 64 Fed. Reg. 63,827, (Nov. 22, 1999) (discussing adverse events reporting requirements under 21 C.F.R. §312.32).

115. William H. Danforth, M.D. et al., *Report of the Independent Panel Reviewing the University of Pennsylvania's Institute for Human Gene Therapy*, Univ. of Pa. Almanac J. Rec., Opinion & News, May 30, 2000, at 1, *available at* http://www.upenn.edu/almanac/v46/n34/IHGT-review.html (last visited Aug. 7, 2008).

116. Comm. on Research Using Humans, *Interim Report*, Univ. of Pa. Almanac J. Rec., Opinion & News, Apr. 25, 2000, at 2, *available at* http://www.upenn.edu/almanac/v46/n30/human-subj.html (last visited Aug. 7, 2008).

117. Univ. of Pa., *Action by the University of Pennsylvania in Response to the Report of the Independent Panel Reviewing the Institute for Human Gene Therapy*, Univ. of Pa. Almanac J. Rec., Opinion & News, May 30, 2000, at 6, *available at* http://www.upenn.edu/almanac/v46/n34/OR-IHGT-actions.html (last visited Aug. 7, 2008).

118. *See* 42 C.F.R. pt.50 (2008) (Public Health Services, Department of Health and Human Services); 45 C.F.R. pt.94 (2008) (Public Welfare) (requiring a research investigator to disclose any significant financial interest she has in the federally-funded research); 60 Fed. Reg. 35,820 (July 11, 1995) (Notice).

119. The federal regulations define a "Significant Financial Interest" as "anything of monetary value, including but not limited to, salary or other payments for services (e.g., consulting fees or honoraria); equity interests (e.g., stocks, stock options or other ownership interests); and intellectual property rights (e.g., patents, copyrights and royalties from such rights)." The definition excludes:

> (5) An equity interest that when aggregated for the Investigator and the Investigator's spouse and dependent children, meets both of the following tests: Does not exceed $10,000 in value as determined through reference to public prices or other reasonable measures of fair market value, and does not represent more than a five percent ownership interest in any single entity; or
>
> (6) Salary, royalties or other payments that when aggregated for the Investigator and the Investigator's spouse and dependent children over the next twelve months, are not expected to exceed $10,000.

42 C.F.R. §50.603 (2008).

120. Telephone interview with Michael Waitzkin, Atty. for James Wilson, M.D., Ph.D., Inst. for Human Gene Therapy, Univ. of Pa. Health Sys. in Lexington, Va. (Mar. 31, 2008) [hereinafter *Waitzkin Interview*].

121. Nelson & Weiss, *supra* note 14.

122. Letter from Barry S. Cooperman, Vice Provost, Research, to James Wilson (June 29, 1995) (on file with author).

123. *See id.*; *compare* Patent and Tangible Research Property Policies and Procedures of the University of Pennsylvania, *available at* http://www.upenn.edu/almanac/issues/past/pdf_files/OR-patent-adobe.pdf (last visited Aug. 6, 2008).

124. CISC Minutes, May 9, 1993 (on file with author).

125. CISC Procedures at Appendix.

126. Memorandum from Kathleen A. Denis, Dir. Ctr. for Tech. Transfer, to Neal Nathanson, Chair, CISC (Dec. 15, 1994) (on file with author).

127. Memorandum from Dale Lombardi, Sec'y, CISC, to CISC (Mar. 3, 1995) (on file with author).

128. Fax from Carol Grande, Dir., Ctr. for Venture & Indus. Relationships, to Dale Lombardi, Sec'y, CISC (Apr. 3, 1995) (commenting on Minutes dated March 13 and 15, 1995, and noting in connection with statement that Dr. Wilson "will not be involved in the design or evaluation of clinical trials" that Lombardi should "check with Kathleen [Denis, Center for Technology Transfer] — I don't think this is correct").

129. Quotes in this paragraph are taken from the Memorandum from Seth Kreimer, Prof. of Law, Univ. of Pa., to Dale Lombardi, Sec'y, CISC, dated May 18, 1995, attached to the Fax from Carol Grande, Dir., Ctr. for Venture & Indus. Relationships, to Dale Lombardi, Sec'y, CISC (June 8, 1995) (commenting on Minutes dated May 18, 1995, which incorporate the Kreimer memorandum) (on file with author).

130. Fax from Neal Nathanson, Chair, CISC, to Barry Cooperman, Vice Provost, Research (Jan. 4, 1995) (on file with author).

131. Fax from Carol Grande, Dir., Ctr. for Venture & Indus. Relationships, *supra* note 129.

132. *Id.*

133. Fax from Neal Nathanson, Chair, CISC, to Dale Lombardi, Sec'y, CISC (Mar. 16, 1995) (on file with author).

134. Fax from Paul Soven, Member, CISC, to Dale Lombardi, Sec'y, CISC (May 31, 1995) (on file with author).

135. Comments on draft CISC recommendations from Robert Terrell, Assoc. Gen. Counsel, Univ. of Pa., to Barry Cooperman, Vice Provost, Research (Apr. 5, 1995).

136. Letter from Paul Gelsinger & Family to David Hoffman, *supra* note 113.

137. *Id.*

138. *Id.*

139. Mello et al., *supra* note 17.

140. Preliminary Objections to Plaintiffs' Complaint of Defendant, The Children's Hospital of Philadelphia, Estate of Gelsinger v. Trustees of the Univ. of Pa., No. 001885 (C.P. Phila. County, Oct. 16, 2000).

141. *See* Arthur Allen, *Bioethics Comes of Age*, Salon.com, Sept. 28, 2000, *available at* http://archive.salon.com/health/feature/2000/09/28/caplan/index.html (last visited Aug. 6, 2008).

142. Interview with Alan Milstein, Esq., in Pennsauken, N.J. (Aug. 3, 2007).

143. *See* David Hyman et al., *Do Defendants Pay What Juries Award? Post-Verdict Haircuts in Texas Medical Malpractice Cases, 1988–2003*, 4 J. Empirical Legal Stud. 3 (2007).

144. E-mail from Paul Gelsinger to author (Mar. 14, 2008) (on file with author).

145. *Id.*

146. *See supra* notes 4, 10–12 and accompanying text.

147. Black's Law Dictionary 1103 (5th ed. 1979).

148. John Duncan et al., *Using Tort Law to Secure Patient Dignity*, Trial, Oct. 2004, at 42, 46–47; Gouse v. Cassel, 615 A.2d 331, 334 (Pa. 1992) (holding that physicians "need not disclose all known information" but are required to advise patients of "those material facts, risks, complications and alternatives to surgery that a reasonable person in the patient's situation would consider significant in deciding whether to have the operation").

149. *See, e.g.*, Canterbury v. Spence, 464 F.2d 772, 791 (D.C. Cir. 1972) (establishing the objective "reasonable person" test for causation but noting that "[t]he patient's testimony is relevant on that score of course but it would not threaten to dominate the findings"); Scott v. Bradford, 606 P.2d 554, 559 (Okla. 1979) (establishing subjective test for causation since the objective test "certainly severely limits the protection granted an injured patient. To the extent the plaintiff, given an adequate disclosure, would have declined the proposed treatment, and a reasonable person in similar circumstances would have consented, a patient's right of self-determination is irrevocably lost. This basic right to know and decide is the reason for the full-disclosure rule. Accordingly, we decline to jeopardize this right by the imposition of the 'reasonable man' standard").

150. Nelson & Weiss, *supra* note 14.

151. *Id.*

152. I am indebted to an anonymous reviewer for the points in this paragraph.

153. *Consent Form, supra* note 25, at 11.

154. *See* Menikoff & Richards, *supra* note 44, at 228 (arguing that research participants usually care most about "the likelihood that the new treatment being tested is actually going to work well" and that the disclosure that "sophisticated investors are willing to bet millions of dollars on a new treatment by investing in a company with rights to it is something that a reasonable research subject might well view as positive").

155. *Id.* at 226–27.

156. Letter from Dennis E. Baker, Assoc. Comm'r for Regulatory Affairs, F.D.A. Ctr. for Biologics Evaluation & Research, *supra* note 2. *Compare supra* notes 2–3 and accompanying text (discussing the FDA's allegations).

157. *Protocol Version 4.0, supra* note 33, at 4-3.

158. Matza, *supra* note 45.

159. Task Force on Financial Conflicts of Interest in Clinical Research, Assoc. of Am. Med. Colleges, Protecting Subjects, Preserving Trust, Promoting Progress–Policy and Guidelines for the Oversight of Individual Financial Interests in Human Subjects Research 3 (2001), *available at* http://ccnmtl.columbia.edu/projects/rcr/rcr_conflicts/misc/Ref/AAMC_FirstReport.pdf (last visited Aug. 26, 2008).

160. In her testimony at NIH's Conference on Human Subject Protection and Financial Conflicts of Interest, Marcia Angell stated "financial conflicts of interest are not inherent to the research enterprise. They are entirely optional, unlike the intellectual or personal conflicts of interest to which they are often compared. . . ." She suggested guidelines for avoiding financial conflicts of interest, including restricting institutions from taking grants "with strings attached," ensuring that investigators with grant support from companies have no other financial ties to those companies, and creating a common policy among institutions to avoid investigators jumping from strict institutions to less restrictive ones. Marcia Angell, Testimony at the National Institutes of Health, Conference on Human Subject Protection and Financial Conflicts of Interest (Aug. 16, 2000).

161. Justin E. Bekelman, Yan Li & Cary P. Gross, *Scope and Impact of Financial Conflicts of Interest in Biomedical Research,* 289 JAMA 454 (2003).

162. I am indebted to an anonymous reviewer for this point.

163. *See, e.g.,* William Sage, *Some Principles Require Principals: Why Banning Conflicts of Interest Won't Solve Incentive Problems in Biomedical Research,* 85 Tex. L. Rev. 1413 (2007); Saver, *supra* note 108, at 724–25 & n.380.

164. *See* Press Release, U.S. Settles Case of Gene Therapy Study That Ended with Teen's Death (Feb. 9, 2005) (on file with author).

165. *See id.*

166. *See id.*

167. Posting of Alan Milstein to blog.bioethics.net (Jan. 29, 2008) (*On Gene Therapy and Informed Consent*), *available at* http://blog.bioethics.net/2008/01/on-gene-therapy-and-informed-consent/ (last visited Nov. 13, 2008).

168. Interview with David Hoffman, Former Assistant U.S. Attorney, in Philadelphia, Pa. (June 6, 2008).

169. *See, e.g.,* Settlement Agreement, at 3 ¶E, *available at* http://www.circare.org/foia3/wilson5_settlementagreement.pdf (last visited Aug. 26, 2008) (unsigned copy of the settlement agreement between the federal government — the U.S. Dep't of Justice acting for F.D.A., C.B.E.R., N.I.H., H.H.S., and H.H.S. Office of Inspector General — and James M. Wilson).

170. University of Pennsylvania, *Editorial: Lessons Learned,* U-Wire, Feb. 11, 2005, at 30.

171. FitzGerald & Smith, *supra* note 48.

172. *Id.*

173. Mara Gordon, *U. Pennsylvania: U. Penn Settles Gene Therapy Lawsuit,* U-Wire, Feb. 10, 2005, at 30.

174. FitzGerald & Smith, *supra* note 48.

175. Gordon, *supra* note 173.

176. FitzGerald & Smith, *supra* note 48.

177. Letter from Paul Gelsinger & Family to David Hoffman, Asst. U.S. Atty, *supra* note 113.

178. Scott Hensley, *Targeted Genetics' Genovo Deal Leads to Windfall for Researcher,* Wall St. J., Aug. 10, 2000, at B12.

179. *See* Agreement and Plan of Merger among Targeted Genetics Corporation, Genovo, Inc., TGC Acquisition Corporation and Biogen, Inc., dated August 8, 2000, filed by Targeted Genetics Corporation as Exhibit 10.34 (Material Contracts) to the 10-K405 10-K on March 21, 2002, at

5.12(b), available through EDGAR Online (discussing the Lockup Agreement under which selling shareholders would not dispose of shares of Targeted Genetics stock during a thirty-month period after the sale); Form S-3 Registration Statement under the Securities Act of 1933 filed by Targeted Genetics Corporation on November 17, 2000, at 8-9, available through EDGAR Online (disclosing the number of shares received by James M. Wilson and Ann Wilson, Trustees, and noting that "All but one of the selling shareholders have agreed not to sell or otherwise dispose of their shares for up to 30 months following the effective date of the Genovo merger, subject to periodic releases"); *Waitzkin Interview,* supra note 120.

180. *See* Hensley, *supra* note 178.

181. *See also* Chris Evans, *Arthritis Gene Therapy Trials and Tribulations,* Hastings Center, Bioethics Forum, *available at* http://www.bioethicsforum.org/Jolee-Mohr-gene-therapy-trial-ethical-issues.asp (noting dispute over the cause of death) (last visited Aug. 6, 2008).

182. *See* Complaint, Mohr v. Targeted Genetics, Inc. (2008) (on file with author).

183. *See supra* note 150 (discussing how removed Wilson was from clinical decision-making).

184. Marcia Angell, Remarks at the H.H.S. Conference on Financial Conflicts of Interest (August 16, 2000) (search "google.com" for "http://aspe.hhs.gov/sp/coi/angell.htm"; follow "Cached" hyperlink) (last visited Aug. 6, 2008).

185. *See* James M. Wilson, Gene Therapy — Bench to Bedside and Back, Med. Grand Rounds, Duke Univ. Sch. of Med. (July 14, 2006) (announcement of presentation *available at* http://medicine.duke.edu/modules/agendax/index.php?op=view&id=934&on=20060714) (last visited Aug. 6, 2008).

186. E-mail from James Wilson, M.D., Ph.D., Inst. For Human Gene Therapy, Univ. of Pa. Health Sys., to author (Feb. 29, 2008).

187. *See* e-mail from David Hoffman, Asst. U.S. Atty., to Paul Gelsinger (May 19, 2005) (attachment entitled "Lessons Learned from the OTC Deficiency Gene Therapy Trial") (on file with author).

188. *Id.*

189. E-mail from Paul Gelsinger to David Hoffman, Asst. U.S. Atty. (May 23, 2005) (on file with author).

190. Letter from Mark Batshaw, Children's Nat'l Med. Ctr., to Paul Gelsinger (Oct. 21, 2003) (on file with author).

191. Nelson & Weiss, *supra* note 14.

192. Letter from Paul Gelsinger & Family to David Hoffman, *supra* note 113.

193. Postscript taken from e-mail from Paul Gelsinger to author (Apr. 12, 2008).

194. FitzGerald & Smith, *supra* note 48.

195. *Id.*

196. I am indebted to an anonymous reviewer for the points in this paragraph.

197. A Lexis search performed on March 8, 2008 for Gelsinger and conflicts of interest yielded 77 law journals articles and 377 news accounts.

Index